S0-ATN-239

EMBATTLED SHADOWS

A History of Canadian Cinema
1895–1939

Peter Morris

McGill-Queen's University Press
Montreal & Kingston • London • Buffalo

© McGill-Queen's University Press 1978
ISBN 0 7735 0323 4 (paper)
Legal deposit 4th quarter 1978
Bibliothèque Nationale du Québec

Reprinted in paper 1992

Design by Naoto Kondo MGDC, AIGA
Printed in Canada

Canadian Cataloguing in Publication Data

Morris, Peter, 1937–
Embattled shadows: a history of
Canadian cinema, 1895–1939

Includes bibliographical references
and indexes.
ISBN 0-7735-0323-4

1. Motion pictures–Canada–History. I. Title.

PN1993.5.C3M67 1992   791.43'0971
C79-2639-2

Contents

Illustrations

Preface

Until recently, the heritage of Canadian film has been virtually ignored. It was popularly assumed that Canadian film began with the founding of the National Film Board of Canada in 1939, and that, if anything happened prior to this, it was neither interesting nor relevant. Thus, for the period covered here, there are no books and such other published material as exists is both sparse and contradictory. Many of the films made before 1939 have been lost. Even the history of the Canadian Government Motion Picture Bureau (the predecessor of the National Film Board) has become obscured. It might be interesting to speculate why we, as Canadians, have ignored our own history; why, in the case of film, we have even assumed that there is *no* history worth considering. But, whatever the reasons, the fact remains that the history of Canadian film before 1939 is largely unknown.

This book, then, is a first attempt to chronicle film activities in Canada before the establishment of the National Film Board. As such, I have intentionally leaned towards trying to encompass as much of these activities as possible in the text while using the chapter notes not only to give references but also to amplify the text or raise questions on which further research is necessary. Though the text is essentially descriptive, I have also attempted to situate events within their social context and distinguish between particular approaches to film making. Most of the material in the book is original and has never been published before. It is based on interviews with the surviving film makers of the period, searches through contemporary documents, archival records, and film trade papers, together with an extensive viewing of the (too few) surviving films that have been gathered and preserved in public collections.

Though most of the material published here is original, I make no claims for the book's definitiveness. It would be arrogant to do so in view of the fact that the study of Canadian film history is still in an embryonic state of development. *Embattled Shadows* is the first attempt to examine comprehensively the early period of Canadian film, to bring certain events and activities to light, and to suggest the significance of those activities. As such, I hope it will serve as a useful point of departure for future research. If it succeeds in stimulating further serious inquiry into film as an aspect of Canadian culture, it will have served its primary purpose.

With the exception of the first chapter, the emphasis throughout is on film production. While there is a need for a study of the distribution and exhibition aspects of the industry, it seemed most useful at this point to concentrate on film making itself. I have, however, included comments designed to illuminate the economic context of the industry and the chapter notes should enable the interested reader to pursue further research.

The genesis of this book lies in some years of personal research paralleled by a professional concern for the preservation of Canadian film while I was curator of the Canadian Film Archives. More precisely, it was made possible through the research undertaken for the production of the film *Dreamland*, for which I was director of research. Barbara Sears was the principal researcher for this project and her painstaking collection of information was essential to its success. Without her contribution, this book could not have appeared in its present form.

I would also like to pay tribute here to two other film historians whose work in the past did much to stimulate my own interest in and concern for the history of film in Canada. The late Hye Bossin who, while editor of *Canadian Film Weekly*, did much to bring together the reminiscences of many film pioneers; and Gordon Sparling, himself a film maker of the period, who has always been a tireless champion of Canadian film and the importance of its heritage.

Several people have read and commented on all or part of versions of this book at various stages: Kirwan Cox, Louise Dompierre, Piers Handling, and Bill Nichols. Each made helpful suggestions on the content and structure of the text and I am indebted to them for assistance so freely given. Other friends and colleagues have contributed, knowingly and unknowingly, to the views expressed in these pages. They all have my gratitude as does the editorial staff at McGill-Queen's University Press, especially Joan Harcourt. Most especially, I am indebted to Kirwan Cox, who first urged on me the importance of writing this book, and to Louise Dompierre who, throughout its preparation, was both my best critic and best friend. Finally, I should like to acknowledge the support of the Canada Council's Explorations Program, firstly for a grant which made the research possible and, secondly, for a grant which helped defray the costs of typing the manuscript.

Peter Morris

Preface to the 1992 reprint

I am pleased that it has proved possible for McGill-Queen's University Press to reprint this book. At the same time, I regret that current financial constraints have eliminated the opportunity to revise and update the text. This Preface, then, must stand as substitute for those emendations and additions I would otherwise have made. It is perhaps obvious that I would not now write this book as it was originally written some fifteen years ago. That aside, however, the intervening years have seen the publication of additional information by other historians of the period. I will draw attention here only to more significant work, primarily books. A revised edition could take full and proper account of these, and other, contributions.

The most fundamental correction would necessitate re-writing the first eleven pages of the book. Germain Lacasse has persuasively documented and demonstrated that the first public film screening in Canada took place in Montreal on 28 June 1896 and involved the Lumière Cinématographe. Lacasse's article "Cultural Amnesia and the Birth of Film in Canada" was published in *Cinema Canada*, 108 (June 1984): 6–7. A translation of the original report in *La Presse*, June 29, 1896, is included in Douglas Fetherling, *Documents in Canadian Film* (Peterborough: Broadview Press, 1988). This useful volume also includes several other articles relevant to pre-1939 Canadian film history. Lacasse has also written an account of the first itinerant projectionists in Quebec: *L'historiographe: les débuts du spectacle cinématographique au Québec* (Montreal: Cinémathèque québécoise, 1985 [Les Dossiers de la Cinémathèque, 15]).

I did not attempt to discuss the economic structure of the film industry in *Embattled Shadows*. This gap has now been filled, especially for the exhibition and distribution aspects, by Manjunath Pendakur in *Canadian Dreams and American Control: The Political Economy of the Canadian Film Industry* (Toronto: Garamond Press, 1990). Similarly, the issue of censorship has been discussed in detail by Malcolm Dean in *Censored! Only in Canada* (Toronto: Virgo Press, 1981).

The history of Quebec cinema has been extensively studied in recent years. Yves Lever (*Histoire générale du cinéma au Québec* [Montréal: Boréal, 1988]) provides a detailed study of the pre-1939 period as well as an extensive bibliography. Statistics relating to Quebec production, distribution and exhibition are analyzed in Yvan Lamonde and Pierre-François Hébert,

Le Cinéma au Québec: Essai de statistique historique (1896 à nos jours) (Québec: Institut québécois de recherche sur la culture, 1981).

A discussion of early cinema in British Columbia and a detailed filmography are included in Colin Browne, *Motion Picture Production in British Columbia: 1898–1940* (Victoria: British Columbia Provincial Museum, 1979). Early film activities in Newfoundland are chronicled in *Film in Newfoundland and Labrador 1904–1980* (St. John's: Newfoundland Independent Filmmakers Cooperative, 1981). The unpublished autobiography by Nell Shipman quoted in chapter 4 has now been published in an edition annotated by Tom Trusky and with an Afterword by Barry Shipman (Nell Shipman, *The Silent Screen & My Talking Heart* [Boise: Boise State University, 1987]). Peter Roffman's monograph details *The Story of "Carry On, Sergeant!"* (Toronto: The Ontario Film Institute, 1979).

In 1978, I wrote somewhat cursorily of John Grierson's arrival in Canada. Recent work by several historians suggests that Grierson's involvement with Canada was more fascinating, controversial, and complex than originally thought. I would refer the interested reader to Gary Evans, *John Grierson and the National Film Board* (Toronto: University of Toronto Press, 1984); Joyce Nelson, *The Colonized Eye: Rethinking the Grierson Legend* (Toronto: Between the Lines, 1988); José Arroyo, "John Grierson: Years of Decision," *Cinema Canada*, 169 (December 1989): 15–19; and Peter Morris, "Praxis into Process: John Grierson and the National Film Board of Canada," *Historical Journal of Film, Radio and Television*, 9, no. 3 (1989): 269–82.

Finally – but not least – the Filmography in this edition should be used in conjunction with D. John Turner's excellent, annotated, *Canadian Feature Films Index 1913–1985* (Ottawa: Public Archives of Canada, 1987). Turner was also the archivist responsible for restoring *Back to God's Country* to its former glory.

I would like to thank those in the film community who have found this book of use in their teaching and research and have supported its reprinting. My hope now – as it was in 1978 – is that it will continue to stimulate "further serious inquiry into film as an aspect of Canadian culture."

Peter Morris
Toronto, January 1992

CHAPTER 1

Came the Dawn

Ottawa, July twenty-first, 1896. The temperature had touched eighty-one degrees during the day and it is still warm at 8:00 p.m. In the open air at West End Park, 1,200 Ottawans are enjoying the tricks of Belsaz the magician and watching the first public exhibition of movies in Canada.[1]

It was a quiet enough occasion, perhaps surprisingly quiet for the first view of a new form of communication that was to change the social and cultural life of Canada. The Ottawa *Daily Citizen*'s report of a preview showing the night before was enthusiastic but the anonymous review was buried at the bottom of page seven:

REALISM ON CANVAS
Marvellous Exhibition of the Vitascope
at West End Park

Out at West End Park last night was given the first exhibition in Canada of the marvellous production of the Vitascope, Edison's latest creation. With this wonderful invention spectacles of life and occurrences are reproduced in a most vivid and realistic manner, and those who witnessed the views projected last evening were not only pleased with the sight, but were enthused to a high degree over the creative genius which made it possible for life-like movements to be depicted on canvass with such extraordinary effect. One can imagine just how wonderful the invention is when it is stated that with the Vitascope it is possible to reproduce every movement in a pugilistic encounter where the motions of the combatants, both in attack and defence, are of lightning rapidity. The necessary adjunct to the Vitascope is, of course, the process of instantaneous photography, whereby these motions are faithfully depicted as they occur. Forty-two photographs to the second preserve an accurate record of the most minute detail of every physical movement and even the facial expression. It is the application of this same process which depicts the very movement of the water in their precipitation. And the transfer of these effects to canvass by means of the Vitascope gives a perfect representation of the cataract in its downward course or the billow as it curls into foam and dashes upon the beach.

Such were some of the delights spread before the spectators at West End Park at a private view last evening. Public exhibitions of the Vitascope will commence this evening and will be given during the week. The Holland Bros. have the Canadian control of this marvellous invention.[2]

West End Park, then the westerly terminus of the Ottawa Electric Railway Company, had been developed on land originally owned by the Holland family in the Hintonburgh district of Ottawa as an encouragement for people to travel on the street railway. Musical and other family entertainments were presented regularly. And for Ahearn and Soper, owners and managers of the Ottawa Electric Railway Company, the movies were only one more additional lure for Ottawans to travel on their street cars. Admission to the film show itself was ten cents, but you could buy a round-trip ticket to the park "including car fares, admission and reserved seat" for only twenty-five cents from Ahearn and Soper's offices at 56 Sparks Street. It was a bargain at a time when traditional theatres charged that much and more for admission alone and when day trips by steamer up the Ottawa River cost fifty cents. The new Vitascope show was a huge success. Long before 8:00 p.m. on that Tuesday evening in 1896 every reserved seat was taken and audiences touched 1,600 on evenings in the first week. The editors of the Ottawa *Daily Citizen* may have thought the movies worth no more than a page 7 review but the forty-five thousand citizens of Ottawa were astonished and delighted at the life-like reproduction of movement and flocked to contribute their dimes and quarters. Though originally scheduled for only two weeks, the show was several times held over. Within six months this Ottawa reaction to the movies was to be echoed in several cities across Canada.

The first movie show was not at all the same experience which it later became. What Ottawans were enjoying was, first, the magical tricks of Belsaz on stage: Belsaz then "transformed" himself into John C. Green and introduced "The New Marvel—Moving Pictures." The films, each running less than a minute, were simple scenic or topical films, untitled, and without stars or stories. "The entire performance consisted of . . . May Irwin and John Rice in a kissing scene, four coloured boys eating watermelons, the Black Diamond Express, a bathing scene at Atlantic City and a coloured film of Lo Lo Fuller's Serpentine Dance."[3] Musical accompaniment was charmingly provided by the Governor General's Foot Guard Band. Unnamed and unsung star of *The Kiss* was Canadian-born May Irwin, then appearing with John C. Rice in the Broadway hit *The Widow Jones*, whose high point was a prolonged kiss between the principals. Considered daring in 1896, today it seems merely quaint. But many then considered it vulgar and disgusting and its presentation in any city "brought on the symptomatic cramps of censorship to come."[4] Inevitably, it was also the biggest hit of the Vitascope movie shows across the continent.

Primitive those first movies may have been but they thrilled their audiences in Ottawa and elsewhere as much as any modern film affects today's movie-goers. The illusion of realistic movement itself created an extraordinary sense of audience participation, of actually *experiencing* the events on the screen. One writer reported in 1897: "The marvellous accuracy of these pictures in depicting natural phenomena is often demonstrated in a curious manner by the audience; a sea-scene in which a large wave breaks through the mouth of a cave, the realism of which is so great that a shudder can hardly be suppressed, and the splash can be quite easily imagined. In another, when a turn out of a fire-engine was being shown, the engine dashed down the street towards the audience, and appears to come right upon them. On one occasion, an old lady in the audience, quite unable to suppress a scream, started up in her seat and tried to scramble out, and in doing so knocked over the person behind her in her endeavour to get away from the horses; many more cases of the same sort have been known."[5]

Enter the Hollands

Ottawans may have been aware that John C. Green (alias Belsaz the magician) presented the movies to them and that Ahearn and Soper's Electric Railway Company ran the park that showed them, but principally responsible for bringing the movies to Canada were two enterprising Ottawa businessmen— Andrew M. and George C. Holland.

The Holland brothers, sons of a pioneer Ottawa businessman, are paradigmatic reflections of the nineteenth century. They typify that special Victorian entrepreneurial urge which, on the one hand, was allied with sig-

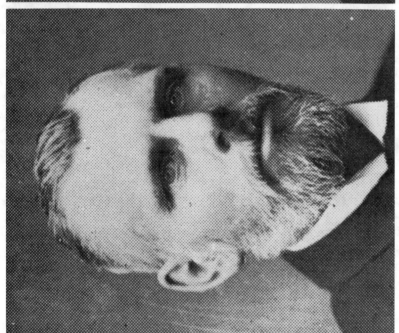

Andrew and George Holland, the entrepreneurs responsible for Canada's First Film Exhibition.

nificant technological advance and, on the other, with an apotheotic dedication to *laissez-faire* capitalism. The Holland brothers—of whom Andrew was the principal partner and driving force—were well known in Ottawa as active and enterprising businessmen. There was little they attempted at which they did not succeed. From their offices at 34 Elgin Street, they were agents for such nineteenth century wonders as the Edison phonograph, the Sorley storage battery, and the Smith Premier typewriter. They had been part-owners of the Ottawa *Daily Citizen* until 1875 when they became the first Senate reporters. They were stenographers, publishers, and booksellers. Andrew had even travelled to Australia where he had been instrumental in establishing a steamship service between Vancouver and Sydney.[6] It surprised their acquaintances not at all when the Holland brothers involved themselves with Thomas Edison and yet another new-fangled contraption—motion pictures.

In fact, their involvement with the movies goes back before the Vitascope—which projected movies on a screen for viewing by large audiences—to the Kinetoscope, a "peep show" device which permitted individual viewing of moving pictures. The Kinetoscope was the key invention in the development of true motion pictures. Others around the world were to become involved in developing projectable moving pictures—among them the Lumière brothers in France and Robert Paul in Britain who presented public film showings before the Edison Vitascope—but all of them based their ideas on the Kinetoscope.

The peep show Kinetoscope had been perfected by W. K. L. Dickson in the laboratories of Thomas Edison in 1889, but Edison was not especially impressed. He was more concerned with exploiting his phonograph and developing slot machine parlours where one might drop in a nickel, put the tubes to one's ear, and hear the band play. The phonograph was the current sensation; as far as Edison was concerned the Kinetoscope was little more than a toy. He did not even patent it until 1891 and then only in the United States, deciding foreign patents would be too expensive. This omission was to cost him dearly in later years. But some others were not so purblind. Among those who saw the possibilities of commercial exploitation was Norman Charles Raff, a young and aggressive former miner.[7] Raff sensed the enormous potential of the new device and was more than willing to take a chance on developing it. He visited Edison in 1893 and finally convinced him that the time was ripe for public exploitation. The Kinetoscope Company was formed with Edison ceding rights of sale to the new company.[8] Norman Raff's Kinetoscope Company did not intend to operate Kinetoscope parlours itself, only to sell territorial rights of use, and the principals of the company now looked for an agent who could launch the first public view of the extraordinary invention. Andrew Holland was not one to let such an opportunity pass and hurried down to New York from Ottawa. The Holland brothers had been Canadian agents for the Edison phonograph and were well known to Raff and his associates. In the spring of 1894, the Holland brothers were named eastern agents for the Kinetoscope Company and the first ten machines were delivered to Andrew Holland.[9]

It is interesting to speculate whether Thomas Edison himself encouraged the decision to give the contract to a Canadian company. He was, after all, the great grandson of a United Empire Loyalist. His father, Samuel Edison, had been a follower of William Lyon Mackenzie in the 1837 Rebellion and had fled with him to the United States when their cause was lost. Thomas Edison began his career as a sixteen-year-old telegrapher for the Grand Trunk Railway at Stratford, Ontario.

Whatever the reasons behind the decision, the Holland brothers justified the faith put in them. On April 14, 1894, only a week after receiving the first ten machines, they opened the world's first Kinetoscope parlour at 1155 Broadway in New York. It was to be the first of hundreds to appear all over the world. The Holland brothers' Kinetoscope parlour was "a Broadway sensation." Thousands queued every day in front of the building "garnished with an illuminated electric dragon with fiery eyes," waiting "to look into the peep hole machines and see the pictures that lived and moved."[10]

On May 1, 1894, Edison wrote to the Holland brothers in Ottawa: "I am pleased to hear that the first public exhibition of my Kinetoscope has been a success under your management and hope your firm will continue to be associated with its further exploitation."

It is likely the Hollands hoped so too. The Kinetoscopes were wholesaled by Edison at $200 and retailed for $300 to $350.

Edison was now convinced that motion pictures had a future—even if a short one. Two years later he put his name to a machine invented by Thomas Armat that could project movies onto a screen for viewing by a large audience and the Vitascope was launched in New York on April 23, 1896, at Koster and Bial's Music Hall. Though projectors developed by the Lumière brothers and Robert Paul had been successfully exhibited to the public earlier in France and Britain, the Vitascope was a great success in the United States under Edison's aegis. Within two months, smart vaudeville promoters across the eastern United States added the Vitascope as a new attraction to their bills. Given the Holland brothers' success with the Kinetoscope, it is not surprising that they were granted sole and exclusive rights to the Vitascope in Canada. And, given their Ottawa origins and close business relationships with Ahearn and Soper of the Ottawa Electric Railway Company, no more surprising that they should choose to launch the Vitascope in Ottawa at a park on land originally owned by them. The street that runs through what was once West End Park is now called Holland Avenue—though nothing marks it as the place where the movies came to Canada.

Movies at the Fair

Several weeks were to pass before Canada's two major metropolitan centres had their first view of "living pictures." The opening of the Toronto Industrial Exhibition—later the Canadian National Exhibition—was an advantageous time to catch Toronto's 145,000 citizens in a festive mood. And, in fact, two competing systems arrived almost simultaneously. The Edison Vitascope—identical to that used earlier in Ottawa—and the Lumière Cinématographe, which had its Canadian première in Toronto, were both on display during September 1896.[11] Ed Houghton (a touring showman like John C. Green) presented the Vitascope show at Robinson's Musee on August 31, 1896. "It was a race from the first," he recalled in 1933, "because a Frenchman named, I think, Lumière, was opening the Cinématographe across the street in an empty store. Old-timers will remember the excitement. . . . You paid a dime to get into the Musee which was a museum of freaks and such. Then you paid another dime to go downstairs and see the pictures."[12]

The movie that opened the Toronto show was the same one that had been such a hit in Ottawa—*The Kiss*, with May Irwin and John C. Rice. Toronto newspapers were hardly ecstatic at the arrival of the latest invention but reported: "The Edison Vitascope has been received with great demonstrations of enthusiasm and will be retained as a feature of next week's show."[13] "Nothing shown in the past has created more interest than Edison's Vitascope with its life-like views which still continues to draw large crowds who go away puzzling themselves as to how it is done. The stage show is also strong."[14]

Robinson's Musee at 81 Yonge Street near King was one of many similar entertainment places in North America in the 1880s and 1890s, most of them patterned on the Barnum Museum in New York. Robinson's had opened in 1884 as McGee's Museum and later became the Eden Musee, then Moore's. As Robinson's Musee, owned in 1896 by M. S. Robinson of Buffalo, it had a menagerie on the roof, a curio shop on the second floor, the Wonderland (offering waxworks) below, and the Bijou Theatre on the main floor, offering vaudeville.[15] The movies were shown downstairs in the Wonderland as one of the many attractions the patron saw for his ten cents. As some measure of the movie's status as a novelty, it is curious to note that a demonstration of "Professor Roentgen's Great X-Rays" commanded a higher admission price (twenty-five cents) and enjoyed a more prominent location in the lobby of the Bijou Theatre where the stage was occupied by the best touring attractions. The X-rays, invented by the German physicist Wilhelm Konrad Roentgen, soon lost their novelty as a theatrical attraction and a similar fate was predicted by many (including Louis Lumière and Thomas Edison) for the movies. The Vitascope show continued until October 16 with a change of films every week or so. During the week of September 19 films were included of "the cataract of Niagara Falls and the whirlpool rapids"— the first time Canadian scenery was depicted on the movie screen, and a foretaste of the deluge of Niagara Falls films and similar exploitations of Canadian scenery that were to follow in the ensuing decade.[16]

Robinson's Musee was to bring back the movies for three weeks beginning December 8, 1896. But in the intervening six weeks, the movies had already become established as a solid attraction with a new status. Reflecting this, Robinson's graduated the movies from the Wonderland in the basement to their prestigious Bijou Theatre. But this time they used, not Edison's machine, but a British device, the Animatographe, invented by Robert Paul of London. It was said to be much superior to the Vitascope, interest in which was already waning barely six months after its launching.

Meanwhile, competition to the Edison Vitascope had arrived. Contrary to Ed Houghton's recollections, the Lumière Cinématographe did not open the same day, nor across the street. It was launched on September 1 by H. J. Hill as part of the grandstand show at the Toronto Industrial Exhibition. Hill, well known as a born showman who, as a manager of the exhibition, had introduced the grandstand show, made a deal with Lumière's agent, Felix Mesguich, for the showing of the Cinématographe not only at the exhibition, but throughout Ontario.[17] The movies led the non-stage attraction at the exhibition that year. Professor Roentgen's X-rays were also on view, along with the newest version of "the Hexiographe, giving a fine selection of pictures" and the Electric Scenic Theatre, direct from the Chicago World's Fair. *The Mail and Empire*, in a preview of the new show, reported: "It is beyond doubt the most marvellous invention of a marvellous age. Scenes and incidents are reproduced with lifelike fidelity, and in motion, the same as in actual existence. Colour is there, animation is there, speech is the only thing wanting, and that will come with the aid of the phonograph before very long."[18] Among the scenes to be shown would be "The Derby and everything about it, the coronation of the Czar, the Henley Regatta."[19] The *Telegram* remarked that the Cinématographe's "photographic figures move in perfectly life-like ways until you wonder whether you are looking at pictures or people."[20]

So successful was the Cinématographe that when the exhibition ended Hill moved the show to 96–98 Yonge Street (opposite the Robinson Musee) on October 23. Admission was twenty-five cents for an adult, ten cents for children. Mr. Hill announced that he had "sixty different views, a series of ten of which will be given every hour, starting at 11:00 a.m. each day . . . until 10 p.m."[21] Though originally scheduled for only ten days, the Cinématographe successfully continued showings through December. Hill also set out to tour Ontario. "Hill refused to show them in the theatres. But he made a pot of money out of them at 25 cents a ticket for 40 minutes of flickers."[22] There was also, on that tour, a portent of things to come. Throughout Ontario's smaller towns live shows often suffered in competition with the movies "because Hill's Cinématographe at 25 cents a head was showing in the Y.M.C.A."[23] Even at this early date, films were exerting the special appeal that was to change the face of entertainment and bring about the end of vaudeville and touring stage shows. And, curiously, it was to be the touring showmen—such as Ed Houghton and John C. Green—who had always presented live shows who grasped the new entertainment medium with great alacrity.

Well satisfied with developments in Ontario, Lumière's agent, Felix Mesguich, returned from Toronto to New York. But he stopped off on the way to photograph—inevitably—Niagara Falls.[24]

If the arrival of the movies had less apparent impact on newspaper editors in Toronto and Ottawa than one might retrospectively expect,[25] Montreal's newspapers—English and French—almost entirely ignored them. Though Canada's largest urban centre was treated to almost every projection device on the market in the fall of 1896, Montreal's newspapers found them worthy only of bare passing mention. Though some felt the movies could be no more than a passing fad, there *was* indeed excitement over them around the world. Audiences everywhere were thrilled and delighted. But Montreal newspaper editors apparently found movies undignified. To notice them through comment could only encourage them. Audiences, however, have a perverse way of going to shows that entertain them whether critics approve or not. To the citizens of Montreal the movies were as exciting as others elsewhere found them. The parochialism of their local newspapers affected their response not one whit.

The Kinematographe made its debut at the Theatre Royal on September 28.[26] This 2,000-seat theatre offered "animated photographs" as a featured attraction on a variety program for admission prices respectively of ten, twenty, thirty, fifty, and seventy-five cents. The cheap (for regular theatres) prices suggests the Theatre Royal was not the most prestigious in Montreal at the time but does hint at the pattern of exhibition the movies were to follow in Canada in the next few years. Many theatres, as an added inducement to their customers to attend live performances, added showings of "moving picture" machines under one or other of their trade names. In Toronto, in 1897, for example, Mr. H. H. Lambin's theatre regularly presented a double bill of vaudeville and moving pictures. At the Theatre Royal, the Kinematographe was the last item on the program—"the chaser"—and the Montreal *Daily Star*'s reviewer merely noted "the series of views by the kinematographe which were very interesting."[27]

On September 30, 1896, Robert Paul's Animatographe opened "every afternoon and evening" at 2223 St. Catherine Street in the Queen's block.[28] On November 19, Montrealers were urged to "see the Prince of Wales' horse win the Derby" at the Theatroscope which had opened at 58 St. Laurent.[29]

Later, in December, the Phantoscope appeared at the Théâtre Français, promoted as "the latest Edison invention."[30] It was not, however, an Edison invention but the machine developed by C. Francis Jenkins who claimed to have invented with Thomas Armat the Vitascope device marketed by Edison. Competition among the early developers of motion pictures was keen and often bitter. The exhibitors of the Phantoscope were running into difficulties in several cities in the United States at the same time, for their attempts to use Edison's name in promotion.[31]

Among the interested spectators at those first film exhibitions in Montreal was a nineteen-year-old electrician, Léo Ernest Ouimet, who was to play a key role within a few years in the development of motion pictures in Montreal. Some sixty years later he recalled his first view of the movies. He was strolling along Rue St. Laurent in 1896 when he was attracted to a showing of movies. It was a space formerly occupied by a shooting gallery, divided so that the movie theatre would be seven feet by fifteen feet, with a real wall on one side and a black cloth on the other. Admission was five cents, standing room only, for a seven minute exhibit of short films. "The exhibitors were Auguste Guay, an electrician with a Paris certificate, and his partner André Vermette. They used a primitive Lumière machine and the now-famed Lumière first subjects."[32] Later "Guay decided to concentrate on electricial work and the equipment and films were sold to the owners of Sohmer Park, an amusement area. There, they were used to offer ten minute programs free to mothers with children during the intermission of the vaude-ville show in the 3,000-seat pavilion."[33]

Something about that first view of the movies intrigued young Ernest Ouimet; a decade later he was to open the first film distribution exchange in Canada, the first luxury movie theatre in the world, and become one of Canada's first film makers.

Living Pictures Now Being Shown

In urban centres, moving pictures quickly found a home in vaudeville theatres. It was natural for them to do so; the film program lasted approxi-mately the same time as a standard vaudeville turn and movies were cheaper than live performers. But if the movies found a natural home in such theatres as Shea's or H. H. Lambin's in Toronto, the Russell in Ottawa, and the Theatre Royal in Montreal, it was the travelling road showmen who brought the motion picture to new audiences and kept the cinema alive during those early years. It was not easy, since travelling showmen had only their own resources and a handful of films to satisfy an audience. The films themselves were often only mildly interesting and it is quite natural that many of the showmen had worked medicine shows and fairs before the movies came along.

"Going to the movies" in those early days was not at all the same expe-rience it later became. Film subjects were rarely more than fifty feet in length, running from one to two minutes. Audiences either stood or sat on make-shift seats during the fifteen to twenty minutes required to present about ten films. The early projection systems caused considerable, and tiring, flicker on the screen. Mechanical shortcomings were common. Appropriate music and sound effects accompanied film presentations in the vaudeville and vari-ety houses from the very beginning—partly because an orchestra was present already for the other acts, partly to drown the noisy projection machines which caused audience discomfort. Film exhibitors operating in other loca-tions than vaudeville theatres resorted to mechanical instruments such as the barrel organ, the music box, or the phonograph to minimize the unpleasant noise.

Toronto's movie shows were characteristic of those evident all over the world during the first years of the motion picture's existence. The Lumière Cinématographe was presented at the exhibition again in 1897 and 1898. Touring showmen arrived in town, with a projector and a collection of films, rented a store, ran their program till audience interest waned, then moved on. During the Toronto Industrial Exhibition of 1897, for example, two Americans rented an empty store at Yonge and Richmond to show movies of the famous title fight between James J. Corbett and Bob Fitzsimmons in the filming of which Ed Houghton (formerly of the Vitascope show at Robinson's) was involved. In 1900, Biograph's special film show covering the Boer War was sponsored at Massey Hall by the Canadian Patriotic Fund. Later *The Passion Play* was presented at Hanlan's Point.

John C. Green who, as Belsaz the magician, had presented Canada's first movie show in Ottawa, typifies those early showmen. Born in 1866, he was already on the road at the age of sixteen, touring with every kind of sideshow, circus, and theatrical stock. At one time he was known as "Green— the original Merry Wizard" as he travelled Canada and the United States. One of his strongest memories was of performing his magic show in an Indian encampment in the days when Indians could still be expected to be hostile. He finished his show as it was growing dark and was packing his trunks when he looked up to see dozens of Indian eyes staring at him. His scalp twitched as they entered the cabin in a rush. Then his interpreter learned their reason. They wanted those magic silk handkerchiefs that changed colour in front of their eyes. What did they matter to him, the Indians asked. He could always make more with his magic! It was three in the morning before he managed to leave.[34]

Green was playing with Dr. Bailey's medicine show along the Ottawa River in June 1896 when he read in the *Ottawa Free Press* that Ahearn and Soper of the Electric Railway Company had arranged with the Holland brothers of Ottawa to bring Edison's new Vitascope to Canada. Green was never one to miss out on a new gimmick. Even though he had never seen the Vitascope, he lost no time in writing to Ahearn and Soper and offering to lecture on the new invention, perform his magic act, and describe the pictures on the screen. In those days the films had no titles, not even an identifying title, since it was common to have someone on stage during the projection identifying the scene the audience was watching and adding his own, often humorous, comments. Though he had never done this before, Green was a great success and he latched onto the movies as a permanent part of his show. After the Ottawa show closed he teamed up with two partners, bought his own projection machine, and set out on tour. Green was the operator and lecturer and gave a magic show to fill out a full two-hour program. He travelled across eastern Canada and the New England States, carrying fourteen trunks of film reels, a hundred sets of song slides, and twenty-six kinds of special lithographed printing. Ottawa was to see him again some years after his first show when the Electric Railway Company extended its line west to Britannia in 1901 and hired him again at a hundred dollars a week all summer to perform at the new Britannia Park. After the show closed on Labour Day, Green presented movies in front of the Grandstand at Almonte and other fall fairs in eastern Ontario. When permanent movie theatres began to appear, his road-show days were over and he settled into managing theatres in Canada and Michigan.[35]

Frederic Conway Edmonds of Lindsay, Ontario, was one of the first travelling showmen in Canada. Born in England on June 2, 1850, he had come to Canada as a young man. He was a ventriloquist, magician, and theatre manager and had managed Larkin Hall in Hamilton as a vaudeville house. When it closed he launched "The Australian Medicine Show," one of the first of its kind to carry a sixty-foot tent with seating and a brass band. A special feature was the free extraction of teeth. After touring Ontario, New England, and the Maritimes, the show closed in 1895. On his return west he saw H. J. Hill's presentation of the Lumière Cinématographe on Yonge Street in Toronto. Intrigued, Edmonds purchased an Edison Vitascope and films and went out on the road. His son recalls his father "premiering" the film of Queen Victoria's funeral in Lindsay only three weeks after the funeral on February 2, 1901. He settled in Lindsay for a few years, designing equipment for slide and movie projection. (The rights to one of his inventions was sold to Thomas Edison.)[36] In 1906 he was back on the road again with his family. His son recalls: "Jim Fairbanks, a Toronto comedian, and myself got the talking picture idea on this trip—worked up a dialogue and sounds for *The River Pirates* and persuaded father to let us try it out in a small Northern town. It wasn't a success—in fact it almost wrecked the show. Opening time, the second night, found all the company sitting on the hall steps in a deserted town. Finally the postmaster came along and, after much persuasion, we found out the cause of the show going flat. He said about as follows: 'You want to know where the people are, do you? Well they are in their homes. Not a man, woman or child, in this town, slept last night and I was till four o'clock this morning seeing people home with the lantern. I will never forget, till my last day, the groans of those dying men. No more pictures for us.' The old gentleman assured us that we would have a full house next night if we promised that there wouldn't be any groans from 'dying men.' Right then we got notice that 'talking pictures' were off."[37]

Such ingenuity was a mark of the itinerant showmen. It had to be. Operating out of tents or "store" theatres, they faced problems no vaudeville exhibitor faced. The pre-1900 films were only mildly interesting: comedies, trick films, vaudeville acts, short melodramas, or scenic films. The vaudeville showman could depend on live performers to ensure that customers got their money's worth. But the itinerant film showman had only his ten or twelve films. In order to supplement his program and ensure an evening's entertainment, the showman necessarily had to adopt techniques of presentation unlike those of vaudeville. They were forced to use greater care in the selection of film subjects and equip themselves with better projectors when they came on the market. One approach was to supplement the film show with lantern slides and sometimes a lecture. Some offered modest vaudeville attractions, often in the form of the showman's wife singing a couple of songs. Others attempted to add sound to the images as did the Edmonds, or H. J. Hill on his first 1897 tour with the Lumière Cinématographe. "He had a man behind the screen, following the flickers. Whenever the blacksmith on the screen struck the picture anvil, down came the backstage hammer on a real anvil." [38] This may well have been the first presentation of "sound" movies in North America.

But soon, all the more enterprising exhibitors began assembling their short films into sets so they had more meaning and perhaps even offered a "theme" for the evening's entertainment. Representative of this approach was John Schuberg's "Spanish American War" show in Vancouver in 1898 during which the movies were supplemented by sound effects created from a bass drum, a large metal sheet, and a pistol with blank shells.

In fact, perhaps no other road showman was more enterprising than John Albert Schuberg, a Swedish-born showman known professionally as Johnny Nash. It was Schuberg who brought the movies to Vancouver, the British Columbia interior, Winnipeg, and many towns across the prairies. But for Johnny Nash, né Schuberg, the movies were only one more step in an already colourful career. Born February 21, 1875, the son of Swedish immigrants in Minneapolis, he was already in showbusiness at the age of thirteen with Kohn and Middleton's Dime Museum in Minneapolis. By the age of eighteen he had taught himself sleight-of-hand tricks and was known as the youngest magician in the profession. After working with circuses for two years, he decided to free-lance, moving to Winnipeg in 1894. There he worked with Fred Burrows, Winnipeg's first showman, playing the fairs and carnivals in the summer and free-lancing in the winter, going as far east as Montreal. In 1898, he married Nettie, youngest daughter of Fred Burrows, and they travelled to Vancouver for the honeymoon. Learning of the new Edison moving picture machine, Schuberg decided to buy one and in the neighbouring city of Seattle stocked up on films and stereopticon slides of the Spanish-American War. "I had reached the age of 23 and my wife was

18, so we really got in on the ground floor of motion pictures," he wrote in his unpublished autobiography "Fifty Years a Showman." [39]

Vancouver was still very much of a frontier town in 1898. Its 18,000 citizens were wary of the movie show Schuberg presented on December 15; they had been caught too often before by fairground hucksters. Schuberg's promise of "living pictures" of the Spanish-American War did not impress them. He had rented an empty store on West Cordova Street near Cambie, "set up equipment near the front and hung the screen at the back. As the show could only run about 30 minutes, seats were not necessary." [40] Admission was ten cents and announcements urged Vancouverites to "see Roosevelt's Roughriders and their trained horses, Sampson's fleet bombarding Matanza's and the burial of the Maine victims at Key West." But Vancouverites were suspicious of the new sideshow gimmick. How could one *see* such things? So Schuberg drew on his circus and dime museum days to tout customers. "People stayed away until I started bally-hooing the shows. I got some thundersheets, guns and drums and used them as background for the war scenes. That got people in." [41] Once inside, they were surprised to discover that the "moving pictures" Schuberg had advertised were really moving. For two weeks, there were capacity crowds.

But Schuberg only had the one set of films and inevitably he had to move on. He and his wife had plans for a black-top tent with which they could tour the fairs and carnivals and show movies. They intended to spend the remainder of the winter in Winnipeg preparing it. On their way back, they worked their passage by putting on shows in the halls of small communities along the CPR line. The first stop in Ashcroft was a disaster: the electrical power was not strong enough to give enough light for the projector and the audience's dimes had to be refunded. Kamloops was better—but not until the showmanship angle had been used again. As in Vancouver, there were no customers when he opened "The War Show" so Schuberg positioned his projector on a balcony overlooking the main street. Passers-by were intrigued enough to pay their dimes to find out what was happening in front of the projector.

In Winnipeg, they bought their twenty feet by sixty feet black-top tent which they called the "Edison Electric Theatre." [42] Its black canvas successfully kept out daylight and it was much imitated.

Their tour began in the spring of 1899 at a street fair in Fargo, North Dakota. Then, in May 1899, in association with W. S. Jones, they showed the first movies in Winnipeg in their black tent. The site was a vacant lot on the west side of Main Street, about 100 yards north of Logen Avenue. The

View of stage at West End Park, Ottawa, 1892, site of
the first public film showing in Canada in July 1896.

A typical black tent Electric Theatre similar to that operated by John Schuberg
in the West. This unidentified photograph is thought to be a British example,
not Canadian.

films were still "The War Show." They returned again to Winnipeg in July and played a week at the Fairgrounds after playing the street fairs in Minnesota and Wisconsin. The same group (Schuberg, Jones, Burrows) had another show at River Park in the spring of 1900 for one month.

For three years, Schuberg was on the road with his movie shows, as were dozens of similar entrepreneurs across Canada.

Not all the showmen were Canadians. Some were, of course, Americans (the border hardly existed for the showmen of the day) but a few travelled from Britain. One such was A. D. Thomas of the Royal Canadian Biograph Company who toured not only Canada but the West Indies in the first years of the century.[43] For some, the film presentations in Canada were better than those south of the border. One British magazine editor reported, "In Toronto, Hamilton and Montreal we saw better performances than in America, and there was desire shown to elevate and instruct by using films with an educational side."[44]

But that was in the urban centres. Smaller towns and settlements fared less well. The showmen ensured that no one was denied access to the new wonder—even if the same group of films were used over and over again. Not even the pioneer settlements of the north were ignored. In fact they were prime areas since the showmen cannily recognized that the inhabitants would welcome some form of diversion to while away the long evenings. An Englishman, Frederick Talbot, has left a striking account of such movie shows in the first years of the century:

> When I visited Cochrane, a town which has sprung up in the wilderness of Ontario, the picture showman had planted himself firmly in its midst. There was only one masonry building in the place, the majority of the 300 inhabitants living in wooden shacks or tents, because the town was in the formative stage. The showman acquired a site upon one of the main streets, and ran up a cheap wooden building with an attractive arched front, gaily bedecked with small red, white, and blue lamps. There was not a unit of electricity or a cubic foot of gas generated in the place, but the indefatigable showman overcame these difficulties by recourse to substitutes. The theatre was thronged the whole evening, a result due in a great measure to the fact that Cochrane was situate in the Prohibition area, and the theatre consequently had not to compete with the lures of the liquor saloon. The ranks of the inhabitants were swelled every day by gangs of workmen passing to and from the great railway construction camps, and the theatre was a distinct success and source of profit to the enterprising operator.

I encountered another quaint outburst of initiative at a far more inaccessible spot—the town of Hazelton around the Hudson Bay post at the head of navigation on the Skeena River in British Columbia. Prince Rupert, 186 miles away, was the nearest town and that post is 550 miles from Vancouver. A cinematograph showman arrived in Hazelton, which at that time boasted a handful of white men, and several Indians. The operator took over an excavation in the side of the hill overlooking the side of the town. . . . In this cramped, unventilated cellar he rigged his screen and lantern. On the wooden door he nailed a large sheet of paper on which was scrawled the name of the "Theatre" and the program of films "now being shown."

The preparations demanded only a few hours. Boxes, barrels, and logs sufficed for seats, while a good many patrons sat or sprawled upon the floor. The little vault was packed to suffocation on the opening night. The Indians were amazed and the whites were amused, though the films would not have been tolerated in London or New York, having long since passed their span of usefulness. The show was kept going day after day until the audience became too small to defray the cost of the illuminant, then the "theatre" was closed, and the showman haunted the verandah of the hotel until he received some new subjects. His supply of films was both uncertain and irregular. He had to order them by post from Vancouver, whence they were brought up by boat. If the fates were kind he received an entire change of program in about a fortnight; if the river were difficult to navigate, a month passed before they reached him, and often the boat came up without his goods, owing to lack of space. Probably no showman ever offered to the public under more difficult conditions. It was doubtful if he would secure any films at all during the winter, as, the river being frozen, communication between Hazelton and Prince Rupert had to be maintained by dog trains, which carry letter mail only.[45]

Catering to the Refined

Even as those shows were running in Cochrane, Hazelton, and a hundred other similar towns, the movies were already undergoing a transformation in the cities. Showmen like Schuberg had had to keep moving on to a new location not only because audience interest soon waned but also because they could not rent the films; they had to buy them. These films soon exhausted their entertainment value in any community long before they were worn out. At a hundred dollars a reel they were expensive to replace and the Schubergs, Greens, and Edmonds of the travelling circuits were bound to get their money's worth out of them. Inevitably they changed location instead of films. Not that this prevented some showmen from trying to establish permanent quarters. But these attempts failed until 1902–1903. It was at this time that not only longer, more dramatic, and more interesting films appeared on the market but—more significantly—the time when several bright showmen hit upon the idea of *renting* their films to others rather than selling them outright. If you could buy a reel of film for a hundred dollars, rent it to two other showmen for fifty dollars a week each, everything else would be profit. So the "film exchange" was born. It was to blossom rapidly into the motion picture industry's distribution arm—a necessary, if often resented, link between the film producer and the showman-exhibitor. The development of the film exchanges was however an essential prelude to the establishment of motion picture theatres as we know them today. With their services, a showman could now change his films instead of his location. By 1906, permanent—if often tawdry—movie theatres had sprung up in cities across Canada.

First of the travelling showmen to settle was John Schuberg. Tiring somewhat of the perpetual travelling, Schuberg and his wife determined to find a fixed location from which to operate. The world's first permanent theatre had come into being on April 16, 1902, in Los Angeles: The Electric Theatre operated by Thomas L. Tally. Returning to Vancouver in 1902, Schuberg decided to try the approach. He rented an empty store at 38 Cordova Street and that October the Electric Theatre became Canada's first "permanent" movie theatre. He opened with a new Edison epic *Mount Pelee in Eruption* and the crowds loved it. The printed program of the theatre for February 16, 1903, suggests the flavour of Schuberg's shows. The Electric Theatre, "Catering to the Refined" is "The Ladies' and Children's Favourite Place of Amusement" with "an Usher in Attendance to see that Ladies get Desirable Seats." Admission was ten cents, "chairs free."[46]

Three months later in Winnipeg he went into partnership with his father-in-law and opened the Dreamland Theatre, located on the west side of Main Street just north of the City Hall. Then he sold the Electric Theatre in Vancouver, moved back to Winnipeg, and opened the Unique Theatre in the fall of 1903 in a former undertaking parlour on the east side of Main Street in the old Cement Block. The opening film was *The Great Train*

The Palace Theatre, Cardston, Alberta, 1907—a typical example of
store-front theatres.

Robbery by Edwin S. Porter. The Unique continued in operation for many
years and was at one time managed by Fatty Arbuckle, the Hollywood slap-
stick comedian.

Over the next few years, Schuberg's career blossomed rapidly. He built
more theatres in Winnipeg, including the Bijou in 1906 (which finally
closed its doors in 1956) and the Province Theatre in 1909 and eventually
owned eight theatres, known as the Nash Circuit, in Manitoba and the central United States. In 1914 he moved back to Vancouver and, in partnership
with W. P. DeWees, obtained the franchise for First National Pictures in
western Canada. By then he was the leading theatre chain operator in the
west. In 1919 he sold out to the fast-growing Allen theatre chain but after
trying his hand at ranching was back in movies in 1921 as operator of the
Strand Theatre in Vancouver. In 1924 he sold out to N. L. Nathanson and
Famous Players Canadian Corporation and settled in Vancouver. He died
December 13, 1958, in Vancouver, one of the few Canadian showmen from

that era able to leave more than a few interesting reminiscences to his children.[47]

Schuberg was smart enough to spot a trend. A decade after its birth, film exhibition in Canada was changing. The days of the travelling showmen and carnival hucksters were nearly over. In urban centres at least, permanent or semi-permanent store-front theatres were making their appearance. Vancouver already had Schuberg's Electric in 1902, the first in Canada; soon it would have the Crystal (1904), Peoples (1904), Edison Grand (1905), and Le Petit (1905). Winnipeg had its Unique (1903), Dreamland (1903), and Roseland (1904). In St. John there was the York (1906), and in Montreal the Nationale (1904) and the Palais Royal (1904). These theatres, though they approximated to regular movie theatres, clearly betrayed their origins as former shops, undertaking parlours, or penny arcades. The audience sat on uncomfortable kitchen chairs, sometimes borrowed from neighbouring businesses. But with the opening of the Nickelodeon in Pittsburgh in November 1905, with its more elegant decor and comfortable theatre seats, there was already a hint of things to come. Audiences were delighted with the comfortable seats and cheap prices. And showmen everywhere quickly capitalized on their delight. "Nickelodeons" sprang up with surprising rapidity across the continent.

First in Canada was John C. Griffin who gave Toronto its first permanent movie theatre, the Theatorium, in March 1906—ten years after that first primitive Vitascope show at Robinson's Musee. Toronto-born John Griffin, a touring circus man, had seen movie theatres on his travels in the United States. He was particularly impressed with the Nickelodeon in Pittsburgh with its fancy house furnishings and comfortable seats. He was probably even more impressed with the fact that though the admission was only a nickel and though there were fewer than 200 seats, the Nickelodeon was yielding almost a thousand dollars a week profit with its opening program of *The Great Train Robbery*, the current film sensation.[48] Returning home for the winter to Toronto, Griffin decided to try to establish a similar theatre. He found a vacant store, 100 feet by seventeen feet, converted it, and named it the Theatorium. The opening attraction was an Edison production, *The Train Wreckers* (1905). He even added vaudeville to make sure the audience was getting its money's worth. The Theatorium was renamed The Red Mill by a later owner, but within a few years Griffin had eleven movie theatres in various parts of Toronto and was a major force on the Toronto entertainment scene. Out of that 1906 Theatorium grew a major Ontario theatre circuit.

Showmen everywhere were settling down to the more ordered and structured life of running their own theatres—though many did so with some reluctance.

One of the last to settle was John C. Green. He far preferred the joys of travel as Belsaz the Magician to the restrictions of running a theatre in one location. He held out until 1917 when even he realized there was no longer a demand for his kind of show. He joined the theatre chain operated by N. L. Nathanson and eventually became district manager in Guelph for several theatres in the Famous Players Canadian chain. Not surprisingly, Green was unhappy in this ordered and structured life, and at one time complained that the treatment he was receiving at the hands of Famous Players "leads me to believe I am serving a life-sentence with them."[49] In 1925 he quit and went back to his first love—magic and live stage. He was still active up to his death in 1951.

As for Frederic Conway Edmonds who had so ingeniously (and ingenuously) attempted to put dialogue onto his films, he too settled down. Throughout his life he attacked the prevalence of Hollywood films in Canadian theatres, advocating the importance of "Empire films" over those from south of the border. He was particularly outspoken during the First World War when he felt American films denigrated or ignored the British and Canadian contributions to the war.[50]

He had earlier opened the Wonderland Theatre in Lindsay (later remodelled and named the Kent Theatre), moved into distribution, and launched the British Canadian Feature Film Company which released European films in Canada. In 1914 he introduced the "talkies" to Canada with equipment manufactured by the Gaumont Company of England to which Edmonds owned Canadian rights. "These pictures were similar to those which are so popular today, only on a smaller scale. [The equipment] consisted of a specially built phonograph and records. The pictures and music were tuned by a dial on both record and film. They were shown for the first time in Wonderland, then were put on the road and played a number of picture theatres throughout the Province."[51]

Two of the earliest showmen to open movie theatres were the brothers Jules and Jay Allen who, with their father, Barney Allen, opened the Theatorium in Brantford in the fall of 1906. The American-born Allen brothers were soon to become major figures in the Canadian film industry. They opened their first film exchange, the Allen Amusement Corporation, in 1908, and in 1911 built their first luxury theatre—the 800-seat Allen Theatre in Calgary. From this grew a nation-wide chain that dominated film exhibition until 1922.

Another showman who became a major figure in the industry was Claire

Hague, later head of Canadian Universal. He had first arrived in Toronto with a carnival company at the turn of the century and eventually joined the Allens at the Brantford Theatorium before moving into distribution.

Movie theatres of greater or lesser elegance continued appearing across the country. In the Maritimes the first movie theatres opened in St. John in 1906 with the York on Carleton Street, and the Unique on Charlotte Street.[52] Halifax had the Imperial, the King Edward, and the Unique. Many of them were operated by former travelling showmen. Kingston had its Wonderland, Edmonton its Bijou, and Ottawa its Peoples and Nationale. Hamilton perhaps topped them all with the opening of The Red Mill in March 1907: the theatre had rainbow-coloured glass stairs with water flowing underneath.

Programs at these "nickelodeon" theatres lasted from twenty minutes to a full hour and usually included a ten-minute melodrama, a comedy, and an "interest" film or travelogue. Sometimes the films were supplemented by a singer or other performer.[53] No theatre was complete without its lecturer who chattered throughout each film, commenting, amplifying, adding colour, and filling in the gaps if anything was lacking in the film. The best spieler had the most vivid imagination. Theatre patrons sometimes sat through two or more performances. To prevent this the owner of the Comique Theatre in Toronto required all patrons to move up one or two seats whenever anybody decided to leave. "Amateur night" was a regular and popular addition to the program, not only with audiences but with the owners, since it was inexpensive. It was common for film programs to be changed frequently and not uncommon for them to change twice a day.[54] Since the theatres only accommodated a couple of hundred people at a time, the films ran continuously from morning to night and had to be changed frequently so people would come back. It seems extraordinary that audiences attended the theatres so often that programs had to be changed once or twice a day. But it was actually the case and suggests that, for some Canadians at least, the movies were already accepted as a major part of their social life.

But only for some Canadians. Despite Schuberg's claim that his Electric Theatre was "Catering to the Refined," movie theatres were not places in which respectable people cared to be seen. Educated people still considered the movies vulgar, low-class entertainment. One man in Montreal was determined to change that. Because Ernest Ouimet—whose interest in movies had first been aroused back in 1896—saw no reason why movie attendance should not be acceptable social entertainment. And he set out to prove it.

Léo Ernest Ouimet was born in St. Martin, Quebec (now part of Ville de Laval) on March 16, 1877. He left school at twelve and worked on his father's farm for five years until 1894 when he moved to Montreal. He found work as a plumber's apprentice and later as an electrician. In 1900 he secured the contract for wiring the Théâtre National in Montreal and became chief stage electrician when he completed the work. By 1904 he had made his first move into the film business when he acquired the Canadian franchise for the Kinetographe Company of New York.[55]

His first efforts were as an itinerant projectionist in and around Montreal. He quickly made a name for himself and was soon a familiar figure at vaudeville theatres and fairs all over the island. But the movies were just emerging from the time when they were mere carnival novelties and vaudeville "chasers." They were becoming serious business enterprises and perspicacious Ernest Ouimet was determined to be among the first to develop them. In fact, he wanted a theatre of his own.

In 1905, with fifty dollars in his pocket, he rented the salle Poiré, a former *café-concert* attached to the Klondike Hotel, at the south-east corner of St. Catherine East and Montcalm, and opened it as the "Ouimetoscope" on January 1, 1906. As was common then, it closed during the summer months so in that time he replaced the kitchen chairs with theatre seats, increased the seating capacity to 600 and created a comfortable atmosphere along the lines of that of the nickelodeons.

Meanwhile, Ouimet's former employer, Georges Gauvreau, had sold his Théâtre National but was being lured out of retirement by the new prospects in the film business. He made an offer to buy the property on which the Ouimetoscope stood. Ouimet was forced to raise counter-financing in order to retain control of his theatre. Eventually, he paid $70,000 for the property, $30,000 for the hotel licence that went with it, plus an additional $50,000 to design and construct a new Ouimetoscope on the site of the old hotel. The work took three months and entailed a cost unheard of at that time for a movie theatre. Nonetheless when the Ouimetoscope opened on August 31, 1907, Ouimet's faith was justified. There was nothing like it anywhere and there was to be nothing comparable until the Warner Theatre opened on Broadway in 1914. It was an imaginative declaration of faith in the future of the motion picture as public entertainment.

The Ouimetoscope had 1200 seats. It had a check-room. Its admission prices were high (the top admission of fifty cents was comparable to vaudeville prices but far higher than the standard five cents to other movie theatres) but it offered reserved seats and encouraged attendance by offering special reduced prices to ladies and children in the afternoons. The auditorium had stalls and a balcony just as in the legitimate theatres. The lobby was spacious with walls of ceramic tiles decorated with appropriate motifs—those on the left represented art and music, those on the right had drama as a theme. The Ouimetoscope offered two shows a day and had a seven piece orchestra which played music for the six reel film program on the screen. The orchestra also accompanied singers who appeared with illustrated slides during the ten-minute *entr'actes* that divided the film presentations. During the *entr'actes*, a corner bar offered drinks (the cost for the hotel licence was probably worth it to Ouimet!) or one could enjoy one of the boxes of candy sold in the theatre. An eight-page magazine, *Le Ouimetoscope*, was also available to patrons.[56]

It was an extraordinary achievement. But, imaginative as it was, it was ahead of its time. Within a few years of its opening, Ouimet's ambitions were shattered. In order to compete with the multitude of nickel theatres that surrounded it, Ouimet was forced to compromise his standards, and the Ouimetoscope became indistinguishable from its neighbours. He rented it out in 1915 and it ceased operation in 1926. The site is now occupied by the Festival and Canadien theatres on the walls of which a small plaque bears tribute to Ouimet's achievement. It was to be nearly another decade before comparable theatres opened and flourished in Canada.

In the meantime, Ouimet's competitor, Georges Gauvreau, financed another theatre, the Nationalscope, four blocks away at the corner of St. Catherine East and Saint-André. Its manager was Arthur Larente, another Montreal pioneer who was to be involved in distribution and exhibition for many years as well as in the production of the first Quebec fiction film *Madeleine de Verchères*.

Ernest Ouimet was to continue in the film business for thirty years—always as a pioneer, always attempting to open new ground. He opened the first film exchange in Canada in May 1906 and established his first branch office in St. John, New Brunswick, where he also acquired another theatre, the Bijou Dream on Union Street. He began to produce his own films in 1908 and in 1915 became exclusive North American representative of the Pathé Film Company of France, launching Speciality Film Import with six offices across Canada. Even when, later, his career in production ended, he was far from idle. He had been one of the first to explore the potential of sound movies in his Ouimetoscope in 1908 and in his later years he was an inveterate experimenter with stereoscopy. He was an extraordinary man, a true pioneer, eager and always curious. It is no surprise that the story of his rise and fall should parallel so closely that of Canadian cinema itself. Always in the vanguard of new developments, whether in production or distribution, he was also to become the most notable victim of the Canadian film industry's inability to control its own destiny.

It was in these first years that the patterns of Canadian cinema were formed. The showmen were Canadian; the theatres, when they developed, were still Canadian owned. But few of the films Canadians saw were Canadian made. Typical programs of the time suggest that Canadians were watching movies, sixty percent of which were of American origin, forty percent of British and French, with a scattering of films from other countries. Canadians, it appears, were content to run the distributorships and operate the theatres but in the years before 1914 there were few Canadians who attempted to make their own films. And this, even including the fact that at the time the terms "Canadian" and "British" were all but interchangeable. If it were not for the stimulus of government and industrial sponsorship it is likely there would have been even fewer.

Among the films Canadians saw there was a fair proportion of images of Canada. Canada's exotic scenery very quickly found a place on the screens of the world as, later, did the adventures of trappers, lumberjacks, and Mounties. But few were Canadian made.

CHAPTER 2

The Early Years

The dearth of production in the first years of the century was a situation not peculiar to Canada. In the first decade after the invention of the movies, it was characteristic of most other countries—even of countries such as Italy, Germany, and Sweden, which were later to develop significant domestic film industries. Those countries which had played key roles in the invention and marketing of film cameras and projectors—Britain, France, and the United States—also dominated production internationally. Not that anyone then paid any attention to a film's country of origin. Stars, directors, and all the later paraphernalia of the movies were totally absent. The films were little more than depictions of interesting scenes drawn from life (what we would now call travelogues, newsreels, or documentaries) or brief comic or dramatic sketches, a few minutes only in length. Even the later well-known "silent" film tradition of explanatory or dialogue titles was absent. Films could, and did, easily cross borders without adaptation.

With the development of permanent movie theatres and the parallel increase in production of "story" films, all this changed. The film histories, proper, of most countries date from this point, when film makers began producing to satisfy domestic demand. Not, of course, that American, British, and French films were suddenly excluded. There was still no language barrier; films had no dialogue and only the titles required translation.

Canada was not, of course, in a comparable situation to most of the European countries nor to the United States. Its urban population was comparatively low and it was the cities which had made possible the multiplication of movie theatres and the consequent growth of a film industry—most notably in the United States. The immigrants who were crowding into the burgeoning cities of the United States in the early years of the century played a significant role in the growth of the American film industry. The movies were not only cheap entertainment—cheaper than vaudeville or the theatre —but, more importantly, required little or no knowledge of English as did other kinds of public entertainment. In contrast, most Canadian immigrants headed for rural areas. In 1905, Canada's population of some six million was strung out across 3,000 miles, hugging the border with the United States. Of its cities, only Toronto and Montreal exceeded populations of 100,000.

But there was a factor which had a more direct influence in shaping the pattern of Canadian cinema though it too stemmed from the population and size of Canada. Countries which developed film industries already had well established vaudeville, music hall, and theatrical traditions. And film producers drew heavily on these traditions when movies began to tell stories. In fact the links between stage and screen in the early years are extremely close and many of the first movie producers and actors had begun their careers on the stage. But Canada had no such traditions. Most of the plays staged in Canada in the nineteenth century were "stock company" productions on tour from Britain, France, or the United States. Canadians who wanted to develop their careers in acting, writing, or producing for the stage almost inevitably found it necessary to base themselves in the United States, Britain, or Europe. Thus, when the movies had developed to the point of needing a particular kind of trained personnel, Canada had none. This is a crucial fact which was to haunt Canadian production.

It was in these years that Canada lost many of those who might have helped establish and sustain a film industry. Among them were pioneer directors Sidney Olcott (a key contributor to the development of the Kalem Company), Allan Dwan (a major film director in a sixty-year career from 1909, including the classic Douglas Fairbanks films), Mack Sennett, and lesser names such as Del Henderson, Harry Edwards, John Murray Anderson, Joseph De Grasse, John Robertson, Reginald Barker, J. Gordon Edwards, and Henry MacRae. Jack Warner (born London, Ontario), Al Christie (born London, Ontario), and Louis B. Mayer (who emigrated to New Brunswick from Russia with his parents) were three producers who made significant contributions to the growth of Hollywood. The names of actors and actresses are too numerous to list comprehensively, but they include Mary Pickford (and her brother and sister, Jack and Lottie), Marie Dressler, Florence Lawrence, Lew Cody, Fay Wray, Walter Pidgeon, Ruby Keeler, Pauline Garon, Walter Huston, Gene Lockhart, Beatrice Lillie, Nell Shipman, Ned Sparks, Berton Churchill, and Norma Shearer. Others include scriptwriters W. Scott Darling, Nell Shipman, and George White, art director Richard Day, photographers James Crosby, Alvin Knechtel, and sound engineer Douglas Shearer. Talented Canadians it would seem, made a far greater contribution to Hollywood than they did to Canada's own films.

Images of Canada

The first films made in Canada, as elsewhere, were "interest" films, brief scenes of Canadian points of interest. Niagara Falls, "the mecca of all early motion picture cameramen,"[1] were the first featured attraction—filmed, separately, by three cameramen in September and October 1896: Felix Mesguich for Lumière, W. K. L. Dickson for the American Mutoscope and Biograph Company, and an unknown cameraman for Edison.[2] Another popular subject was the Rockies. Scenes were most often photographed from a moving railway train, with the friendly cooperation of the Canadian Pacific Railway. G. W. ("Billy") Bitzer—later famous as D. W. Griffith's cameraman—photographed a series of five films for American Mutoscope and Biograph in October 1899.[3] Edison's cameraman shot another series of six films on the Rockies in 1901.[4] Not surprisingly, films of Canadian winter scenes were also a popular attraction, as were "newsreels" of visits by royalty together with other Canadian activities that might interest American audiences.[5] Among these were films of Canadian troops leaving for the Boer War in 1899 and films of the visit of the Duke of York to Canada in 1902, all released by Edison.

The names of many of the early cameramen who filmed Canadian subjects have not survived. Certainly some, such as Billy Bitzer, were sent into Canada by the parent company; others may have been Canadians who photographed scenes on a free-lance basis and sold their films to Edison, Biograph, or another company. One such may have been Robert Bonine. In October 1897, the Edison Company began releasing a series of films on the Klondike Gold Rush, scenes first of the loading of baggage and horses and later scenes in the Klondike itself.[6] Eight films in all, priceless records of one of the most extraordinary events of modern times. The photographer was Robert Bonine, a cameraman who supplied film to both Edison and Biograph. Nothing is known of his origin; but his name and the fact that most of the material he obtained for these companies was of Canadian origin suggest that he was himself Canadian. The films of life in the Klondike were not released by Edison until May 1901, presumably after Bonine's return from the gold fields. In early 1902, both Edison and Biograph released an unusually large number of films set in Montreal and Quebec. The records of Biograph show that Bonine photographed three films for the company in February 1902: *Run of a Snowshoe Club*, *Quebec Fire Department on Sleds*, and *What Ho, She Bumps!*[7] At the same time, the Edison Company released several very similar films: *Skiing in Quebec*, *Skiing in Montreal*, *Tobogganing in Canada*, and *Coasting at Montmorency Falls*. It seems likely that Bonine also photographed these as it does that he was the cameraman for *Arrival of the Governor General, Lord Minto, at Quebec* (February 1902).[8] Bonine's work immediately after this was entirely outside Canada; in August 1902 he photographed the coronation of King Edward VII and in 1906 he filmed the San Francisco earthquake, but his later career is unknown.

Almost certainly the first Canadian to produce his own films was James S. Freer, a farmer from Brandon, Manitoba, who had purchased an Edison camera and projector. Freer, a former printer and newspaper publisher in Bristol, England, had settled in Manitoba in 1888.[9] By the fall of 1897 he was filming scenes of life in Manitoba, including harvesting and the arrival of the CPR trains, and by April 1898 was on tour with his films in Britain.[10] Freer's tour was sponsored by the Canadian Pacific Railway Company and his show, "Ten Years in Manitoba" included not only movies but lectures on "the value of agricultural pursuits in Canada . . . the richness of the Canadian soil and the large free grants of land which are given to emigrants by the Canadian government."[11] How the CPR became involved with this venture is not known.[12] However, William Van Horne, builder and then head of the CPR, was a great believer in modern promotional methods; it appears not unlikely to have been his personal decision to back Freer's tour. Certainly, this was only the first involvement by the CPR in using film as a tool in its land settlement policies. Over the next two decades the company was to be increasingly involved in motion pictures, eventually establishing its own production company in Montreal.

Freer's films included: *Arrival of CPR Express at Winnipeg*; *Pacific and Atlantic Mail Trains*; *Harnessing the Virgin Prairie*; *Canadian Continental Jubilee*; *Premier Greenway Stooking Grain*; *Six Binders at Work in Hundred Acre Wheatfield*; *Typical Stooking Scene*; *Harvesting Scene, with Trains Passing By*; *Cyclone Thresher at Work*; *Coming thru' the Rye* [Children playing in the hay]; *Winnipeg Fire Boys on the Warpath*, and *Canadian Militia Charging Fortified Wall*. While in Britain, Freer photographed *Canadian Contingent at the Jubilee* and *Changing Guards at St. James Palace*, which he added to his program. His tour was a great success, drawing praise from newspapers for the novel use of the motion picture as an "emigration agent." The London *Daily Mail* admired Freer's "capital series of cinematograph pictures" while the Norwich

READING Y.M.C.A.

LECTURE HALL,

THURSDAY, FEBRUARY 9th, 1899,

At 8 p.m.

CINEMATOGRAPH

❈ LECTURE ❈

ILLUSTRATED BY . . .

ANIMATED PICTURES

"Ten Years in Manitoba"

BY

Mr. JAMES S. FREER,

Of Brandon, Manitoba, Canada.

25,000 Instantaneous Photos upon Half-a-Mile of Edison Films, *representing the following amongst other scenes :—*

Arrival of C.P.R. Express at Winnipeg; Pacific and Atlantic Mail Trains; Premier Greenway stooking grain; Six Binders at work in 100 acre Wheat Field; Typical Stacking Scene; Harvesting Scene, with Trains passing; Cyclone Thresher at work; Coming thro' the Rye (Children play in the Hay); Winnipeg Fire Boys on the Warpath; Canadian Militia charging Fortified Wall; Canadian Contingent at the Jubilee; Harnessing the Virgin Prairie; Changing Guards at St. James's Palace (as exhibited at Windsor Castle); and other subjects.

MUSICAL ACCOMPANIMENTS.

Admission by Member's Pass or by Tickets 1/- and 6d. To be obtained of Members, or at Office.

An example of the handbills used to promote the British tour of
James Freer in 1899.

Eastern Daily Press described his films as "reproducing in realistic manner the conditions of life in the Far West from the interior of a bachelor's shanty to Mr. Freer's pretty and attractive family residence with the family assembled outside."[13]

How many Britons were convinced to emigrate to Canada as a result of Freer's films and lectures is unknown. They must have had some effect because, in December 1901, the federal minister of the interior, Clifford Sifton, agreed to sponsor a second tour, "under the auspices of the Canadian Government."

James Freer had returned to Manitoba in the spring of 1899. He attempted to make additional films but without much apparent success and increasingly he turned his activities toward exhibitions, showing films of the "Old Country" in Manitoba. He attempted to obtain the federal government's co-operation in his planned filming of the Duke of York's visit to Ottawa.[14] He received no reply to his letter and the visit was filmed instead by a cameraman for Edison, films which Freer then had to purchase for his collection. He may have attempted other film projects but, if so, they failed. For his 1902 tour, Freer used again the films he had used in 1898–99 with the addition of new films purchased from other producers: *Canadian Mounted Rifles Cutting Off a Boer Commando*; *Arrival of the Duke of York in Canada*; *Shooting the Chutes*. The only new Freer film was of a trip across the Atlantic from Liverpool to Quebec City, probably photographed on his return from the 1898–99 tour. This second tour was less successful than the first, possibly because Freer visited many of the same towns, and audiences must have been disappointed to discover they were watching the same scenes they had seen three years earlier. In any case, neither the Canadian government nor the CPR repeated the experience with Freer. When the CPR, liking the idea but wanting new films, decided to sponsor their own they went not to James Freer but to a British producer, Charles Urban. Freer himself returned to Manitoba and apparently abandoned film production though he continued running film shows.

The CPR was not alone in discovering the potential of motion pictures for promotion and advertising. By 1898, several commercial companies (notably the soap companies) were taking advantage of films to promote their products.[15] Among the first was the Massey-Harris Company of Toronto which, in 1898, commissioned the Edison Company to produce films of its agricultural machinery at work on Ontario farms.[16] A by-product of Walter Massey's interest in photography, the films were shown at the Toronto, Ottawa, and Montreal exhibitions of 1898 and later exported to Britain from where it was "anticipated that large orders for goods will follow." This early involvement by both commercial companies and government is of interest because it, too, set a pattern that continued to mark Canadian production over many decades. Indeed, it seems to have been realized almost from the beginning in Canada that film could be used for more than just entertainment. The Massey-Harris films are an example of this, as are the two tours by James Freer to promote immigration. In fact, the CPR's inevitable need to promote settlement of "The Last Best West" was to be a key element in Canadian film production until 1910.

"But No Snow or Ice Scenes"

At the turn of the century, Canada had a population of just over five million. Between then and 1914 the combined efforts of the CPR, other railways, and the federal government lured more than three million immigrants to Canada. "Nothing to compare with the great mass migration into Western Canada during the first decades of the twentieth century ever happened before. . . . Nowhere were more people enticed, cajoled, persuaded, induced, gulled, or just plain bamboozled into tearing themselves up by their roots to journey . . . to a land where not a single constructive step had been taken by anybody to prepare for their arrival." [17]

In this process of persuasion, the motion picture was to play a key role, being used first by the CPR and later by governments themselves and other railways. The effectiveness of these films was to be remembered later by officials of the federal government when they were considering the establishment of a permanent government film bureau in 1917.

Most of the films were directed principally at British audiences. This was a deliberate policy decision. In the first five years of the century immigrants from the United States outnumbered those from Britain. There was concern in Ottawa that the "British" character of the Canadian west might be lost, indeed that the west itself might be lost to the United States, if British immigration were not stepped up. [18]

First in the motion picture field was the CPR, whose commercial viability depended on the rapid settlement of the Canadian west. In 1902, soon after Freer's second tour, the CPR hired a British group to travel across Canada filming scenes of Canadian life. The films were guaranteed release in Britain through the Charles Urban Trading Company and were designed to stimulate emigration from Britain. [19] Charles Urban also supplied the personnel of the group: F. Guy Bradford, a cameraman, technician, and later an executive with Urban's company; Clifford Denham, Bradford's brother-

The Bioscope Company of Canada (Joe Rosenthal, Cliff Denham, Guy Bradford, and an unidentified man) established by Charles Urban to make films for the CPR in 1903. This photograph was taken on the CPR tracks near Dorval.

in-law; and Joe Rosenthal, the most famous cameraman of his day, whose reputation had been established by his coverage of the Boer War in South Africa. The group called themselves the Bioscope Company of Canada following Urban's general practice.[20] They had strict instructions from the CPR, according to Cliff Denham, "not to take any winter scenes under any conditions." Canada was—already—thought of too much as a land of ice and snow. CPR liaison for the filming was handled by Mr. Kerr, general passenger agent, and Mr. Armstrong, colonization agent.[21]

Filming began in the early fall of 1902, continued through the summer of 1903, and covered the country from Quebec to Victoria—following, of course, the CPR railroad. "The railroad scenes were taken from a flat car pushed by an engine and the others were usually picked out by Tourist Bureaus, etc., as we visited different cities in turn."[22] Guy Bradford set up processing facilities in downtown Montreal to print the film as it was shot. His assistant was Maurice Metzger who later became superintendent of Associated Screen News' film laboratory.

The first films to arrive in Britain in January 1903 were given a major première at the Palace Theatre, London in the presence of the Canadian high commissioner, Lord Strathcona (formerly Donald Alexander Smith of the CPR) who "has so materially assisted in developing the resources of Canada."[23] The series, eventually to be called *Living Canada*, pictured Canada from coast to coast, from the arrival of immigrants at Quebec City, through the Canadian Shield, across the prairies, and down the Fraser River Canyon to Vancouver. The first night audience gave the films a "hearty reception"; London's critics were also kind. The films "included some of the finest we have seen; the Fraser River 'run' took twelve minutes to pass through, and, photographically was remarkably good. The harvesting, ranching, and lumbering views are, besides, full of instruction in characteristic phases of Canadian life, and altogether we congratulate those concerned on a display of animated photographs which, for technical excellence and deep interest, we have not seen excelled."[24]

True to his covenant with the CPR, Charles Urban diligently avoided displaying any winter scenes at that première performance. The CPR itself and Canadian immigration agents used that series in special presentations throughout Britain, often accompanied by a lecturer, in the manner of James Freer. But when Urban came to release the films of his own account for general theatrical release in June 1903, it was apparent that the trio at work in Canada had not taken the CPR's instructions too seriously. Such films as *Montreal on Skates*, *Ice Yachting on the St. Lawrence*, and *The Outing of the "Old Tuque Blue" Snow-Shoeing Club of Montreal* were listed in Urban's catalogue under the heading "*Living Canada* by Joseph Rosenthal."[25] Other films were more what had been expected, including items on the lumber industry, threshing wheat, Indian canoe races, the Labour Day Parade in Vancouver, CPR trains in the Rockies, and, inevitably, *Niagara, the World's Wonder*. The trio also took advantage of additional financing from the Anglo-British Columbia Packing Company to produce *Catching Fifty Thousand Salmon in Two Hours*. In all, Charles Urban released thirty-five *Living Canada* films in 1903–1904. In 1906, several of the films were re-edited, condensed, and re-released under the title *Wonders of Canada*.[26]

Living Canada was also exhibited in Canada in programs organized by Denham and Bradford.[27] Their two and a half hour show opened at the Windsor Hall in Montreal in 1903, ran for six weeks, moved to Massey Hall in Toronto for two weeks, and then toured the country. Joe Rosenthal left

Canada at the end of his assignment in order to film the Russo-Japanese War. Both Bradford and Denham remained in Canada, and both developed careers in exhibition. Denham settled in Victoria B.C., and eventually managed several theatres for Famous Players Canadian Corporation. Bradford, "a very fine type of cultured English gentleman with a real genius for creating enthusiasm," moved to the Maritimes and was instrumental in starting St. John's first deluxe movie theatre, the Nickel.[28] Later he opened other theatres in the Maritimes and became a distributor himself.

While in Canada, Rosenthal produced what is certainly the first film drama made in Canada: *"Hiawatha", The Messiah of the Ojibway.* Released by Urban in the fall of 1903, it was described as a dramatized presentation of Longfellow's poem *The Song of Hiawatha* "enacted by North American Indians of the Ojibway Tribe at Desbarats, Ontario." The makers are unknown but Urban's catalogue acknowledges the conception as the work of Mr. E. A. Armstrong of Montreal—who may well have been the same Armstrong who was the CPR's colonization agent. At 800 feet (fifteen minutes) *Hiawatha* was considerably longer than the usual production of 1903 which rarely exceeded 200 feet. Urban subtitled the film *The Passion Play of America* ("There is but one Oberammergau. There is but one Desbarats.") and it is evident that the film was largely a photographed stage play though set in natural surroundings. The nine-page description which Urban included in his catalogue is in fact a rapturous description of the original stage play since it includes references to the play's music (by Frederick R. Burton) and the spoken words of Longfellow's poem. The anonymous author concluded: "Never had play such a setting. Never had actors such splendid distances, such a glorious background. The picture stamps itself indelibly upon the mind of every beholder, a perpetual memory, odorous with the unameable [*sic*] fragrance of pine and cedar and balsam, and shelving rock and shimmering water."[29] While on the West Coast Rosenthal also made a short one-minute drama, *Indians Gambling for Furs—Is it Peace or War?*, released also in September 1903.

Urban's success with the CPR films was to lead to two other Canadian contracts. These were, first, with the British Columbia government in June 1908 for the purposes "of making known the advantages and resources of British Columbia to the outside world,"[30] and second, with the Canadian Northern Railway Company in 1909 which, not to be outdone by the CPR, also wanted "to induce settlers of the right kind to emigrate from [Britain]."[31] The films resulting from these ventures were less scenic and tended to concentrate more on industrial and agricultural aspects of Canada with such titles as *Pulp Mills in the Province of Quebec*, *Canadian Iron Centre*, *Port*

Arthur, *Modern Methods of Harvesting*, and *Stripping a Forest in Winter*.[32] A British reviewer commented that the industrial processes could be seen "to better advantage in this country and we failed to detect anything exceptional in the Canadian films." He was somewhat doubtful of *The Emigrant's Progress* in Canada which showed him "from the time of selecting his free land grant till we see him with his motor-car and fifty horses (plus a very imposing house) representing a piece of good fortune which the sceptical stay-at-home may consider too good to be true."[33]

Other railway companies intended to do their bit. In 1909, the Grand Trunk Railway Company hired Butcher's Film Service. Frank Butcher and E. L. Lauste travelled from London to spend four months filming along the routes served by the Grand Trunk and Grand Trunk Pacific Railroads. The films were premièred in London in January 1910, introduced by speeches from several Canadian and British representatives who stressed Canada's need for "five million workers at once" to join the "fine specimens of the Anglo-Saxon race" already settled there.[34] Similar to the Urban efforts, the films included the traditional views of Niagara Falls, of harvesting, lumbering, and of Indian life together with "one of the most wonderful pictures ever produced," *Building of a Transcontinental Railway in Canada*, which depicted the techniques of track-laying.[35]

Meanwhile foreign producers were continuing to make "interest" films in Canada which varied little from earlier efforts, except in length. Typical of these are the Edison releases *Stalking and Shooting Caribou, Newfoundland* (1907); *Honeymoon at Niagara Falls* (1907); *A Canadian Winter Carnival* (1909, photographed by James White); *The Codfish Industry in Newfoundland* (1911); and *Eskimos in Labrador* (1911); Biograph releases *Moose Hunt in New Brunswick* (1905), and *Salmon Fishing Nipissiquit River* (1906) both photographed by Billy Bitzer; Solax releases *Caribou Hunting* (1911); *Salmon Fishing in Canada* (1911) and *Highlands of New Brunswick, Canada* (1911); British and Colonial Kinematograph release *Seal Hunting in Newfoundland* (1912); and Pathé releases *Picturesque Canada* (1907); *Bear Hunt in Canada* (1908) and *Montréal, Québec and Halifax* (1913). Audiences, it would appear, never tired of viewing Canada's stereotyped image.

The spectacular vistas of the Arctic were also favoured images for cinematographers. James H. Avery accompanied the Wellman expedition to the North Pole in the summer of 1906, though his film was apparently never released. Another British cameraman travelled with the Ziegler expedition in late 1909. In 1911, the Warwick Trading Company released Rayleigh and Robert's films of the 1909 *Arctic Voyage of H. R. H. Prince Imperial Henry of Prussia and Count Zeppelin*, photographed by I. Roseman.[36] It was not until

1913–16 that a Canadian, George H. Wilkins, photographed Arctic scenes during the Stefansson Canadian Arctic Expedition.[37] Of somewhat more significance were serious ethnological films recording the way of life of Indians and Eskimos.

Robert Flaherty made a six-reel film of Eskimo life during the Sir William MacKenzie expedition to Baffin Island in 1913–15.[38] It was shown at the University of Toronto in April 1915 but later destroyed in a fire. Its loss was propitious. It ensured that Flaherty made a second film on his next Arctic expedition: the classic *Nanook of the North*.

Notable among the ethnological films is *In the Land of War Canoe* (1914) a six-reel dramatic recording of Kwakiutl Indian life, filmed by Edward S. Curtiss on Vancouver Island.[39] This drama of love and war, part document, part fiction, predates Flaherty's *Nanook of the North* but bears comparison with both this classic and the later *The Silent Enemy* in its manner of dramatizing actuality.

Those few Canadians who managed to make films on their own account at least avoided the almost mindless simplicity of the image of Canada that was being projected abroad. A Toronto photographer, George Scott, filmed *The Great Toronto Fire* of April 1904 during which 114 buildings were destroyed in eight hours. He released the film himself in the United States, but sold British rights to Charles Urban. Scott also produced several other short "interest" films: *Glimpses of High Life* (1905) depicting holiday scenes in Toronto; and *Scenes in and about Toronto* (1907). He almost certainly shot other films but, if so, no records have survived.

In Newfoundland, Judge Harry Winter was actively filming from 1904, creating records of various royal and vice-regal visits, celebrated local events, and particularly the training and embarkation of the Royal Newfoundland Regiment in 1914–15 and the Victory Parade of 1919.

Ernest Ouimet of Montreal began filming in 1908, first by recording a touching portrait of the lives of his own children, *Mes espérances*, then by taking his camera into the streets to record the life around him. Among the events he filmed were: *Quebec: The Tercentenary Celebration* (1908) which he sold to Charles Urban and *The Eucharist Congress in Montreal* (1910) which was released by Butcher's Film Service. Ouimet also filmed Sir Wilfred Laurier during the 1911 federal election campaign and the construction of the Quebec Bridge among other newsworthy items, films which he showed in his own theatres. Unfortunately, illness forced Ouimet to withdraw from active production and other film activities from about 1912 until 1915 when he founded Speciality Film Import to distribute the films of the French Pathé

Company, including the Pearl White and Ruth Roland serials. Later, he was to return again to active production.

The Kinemacolor Company of Canada, headed by Henry J. Brock, is one of the curiosities of the time.[40] Established in 1911 to distribute British films produced with the patented Kinemacolor process, it quickly moved into filming on its own account.[41] Sometime during 1911, film of "the gorgeous beauties of nature among the Rocky Mountains" was produced. The ever cooperative CPR provided a "Kinemacolor special"—a "special engine attached to a dark room on wheels."[42] In 1912 a film of *The Canadian National Exhibition at Toronto* was released.[43] A two-reel drama, *A Romance of the Canadian Wilds* (1912), may or may not have been a Canadian Kinemacolor production. Not untypical of its times, this was the story of a New York artist who decides to settle among the French Canadians in "close commune with unmolested nature." There he falls in love with a local girl and arouses the jealousy of Pierre, "a native admirer," who attempts to kill him. The girl saves the artist's life, "Pierre repents and by death pays the penalty of his wickedness, the stern father is persuaded by the village priest to forgive his daughter" and all ends happily for the young lovers.[44]

Adventures in the Northwoods

A Romance of the Canadian Wilds was not untypical because for some five years previously there had been evidenced a proclivity on the part of American producers to make "Canada-as-content" dramas. The films, even down to their titles, are all "much of a muchness." They all tend to emphasize the romantic, awesome vastness of the land: Canada as wilderness. The same stock characters appear first in 1908 and crop up again and again in Hollywood films about Canada right through the Fifties: French-Canadian lumberjacks or trappers (who usually play the villain of the piece), the almost invariably vicious "half-breed," whisky runners, the odd miner or gold prospector, and the inevitable noble Mountie who not only always gets his man but usually his woman, too. The heroines are often the daughters of trading post managers, NWMP officers, or of pioneers hacking a bare living out of the wilderness. Refugees from justice, "across the border," occur with remarkable frequency in the northwoods films. As William Gladish wrote in the Toronto *Daily News* in 1918: "Canadians may soon become as tired of Canadian characterizations in moving pictures as they have disliked Kipling's *Our Lady of the Snows*. It is being poured out that every so-called Canadian film story depicts life at a Hudson's Bay trading post with the players wearing furs, snowshoes and Red River costumes and using firearms and dogsleighs freely."[45] The writer was incensed about *That Devil, Bateese* [*sic*, presumably "Baptiste"].

The Kalem Company was the first American company to travel into Canada to film Canadian dramas on location. The Kalem Company was established in 1907 and much of its continuing historical significance rests on the company's willingness to travel around the world to film stories in their natural locations. They had a company of players in Florida in 1908, and in 1910 and 1911 were to film dramas in Ireland and the Middle East. But their production of nine films in Canada in the summer and fall of 1909 was their first foreign venture. Frank Marion, one of the heads of the company, was involved in the production but the cast and directors who worked on the films are unknown.[46] Toronto-born Sidney Olcott was Kalem's principal director at the time and it is not unlikely that he was involved. Their first release was to be also the first Mountie drama. *The Cattle Thieves* (1909) was "a magnificent story of the Northwest introducing the Northwest Mounted Police . . . for the first time to the American public."[47] It was followed by *The Canadian Moonshiners* (1910) "A French Canadian Story" with "real Canadian Indians"; *Fighting the Iroquois in Canada* (1910); *A Leap for Life* (1910) "The story of a trapper's leap to escape from the Indians"; *The Perversity of Fate* (1910) "full of primitive splendor"; *Her Indian Mother* (1910), the story of a half-breed whose response "to the call of her Indian blood is strong"; *White Man's Money, The Red Man's Curse* (1910), a story of "The influence of the white upon the redskins"; and *For the Flag* (1911) the story of a French-Canadian girl who defends the honour of the French flag against the English invaders. Kalem also departed from the usual "Canadian content" plots by filming a story of Canadian participation in the Boer War —*The Girl Scout* (1909).[48]

Other American companies tended to follow the more common pattern of producing films with Canadian plots but filming them on sets or on location in the United States. The Biograph Company had set this pattern, before Kalem's venture, with *An Acadian Elopement* (1907), *The Ingrate* (1908), and *A Woman's Way* (1908). The two latter films were directed by D. W. Griffith in his first year as a film director and did little to assist his reputation. Both feature embattled heroines denying their favours to intemperate French-Canadian trappers.[49]

Other companies including Selig, Lubin, Essanay, and Vitagraph moved quickly into the field. Between 1907 and 1914 approximately one hundred Canadian content films were produced by American companies. A detailed discussion of these films lies outside the scope of this book but it is worth noting that the first shapes of the developing Hollywood image of Canada were already formed in the early years.[50] That the films were made should perhaps not be surprising. The Americans, had no "northwoods," no French-Canadian lumberjacks and, most importantly, no romantic law-and-order frontier police force comparable to the North West Mounted Police. It was perhaps inevitable that Hollywood would choose to exploit these differences; if there had been also a different perception at work in Canada it might not have mattered. As it was, Hollywood's image of Canada quickly became the world's image. And, it might be argued, Canada's image of itself.

A few of these Canadian content fiction films, such as *Pierre of the North* (1913 and 1914), *The Dollar Mark* (1914), and *The Way of the Eskimo* (1911) were shot on location but most were photographed in studios or in "Canadian-like" exteriors in the United States. Those shot in Canada tend to minimize plot in favour of scenery and action. A contemporary reaction to *The Way of the Eskimo* typifies many such films. "The plot was slender, but the scenes portrayed the life of the frozen north with great fidelity and vigour, showing the Eskimo fishing through the ice, and hunting the polar bear and walrus by his primitive methods. A valuable polar bear was sacrificed in the desire for realism."[51]

Many other films, requiring snow or striking scenery were shot in part in Canada. Directors intending such location shooting were commonly reported as travelling "to the wilds of Canada" where "impressive backgrounds" for their new production would be obtained. Quebec City was also a favourite location, being used not only in itself as a setting for such films as Kalem's *Wolfe, or the Conquest of Quebec* (1914)—"the townspeople were delighted with the flood of American dollars poured into the old town"[52]— but also as a substitute for old French towns as in *The Man of Shame* (1915).[53] But snow and ice were the commonest reasons for Americans to film in Canada. Unfortunately one company at least was to be disappointed: Canadian-born director J. Gordon Edwards took his cast to home-town Montreal to film snow scenes for *Anna Karenina*, to be greeted only by slush and mud.[54]

The Canadian Pacific Railway, still true to its early commitment to the movies, was not tardy in exploiting the newer dramatic forms of film. The railway was still intent on colonizing the West. But CPR officials were aware that "the great mass of the [movie] public . . . want to be amused and entertained not instructed, and if they are to be educated it must be in a subtle, delicate manner . . . through the interest that the story itself creates in the minds of the audience."[55] The CPR recognized that the "interest" films it had sponsored in 1902–1903 could no longer reach the same numbers of people. Audiences had changed. Movie-goers wanted drama; routine travelogues would only bore them. "What does Johnny the conductor from East Harlem care about the mining industry in southern British Columbia, or the ranching industry in Alberta? Not a rap. . . . But if the class of story that appeals to Johnny and his girl runs prominently through mining, or lumbering, or fishing, or ranching films, they will unconsciously swallow the knowledge." [56]

At the instigation of J. S. Dennis, head of the CPR's Colonization Department in Calgary, the railway contracted with the Edison Company of New York to produce a series of dramatic, comic, and scenic films which would picture the "actual conditions" of western Canada. [57] This, Dennis felt, would be the "very highest class of advertising." [58]

Nine members of the Edison Company left New York on June 22, 1910. Among the company were director J. Searle Dawley, cameraman Henry Cronjager (who had developed a special camera case that reduced the effects of cold temperatures on film), and Mabel Trunnelle, who was to play the lead in most of the films. [59] A stage actress who had only recently joined the Edison Company, she was to return to Canada eight years later to star in *Power*.

The company spent two months filming across Canada from Montreal to Victoria. The CPR not only provided them with a special train but "placed at their disposal" hotels, mountain guides, and even the 10,000-ton *Empress of India* liner. [60] A wide variety of locations was used: a lumber camp in B.C., an Alberta coal mine, an isolated railroad depot, a ranch at Red Deer, the Monarch silver mine at Field B.C., the RCMP headquarters at Regina, and the 7,000-feet high glacier at Mount Lefroy, Lake Louise. [61]

Thirteen one-reel films were produced in those two months. All of them expressed the attractions of western Canada; each of them in its own way and more or less subtly, was designed to encourage immigration.

At the New York press preview of the films in September 1910, one reviewer recalled being present at the successful 1903 London première of the CPR-Urban films and praised the CPR for "the very effective use" it was making of the movies. The films themselves also came in for high praise. "Their delicacy of tone rendering, their fidelity to nature are simply remarkable. . . . All the local colour is there, all the territorial idiosyncrasies of the Dominion are there. It is all, in fact, Canada on the moving picture screen." The *Moving Picture World's* reviewer would not "be a bit surprised" if this "splendid series of pictures—splendid in photography, splendidly simple and natural in theme" did not succeed in its object of "attracting immigrants from the United States into Canada." This process, he noted darkly, would "one day not far distant bring about some interesting political developments."[62]

Two of the films, *A Trip over the Rocky and Selkirk Mountains in Canada*[63] and *The Life of a Salmon*,[64] are traditional "scenics," while a third, *A Wedding Trip from Montreal through Canada to Hong Kong*, uses the slight, comic story of a honeymoon trip to depict Canadian scenery and "the splendid mountain hotel system of the Canadian Pacific Railway."[65] The other ten are dramas, or, rather, short melodramas that belong very much to their time. All involve love stories, lovers' misunderstandings, or matrimonial mix-ups, combined with adventure or crime. The two films which have survived the years are typical. *An Unselfish Love* is the story of John, an American who cannot marry Mabel, the girl he loves, because her father thinks him not sufficiently wealthy. He sets out to seek his fortune in farming in southern Alberta. Not surprisingly, he prospers. He also meets "a lady by no means unattractive but of the type and age popularly designated as an old maid." She falls for him but "her attentions become quite unwelcome" especially since he is not receiving letters from his fiancée. Meanwhile, the girl's father is doing his evil best to break up the attachment since a very wealthy suitor has appeared on the scene. He inserts a notice in the local paper announcing that John is marrying an Alberta girl and Mabel, soon after, accepts the new suitor and sends John a wedding invitation. John is heartbroken when he receives it and starts to write a letter. The spinster arrives with "her customary floral offering" but John has seen her coming and leaves. She discovers the half-written letter and "here, her noble heart, though beating under an old-fashioned exterior, becomes evident." She sets off for the east to tell Mabel the truth and persuades her to come to Alberta (via CPR, of course). The lovers are reunited but "our joy is almost overpowered by the sympathy we feel for the 'old maid' as she furtively wipes her eye and turns away."[66] Canadians, it would seem, are nothing if not unselfish and Americans planning immigration need not fear they will be snared by "unwelcome attentions" from our good Canadian womenfolk.

The Song that Reached His Heart is the tale of "a man of brawn and muscle made rough and rude by his life and surroundings" in a B.C. lumber camp, whose nostalgia for his childhood is aroused by a song. He buys an Edison phonograph and spends the evening listening to the old-time songs. When he hears the strains of *Annie Laurie* a split-screen effect shows him thinking of his childhood in a more civilized world back east when his boyhood sweetheart used to sing that same song. He is extremely upset by the memory and "seeks forgetfulness at a gambling table in a hotel." Meanwhile, the singer of the song—none other than his boyhood sweetheart, now famous —travels West (via CPR) "for her health." Unknown to the lumberjack she arrives in the same hotel. "Just as the lumberjack is about to commit a theft [to pay his gambling debts] the song reaches him again from the room above. . . . Drawn by the charm of its spell," he listens at her door and discovers a plot to rob the singer. He bravely defeats the villains and rediscovers his sweetheart whose song "will find echoes in the chime of wedding bells."[67] Western Canada, the film suggests, may indeed be brutalizing, but if immigrants fight off temptation, the east will stretch out civilizing hands to bring back the joys of a former way of life.

Two of the films are Mountie dramas. *Riders of the Plains*, staged "by real officers and real Indians," depicts the capture of a band of Indian horsethieves.[68] *More Than His Duty* tells of a constable in love with the superintendent's daughter but prevented from marrying her by her brother's hostility. In solving a robbery, he discovers the criminal is the brother. He lets the criminal go free but the girl discovers the truth and refuses to accept her lover's sacrifice.[69]

In several of the films there is a continuing implication of success for the honest worker, even if poor, in western Canada. Most commonly this is expressed through the man falling in love with a richer woman. There are, we note, no class or economic barriers in western Canada to the course of true love and the lovers invariably marry. The constable in *More Than his Duty* loves—and wins—his superintendent's daughter. *The Cowpuncher's Glove*, set on an Alberta ranch, has a "poor but honest" man seeking the love of the daughter of a wealthy rancher but prevented from winning her, until the dramatic climax, by a series of complications and a jealous, criminal, rival.[70] *A Daughter of the Mines* is a Romeo and Juliet story of the rivalry between two miners, one rich and one poor, whose son and daughter fall in love and overcome their respective fathers' opposition.[71] *The Stolen Claim* is "a tale of love and deception resorted to by one man to win the desired girl"—and a rich mine.[72]

One film even suggests that there are opportunities in the west for independently minded women. *The Little Station Agent* is a nineteen-year-old woman who operates, on her own, a small wayside railroad depot in the Rockies. She is loved by two freight-men, one of whom tries to kill the other and stage a wreck to hide the crime. But the "little station agent" prevents the wreck between the freight and the trans-Canadian passenger train, Imperial Ltd. "The usual happy ending closes in a pretty way."[73]

In only one film is there a hint that Canadians might be less than moral. Set in the Lake Louise district "amidst snow-capped peaks and eternal glaciers," *The Swiss Guide* tells the story of a mountain guide who falls in love with a pretty woman tourist—"quite forgetting his duty to his young wife." But the tourist does not intend to be seduced. She rejects him while they are up a mountain, gets herself lost, and has to be rescued by the guide's wife and his "faithful dog."[74]

The single comedy of the series, *The Ship's Husband*, is also the least related to extolling the virtues of western Canada. It was staged on the CPR's Vancouver-Victoria ferry but the plot is a comic matrimonial mix-up in which two husbands and two wives each think their respective mates have eloped by sailing away with someone named "The Charmer"—which, of course, turns out to be the name of the ferry-boat. Though "the comedy fairly bubbles over with good humour and human nature" it was in fact the least successful of the thirteen films.[75]

For the CPR, the venture was a great success. The films were widely seen in theatres throughout the United States, Britain, and Canada and later used by CPR lecturers in their presentations.[76] It had indeed been a remarkably sophisticated idea. Its success enabled the CPR to reach an audience who would most certainly have been uninterested in a repetition of their earlier documentary-type scenic and industrial films. Undeniably the films played a role in encouraging the intensive pre-1914 American immigration into western Canada.

"It Surely Is a Good Beginning"

Up to this point, Canada's role in moving picture history had been largely a passive one. There were exceptions: the enterprising Holland Brothers, Ernest Ouimet, George Scott, Harry Winter, James Freer. But Canada's role was principally to have been used as a piece of exotic scenery. Though the scenery was used to good advantage by the CPR in the form of immigration films, these films were almost entirely the work of British and American film makers. Canadian contribution was minimal. What Canadian initiative had been taken saw film as a means to an end, and not an end in itself as either art or entertainment. It was not until 1911 that domestic production companies began to appear across the country whose aim was simply to make films, fiction or non-fiction.

It is worth speculating why the CPR chose to hire British and American film companies rather than Canadian. Certainly they could have stimulated domestic production by hiring Canadians to do the work, or by forming their own film company as they were to do later. There were Canadians around capable of the job and more would have been trained. Canada could have developed a pool of qualified craftsmen—something sadly lacking until the First World War. The answer, quite apart from questions of the possible relative merit of the films that might have been made, is simple. Both Urban and Edison could guarantee release of their films in the markets the CPR wanted to reach. No Canadian could do so. Once the films were made, the Canadian company would have had to sell them to American and British distributors or establish distribution systems of its own in New York and London.

This was a problem that plagued Canadian film makers almost from the start. As Canadian production companies began to appear after 1911 it became increasingly onerous. The Canadian domestic market was, simply, too small and the potential audiences too scattered across the country, for production to be viable without foreign release. The Canadian response to this was in one of two directions. Either the production company geared its fiction films to American release (most often reflected in the number of Americans in cast and crew) or it announced major plans for producing dramas "using Canadian talent" but in practice produced only scenics and sponsored films.

Among the second group were such companies as Starland Ltd., motion picture photographers of Winnipeg who also controlled the Starland Theatre in Winnipeg and made two short films in 1912, *The Calgary Stampede* and *Sovereign Grand Lodge Oddfellows Annual Parade*.[77] Though their activities were restricted initially to "Western Canadian topicals" they planned "regular releases in the near future." The Canadian Film Manufacturing Company, also of Winnipeg, announced its intention in 1911 of "making regular releases which will consist of educational, dramatic, comic, western, and cowboy subjects."[78] In 1914 the company acquired Royal Films which had been producing films "in and about Montreal for use abroad."[79] Royal Films was apparently operated by Maurice Marcelot and John William Peachy as part of the Canadian Cinematograph Company of Montreal. Montreal Motion Pictures was established by Albert Joseph Gariepy and William Henry Zalde in 1912 "to engage in the manufacture of motion pictures" though there is no record of any actual production.[80] The Premier Film Manufacturing Company established studios in Lachine, Quebec, in 1913, announced it would produce "photoplays of every description using Canadian talent" but, in fact, released only a short documentary, *Montreal Sports and Ice Harvest*, in 1914.[81] The Canadian Cinematograph Company, established in Longueuil in 1914, planned both a weekly newsreel and several drama projects, announced it would bring "an experienced producer from

New York," but seems to have produced nothing.[82] The two Canadian directors of the company, Maurice Marcelot and John William Peachy, secured some American investment, re-formed the company as the Dominion General Film Corporation, and announced the production of "educational" films under an advisory board.[83] Again nothing seems to have been produced, though in late 1914 the company sent a cameraman, J. O'Neil Farrell, to film Canadian troops in action in Europe. By mid-1915 the Longueuil studios were taken over by "Mr. Goldie" for Canadian Art Photoplays in order to produce comedies.[84] Again no films apparently resulted.

In the west, Arthur J. Aylesworth Pictures produced a series of wild life films whose release was handled in the United States by Ernest Shipman.[85] Arthur Aylesworth had been manager of the Lyceum Theatre in Edmonton and in 1913–14 went on a hunting trip through the Mackenzie Basin, a trip which he photographed. The six-reel film, titled Aylesworth Animal Pictures, was released in the United States to less than ecstatic reviews. Noting the "less than high standard" of Aylesworth's photography, reviews also objected to the depiction of killings. "He not only shows a great number of killings but he spreads even the most unpleasant details before the camera. We see animals mutilated, skinned, and disembowelled."[86] Though the film was to be "preserved for the edification of posterity and the United States' government's records," Aylesworth made no more films. The film, in fact, seems to have been a disaster; the hyperbole associated with its promotion can only be credited to the wiles of Ernest Shipman—later to be more constructively associated with Canadian films.

Four pre-World War 1 companies which produced fiction films were to make somewhat more of an impact on the outside world, even if the films themselves seem hardly distinguishable from those Canadian content films produced by American companies. Though the companies argued for, and announced, "Canadian production of Canadian stories," by and large they were to accept without question the American definition of what was a Canadian story. Perhaps this should not be surprising. American personnel were heavily involved in all four of the Canadian companies active in fiction film production before the war: the British American Film Company of Montreal (incorporated in July 1912), the Canadian Bioscope Company of Halifax (incorporated in November 1912), the Conness Till Film Company of Toronto (incorporated in April 1914), and the All-Red Feature Company of Windsor (incorporated in July 1914).

The British American Film Company was to be responsible for the first drama produced by a Canadian film company. It was to be an Indian drama as had been Joe Rosenthal's *Hiawatha*, the first drama filmed in Canada a decade earlier. *The Battle of the Long Sault* depicted the Iroquois expedition against the French settlement at Montreal in 1660 and the resistance by the seventeen colonists led by Adam Dollard des Ormeaux who defended the stockade at Long Sault. The company had been organized locally and had offices in the New Birks Building but their "representative" and active voice was an American theatrical promoter, Frank Beresford. In the fall of 1912 he was in New York "engaging people for picture stock" in Montreal, one of whom was to be Frank Crane, a former actor who was hired as director.[87] By November the film was in production and Frank Crane was complaining bitterly about the weather: "It's so cold the film freezes onto the camera."[88] The major set—the colonists' stockade—was constructed in Lachine and Indians from the Caughnawaga reservation were hired as extras. The completed two-reel drama was released in April 1913 to good reviews. An American critic congratulated the company, noted the good photography and praised the "thrilling" scenes—the war expedition of the Iroquois in the canoes and the fighting around the stockade. "It surely is a good beginning and can be commended as a first class feature."[89] Unfortunately the "good beginning" of British American was also its end; no other films were produced. However, when the famous 22nd Regiment was founded in September 1914, Prime Minister Laurier made a reference to the heroism and sacrifice of Dollard des Ormeaux as reflected in the film: "If there still flows in veins of Canadians some drops of the blood of Dollard and his companions you will join [the new regiment] *en masse.*" Frank Crane was later to work for the Conness Till Company in Toronto while Frank Beresford was involved in Kalem's *Wolfe, or the Conquest of Quebec* and the location shooting of *The Man of Shame* in Quebec City. The studios and equipment were taken over by the *Canadian Animated Weekly* headed by John Boldt, formerly with the Canadian Cinematograph Company.

Arthur Larente, a pioneer Montreal distributor and exhibitor, was also involved in the production of a four-reel historical drama, *Madeleine de Verchères.* Yet another Indian drama, this was based on the true story of Marie-Madeleine Jarret de Verchères who, in 1693 at the age of fourteen, led the defence of the fort at Verchères, twenty miles from Montreal, against an Iroquois attack and helped to prevent the fall of Montreal. Madeleine was played by A. R. Thibault and again Indians from Caughnawaga played extras, invading the fort in canoes. The photography was by J. Arthur Homier, a former still photographer. It seems possible that the same sets constructed for *The Battle of the Long Sault* were used for *Madeleine.* The completed film was shown in Larente's own theatre and one print sold in France but had no wider release.[90]

Scene from *Madeleine de Verchères*.

As with the British American Film Company, the first film produced by the Canadian Bioscope Company was to deal with an event in Canadian history—the expulsion of the Acadians. And, as with *The Battle of the Long Sault*, *Evangeline*, based on Longfellow's poem, was to make considerable use of imported American talent—including two American stage and film actors, William H. Cavanaugh and E. P. Sullivan, who were responsible for "staging" *Evangeline*.

The Canadian Bioscope Company was organized in Halifax in 1912 with studios and offices at 108 Pleasant Street (now Barrington Street) by

Captain H. H. B. Holland. General manager, vice-president, and cinematographer was H. T. Oliver, an American who had worked for the Edison Company.[91] The company's first film was to be written by Marguerite Marquis from Longfellow's famous poem describing the expulsion of the Acadians in 1755 and the undying love of Evangeline and Gabriel. The story had already been filmed in 1911 by an American company, Selig, and was to be filmed twice more in 1919 and 1929. It was a popular romantic tale and obviously a wise choice by the company, especially since they intended to film it in the actual locations described by Longfellow: Grand Pré, the Annapolis Valley, Cow Bay, and Eastern Passage. The CPR contributed its facilities. Two American actors, Laura Lyman and John F. Carleton, were brought in to play Evangeline and Gabriel while some local actors (including R. J. Leary and Rhea Rafuse) were used in supporting roles. Production spanned the summer of 1913 and cost $30,000: high for its time. The film's titles were all quotations from the poem and the images were given a colour effect through tinting and toning. It was a long film for 1913; at 5,000 feet it ran about seventy-five minutes on the screen. But the effort was worth it. The film was previewed in Halifax in 1913 to, not surprisingly, an ecstatic reception. But the Halifax audience's reaction was borne out elsewhere. Canadian and American critics were unanimous in their praise and audiences loved it. Described as "a work of art" using "everything known to the art of stage direction and the mechanics of photographic skill," together with "strict adherence to historical detail,"[92] *Evangeline* was "a good picture," "well acted," and "intensely dramatic, appealing and moving."[93] Canadian Bioscope's first production was, in short, a great artistic and financial success.

Their next productions were to be less successful. By the spring of 1914, soon after *Evangeline*'s American release, Canadian Bioscope had completed six more films, three of which were to gain general theatrical release. *Saved from Himself*, a three-reel drama, told the somewhat familiar story of an American fugitive from justice who escapes to British Columbia where his younger brother is head cashier of a mining company. After various altercations, the younger reforms his brother and we see him at the end, "making good" as a real estate agent in the west.[94] *Mariner's Compass*, a sea-coast drama in three-reels, was a highly convoluted story of an American coast-guard who adopts a baby girl and years later falls in love with her only to lose her in the end to a young man to whom he had also given a home.[95] *In the Enemy's Power* (also called *The Mexican Sniper's Revenge*) was somewhat unusual for Canadian producers of the time in that it was set in Mexico, a three-reel drama of an American who falls in love with a Mexican woman and gets caught up and dies in the revolutionary war between President

Modero and Porfirio Diaz.[96] All three of these films were released to theatres but created far less impact than *Evangeline*. Canadian Bioscope also produced three short one-reel comedies, *A Neglected Wife*, *Willie's Birthday Present*, and *Thou Shalt Not Steal*, featuring mainly local actors including William "Pud" Johnson, Anna Doherty, Lillie Leslie, Jack Cowell, and William Vaughan.[97] These seem to have been made purely for local consumption and were not offered elsewhere. When war broke out, the personnel of Canadian Bioscope dispersed, the company went out of business, and its films were auctioned off.

In naming the All-Red Feature Company, based in Windsor, American cinematographer Frederic Colburn Clarke was referring not to the Red of Bolshevism but to the Red of the British Empire.[98] The company's first, and only, drama was a three-reel historical epic set in the Niagara Peninsula during the War of 1812. *The War Pigeon* was written and directed by Clarke from a story by Canadian novelist Arthur Stringer and told of a Canadian traitor, William Crandall, who agrees to act as a spy for the Americans and compels his daughter, Alice, to help him. Information is carried to the Americans by the pigeons Alice keeps as pets. Unfortunately for Crandall, Lieutenant Fitzgibbon discovers his technique and also falls in love with Alice. When Alice learns Fitzgibbon and his men are to be attacked, she betrays her father and sends word to Fitzgibbon who then "seeks Alice and receives his reward." Released with some success in Canada in November 1914, it was described as "full of stirring action" while "the scenery and costumes of the period contribute to make an artistic as well as historic production."[99] The British American Film Company of Detroit released the film in the United States, but it made little impact. The All-Red Feature Company also released a weekly newsreel, *All-Red Weekly*, soon after the war started and was pleased that its newsreel was exempt from the "government edict" banning newsreels of the war since the *All-Red Weekly* "promoted enlistment."[100] It may, indeed, have done so but it lasted only a few, brief, weeks. With its demise, Frederic Colburn Clark returned to the United States where he became head of still photography for the Goldwyn Company and, later, was special photographer to Nazimova and Florence Turner.

The Conness Till Film Company of Toronto was to be typical of much later production. With adequate financial backing, a studio, and talent this company produced several dramas that were well received by theatrical audiences but nonetheless survived only twelve months. Its financing was largely American and when financial returns did not work out as they expected they removed their backing and went home.

The company was formed in April 1914, on the initiative of Philadelphia-born actor Edward H. Robins who played summer stock with the Robins Players in Toronto.[101] He convinced American theatrical promoter Luke Edwin Conness, Toronto businessman Louis A. Till, and Philadelphia financiers, James and Charles Beury, that Toronto was a fine site for a movie studio. The Beury brothers put up $150,000 and Conness, Till, and Robins himself also invested in the company. Conness was president and general manager, Till was secretary, James Beury treasurer, and Robins and Charles Beury vice-presidents. American actress Clara Whipple was brought in to play lead roles opposite Robins and a mixture of Toronto and American actors, including Frank Crane (recently of the British American Film Company), Marie Cummings, Dorothy Millette, and Eugene Frazier were hired for supporting roles. Chief director was A. J. Edwards, assisted by former actor Tom McKnight. Cameraman and technical director was Louis W. Physioc, formerly with Pathé, who was joined later by one-time Edison cameraman Ned Van Buren. Scriptwriters were Torontonian Archie McKishney, together with Paul Bern who made his debut in the industry with Conness Till. (In 1932, while Bern was general assistant to Irving Thalberg at MGM, he married Jean Harlow and killed himself two months later.)

Conness Till launched itself in the summer of 1914 with an extensive advertising campaign in Canadian magazines and a film script contest with $350 in prizes—which brought in over 500 entries from Toronto alone.[102] Describing itself as "a Canadian firm established in Canada for the purpose of producing Canadian plays with distinctive Canadian settings and written by Canadians,"[103] its first releases were factual films: newsreels of an exhibition rugby game and of the 2nd Canadian contingent camped at the CNE in Toronto which were used to encourage enlistment.[104] But by October 1914, the company's studio on the Humber River just outside the Toronto city limits had been completed at a cost of $50,000 and production began in earnest, if not entirely free from difficulties.[105] There were rumours of "disgruntled actors" complaining of both salary and working conditions. In January 1915, a weekly magazine, *Jack Canuck*, reported that Clara Whipple had been "obliged to work in a low-cut dress in weather almost down to the zero mark" and for seventeen days work was paid "the niggardly sum of $13.50." Moreover, working conditions were bad, "lacking the ordinary accommodations which decency demands where men and women are constantly changing their costumes."[106]

Despite these difficulties, in February 1915, Conness Till released its first drama, a three-reel "well-acted and well-photographed" Mountie story, *On the King's Highway*, featuring Edward Robins and Clara Whipple, and directed by A. J. Edwards.[107] Distribution in Canada was handled by the

B. and C. Feature Company, whose general manager was George Brownridge, who was later to play a more direct role in Canadian production. As part of the deal, Brownridge moved the offices of B. and C. to those of Conness Till at 1 Adelaide Street East in Toronto. Plans were also announced for British release, presumably through B. and C.'s British parent company.

From February until April, Conness Till were to release a two- or three-reel film every week.[108] Some were news films such as the previously photographed film of manoeuvers of the Canadian expeditionary forces and of the governor-general reviewing the troops, but most were dramas. Among them were *His Awakening*, a comedy about an artist who falls asleep and dreams he is a great lover in the Egypt of the Pharaohs, which was directed by Tom McKnight, written by Paul Bern, and starred Clara Whipple and Edward Robins; *Canada in Peace and War*, a war drama directed by McKnight, with Clara Whipple, Edward Robins, Gene Frazier, and "real" Canadian troops; *The Better Man*; *Motto on the Wall*; *To Err is Human*; and *A Soul's Affinity*.[109] The company's last release, *The Faithful Servant*, appeared in late April.[110] Relations had not been smooth for some time between James P. Beury, principal shareholder in the company, and Luke Conness and Lou Till. Beury apparently felt the Conness Till production policies were designed only to lose his money and, finally, he bought out Conness and Till together with the liabilities of the company and reorganized it in May 1915 as the Beury Feature Film Company.[111] Edward Robins retained his financial interest and Tom McKnight, Louis Physioc, and Ned Van Buren remained on staff. Production would be resumed in "about eight weeks" on a "big feature" with several well-known actors joining the company "along with the local actors." Beury did in fact meet with Ralph Connor to consider filming Connor's novels, beginning with *The Prospector*.

However, the first activity of the company was its involvement in a curiously shady scheme to release film of the 1915 prize fight between Jess Willard and Jack Johnson in Havana, Cuba. Prizefight films had been banned in the United States since 1912 as a direct result of race riots accompaning showings of film of the Jack Johnson-Jim Jeffries fight in 1910.[112] Johnson had appeared in Beury's Philadelphia theatre and, as a result, a scheme was developed to get round the American law. Cameras recorded all twenty-six rounds of the fight in Havana and the negatives were processed at Beury's studios in Toronto. The film was shown to the Ontario censor board which "acknowledged that there was nothing of a brutal nature or unpleasant in any of the seven reels" but regretted "it was not in their power to pass favourably upon the pictures."[113] Ten prints of the film went out from Toronto to satisfy European and South American demand but as Beury well knew, "a fortune was waiting" if the film could be got into the United States. "A scheme of amazing cleverness was evolved . . . to import the picture without bringing in the film." Beury's technicians built a device which could project the negative across the border where it could be copied onto positive film in the United States. A tent was set up straddling the border between New York State and Quebec. The Canadians with the negative "gingerly moved about placing it in the machine with careful steps that they might not touch by so much as a fraction of an inch the forbidden soil of the United States."[114] The copying process was a great success but the resulting print was promptly seized by the American Customs officers who had been present throughout. The American public never saw the film.

Beury's "big feature" when it got underway in late May would have been a curiosity had it ever been completed. *Nicotine* was planned as a six-reel drama featuring Ethel Kaufman and directed by Tom McKnight. Beury got financial sponsorship from the Medical Review of Reviews and *Nicotine* was to be an anti-smoking film. But on May 31 a fire completely destroyed the studios, though the two reels of the film already shot were saved.[115] Insurance fully covered the estimated $100,000 loss of the studio—which had cost $50,000 to build a year earlier. Jim Beury took the insurance money, forgot his idea of filming the Ralph Connor stories, and returned to Philadelphia. Edward Robins returned to the theatre where Tom McKnight directed him in stock at the Royal Alexander Theatre in the summer of 1915.

None of these four companies produced anything that stretched the imagination. None survived much longer than a year. None of their films, with the exception of *Evangeline*, created much impact. Those of Conness Till and the All-Red Feature Company had a modest release in Canada; those of British American and Canadian Bioscope enjoyed a somewhat wider international release. But, in retrospect, only *Evangeline* seems noteworthy.

On the other hand, there was, then, nothing surprising in the functioning of the embryonic Canadian film industry. Similar patterns were evident in other countries at the time, and not only in countries with a developing industry. Film companies sprang up and disappeared almost overnight and those with longevity were the exception, not the rule.

What was different in Canada was that there was no focal point for the developing film activity. Each of the four companies established before the war was in a different city: Montreal, Halifax, Windsor, and Toronto.[116] This was in complete contrast to the pattern in all the European countries—and in the United States itself—where production centred first on New York and later on Hollywood.

And not only were the production companies strung out across the country but so also was the population—and the potential market for the films. Combine this with the absence of an established theatrical tradition, the lack—or loss—of trained writers, actors, and technicians, plus the difficulties in raising capital to finance inexperienced production and the impossibility of recouping that investment within Canada alone, and you end up with a pretty cogent case for not attempting any production in the first place. Indeed, it is perhaps more surprising that there was *any* production rather than that there was so little.

To an extent, those first efforts were a result of a growing anti-American climate, clearly evident in the debate on trade reciprocity with the United States during the 1911 federal election.

Author Rudyard Kipling was only one of many leading figures who felt that Canada was risking its "national soul" if it accepted the treaty. "Once that soul is pawned for any consideration," wrote Kipling, "Canada must inevitably conform to the commercial, legal, financial, social and ethical standards which will be imposed upon her by the sheer admitted weight of the U.S."[117] Across the country, Canadians agreed with Kipling and heavily rejected Sir Wilfrid Laurier's Liberals who had negotiated the treaty in favour of Robert Borden's Conservatives who opposed it.

In relation to the movies, this anti-Americanism was expressed in an increasing impatience with American-produced dramas which displayed attitudes not always sympathetic to Canadians. Though Canadians had been content to watch American-made "interest" films, they wanted story films that related more closely to their own lives and backgrounds. American films would, to quote one commentator, "encourage a misdirected idea nationally."[118] The most glaring example of lack of consideration of foreign sensitivities was the, often gratuitous, insertion of the Stars and Stripes as an audience rallying device. Producers were urged, in 1911, "to reproduce some pictures of English and Canadian heroism, which have a direct effect on the patriotism of Canadian children."[119] But reactions went beyond complaints and urgings. Film censorship boards had been established in Ontario, Quebec, and Manitoba by 1911 and in British Columbia and Alberta by 1913.[120] Almost their first act was the banning or cutting of films containing "an unnecessary display of U.S. flags." In 1914, the B.C. censor was to ban fifty reels for this offence—which made it third behind infidelity and seduction as the most banned offence. Though the American film trade paper *Moving Picture World*, was sympathetic to this action on the part of Canadian censors, it was to comment acidly: "Canadian Imperialists are complaining about having to witness too many deeds of Yankee valour in moving pictures. No reciprocity wanted—excepting Yankee dollars."[121]

The outbreak of the war in September 1914 was to intensify this anti-American feeling. The Americans were not involved in the war until 1917 and there was an understandable demand by Canadians for documentaries and dramas that reflected the "British Empire" perception of the war. The mood was to become even more acute after the American entry into the war touched off a flood of films depicting, not surprisingly, the contributions of the United States itself. By 1918, almost every Canadian newspaper had printed editorials condemning the quantity and quality of American war films.

More positively, the war was to create a new awareness of the Canadian identity as something distinct from "British" or "North American." Those same editorials which condemned American films also urged the production and exhibition of more British and Canadian films. It was in this atmosphere of heightened nationalism and awareness of cultural identity that the federal government and the Ontario government created their motion picture bureaus, that the first all-Canadian newsreels appeared, and that the general level of feature film production jumped sharply. The years from 1914 to 1922 were to be the most active years in Canadian film production. They were also to be the years in which Hollywood noticeably increased its production of "Canadian content" films.

CHAPTER 3

The Years of Promise

In 1922, pioneer American producer and distributor, Lewis Selznick, wondered aloud why Canadians bothered producing films. "If Canadian stories are worthwhile making into films," he commented, "companies will be sent into Canada to make them." [1] Though he could not have known it, his words were prophetic. That year was perhaps the most active for Canada's private producers with more features and shorts made for theatrical release than ever before. But though 1922 was the most active year it also marked the end of a period of intensive production that had begun early in the First World War and peaked in the four years between 1918 and 1922. Only one feature was in production in 1923 (in contrast to seven in 1922) and even the production of short films showed a sharp decline. There is something symbolic of this decline in the departure from Canada of Ernest Shipman—the producer responsible for a significant share of the feature production activity in those four years. Thereafter, apart from a brief flurry in the late Twenties, film production was restricted to the federal and Ontario governments' film bureaus and to a handful of private companies whose work was principally the production of industrially sponsored documentaries.

But for some eight years there was no doubt of Canada's desire to have a domestic film industry reflecting its own image. The mood, a new self-aware nationalism, was exactly right.

The first emanation of the new self-awareness was the appearance of several uniquely Canadian newsreels. With the outbreak of the war, Canadians had a natural interest in seeing events related to it, and the newsreels were created to satisfy this demand in a manner American newsreels could not or would not. There had been films of news events shot by Canadians before this but they were usually destined for local screenings (several theatres had their own newsreels) and only if the event were of wider significance did the film find its way to national or continental release.[2] The war changed this. By late 1914, Canadians were watching newsreels produced and released in Canada of events that had special significance to them.

The first war films were produced by private companies or individuals and were most often films of Canadian troop units training and departing Canada for the war front in Europe. Footage of this kind cropped up widely in newsreels both Canadian and foreign in the first months of the war. Within two months after the outbreak of war, the Lubin Company of the United States had put together a collection of this footage under the title *Canadians Rally Round the Flag*, which had a wide release in Canada, Britain, and the United States.[3] In October 1914 the first of the Canadian newsreels, *Canadian Animated Weekly*, appeared, taking over the studios and equipment of the British American Film Company of Montreal. Their first production, *Events in Canada During War Time*, had a wide release across Canada through the offices of Canadian Universal. John E. Boldt, who was responsible for the *Weekly*, reported that the first release played twenty-nine theatres in Montreal alone.[4] The *All-Red Weekly* produced by the All-Red Feature Company under Frederic Colburn Clarke showed "exclusive Canadian pictures, mostly of Canadian troops at present."[5] The Dominion General Film Corporation with studios at Longueuil announced in September 1914 that their J. O'Neil Farrell "is now ready to follow the Canadian troops for the Dominion."[6] In December 1914 the Conness Till Film Company of Toronto filmed the second Canadian Contingent training at the Toronto Exhibition grounds, and later, reviews of the troops in Toronto by the governor general, the Duke of Connaught, and Prime Minister Robert Borden. The weekly releases of Conness Till were compiled into a three-reel featurette *Canada in Peace and War* and included a mock battle by troops of the Second Canadian Contingent. On its release, these scenes "created a big sensation both in public and press."[7]

Such productions by Canadian companies were stimulated by official concern over the screening of real battle scenes in Canadian theatres; the authorities felt that scenes of troops being wounded and killed would discourage recruitment.[8] In November 1914 all war films were banned in Ontario and three months later the Dominion Militia Department ordered the censor boards of every province to condemn all war films.[9] Frederic Colburn Clarke was delighted that his *All-Red Weekly* was exempt from the edict since it was considered to "encourage enlistment."[10] In any case, the edict does not appear to have had much effect, since by August 1915 a movie trade paper could report that, "*Canada Wants War Films*: Pictures of real and officially vouched for events, troops fighting and war's devastation are eagerly watched by audiences in Ontario."[11] The reaction of the Dominion Militia Department to this is not recorded but when the department exhibited its own official war films for the first time in December 1915 all scenes of actual warfare were carefully excluded. *Canada's Fighting Forces*, in six reels, was photographed by Lieutenant D. S. Dwyer of Victoria, B.C., the official government photographer. The film showed the life of a Canadian soldier, "Jack Canuck," from the time of enlistment, through his training period, to the arrival at the front. Though there were scenes of military hospitals where soldiers were seen recovering from wounds, the battle of Ypres was depicted only through animated diagrams. The film premièred at Massey Hall in Toronto on December 6, 1915, and then went on an extensive tour across Canada before moving to Boston on June 12, 1916, for an American tour. It was accompanied by a lecture by Sergeant Fred Wells who had lost his left arm in the fighting. Reviews stressed that Wells' personality and sense of humour were instrumental in raising "the entire performance to its high plane of sustained interest."[12]

From 1916 on, the government was to play an increasing role in films relating to war. This arose not only because of the desire to use film for official propaganda purposes but also for the simple reason that military authorities controlled access to the war front and to military establishments. It was natural for the military mind to insist on control over what was photographed. Early in the war, cameramen, like journalists, found facilities nonexistent and even had difficulties securing permission to visit the front.[13] One of the early film journalists, Geoffrey Malins, wrote a bitter account of the first months when he had to find his own transportation, carry all his own heavy equipment, and argue "every step of the way with incredulous soldiers of the old school."[14] In London, the various companies involved in actuality production decided to band together to negotiate jointly with military authorities for facilities. The Cinematograph Trade Topical Committee was established in October 1915 and, in return for the cooperation of the military, the members agreed to pay a royalty fee to military charities for any films obtained. Early in 1916 the Imperial War Office decided the committee was not satisfactory and established its own War Office Cinematograph Committee under the chairmanship of Sir Max Aitken (later Lord Beaverbrook) with representatives from both the War Office and the film industry.[15] Film cameramen were sent to the front under official sponsorship and the footage they shot was sent to London and edited into both newsreels and longer films. A regular newsreel was started in 1917 when the committee first took control of, then later bought, the Topical Film Company.

In July 1916 the Canadian government joined the committee and all official Canadian war films from that time were made under the auspices of the Imperial War Office Committee. Several films were made and shown widely in Canada including *Canada at Mons*, *Canadian Officers in the Making*, and the two series, *With the Canadian Regiments* and *Famous Canadian Regiments in France*.

Meanwhile the Canadian government was also sponsoring war films of purely domestic interest. The Pathescope Company produced *War Gardens* (1918) for the Motion Picture Committee of the Food Controller's Office, a film designed to encourage backyard gardens.[16] The Department of Soldiers' Civil Re-establishment sponsored a five-reel film photographed by William J. Craft of Pathescope, *Canada's Work for Wounded Soldiers* (1918).[17] Released the same year were *Waste Not, Want Not* and *Everybody's Business*.[18] All these films were distributed free of charge to theatres and were widely used.

Also available free to theatres were the films sponsored by the Dominion Victory Loan Committee, films exhorting Canadians to buy war bonds. Though a few of these were the work of Canadian producers (including Pathescope's *Victory Loan 1919*) most were Canadian adaptations of Hollywood produced "Liberty Loan" films, featuring famous film stars. Among them were Mary Pickford in *100% Canadian* (understandably, retitled from *100% American*), Douglas Fairbanks in *Sic 'Em, Jack Canuck* (adapted from *Sic 'Em Sam*) and a most unusual Charlie Chaplin film, *The Bond*, which has Chaplin playing a comedy scene against highly abstracted sets. Most of the films adapted for Canadian use were produced by Adolph Zukor's Famous Players-Lasky company.[19] The difficulties encountered are well illustrated by *His Extra Bit* which features Wallace Reid and Dorothy Davenport in a family squabble about buying bonds. But the family has black servants ("even Mandy the cook prevents Rastus from buying a watermelon so as to save for the bonds") and for Canadian audiences this must have, at the least, seemed strange.

During the war there was also a brief flurry of locally produced films destined for soldiers overseas to give them a glimpse of their hometown and families. Among the most successful were *Hello, Dad!* produced in Calgary by R. W. Marshall of the Imperial Film Company for the local Rotary Club[20] and *The New Teacher* produced in Woodstock, Ontario, under the auspices of the local chapter of the IODE in which the performance of lead actress Aveleigh Wallace "would do justice to Mary Pickford."[21] In London, Ontario, enterprising local amateurs produced a two-reel science fiction-adventure film, *The Adventures of Dot*. In it, the leader of a gang of anarchists steals a new, ultra-powerful explosive invented by Dot's father and threatens to blow up London unless paid a very large ransom. Dot discovers the plot and with her sweetheart, a newspaper reporter, locates the gang's hideout. After an exciting car chase, the anarchist chief dies when his car falls spectacularly over a cliff. Dot and her lover marry just before he enlists in the Canadian Army.[22] All of these films were shown with great success in local movie theatres before being sent to Europe for viewing by Canadian soldiers at the front.

Canadian newsreels continued appearing through the latter part of the war, though some had only a brief existence. An Ontario theatre owner, R. S. Marvin, founded the *Strand Star Weekly* in 1916, replaced it with the *Canadian Topical Review* early in 1917, and sold it late in December.[23] Commercial Films of Montreal produced the *All Canada Weekly* in 1917[24] and the Pan American Film Corporation of Trenton began releasing its own newsreel in March 1918.[25] The Pathescope Company of Toronto used deft lobbying in Ottawa to persuade the federal government to subsidise its own newsreel, *Canadian National Pictorial*.[26] Its first release was in August 1919 and it continued appearing regularly until 1921—a longer life than most Canadian newsreels of the time.

All these newsreels showed exclusively Canadian items; not out of chauvinism but simply because they had no cameramen outside the country. This was an obvious defect for Canadian movie patrons who, though interested in Canadian news, wanted also to see something of the outside world. It was the always enterprising Ernest Ouimet who devised a better approach with his *British Canadian Pathé News*, founded in January 1919.[27] Ouimet's company, Speciality Film Import, held distribution rights to the British Pathé newsreel and Ouimet decided to combine international material from this with news shot by his own cameramen across Canada. It was a great success and, at its peak, was seen twice weekly by one-and-a-half-million Canadians. In fact it was so successful that the Fox and Kinograms newsreels of the United States decided to emulate it with *Fox Canadian News* and *Canadian Kinograms* respectively, consisting of the original American newsreel with Canadian "inserts."[28] Not untypically, both were to survive long after Ouimet's newsreel folded. In fact, most of the Canadian newsreels did not survive the end of the war. Only *Canadian National Pictorial* and *British Canadian Pathé News* were released in the ensuing years and even they did not survive the hiatus of 1922. Thereafter, the newsreels shown in Canada were entirely foreign controlled, though most had "Canadian editions" which included items of purely domestic interest. Not that they did this out

Main title for Ernest Ouimet's newsreel.

of a generous feeling; in Ontario at least, the provincial Censor Board imposed a strict minimum quota of Canadian and British items in foreign newsreels.

Among the newsreel cameramen of the time were Dick Bird, Roy Tash, Blaine Irish, Bert Mason, Frank O'Byrne, Bill Brenon, Michael Shiels, Marcel Tanguay, Mervin LaRue, Bill Craft, Charlie Quick, George Bastier, and the brothers Len and Charles Roos. Many were Americans who had worked on newsreels in the United States and were brought into the country by R. S. Marvin, Ernest Ouimet, and others. British-born Dick Bird had worked for the *Selig Tribune* newsreel in the United States; Roy Tash and Blaine Irish had worked for the *Pathé* newsreel. Bill Craft had photographed the *Hazards of Helen* serial and worked for Pathé. Mervin LaRue worked for Kalem. Some of those not Canadian born were to remain in Canada and make a continuing contribution to the industry: Dick Bird, Roy Tash, Michael Shiels, and Blaine Irish. Others such as Mervin LaRue and Bill Craft returned to the United States. Of the Canadians, Len and Charles Roos were to make the most significant contribution—though Len eventually left for Hollywood. Both were born in Galt, Ontario, and began their film careers with the Atlas Film Company in Detroit before moving back to Canada during the war.[29] Both filmed for the *Strand Star Weekly*, *Canadian Topical Review*, and *All Canada Weekly* but, more significantly, they were to be prime movers in the first dramatic films to be produced during the war, notably *Self Defence* produced for their own company, United Films of Galt, in 1916. After the war, both returned to documentary and newsreel work.

Hollywood of the North

Newsreels were by no means the only emanation of the new Canadian nationalism. No fewer than three dozen film companies were established between 1914 and 1922, an unrealistic number for any country with Canada's scattered population. It is not surprising to discover that fewer than half actually produced anything.[30] Many of those that failed to do so were undoubtedly stock promotion swindles. Such operations were common across the continent at the time and Canada was not excepted. Indeed, Canada was a favoured hunting ground. Canadians were expressing a decided interest in producing their own films; in the post-war investment boom, Canadian investors, inexperienced in the movie business but willing to back Canadian film production, could readily be trapped. There is more than a handful of examples of Canadians being hoodwinked, bamboozled, and just plain cheated out of their money in these stock promotion deals.

By and large, the Canadians involved in most of the film companies were well-intentioned and sincere if, too often, inexperienced in the business of making and selling movies. In fact, their inexperience and good intentions were to be exploited more than once by skilful promoters: the Conness Till-Beury experience was to be repeated several times over the years, each time with the same pattern. When the company went bankrupt, the principal promoter involved was certain not to be one of the losers. In the end, this pattern was to have the inevitable self-destructive effect: investors became increasingly wary as the number of failures mounted and the impossibility of recouping investment through distribution in Canada alone became apparent. By 1923, film companies were anathema for investors and the failure following the optimistic financing of *Carry On, Sergeant* in 1927 capped it all.

As in the earlier period, no single major production centre developed. The active companies were scattered across the country: St. John, Sydney, Montreal, Trenton, Toronto, Galt, Ottawa, Sault Ste. Marie, Winnipeg, and Calgary. It was not a pattern calculated to build a stable industry—

certainly not at a time when other countries were rapidly orienting themselves towards centralized studio production. Only one Canadian town was to come close to the Hollywood studio pattern: the small Ontario town of Trenton, much-vaunted over nearly twenty years as "the Hollywood of the North," and the only Canadian studios to continue in active service more than a year or two. Why Trenton was selected over other sites is a mystery. It was reasonably accessible to Toronto. It had a range of scenery including mountains, bush, and lakes within easy reach. But otherwise it had little to offer. The most likely reason is the sheer chance of one company building a studio there in 1916 and the same studio offering convenient facilities to a continuing series of film companies. The same kind of "chance" lay behind the growth of Hollywood; its growth as the movie capital was dependent more on circumstances than on deliberate choice.

The fact that the studios were in a small town is significant. Had they been in a larger urban centre it is likely that, when a company folded, the studios would have been sold and used for some other purpose. This was true of studios in Montreal and Toronto. The story of the production activities of Trenton offers considerable insight into the patterns of Canadian film production, its rise and fall, its successes and failures, and into the problems that beleaguered Canadian film makers.

Canadian National Features was the company responsible for the construction of the Trenton studios. This company, one of several established in 1916 to produce fiction films, was the brainchild of George Brownridge, a fast-talking Toronto distributor and promoter whose first direct link with Canadian production had been through his releasing the films of the Conness Till company. Brownridge was general manager and vice-president of Canadian National Features and J. J. Shea, a Buffalo and Toronto theatre owner, was president and a major stockholder.[31]

Brownridge's appeal for funds anticipated that of Ernest Shipman. Pointing out that Canadian branches of American distributors were taking "millions of dollars per year out of the Dominion," he urged investment on patriotic grounds.[32] Capitalization was $500,000, of which $278,000 was subscribed within weeks of the company's incorporation in June 1916.[33] Brownridge and Shea originally planned to build a studio on the Kingston fairgrounds but when negotiations with the City Council fell through, they settled on Trenton in November 1916. By the spring of 1917, a two storey studio, 140 feet by 60 feet had been completed just west of the intersection of Highways 2 and 33. In addition to the main building there was also an open air stage and two large houses used as "clubhouses" for cast and crew. The studios alone cost $24,000, plus another $12,000 for equipment.[34]

The studios at Trenton, Ontario, in the early Twenties.

Louis W. Physioc and Archie McKishney, late of Conness Till, were hired as technical director and writer respectively. Brownridge made several trips to New York where he signed contracts with Barry O'Neill as director, and Mabel Trunnelle (on her second Canadian job), Herbert Prior, Marguerite Snow, Holbrook Blinn, Clifford Bruce, Sadie Weston, Fred Tidmarsh, and several others to play leading, supporting, or character roles.[35] By March the first feature was in production and European and American distribution deals were set. But suddenly, before the second feature was completed, the company ran out of cash to handle its payroll and operating expenses.[36] Cast and crew worked for a while without salary but soon quit. Most returned to New York but Holbrook Blinn, Clifford Bruce, and Sadie Weston stayed on to sue for monies owed them. Canadian National Features suspended operations having spent some $43,000 on its first two five-reel features, *The Marriage Trap* and *Power*. Given assets at bankruptcy of $79,000, plus the costs of the studio and of the first two films (a total of some $146,000) it is a puzzle what happened to the rest of the $278,000 invested in the company.

George Brownridge was nothing if not optimistic. A year later he was back in production with another company, Adanac Producing Company. "Adanac" is, of course, Canada spelt backwards and has often been a popular name for Canadian companies. Through Adanac he released *Power* and *The Marriage Trap* in September 1918. *Power*, "a story of politics and business," featured Holbrook Blinn, Mabel Trunnelle, Clifford Bruce, and Albert E. H. Grupe.[37] *The Marriage Trap*, a love story, featured Marguerite Snow, Herbert Prior, Carleton Macy, Clifford Bruce and Albert E. H. Grupe.[38] Neither received a more than lukewarm critical and public welcome, though by April 1919 they had been seen extensively throughout Central Canada[39] and Brownridge had claimed the sale of foreign rights "at a good price."[40]

Brownridge was to return to the Trenton studios, but in the meantime another company, Pan American Film Corporation, took possession in January 1918.[41] It planned to produce "photoplays of the Canadian Northwest and its mounted police" and a newsreel which would "include an animated cartoon by Bert Cob." Featured players in the dramas would be David B. Gally and Marie Lambert, both American stage and film actors. Gally, "brought from New York at a large salary," would direct the films which were to be written by Marie Lambert.[42] General Manager was A. J. LaFay. By March, the first newsreel was released and the company was preparing two-reel comedies and a series of six-reel features about the Northwest Mounted Police, *The Riders of the Plains*. They were to be "true stories . . . told by a Northerner who knows," the first of which was to be *When He Brought Back His Man*.[43] In the event, the film was not completed and the company's only release was a ten minute rural comedy short, *Modern Eden*, which appeared in April.[44] Despite promises of new releases "every two weeks," Pan American Film Corporation quietly folded.

George Brownridge had not lost his optimism. He was convinced that Canadian National Features had been "doomed to failure by poor financing." With "proper financing, with a strong board of directors . . . who will not allow petty jealousies to interfere with their work," together with a "properly equipped studio," then, Brownridge argued, films could be successfully —and profitably—produced in Canada. Of course, cast, directors, and technicians "for the time being" would have to be obtained from the United States, "as we have not had the opportunities to learn this business."[45]

Brownridge was determined not to under-finance his next venture and when he formed the Adanac Producing Company in the summer of 1918 it was in order to produce "educational and industrial films."[46] He had also devised a remarkable stunt to promote attendance at movie theatres and, at the same time, have the theatre pay the production costs of a short dramatic film. Contest entrants were to sell tickets for the theatre and the one selling the most was given the leading role in a drama. The Oakwood Theatre in Toronto was the first to offer the photoplay contest and "as a box-office stimulator it was a great success."[47] Beverly Redfern was the winner and she appeared in a two-reel railroad drama, "full of thrills and fast action," directed and photographed by William J. Craft.[48] The completed film, *Freight 249*, was shown at the Oakwood Theatre in August and later released successfully across Canada. Brownridge planned other "photoplay contests" but whether there were others is not known.

In any case, Brownridge had a new idea: the production of dramatic shorts, sponsored by commercial companies. Sponsored industrial documentaries were, of course, common. Pathescope and Commercial Films of Toronto and Canadian Films of Montreal were all active in the field. But the idea of promoting commercial products in a dramatized form was less well known. Brownridge had undoubtedly seen Ernest Ouimet's five-reel production of *The Scorching Flame* in the summer of 1918, a film which dramatized the daily lives of Montreal's firemen and which had enjoyed a successful commercial release.[49] Brownridge only produced one short film in this manner (a single reel drama for the Canadian Chewing Gum Company)[50] but the idea was to lead Brownridge back into feature film production by a somewhat circuitous route.

In the fall of 1918, Brownridge approached John Murray Gibbon, publicity director for the CPR, with his idea for dramatized publicity shorts.[51] Gibbon was not encouraging but he had just seen *Power*, the political drama produced at Trenton by Brownridge.

As he and Brownridge were returning from the theatre, Gibbon suddenly stopped and put his arm around Brownridge. Then, as Brownridge recollected it some forty years later, he told Brownridge: "The C.P.R. and others have a problem and you may be able to solve it." That problem was "Bolsheviks entering the ranks of labour."[52] Gibbon was not understating the issue. There was indeed a post-war "red scare" hysteria across North America. Not surprisingly, the mood was reflected in the movies and the red scare gave rise to at least nine features depicting the insidious, and immediate, Bolshevik threat to the American way of life. (Characteristically, all advocates of strike action had mysteriously Russian sounding names.) Among these films was *The Great Shadow*, produced by Adanac at the Trenton studios.

How literally Gibbon intended Brownridge take him at that meeting is unclear. In any case, Brownridge reorganized his Adanac Producing Company in January 1919 with himself as managing director, Denis Tansey, M.P. as president, and J. J. Shea (former president of Canadian National Features) as secretary-treasurer. Rudolph Berliner was brought in as artistic supervisor. Studios established "on nine acres of ground . . . at a cost of approximately $90,000" were at Trenton and the Montreal head office was in the CPR Telegraph Building.[53] By March, Rudolph Berliner and Brownridge had prepared the outline for a script which depicted the attempt by a group of Bolsheviks to take over a union in a shipbuilding plant, only to be defeated by an honest labour leader "always looking out for the good of his men." Armed with this he went back to the CPR for financing. But the CPR were a little wary of Adanac. Perhaps the film should be made in New York? Brownridge refused, since one of his oft-stated aims was to help "establish a motion picture industry in Canada." On March 10, the president of the

CPR, Edward Beatty, wrote to Sir John Willison, head of the Canadian Reconstruction Association. Pointing out that Brownridge was seeking "the financial cooperation of some of the larger Employers of Labour in the preparation of this film," he said he had recommended that Brownridge "submit his proposal for your consideration" since this was a question "on which such Employers would probably consult you before taking action."[54] Brownridge asked for the association's endorsement on April 11. With it, he said, the CPR would "subscribe their share toward the cost of production [and] we could complete the financing within a week."[55] The association did endorse the project and later made a financial contribution.[56] As a result, several employers subscribed to a fund held by Price Waterhouse which was used to finance the film.

For the leading role, Brownridge signed Tyrone Power, an American stage actor and father of his more famous namesake. *The Great Shadow* was to be his first film. In May, Travers Vale, British born actor-director in the USA, was hired to direct but was later forced to withdraw because of a prior contract.[57] To replace him, Brownridge brought in British born Harley Knoles, a minor director who had recently completed one of the red scare films, *Bolshevism on Trial*. Rudolph Berliner's story was scripted by Eve Unsell and the film went into production in mid-July 1919.[58] In its final form, it told the story of a union headed by Jim McDonald (played by Tyrone Power) struggling with a gang of Bolsheviks led by Klimoff (Louis Sterne) "planning to wreck the government and society by poisoning the mind of organized labour." In sympathy with the reasonable demands of his men is capitalist Donald Alexander (Donald Hall) whose daughter Elsie (Dorothy Bernard) is in love with a secret service agent (John Rutherford). The propaganda of the Bolsheviks sweeps aside McDonald's reasoned arguments and a strike is called. Incendiarism and sabotage follow and McDonald's child is killed. Elsie is kidnapped by the Bolsheviks and rescued by her lover who captures the agitators. Public opinion is stirred and at a union meeting, McDonald wins over the men and "an armistice between capital and labour providing no strikes for twelve months is arranged."[59]

Production took about six weeks at a cost of $86,000.[60] Most scenes were shot at the Trenton studios with location scenes in Toronto and Montreal—including the Vickers Company factory at Maisonneuve where 600 members of the union were persuaded to act as unpaid extras after their regular work day and until 3:00 a.m. the next morning. The CPR was associated with the film in Adanac's publicity for over a year—without protest from the CPR. But when the film was released the CPR appears to have become nervous about its involvement. In January 1920, Adanac issued a statement denying the CPR's financial participation.[61]

The Great Shadow was previewed in Ottawa on November 17, 1919, and in Montreal on December 12.[62] Press reaction following these screenings and the general release in March 1920 was adulatory. "Timely in theme, vigorous in treatment and absolutely convincing," wrote C. H. Hamilton in the Montreal Herald, noting that, although written in May 1919, it was "a wonderful case of verified prophecy in the light of subsequent events in this country [presumably the Winnipeg General Strike] and the U.S.A."[63] Morgan Powell in the Montreal Star described it as "timely . . . of the highest quality as propaganda. . . . It is unquestionably a notable picture and may mark the beginning of a new industry for the Dominion."[64] Hector Charlesworth in Saturday Night waxed eloquent, comparing the film to The Birth of a Nation and Intolerance. "The Great Shadow is a more valuable contribution to the motion picture craft than these, because it deals with an issue of greater moment to everyone and presents contemporary history in an impartial and graphic way. . . . It is replete with touches of human interest, and sensational pictures that have never been surpassed in the history of the art. The mob episodes and other ensemble scenes are the best that one has witnessed because they are obviously the real thing and not the result of theatrical artifice."[65] The Toronto Telegram's critic agreed: Considered "from a point of view of heart interest and sensational episodes with beautiful photography and settings, then it certainly is a masterpiece."[66]

World distribution rights outside Canada were sold to Lewis J. Selznick for release by Republic.[67] American critical response, though not as adulatory, was warm. The acting was praised and, though there was a lack of "heart interest . . . the melodramatic climaxes and spectacular scenes will make up for this . . . The picture is excellent as propaganda against industrial unrest."[68] Variety, with keen insight, felt the conventional story only "a transparent covering" for the propaganda message: "the insidious methods of Russian aliens disseminating the gospel of Bolshevism among Labor organizations."[69] The reviewer however was somewhat puzzled over the prominent display of a Union Jack in the film. Unaware of its Canadian origin, he thought the film was set in the United States and suggested the Stars and Stripes would have been more appropriate.

Box-office results, in Canada at least, were good; though this may have been helped by the fact that several Toronto companies provided their employees with free tickets so they could "observe the moral depicted in the picture."[70] New productions by Adanac were announced, variously described as *Canada, A Nation* (the history of Canada from Jacques Cartier up to the present!) and *The Soul of a Woman*. One short comedy, *Oh, Joy!* featuring two Trenton actors, was released late in 1919, but no other films were even begun.[71] By the fall of 1920, Adanac was in precisely the same difficulty as Canadian National Features. A shortage of cash to meet immediate liabilities was creating difficulties and Brownridge wrote to subscribers requesting their agreement to the company's taking the first $15,000 of revenue to liquidate its more pressing debts.[72] Whether they agreed or not is unknown, but in any event Adanac ceased activities and the Trenton studios were again dark.

Why the Adanac Producing Company should have failed is a mystery, given the overwhelming response to *The Great Shadow*. Brownridge blames it on "wasteful tactics" by Harley Knoles and on the sale of the film to Selznick who did not give the film an adequate release and promotion. Even accepting these arguments, the financial mismanagement must have been, to say the least, of an order with that of Canadian National Features. Brownridge may have been sincere and well intentioned in his desire to produce films in Canada but someone, somewhere, had skimmed the cream off the two Brownridge-promoted companies. The financial failure of Adanac, after the evident qualities of *The Great Shadow*, did much to sour Canadian investors on the financing of Canadian production. Not the least embittered were investors in Trenton itself, among whom were Father J. J. Connolly and Dr. F. J. Farley who had not only invested in the company but also held substantial chattel mortgages.[73] Both were later to recoup their investments, with interest, when Brownridge sold the studio to the Ontario government.

Another reason why *The Great Shadow* failed to recoup a substantial return from the American market may also lie in the fact that it was released late in the cycle of red scare films. In fact, only two months before its release in the United States, an American film with a strangely similar plot, *Dangerous Hours*, had hit the theatres. Coincidentally (one assumes) it too depicted Bolshevik agitators poisoning an honest labour union.[74]

Brownridge's career as a major film promoter was ended. He was to be involved peripherally, though not inconsequentially, with the Ontario Government Motion Picture Bureau in its years at Trenton. In 1930 he was operating a distributing company in New York and was instrumental in promoting *Canadian Sound News*, an all-Canadian newsreel which used considerable political pressure to get American sound trucks barred from entry into Canada as a protection for their own intended production.[75] Brownridge left Canada again in 1932. He was never again involved in film production and spent the rest of his career in publicity and promotion.

As for the CPR, soon after the release of *The Great Shadow*, they established their own film production company—Associated Screen News.

The Trenton studios remained dark for almost four years though there were occasional rumours of its reopening. Ottawa lumber baron, J. R. Booth, was one of the backers of Tesa Films of Ottawa which planned to use the Trenton studios in 1922 but the project never got underway.[76]

In 1923, George Brownridge persuaded the Ontario government to purchase the studio for its Motion Picture Bureau. The Bureau had had considerable difficulties with the two commercial companies producing films for it and had determined to make its own films. The idea of purchasing the Trenton studios appealed to the new provincial treasurer, Colonel W. H. Price. Brownridge went to the principal creditor, Father Connolly, in Trenton and induced him to act as principal in the sale. They agreed on a figure of approximately $29,000 (a bargain for the province) to cover Connolly's investments and mortgages plus those of others together with (so Brownridge claimed) monies owing to him personally.[77] Presumably Brownridge did not want the Ontario government to know that he would personally benefit from the sale he had negotiated. The sale went through in late 1923 but, said Brownridge later, Father Connolly never gave him the money owed him. For years later, Brownridge felt himself to have been badly treated by his associates throughout his attempts to produce at Trenton—and indeed during the sale of the studios. It was with some glee that he later recalled Father Connolly's dying soon after failing to pay him the money he claimed as his due.[78]

The Ontario Government Motion Picture Bureau was to use the studio until its closure in 1934. During that decade, several companies expressed interest in using the studio to produce fiction films but only one was to put its interest into practice. In 1927, Canadian International Films were to produce at Trenton the feature *Carry On, Sergeant* and a series of short comedies.

The saga of this company is not dissimilar to those of earlier companies at Trenton and exemplifies much Canadian production activity in this period. It involved one group of Canadians genuinely concerned with the development of a Canadian film industry and a second group, less concerned with the films than with the money to be made by promoting a film company. With *Carry On, Sergeant*, it was to produce the Canadian cinema's most expensive flop. Many influential Canadians—among them Arthur Meighen and R. B. Bennett—subscribed or loaned funds to the company on altruistic grounds or as a means of offsetting American cultural influences.[79] All lost their investments. It was not quiet failure, either, as was that of some earlier companies; it was a noisy, public failure that aroused much acrimony among those involved. Raising funds for Canadian feature film production after *Carry On, Sergeant* was a practical impossibility. As an abortive attempt, amid much goodwill and ample funds, to establish a continuing Canadian feature film industry, Canadian International Films was to bring about a quietus in the industry from which it did not recover until after the Second World War. It was, in short and on several levels, an unmitigated disaster.

None of this is a reflection on the qualities of *Carry On, Sergeant*. It is at least as good a war film as most of its Hollywood contemporaries—which were numerous. But it was not better. It does not bear comparison with, say, the earlier *The Big Parade* and *What Price Glory*, or the later *Wings*. And that was part of the problem. War films were a glut on the market and *Carry On, Sergeant* was simply not good enough to rise above the general level which surrounded it. Given a more modest production, greater efficiency, less waste (and a great deal less skimming of funds by the promoters for nonproduction purposes), there is no reason why its release could not have been successful enough to enable the company to continue producing. But a not inconsiderable share of the invested funds found its way into the pockets of the principals involved in the company and there *was* wastage and poor management. And Canadian International Films collapsed.

The story begins, interestingly enough, with George Brownridge. In 1925, Brownridge had been sent to New York by the Ontario Government Motion Picture Bureau to negotiate for the American theatrical release of the Bureau's films. More than a year, and a large expense account, later he had still not made a sale.[80] Pressed by the minister in Toronto, Brownridge finally recommended a contract for world-wide distribution with the firm of Cranfield and Clarke, independent distributors in London and New York. Partners in the company were both English: Colonel W. F. Clarke and R. T. Cranfield. The Ontario government was not to know it, but the company was not exactly the most well based and would collapse in bankruptcy within two years—still owing money to the province of Ontario. Colonel Clarke was held largely to blame for the failure by his partners. Cranfield later wrote of "the painful experience" of working with him and of "his want of concentration, absolute lack of business acumen, added to impatience at any help, advice or even consultation."[81] An investor who lost funds in Cranfield and Clarke felt Clarke would make "an awful mess" of running a company in Canada.[82]

But for now, the Ontario government relied on Brownridge's judgement of the company and on the fact that—as George Patton, head of the Motion Picture Bureau, put it—"There are no Jews" in the company.[83] A contract was signed in May 1926 with Cranfield and Clarke, who opened a branch office in Toronto. Almost immediately, Colonel Clarke began promoting the idea of film production in Canada. He found receptive ears. This was again a time of increasing concern over the dominant influence of the American film industry in Canada, Britain, Australia, and other countries. The British film industry had well-nigh collapsed under the pressures of Hollywood; Britain was considering a law—the "quota law"—to ensure that British movie theatres exhibited a certain number of British made films. Similar concerns were expressed in Canada, though they related more to "British" interests than to "Canadian" *per se*.

Cranfield sensed that the greatest Canadian resentment of Hollywood films focused on war films. The British and Canadians were annoyed at the fact that, although the United States had entered the war only in 1917, the world was flooded with films depicting only the American involvement in the victory. By late 1926, just months after his arrival in Canada, Clarke was already touting the idea of a company to be called British Empire Films of Canada, the first production of which would be "a dramatic story written by an eminent authority around the part played by the Canadians in the World War." The company had "already begun operations" on a series of twelve animated silhouette films, *The Shadow Laughs*, which would be made at Trenton.[84] Rumours spread that the Ontario government would advance five million dollars to the company. Understandably, government officials laughed off the notion since the government did not have that kind of money to advance to anyone.[85] It was purely, as one journalist later described it, "cheap publicity,"[86] and on a par with the later attempt to claim former Canadian prime minister, Arthur Meighen, as president of the company— a claim immediately denied as "entirely false" by Meighen.[87] Nonetheless, the idea persisted that "important government officials" were backing the company. The idea was at least encouraged by a dinner for leading businessmen organized by Clarke at the National Club in Toronto—a dinner attended by Arthur Meighen, Ontario Premier Howard Ferguson, the provincial treasurer, and the attorney-general. Meighen made a speech urging the production of Canadian films while Premier Ferguson made a strong plea for the businessmen's support and promised the "closest cooperation of the government in connection with British Empire Films of Canada."[88] This was to extend to lending the Trenton studios to the company at a nominal rental.[89]

Clarke incorporated his company in June 1927—not, somewhat suspiciously, under federal law but under the less onerous jurisdiction of New Brunswick. Clarke had "so much confidence in the future" of British Empire Films of Canada that he intended "remaining in Canada as Managing Director, devoting all his time to its operation and development." One-quarter-of-a-million dollars was required to produce the "first super picture" whose net profits would be "100% at an extremely conservative estimate." The company would have links with a similar British company, British Incorporated Pictures which "had options on the film rights" of thirteen British authors including Arnold Bennett, John Galsworthy, and Arthur Conan Doyle.[90] In fact, British Incorporated Pictures (unknown to the potential investors in Canada) was a somewhat dubious 1927 scheme to raise funds to build a "British Hollywood" at Wembley, a scheme which foundered in less than a year.[91]

But undoubtedly the most appealing bait for investors was the name of the British author who had agreed to write the first film. Bruce Bairnsfather was not only popular through his biting cartoons of "Ole Bill" and trench life in the war, but four films based on his plays and stories had been enormously successful in Canada and were well remembered.

The 1918 film version of his play *The Better 'Ole* had been released through the Allen Theatre chain in Canada under the title *Carry On!* It had been one of the most financially successful films shown in Canada up to that time and made a fortune for the Allen brothers. The second film version of the play had been released only a year earlier with equal success. And, more than that, he was familiar with Canada, having lived in St. John's, Newfoundland, before the war and having travelled across Canada in 1923 on a stage tour. It was a stroke of genius to hire him—at least from the point of view of raising funds. From other viewpoints it was to be proved a mistake. But, in the summer of 1927, there were undoubtedly many who subscribed to the company on the strength of Bairnsfather's name—particularly when it was known that he had written a film story about Canadians at war called *Carry On, Sergeant*. A key element in the story was to be the German gas attack at Ypres in 1915 during which the Canadian Expeditionary Force held its ground while others fled. Bairnsfather's contract with Clarke was for twelve months at $2,000 per month plus a car allowance, a private secretary, and, later, a chauffeur—not excessive for a man of his stature nor excessive by Hollywood standards, but enormous by comparative Canadian standards.[92] He was to be not only author but "supervising director" with over-all artistic responsibility and the right to hire his own cast and crew. He was, in fact, allowed far more control than was usually given a director at the time. Though his reputation as an author was unimpeachable he had had no direct experience of film production. That lack of practical knowledge was to cost the company dearly.

In July, Bairnsfather joined Clarke on the provincial round of Rotary Clubs, Kiwanis Clubs, and businessmen's luncheons in order to raise money for the production. Bairnsfather seems genuinely to have wanted to give Canada a major film of which she could be proud, one which would not perpetuate the stereotyped image given it by Hollywood. In a more general sense, he wanted his film to be "the foundation of a sound and invulnerable motion picture industry for Canada"[93]—as his statements and speeches both before and after the production make clear. Unfortunately, he was not aware until much later that he was involved in an enterprise promoted by men whose principal aim was their own remuneration.

Two months later, Clarke decided to organize a "subsidiary" of British Empire Films of Canada—Canadian International Films—which would be responsible for actually producing *Carry On, Sergeant*. Vice-president and general manager at a salary of $1,000 per month was Colonel W. F. Clarke. President, at the same salary was Major Edward P. Johnston, a Toronto financier whom Clarke met in 1927 and who had no prior knowledge of film production or even of the theatre. Secretary was B. K. Johnston and the board of directors was completed by Bairnsfather, Henry S. Gooderham, and G. F. McFarland.[94] Already, the financial affairs of the two companies were highly complex with stock and promissory notes issued under both names. They were to become more so, to the point where it became impossible to disentangle the actual production costs of the film—though certainly a considerable proportion of the later quoted half-million dollar production cost went into capital expenditures at the Trenton studios.

However, with the money raised, filming started in November 1927 and lasted until the following May—an inordinate production time that itself indicates something of the problems, delays, crises, and quarrelling that beset the production. Bairnsfather had been given a large measure of control and his personality demanded that this control should be complete. From the start this created difficulties. Since Bairnsfather had no practical film experience, Clarke had brought in an American associate director, Don Bartlett, to work with him. Bartlett was not an established film director but at least he had some technical knowledge. Bairnsfather pointedly ignored him and Bartlett sat around the set for a month, doing nothing, until his contract was bought off (for $2,100) and he returned to New York.

Bairnsfather was not only inexperienced. He had a rather paranoiac inability to accept advice from anyone, including the technicians involved

Technicians on the set of *Carry On, Sergeant* during the shooting of the *estaminet* scene.

and, increasingly, Clarke and Johnston. His ignorance of film production was to lead to considerable wastage. Six weeks was spent on location in Kingston shooting a sequence that lasted only a few minutes on the screen. Sets were constructed and never used. Bairnsfather was allowed to hire his own cast and did so, giving contracts for the duration of production (itself unusual) to actors, none of whom except Niles Welch, had practical film experience. Jimmy Savo, a vaudeville comedian, was hired at $1,100 a week and eventually received some $30,000 for his contribution—many scenes of which ended up on the cutting room floor. Niles Welch (a handsome Hollywood actor) and Hugh Buckler received $400 a week for seven months—about $10,000 each. Bert Cann, a well established British cameraman, received $300 a week, B. Rothe, the art director $250 a week, and even minor technicians were paid well above the usual Canadian salaries. Gordon Sparling, formerly with the Ontario Motion Picture Bureau, was paid seventy-five dollars a week to build a model of Ypres—which was not used in the film. A continuity writer, the daughter of Mr. Cranfield, was brought from Britain, all expenses paid, and discharged after three months because of quarrels with Bairnsfather. Over $150,000 was spent on the salaries of the promoters, principal cast, and crew.[95] Meanwhile, even with close to half-a-million dollars subscribed, the company was constantly in arrears in paying the modest rent on the Trenton studios and in paying Trenton tradespeople for goods and services.[96]

By the spring of 1928, the acrimony between Bairnsfather and Colonel Clarke and Major Johnston was common knowledge and the production unit was split into two camps. Clarke and Johnston were, not unnaturally, incensed at Bairnsfather's autocratic control over the production, his exclusion of both of them from the studios, and his refusal to show either (or anyone else) a shooting script. No one ever saw a final script and no one except Bairnsfather knew which scene would be shot next. Conversely, Bairnsfather complained bitterly to Provincial Treasurer J. D. Monteith and to shareholders of the company about Clarke's and Johnston's treatment of him. He had "suffered much" at their hands. When he heard on May 14 that Clarke planned to produce a series of comedy shorts at Trenton, he resigned from the board of Canadian International Films. It was, he felt "undignified" to follow his epic with a series of cheap comedies.[97] Johnston responded by swearing out a writ to take possession of "the continuity and still pictures" connected with *Carry On, Sergeant* from Bairnsfather's Trenton home.[98] Bairnsfather's complaints finally brought about a shareholder's meeting and some changes on the board. Clarke lost his job as general manager but remained as vice-president and E. P. Johnston became chairman of the board, being replaced as president by J. Smith, previously a stock salesman. B. K. Johnston resigned as secretary and was replaced by Mr. Berkinshaw of the Goodyear Tire Company. This group continued Bairnsfather's authority over the film, in particular allowing him to edit it: an almost unheard of privilege for a director in North America at the time. He was to spend nearly three months cutting *Carry On, Sergeant* and, after a preview showing in Toronto in late August, shortening and revising it to its final release length of 9,700 feet.[99]

Meanwhile, production of the short comedies got underway at Trenton on July 12, 1928. They were to star Bozo Snyder, a burlesque comedian, and Mona Kingsley, an American actress of little repute. Directing them was Douglas Bright, described as "formerly with the Harold Lloyd Corporation of Hollywood." In fact, he was once employed there as an extra on one film.[100] Three of these comedies were produced that summer but quickly disappeared from view and the contracts were cancelled. As Bairnsfather had said, there was a very limited market for comedy shorts, even the best of them. Simultaneously, the Ontario Motion Picture Bureau produced at Trenton *Little Gray Doors*, a half-hour fantasy for children.[101]

Carry On, Sergeant was given its première at the Regent Theatre in Toronto on Saturday November 10, 1928, the day before Armistice Day. It was, of course, without synchronized sound or dialogue and Ernest Dainty had composed a special music score to accompany the film. (The theme of this later became the most popular Canadian song of the Second World War.)[102] Public response was strong during its two week run. Critical reaction in the press was more mixed. Merrill Denison in the Toronto *Daily Star* gave the film an absolutely glowing review, arguing that it proved once and for all that good feature films could be made in Canada. Its story of an ordinary Canadian, Jim McKay (played by Hugh Buckler), who leaves his wife (Nancy Ann Hargreaves) when war breaks out and joins the Canadian Scottish, depicted "the trenches as one remembers them and men behaving as one remembers them behaving." The comic scenes with Jimmy Savo "are among the most enjoyable in the picture" while the photography by Bert Cann was "amazingly beautiful" especially in the trench scenes and during the gas attack at Ypres. Denison wondered how the film would be received in the United States, but felt the generous scenes depicting "the American entrance into the war can do no harm."[103] In fact, the American scenes were to stir up some indignation among Canadian audiences. Bairnsfather had included in the film a parallel story to that of the "ordinary" Jim McKay. This was the story of two rich families, the Camerons (Canadian) and the Sinclairs (American) whose sons also enlist but, of course, become officers. One critic was to object to scenes of Americans "in full war-time array marching through the streets of Gotham before even the Battle of Vimy Ridge."[104] Another objected to "the Stars and Stripes waved under our very noses on at least two occasions" after Bairnsfather had promised a "purely Canadian film."[105]

Other criticisms were to be more telling. *The Evening Telegram* found the story "vague and rambling," the construction "too evenly paced and unvaried" despite many excellent scenes and an admirable cast. But its principal defect was a scene set in a French *estaminet* towards the end of the film: Sergeant McKay "keeps a clean heart, a fine pose for three long years. Then he succumbs to the wiles of an *estaminet* girl." The scenes of his downfall "might have been taken from the pages of Guy de Maupassant at his sordid worst." Even though "thoughts of his wife at home fill him with remorse and despair [until] a German bullet ultimately solves his problem," the inclusion of these scenes was "little short of blasphemy." The mixing of "immorality and gallantry only serves to make the hero look ridiculous."[106] The scene in question—understated, if explicit—showed only McKay and the woman walking upstairs together; similar scenes were not uncommon in other films. Bairnsfather had already shortened the scene after the preview screening in September but now it did no good for him to say the film "depicts war as it was" to point to "the tremendous theme underlying the picture."[107]

Rumours spread that the film would be withdrawn from distribution because of its reflection "on the morals of the Canadian Expeditionary Force."[108] It was even said that the provincial attorney-general, Colonel W. H. Price, had asked for the film to be shelved. Though Price denied it, the rumours persisted and the consistently reiterated stories most assuredly did not help at the box-office. Price even went so far as, in early December, to suggest that American interests were "behind some of the objections to the picture" since "they would naturally desire to see their own pictures continue to control the Canadian market." "American interests" in this case meant Famous Players Canadian Corporation and, during the ensuing battle over the film's exhibition, they were to defend themselves vigorously. They had, they claimed, given the film every opportunity in their theatres but it had still lost money despite this. Even the two-week opening run in Toronto had lost money. (This is difficult to credit unless the theatre's expenses were padded, since there were almost full houses during this run.)[109] To what extent they tried with the film is impossible to say but, after runs in Montreal and several Ontario towns, *Carry On, Sergeant* disappeared from view.

It was also said that its release was hampered because it was a silent film produced after sound films had been introduced. This may well have had an effect in some larger centres but not in most towns. By late 1928 and early 1929 relatively few theatres were equipped to show sound films. In any case, no American sale was made and it was reported that the previously announced British sale was cancelled for fear of "prejudicing the standing of future Canadian production."[110] In January 1929, writs were served on Canadian International Films for debts incurred during the production and by May the company was declared bankrupt.[111] Colonel Clarke had long since left Canada and was heard of no more. His presence on the Canadian film scene left many smarting. In March 1929 when another film stock promotion, Canadian Classic Productions of Montreal headed by Colonel W. F. Stewart, folded, one journalist was to comment acidly: "It would be an excellent thing if some of the Colonels with film ambitions and get-rich-quick ideas would be de-colonelized."[112]

Carry On, Sergeant resurfaced briefly in 1930 as yet another George Brownridge project. Brownridge planned to re-cut it, add a sound track, and shoot several new scenes which would include giving Sergeant McKay's wife a child. The objectionable *estaminet* scene would be eliminated. The newly titled film "would gross at least $200,000."[113] As with the other contemporary Brownridge project, *Canadian Sound News*, nothing happened and *Carry On, Sergeant* was buried again.

The Ontario government repossessed the Trenton studios and the Motion Picture Bureau moved back to produce its documentaries and travelogues. There were to be continuing stories of companies planning to produce fiction films at Trenton, most of the proposals relating to producing for the British quota market. The Calgary-based company, British Canadian Pictures, considered using Trenton in 1929.[114] The Canadian Motion Picture Company planned to produce shorts in 1930 under the direction of Len Humphries,[115] as did Booth Canadian Films in 1931.[116] None of these companies produced anything except Booth Canadian Films—and that not at Trenton.

In 1932, the spectre of Canadian International Films arose again with the announcement of "a million dollar movie company" which would "put Canada on the movie map." The Ontario government had indicated "sympathetic interest" and would rent the studios at "a nominal figure." Several important Canadian businessmen were reported to be interested, including Sir Edward Beatty and Sir Herbert Holt. A whole string of well-known actors, actresses, and directors would "shortly be making feature productions at Trenton."[117] But investors could not be lured a second time by the same bait, especially during the Depression, and the project came to nothing.

There was, however, to be yet one more feature produced at Trenton, albeit quietly—so quietly indeed that the event passed almost unnoticed. This was *Cinderella of the Farms*, a sixty-minute dramatized documentary produced, somewhat surprisingly, by the Ontario Motion Picture Bureau in 1930.[118] Though ostensibly a romantic tale of a young immigrant's love for the adopted daughter of his neighbour and the entanglements that follow through his wish to keep secret his ownership of his farm, it was in fact thinly disguised propaganda designed to encourage immigration from Britain and foster good farming practises. It was the almost single-handed creation of one man, John McLean French, who conceived it, wrote it, produced, directed, and edited it. Sixty-seven-year-old French was a writer who had been attempting for some time to become involved with films. His 1924 novel, *The Trail of Destiny*, had been accepted for filming by Canadian International Films (as had the works of other Canadian authors such as W. A. Frazer). He himself withdrew when Bruce Bairnsfather made known Colonel Clarke's mismanagement of the company.[119] He was several times associated with (inactive) production companies and in 1932 wrote a three-reel drama, *Under the Circumstances*, for Booth Canadian Films.[120] He had submitted his script for *Cinderella of the Farms* to Provincial Treasurer Monteith in January 1930 and, in the absence of the Bureau's director, George Patton, the film went into production that May with a cast of Toronto actors (including French himself) and with French in complete charge.

Production, which was planned to take no more than a couple of months, dragged on through January 1931. And when it was completed, no one knew what to do with the film.[121] Theatrical distribution was out of the question—though French tried. *Cinderella of the Farms* was silent and in 1931 silent movies were anathema to almost every theatre. So *Cinderella of the Farms* was slipped out, without fanfare, onto the Ontario Motion Picture Bureau's non-theatrical circuit in Ontario and into the Ontario agent general's office in London. There was no evident reaction.

Such a demise for the film was undeserved. It had many qualities not only in its photography but in its subtle integration of drama and documentary, its blend of fiction and reality, its use of natural locations. It was an approach which had marked many other successful Canadian films—notably those of Ernest Shipman—and was to mark others in the future. It was, indeed an approach being used at precisely the same time by Varick Frissell in Newfoundland on his film *The Viking*.

But, deservedly or not, *Cinderella of the Farms* was a failure in the sense that hardly anybody saw it. As the last major production at the Trenton studios its failure seems that much more acute.

For three more years, the Ontario Motion Picture Bureau continued to operate the studios until the new Liberal government under Mitchell Hepburn closed the Bureau in October 1934. The studios themselves were donated to the town of Trenton as a community centre.[122] All that remains today is the building itself, now the premises of the Bayside Dyeing and

Finishing Company, and the street that runs past its door which is still called Film Street. It was an ignoble end for studios which had focused so much of Canada's film production activity, an ironic end for a film town which had once boasted of being "the Hollywood of the North."

In the successive occupations of the Trenton studios there are some suggestions why, despite numerous attempts, a self-perpetuating feature film industry did not develop in Canada. Each of the efforts remained self-contained, isolated, the product of the efforts and energies of different groups of people. Directors, writers, and actors were often imported from the United States or Britain; supporting acting roles and minor technical tasks were handled by Canadians. When a film was completed, those involved in its production dispersed. There was never enough money, for whatever reason, to finance continuing production and help establish the essential continuity of personnel.

Blooms in Innocence

The same pattern was apparent in fiction production outside Trenton. Seven companies, apart from those of Ernest Shipman, were to produce feature films between 1915 and 1922; six of these were to produce only one feature each. Given the mood of Canadian nationalism at the time, there is a certain bitter irony in this. And, given the optimism of the period and the failures that resulted, the pessimism many later felt about the possibilities of a viable Canadian film industry become more understandable.

But the desire to create an indigenous film industry was very much in evidence during those years. The signs were everywhere. Newspapers editorialized, politicians debated, the public wrote letters, and the financiers bought shares in Canadian film companies. In 1916, following showings of D. W. Griffith's *The Birth of a Nation*, "a movement was started to bring about the making of a big picture play dealing comprehensively with certain phases of Canada's history."[123] In 1919 there was even a debate in the British Columbia Legislature about the excessive domination of Hollywood films in Canadian theatres.[124] Inevitably, the mood gave rise to numerous stillborn productions such as the epic feature on Louis Riel and the 1885 Rebellion planned for filming in Regina[125] or *The Little Canuck*, a film on the Canadian contribution to the war.[126] And, just as inevitably, the mood attracted numerous stock promoters who, hungrily, were able to exploit it. Almost always such promoters made their appeal for funds on nationalistic grounds, pointing out that the United States "took six million dollars annually out of Canada and offered nothing tangible in return." [127]

Hollywood, too, responded magnificently. There had always been "Canadian content" films made in the United States. But now, Hollywood began to pay attention to Canadian complaints about "undue exploitation of the American Flag" and the ways in which Canadian contributions to the war were being ignored. Suddenly, after 1917, there began to appear "Canadian adaptations" of Hollywood films and there were even Hollywood films in which Canadians were the heroes. Canadian reaction to the adaptations of the Victory Loan Films featuring Hollywood stars had been warm; now the approach was tried in other films. In the Pathé war serial, *Pearl of the Army*, for example, Pathé inserted scenes of Canadian troops and of Canadian flags. Examples of Hollywood films featuring Canadian soldiers included *Private Peat*, *The Great Love*, *Over the Top* and—by far the best of its type— *The Heart of Humanity*. It was even suggested this film should be presented officially by the United States government to the government of Canada "as a tribute to her splendid spirit of sacrifice." [128]

In Canada, the greatest beneficiaries of the conscious drives to create a domestic film industry were by far the stock promoters. Ernest Shipman, though always remaining on the right side of the law, was to take advantage of this mood in promoting his Canadian companies between 1919 and 1922. But more typical of the stock promoters of the time was Harold J. Binney. This twenty-nine-year-old American arrived in Toronto in late 1918, claiming a career as an "independent producer-director since 1916" and trailing in his wake several independent companies already foreclosed by creditors— or soon to be so. [129] His first act as Harold J. Binney Productions, Toronto, was to produce a feature, *Polly at the Circus*, at the CNE. Photographed by Charles Roos, assisted by Frank O'Byrne with Charlie Quick as "associate," and a cast of local actors, it received no theatrical release. Binney's evident purpose was to use it as "a means of promoting finance." [130] In March 1919 he incorporated Canadian Photoplay Productions (no relation to Ernest Shipman's Canadian Photoplays of Calgary) and announced that he would build a half-a-million dollar studio in Toronto. [131] Of course, Torontonians were expected to subscribe to the cost of this and, for a time, Binney was a familiar figure around town, clutching a roll of "plans" for his studio (which, rumour had it, were actually the blueprints for a dry-cleaning plant), and tempting potential investors. Students at the University of Toronto were lured into spending their summers selling movie stock to their friends and relations. At this time he claimed to have on staff Philip Van Loon as script editor,

Arthur Porchet as cameraman, and actors Fred Bezerril, Vangie Valentine, and Neil Hamilton.[132] How many Torontonians were seduced by his winning ways is unknown but Harold Binney eventually left Toronto and was heard of no more.

On the other side of the country, in Victoria, B.C., a similar series of events was taking place. Victoria has often been a favoured site for the location of film studios. Certainly, in climate and locale, it offers many advantages. But its greatest attraction over some forty years seems to have been a city council willing to offer tangible and intangible assistance to film promoters proposing to build studios in Victoria. The proposed studios often had such grandiose names as "Cinema City" or "Maple Leaf City." But, until the arrival of Commonwealth Pictures and Central Films in the Thirties, they were more imaginative than practical.

One of the more persuasive of these promoters was J. Arthur Nelson who arrived in British Columbia in the fall of 1916 as president and general manager of the Dominion Film Corporation, whose head offices were in Vancouver.[133] Nelson was English born but had lived for many years in the United States. Like Binney, he claimed to have worked for several American film companies. On his arrival he expressed surprise at the "primitive condition" of the film industry in Canada and urged Canadians to spend some of the fifteen million dollars invested in Canadian movie theatres on producing Canadian films to put in them.[134] By January 1917 he had located a twenty-three acre site for the studio just outside Victoria which could be purchased for $18,400. He was prepared to start production almost immediately in Victoria if the city would "make a grant or loan of one-half this amount." He already had his first "star" under contract: Marion Swayne, a Hollywood actress of small repute who was later to appear in Shipman's *The Man from Glengarry*. In return he guaranteed to spend "at least $100,000 on production work in Victoria within two years." A public meeting was called in Victoria to consider Nelson's proposal, a meeting attended by four B.C. cabinet ministers, the Victoria representatives in the provincial Legislature, members of the City Council, and local businessmen. The mayor of Victoria chaired the meeting at which it was unanimously decided to support Nelson's proposal. The city then discovered it could not provide assistance directly to the company and attempted to channel the funds through the Victoria and Island Development Association as a donation ostensibly for "publicity purposes." When the city solicitor advised the council that this too would be illegal, a public subscription campaign was launched to raise the necessary $9,200. Throughout all this, Nelson alternated between denying he was "just a promoter" and threatening to take the studio elsewhere.[135]

The citizens of Victoria were wiser than their council and, by the summer of 1917, only a small percentage of the required funds had been raised.[136] Nelson made good his threat and took Dominion Film Corporation to Burnaby, a suburb of Vancouver. Here, he requested the city donate the site (valued at $41,000) for Dominion's studio. Though accepted by one of its committees, the City Council itself wisely rejected the deal.[137] Dominion Film Corporation and J. Arthur Nelson were heard of no more in B.C.

In Montreal, Patricia Photoplays produced a five-reel feature, *The Vow*, and a travelogue on Montreal, *The City Beautiful*, from "a provisional studio" on Alexander Street in 1920. The company was promoted by a self-proclaimed British playwright, J. Reynolds Allison, and a former Montrealer, Maurice R. Coste who claimed to have been "associated with the picture industry since its inception." Though the board of directors included several well known Montreal names (J. C. Gagné of La Prévoyance and the Sun Trust Company, J. L. Tarté, president of *La Patrie*, and J. L. Perron of Perron, Taschereau, Renfret and Genest) the company was clearly a stock promotion swindle.[138]

Though several Canadian cities had similar experiences with stock promoters who scoured their communities for money with which to build studios, there were many legitimate enterprises established with a genuine desire to produce fiction films. Some succeeded.

Among these was United Films of Galt, Ontario, a company founded and operated by Charles and Len Roos. They were to be jointly responsible for producing Canada's first major feature during the war. In fact, *Self Defence* was a patriotic film produced in cooperation with the Department of Militia and Defence. Written, produced, and photographed by Charles and Len Roos in 1916, *Self Defence* was a nine-reel drama depicting an imaginary invasion of Canada by the Germans. Featuring Toronto actor Albert E. H. Grupe, it had "a well developed plot enfolded in a striking theme" that blended staged dramatic scenes with documentary and newsreel footage. Twenty-five-thousand Canadian troops in training were used in some scenes while the invading German army was depicted through newsreel footage of German soldiers on the Eastern Front. It was "vital and vivid," "cogent and compelling," and "a wonderful success."[139] United Films produced no more features though they did make the documentaries *Across Canada* and *Seeing Canada First*, both in 1916. Charles and Len Roos were to work the following year for Atlas Films of Canada, which was organized by Alex

Dunbar, and they made at least one two-reel comedy.[140] Later, Charles joined the Pathescope Company and worked for Harold Binney while Len became editor of the *Fox Canadian News*.[141]

In Sydney, Nova Scotia, several local businessmen financed the establishment of the Maritime Motion Picture Company of Canada in March 1920, with Wallace MacDonald (who had organized the company) as general manager.[142] *A Ten Days' Trip Through New Brunswick*, a travelogue photographed by H. B. McNeil, was the company's first production in early 1921 and a feature-length drama went into production in the late summer of 1921. *Big Timber* (later retitled *Clansman of the North*) was directed by American John W. Noble and starred Richard C. Travers, but was never released.[143] In March 1922, John Noble sued the company in the United States for breach of contract and a receiver was appointed to take over the film.[144] That was the last anyone heard of it. The company continued nevertheless, producing in 1922 a feature-length travelogue on Newfoundland, *Port aux Basques*, and a second feature-length drama. *The Sea Riders* was directed and scripted by Hollywood director Edward H. Griffith from a story by Wallace MacDonald and starred Americans Edward Phillips and Betty Bouton, with Ed. Lawrence, Mike Brennan, and America Chedister (the wife of E. H. Griffith) in supporting roles.[145] This story of "romance and adventure in a picturesque little Cape Breton fishing village" was completed in September 1922, shown in Halifax in November, and released in the United States— without much impact—in 1923.[146] Less than a year later the company was dissolved.

Roy Mitchell and John A. Martin had incorporated their Toronto-based Canadian Feature and Production Company in 1920. Initially a distribution company, it was to produce one feature drama in 1922: an unusual drama for a Canadian company at the time, in that its plot had nothing whatsoever to do with Canada. Roy Mitchell, a former director of Hart House, and John Martin, a Toronto financier, were respectively president and general manager of the company; jointly they were to supervise the production of *The Proof of Innocence*.[147] Associated with them was John L. Hunter, a former Toronto distributor and then head of the distribution department of the American Releasing Corporation in New York—the company that was to release the film in the United States. Directed by B. C. Rule from a script by Charles Rich, *The Proof of Innocence* told the story of Mignon, an orphan rescued from a Greenwich Village tenement by artist John Courtney, who later poses for him and inspires him to his greatest work. He becomes famous, "the idol of the smart set," falls in love with "society butterfly" Marion Wesley, and amasses debts trying to keep up with his new friends.

When a wealthy art collector is murdered, Courtney is accused of the crime but Mignon solves the mystery and proves him innocent. Louise Du Pré played Mignon, John Hopkins appeared as John Courtney, and supporting actors included Dorothea Teal as Marion Wesley, J. Francis O'Reilly as the art collector, and Carl Sodders, Oliver Putnam, and Don Merrifield.[148]

Though essentially a mystery drama, there was "too little suspense" in *The Proof of Innocence*—a failing, one reviewer felt, in the dramatic construction rather than in the story itself. Louise Du Pré, "a pretty type, expressive of a popular ideal in feminine beauty," gave a performance that lacked "real emotional quality." Others found the "lavish settings" and "plausible story" created a pleasing film.[149] *The Proof of Innocence* enjoyed a modest success in Canada, less of one in the United States. Mitchell and Martin produced no more films and later changed the name of their company to United Exhibitors of Canada.

Blaine Irish's Filmcraft Industries had been actively and successfully producing documentary and educational films since 1919, had introduced the theatrical short film series *Nature Classics* in 1920, and the much praised *Camera Classics* series in 1922. Now, the thirty-one-year-old Canadian producer decided to embark on a feature. Directed and photographed by Roy Tash, *Satan's Paradise* was to "combine entertainment and education with entertainment predominant."[150] Its cast, including Rance Quarrington and Harold Taperty, was entirely from Toronto as were the story and locale. Designed to expose the charlatans of Spiritualism, it told the story of a Canadian soldier who is reported missing in action during the war. His mother attempts to find the truth of her son's fate and "is drawn into the meshes of Spiritualism . . . which has gained such a footing at the expense of war-bereaved womanhood." She is seduced into thinking herself able to communicate with him while at the same time his girl friend receives letters "sent from beyond." One medium even attempts to persuade the mother to commit suicide in order to rejoin her son. During an investigation, the mysterious practises of the mediums are exposed as fraudulent, mere magical tricks. The son is not even dead, only shell-shocked, and eventually returns home.

Toronto critics were unanimous in their praise for the film when it was released in December 1922, not only because of its important theme "but for its technical and pictorial qualities." The Toronto *Globe* felt it compared well "with the best importations from Hollywood and the big foreign studios" while Ray Lewis was "flabbergasted" at its quality, finding it "among the very best pictures yet produced in Canada." Its merits were such, she wrote, that theatres need not play it only for nationalistic reasons because it was "home product."[151] *Satan's Paradise* was released by Famous Players Film Service but, despite the warm praise from critics, had only a minimal distribution. Filmcraft Industries produced no more features. Its studios were destroyed in a fire in September 1923 and Blaine Irish, a producer who had only just begun to make a mark on the Canadian film scene, died of erysipelas that October.[152]

For some years, Ernest Ouimet had been operating his distribution company, Speciality Film Import, producing *British Canadian Pathé News* and the occasional sponsored industrial film in Montreal. He had been active in producing sponsored films since making a film on the construction of the Quebec Bridge for the Dominion Bridge Company and the federal government. He was also to produce films for, among others, Holt Renfrew in 1915, and for Henry Birks and Sons in 1918. But, imaginative as always, he was to expand the form of such films in 1918 by blending drama and documentary, fiction and reality. His approach anticipated that of several later Canadian films. In fact, it was the first shape in a pattern that was to continue to mark much Canadian production. In the summer of 1918 he produced *The Scorching Flame*, a five-reel dramatized portrait of the life of Montreal's firemen. Directed by Armand Robi, of Montreal's Théâtre National, photographed by Bert Mason, and sponsored by the Montreal Firemen's Association, it was to enjoy a successful commercial showing at the Théâtre français.[153] Later that same summer he filmed *Sauvons nos bébés*, a dramatized documentary, directed by Henri Dorval, and designed to promote the campaign against infantile mortality.

Now, in 1921, he, too, decided to embark on the production of dramatic features, the first of which was to be an adaptation of a story by Sir Gilbert Parker.[154] However, when he incorporated Laval Photoplays in February 1922, following a visit to Hollywood, he announced that he planned to film there and not in Montreal.[155] Ouimet had evidently concluded that one of the difficulties with Canadian production was that the films were made outside of the Hollywood system. Perhaps producing in the film capital itself would solve that. In May 1922, he sold his Speciality Film Import to N. L. Nathanson's Regal Films for $200,000 and moved to California, though the head office of Laval Photoplays remained in Montreal.[156] Eighteen months later his first feature, *Why Get Married?* was completed and was previewed in Montreal in December 1923.[157] Directed by Paul Cazeneuve from a script by William M. Conselman (who had earlier worked together in Hollywood on the not dissimilar *Why Trust Your Husband?*) it told the story of two young (American) couples who get married at about the same time. One wife, Marcia, insists on continuing working in a business office while

Scene from Ernest Ouimet's *Why Get Married?*

Janet, the other, resigns "to devote herself entirely to her domestic duties."
Both couples have difficulties. Marcia's husband, though only able at first
to get a job as a railway porter, soon climbs to the position of manager of
the line and "Marcia has the good sense to resign her post and go with him"
to Chicago. Janet gets jealous of her husband and leaves him to return to

mother "but James is easily able to persuade her she has no grounds for complaint." [158]

Andrée Lafayette, a French actress who had scored a mild success in Hollywood for her performance in *Trilby*, played Marcia with Helen Ferguson as Janet, and Jack Perrin and Bernard Randall as the husbands. All of the performers, including Edwin B. Tilton, William Turner, Max Constant, and Orpha Alba in supporting roles, were Hollywood based.

Released in March 1924, it was immediately characterized as "cheaply done" (it cost $27,000), of "stereotyped programme quality" and "a second feature for average houses." [159] The British *Bioscope* found the acting "adequate but by no means distinguished." Andrée Lafayette was "handsome" but "the cold unemotional businesswoman is hardly a sympathetic character and affords little scope for acting." [160] Box office returns matched this critical reaction in Canada, the United States, and Britain—though it did well in Montreal. Only in Europe did it enjoy a modest success because of the momentary popularity of Andrée Lafayette. [161]

As for Ernest Ouimet, his film making career was ended, as indeed was his career as a distributor. It is a somewhat telling point that the active career of perhaps the most creative contributor to Canadian film should end exactly as the nascent Canadian film industry itself was collapsing. Ouimet continued working on the fringes of the industry in both Hollywood and Montreal until 1934 when he returned to the city permanently. He was manager for two years of the Imperial Theatre on Bleury Street but when two young girls lost their lives in a theatre fire his film career was ended. A position was obtained for him as manager of a Quebec Liquor Board outlet and he remained there until his retirement in 1956. He died March 3, 1972, in a Montreal hospital at the age of 94.

On the West Coast, Vancouver-born Arthur D. Kean (sometimes known as "Cowboy" Kean) had established himself as a photographer and film maker of some standing. His first films had been of the Calgary Stampede in 1912 and he had worked since then shooting films for the provincial government, the CPR, and the Vancouver Exhibition. [162] He had produced a complete film record of every B.C. battalion to leave for the war—released as the four-reel *B.C. For the Empire* in 1916. His 1916 documentary on the whaling industry off Vancouver Island had had considerable commercial success, being released as part of the *Ford Canadian Monthly*. [163] He had worked as a cameraman on westerns in the United States and, in Vancouver, had his own film laboratory and distribution company, Kean's Canada Film Exchange. In 1917, he had made a short comedy, *The Adventures of Count E. Z. Kisser*, and in 1922 was to embark on a major feature production. [164]

Through his company, Canadian Historic Features, he planned to produce a dramatized documentary, *Policing the Plains*, which would depict the role of the Royal Northwest Mounted Police in the settling of the Canadian West.[165] Based on the book by R. G. MacBeth, it was to include both documentary sequences and dramatic reconstructions, plus a romantic story.[166] It was not finally completed until August 1927, five years later, at a reported cost of $100,000, with shooting taking place intermittently over the intervening years.[167] Kean was later to speak angrily of the difficulties in completing and releasing his film, difficulties which he blamed on Famous Players Canadian Corporation and their associated distributors who, he claimed, "blocked" the film.[168] Eventually, he himself rented the Royal Alexandra Theatre in Toronto and *Policing the Plains* had a two-week run in December 1927.[169] The Toronto critics admired the film but pointed out the weaknesses others had already described to Kean, notably its lack of dramatic continuity. Though the chief roles were "capably enacted" and the film had "a splendid veracity . . . packed with native Canadian colour down to the least historical detail," it lacked "dramatic technique." With "some of the finest material available" for a Canadian epic, *Policing the Plains* failed for want of "a big dramatic director."[170] In fact, the film consisted of eight reels depicting various historical events, loosely tied together through the story of two men who join the RNWMP and who both love the same girl. *Policing the Plains* enjoyed a modest release across Canada; Kean recouped his investment but produced no more features.

In fact, the delayed release of Kean's film was the last testament of Canada's still-born feature film industry.[171] In 1918 there had been real promise of developing a viable film industry. Yet, by 1923, that promise had proved itself illusory. No features were produced after this time (excepting the atypical *Carry On, Sergeant*) until the introduction of the British quota revived feature film production of quite a different kind in the late Twenties and Thirties. It did no good for newspapers editorially to urge Canadians to "wake up, and make Canadian films,"[172] nor for *Canadian Forum* to advocate the establishment "of a moving picture industry of our own, by Government assistance to whatever degree is necessary."[173]

Investors had been burnt too often, the brief flurry of nationalism in film production died down and Canada increasingly turned to Hollywood films with Canadian plots as a substitute for the—obviously—doomed domestic production. Hollywood responded magnificently. Already in 1918, Hollywood had reacted to Canadian complaints about American war films by producing films such as *The Heart of Humanity* and *The Great Love* which depicted Canadian participation in the war. After the war, the number of

Hollywood features set in Canada increased sharply, reached a peak in 1922, and continued at a high level through the mid-Twenties. Almost all were films about the Northwest, Mounties, trappers, Hudson's Bay, or the Klondike. Several were shot in Canada including *The Valley of Silent Men* (1922), *Unseeing Eyes* (1923), *The Snow Bride* (1923), *The Calgary Stampede* (1925), *Winds of Chance* (1925), and *The Canadian* (1926), but many dozens more were produced in American locations. Canadian newspapers increasingly turned from promoting domestic production to praising Hollywood companies for producing "Canadian" stories. During Canadian Book Week in 1925, one Canadian newspaper commended the Vitagraph company for including in "its current schedule, the production of four Canadian books, two of which are by members of the Canadian Authors' Association and two by a popular writer [James Oliver Curwood] who lays all his scenes in the Canadian Northland."[174] When, in 1925, director D. W. Griffith urged Canadians to produce their own feature films,[175] he was already speaking to a people whose image on the world screen—at least in fiction films—was being reflected in films by producers "sent into Canada to make them." As Lewis Selznick had predicted, Hollywood producers were more than happy to film our stories for us. Ironically, Selznick himself was to be a victim of the massive Hollywood thrust to control the world's film industries, the same thrust he was espousing in 1922. In 1923 his own company was swallowed in a take-over bid.

Production was not the only aspect of Canada's nascent film industry to suffer. The distributorships gradually fell under direct Hollywood control or domination as, in parallel embrace, did the theatres. The single, most telling, example of this occurs, perhaps not coincidentally, also in 1922–23 with the demise of the Canadian owned Allen Theatres chain. The Allen family had opened their first theatre in Brantford in 1906 and had taken fifteen years to build up a nationwide theatre chain. They had even made tentative forays onto the international scene. Their only competitor, N. L. Nathanson's Famous Players Canadian Corporation, was initially much smaller. But Famous Players was backed by Adolph Zukor and New York financial interests while the Allens built each of their theatres with shares floated locally as a popular investment. Eventually the war with Nathanson's well-financed company took its toll, the Allens overextended themselves, and bankruptcy became inevitable in 1922. Finally, in June 1923, Nathanson bought the Allen theatres for an almost unbelievably low price and Famous Players won control of the Canadian exhibition market.[176]

The Canadian film industry was not the only national film industry to fall under Hollywood domination. The British industry and those of most

European countries were experiencing similar, if less acute, difficulties. Some Canadians, including the federal government's film officials, were to argue that Hollywood's international influence was a precise reflection of the quality of its production; if other countries could produce equally good films that appealed to audiences, their domestic film industries would not have problems. Others, in less influential positions, felt Hollywood's domination stemmed more from economic forces than from artistic ones.

If one considers the films produced by Canadians in Canada during this period, there is nothing like the same coherence of output that one sees in the Hollywood films with Canadian content. The Americans were to see Canada with an almost mindless simplicity as a land of ice and snow, mountains and Mounties. Canada's own production was less clearly defined and the films, though they included some stereotyped Canadian stories, offered a wide diversity of content, running from domestic comedies to anti-Bolshevik dramas and war films. If there was a definable quality—and it was a tentative one—it lay in relating fiction and reality, in the idea that stories should be filmed not on sets but in natural locations, in applying a documentary approach to drama. Such an approach characterized many of the most successful Canadian films of the period, notably those of Ernest Shipman, and was to find its most potent expression in three quasi-Canadian films: *Nanook of the North*, *The Silent Enemy*, and *The Viking*. It is perhaps not surprising that, denied access to producing feature films, Canadians should excel in the documentary film. But neither the documentary nor the dramatized documentary has ever had much, in Hollywood's terms, mass audience appeal.

CHAPTER 4

Ten Percent Ernie

With me, the making of pictures in Canada first appealed as a business, then it became a hobby, now I might fairly say it is a religion. I welcome the opportunity of addressing myself to the Canadian Clubs, believing that I find here perfect understanding from a movement founded for the purpose of quickening a Canadian national consciousness—the spirit which now finds expression not only in a new and distinctive note in Canadian literature, but in a demand for Canadian-made motion pictures, as real and free and wholesome as is Canadian life at its best.[1]
 –Ernest Shipman
 March 1923

It is difficult in retrospect to decide whether Ernest Shipman was a rogue or a genius. Perhaps like all great entrepreneurs he was a little of both. A typical example of the "Diamond Jim" kind of opportunistic promoter who flourished in North America in the late nineteenth century, he went through two fortunes and five wives during the course of his chequered career—eventually dying at fifty-nine of the *bon viveur*'s disease, cirrhosis of the liver.[2] Nell Shipman, the fourth Mrs. Shipman and herself a talented producer, actress, and writer, described him affectionately. "Men like Ernie Shipman made the Nineties gay. A vanished breed. He had the bounce of a rubber ball, the buoyance of a balloon. . . . He was one of the great cocksmen of his time, not immoral but amoral, not lascivious but lusty. If they named him dishonest he was always within the law's fences contractually and the ten percent he required of his minions' wages he considered a fair return for his efforts on their behalf."[3] It is possible, of course, to dismiss him as an opportunist who used the lure of Canadian film production during a period of heightened nationalism to extract money from naive investors in cities across Canada. And he did, indeed, have a remarkable talent for separating Canadians from their bankrolls. But this does not tell the full story. He did, after all, produce seven feature films in Canada in three years and in achieving this he stands alone. He realized his films had to be seen outside Canada in the American market if they were to be financial successes. He paid strict and efficient attention to the marketing and promotion of all of them. None (except *Blue Water*) failed on this level as so many previous Canadian films had—and as they were to fail again in the future. His basic theory that films should be produced directly in the locations with which they dealt was faithfully put into practice on all seven films. "Telling the Truth in Motion Pictures," Shipman called it. This in itself was something, given the misrepresentations of Canada that were being perpetrated in contemporary Hollywood films. The content of the films was nothing if not Canadian: the life of Bay of Fundy fishermen, the Glengarry lumber industry, Russian immigrants on the prairies, not to forget, of course, the North West Mounted Police and north-woods adventure. And more, there was something about his approach to filming that seems rather specially Canadian.

Shipman never varied his mode of operation. The formula was to find a Canadian story, raise money for its production as a film in the locale in which it was set, excite community participation in the production, and promote "in kind" assistance in the form of locations, facilities, and personnel. The lead actors and technicians were imported though they were often, as he was, Canadian-born. He spoke many times of repatriating—permanently—the many Canadians working in movies in Hollywood. He prophesied that new Canadian actors and technicians would not have to leave the country to find work in movies. He promised the construction of permanent production centres, spread across the country, regionally based. Canada had almost limitless potential as a major film producing nation. "There is a market for thirty Canadian features in Canada," he said in April 1922, "but I can make only ten and may make only seven. Centres all over the Dominion will be selected for production. Preference will be given to Canadian authors, Canadian players, and the necessary technical staff will be recruited from Canadians also. . . . A Canadian picture will not necessarily mean that we are to have snow scenes. In fact, we intend to eliminate the snow scenes and picture Canada during her Summer and Autumn months." [4] A year later his vision had become more grandiose. Comparing the Canadian film industry to a "young giant" which had "no past to live down, no mistakes to apologize for," he noted that he had "carefully estimated that at least one hundred features could be made without duplication of scenery or background." [5]

He was an indefatigable defender of Canadian national interests in the film field. His most forceful statement on this was written in September 1921, soon after completing *Cameron of the Royal Mounted*, in response to news that the United States would impose a special tariff on the importation of foreign films. He predicted that Canada would respond to this with a "retaliatory tariff" which would "practically prohibit the export of American-made pictures into Canada and give to Canadian producers a great opportunity and full protection for the making of an increased number of pictures for home consumption." Canadian exhibitors, he wrote, "figure that an increased activity in the making of Canadian pictures would open to them the doors for investment through which they would receive their share of profits from the export of these pictures to all other countries, and at the same time have some voice in the subject matter and the making of these pictures.

The attitude assumed by the big business interests of the Dominion is that instead of paying so many millions of dollars a year to American producers for entertainment [the business men] will instead receive from foreign markets many millions of dollars, and at the same time demonstrate to the world at large the beauty, resources and virility of the nation."

The films "would be treated from the artistic rather than the commercial standpoint;" free trade relations "would consequently be established between all countries which had not discriminated in their tariff laws against Canadian-made productions." Canadian films would be exported to Britain, France, Scandinavia, Italy, Spain, and Australia, and Canadian exhibitors would purchase from these countries films "in sufficient quantities to fulfill all needs until such time as the Canadian producing units have developed to a point where they can be relied upon for a considerable number of high grade pictures each year." Meanwhile, markets in the United States would not be closed to the best Canadian films. All that was necessary was to pay "a duty of $30,000 on each $100,000 production"—since *Back to God's Country* had already earned over $500,000 that was hardly a problem.[6]

Canada also would establish a film school. "A certain educational institution located in one of the Canadian border cities has already suggested the establishment of a school for the teaching of all branches of the motion picture art." Such a school, headed by experienced film makers, "would effectually safeguard the study body from all dangers of studio life and lay a practical foundation for the picture industry."[7] (The dislike of "studios" was in accord with his oft-expressed belief in "realism with nature backgrounds.")

For a country in the first flush of discovering its existence as a nation following World War I, Shipman's words were heady stuff. Investors were ready to believe his prophecies. But then, of course, he had an amazing talent for promotion, especially self-promotion. His advertisements were highly imaginative and visually striking—and Shipman's name was itself always prominent. But, more than this, he managed to keep himself consistently in the news section of the movie trade papers. Such stories usually included his name in the headline and more often than not were accompanied by a photograph. Typical headlines from 1913 on include: "Ernest Shipman's World Plans"; "Ernest Shipman's World Tour"; "Shipman Organizes Money-Making Plan"; "Shipman Records Activities"; "Shipman Completes Large Plans"; "Shipman Family Reunion"; "Ernest Shipman Sails for Continental Conferences"; "Ernest Shipman Will Produce a Series of Pictures in the South"; "Independent Studios Soon Will Dot Florida, Shipman Predicts." Such stories, though most of them were obviously planted, are a tribute to his promotional talents, as, conversely, is the fact that no stories ever appeared in the trade papers describing his several failures. For example, not a word appeared in print after the collapse of his Canadian ventures. Instead there are stories about his latest idea: to turn Florida into a rival of Hollywood.

Typical of his proclivity for self-promotion is the coverage of the première of *Cameron of the Royal Mounted* in Ottawa. Shipman had organized the première at the Imperial Theatre under the auspices of the Canadian Authors' Association. But the stories that appeared in the American movie trade paper, *Moving Picture World*, concentrated their attention on Shipman's involvement with the production and his "personal appearance" at the première. "Shipman permitted himself to be persuaded into a public appearance. He knew just the line of talk to employ, and the Ottawa papers got solidly behind the idea and played it up, down, and across. At the public showings the place was packed and not to have seen *Cameron* was almost akin to disloyalty, treason, and regicide. . . . It was the culmination of one of the best publicity campaigns that has ever launched a picture and it must be remembered that Mr. Shipman has boosted more than one play to success before this." With his personal appearance, continued the story, Shipman had started something new. "And Shipman has it all over Clara Kimball Young and Viola Dane and all the rest of the personal appearance stars. He does not have to advertise that he will wear a new suit at each show . . . and you couldn't hire him to write a corset ad. He makes his hit on the strength of his manly beauty—and his nerve, mostly his nerve, but he is paving the way for Cecil B. DeMille and Maurice Tourneur and the rest of them. . . .

And, as has happened before, he is first in the field." [8]

To read this piece is to see Shipman's own deft hand at work. It is not impossible that he filed the story himself under an assumed name. But whatever the techniques he used, the fact remains that similar laudatory stories continued to appear throughout his career. At the very least, the editors of the magazines liked him.

He seems to have been liked, if not exactly trusted, by most of his contemporaries. Rogues like him with an eye always out for the main chance do not survive without a quality of charm to take the sting out of the con. Certainly women found him lovable—as his sobriquet "The Petticoat Pet of Broadway" suggests.

His son, Barry Shipman (who himself became a Hollywood scriptwriter), recalls that he "was not a businessman." [9] Ernest's penchant was in promoting schemes that remained just on the right side of the law. Out of them, Ernest took his cut, as he did from the theatrical stock companies he managed in his early career. Hence the name, "Ten Percent Ernie," which stuck to him throughout his life. The monopolistic drive of twentieth-century capitalists was beyond him. He had none of the hunger for power and control that motivated the Adolph Zukors of the film industry. Though he liked money, he lost it almost as quickly as he made it. His methods and peculiar sense of independence were out-of-date in an industry already falling prey to the thrust for massive centralization that characterized so much of American industrial development. And it was the new tycoons of that industry—Adolph Zukor, William Fox, Marcus Loew, and Joseph Schenck—who were eventually to force him out into the cold.

Search for a Dream

Ernest G. Shipman was born in Hull, Quebec, December 16, 1871. He was the eldest of four brothers, two of whom, besides himself, had careers in show-business. [10] His father, Montague, was a descendent of the Shipman family that founded Almonte, a small town near Ottawa. [11] He was educated at the Ryerson School in Toronto and became interested at an early age in promotion and publicity. At twenty-six he was running the Canadian Entertainment Bureau in Toronto and soon after was president and general manager of the Amalgamated Amusement Company with offices on Broadway in New York. Staging Shakespeare plays was his favourite approach to theatrical stock promotion since it did not involve the payment of royalties, but he also staged many other successful shows. "He toured the Kilties Band around the world. He brought Albert Chevalier to Canada. Theodore Roberts and Florence Roberts (unrelated but both ranking stars) toured

Canada under his aegis. Many others including a note-worthy tour [in 1912] of Lawrence D'Orsay in the *Earl of Pawtucket*."[12] His closest friend, "slave, mentor, and Boswell," William Colvin, began to work with him at this time and stayed faithfully by his side for some thirty years. He acted in several of Shipman's films but his managerial role was more important: he soothed investors, handled minor but essential details of organizing a production, and generally helped Shipman keep control of his multifarious operations. Shipman trusted him completely and relied on him totally.[13]

In 1907 he married his third wife, Rosalie Knott, an established actress on Broadway and in theatrical stock.[14] Their marriage lasted a bare four years because in 1910 Ernest met Helen Foster Barham, better known in later years as Nell Shipman.

Helen Barham was born in Victoria, B.C., October 25, 1892. She was eighteen when she met Ernest and had already been in showbusiness four years, touring Canada and the United States as an actress and vaudeville performer. She was a strikingly impressive woman; perhaps not beautiful in the conventional sense, but with a face of great charm and character. More importantly, she had talent both as an actress and as a writer—and had faith in that talent. Though her middle-class parents did not approve of her career, she persisted. And for those first four years her career could not be considered a success: her one claim to fame was that Charles Taylor had written a play for her, *The Girl from Alaska*. In October 1910 she went to look for work with the George Baker stock company, which featured the popular Joseph Galbraith, Ethel Clayton, and Fay Bainter. The man who interviewed her was Ernest Shipman, manager of the company. "A man wearing a rakish little red hunting cap aslant his blonde hair was seated at a desk in the room back of the box-office. He looked up and his eyes were Saxon-blue, his complexion that healthy underlying pink of your Canadian-born. He had a wide humorous mouth and he grinned at the applicant in the black fur coat and green velvet tocque."[15] He was thirty-nine, she was eighteen, and he gave her a lead role in the upcoming tour of Rex Beach's *The Barrier*. He financed the tour with ten thousand dollars raised from a wealthy backer. "Seamy-side gossip had it that the ten grand was to include an inning with the leading lady," wrote Nell Shipman. "I do not believe this *canard*. It may have been a vague hint, but not a promise. The man was no procurer. His women, if plural, were protected. He cared for his new girl, worked hard for her career, married her [in 1911] as best he might—twice according to the vital statistics—but he must have wished her more adept bed company. I doubt mine the first maidenhead taken for he had the flair of a grand Seigneur and any woman was fair game. Our initial matrimonial fling occurred during the tour of his show and was romantically staged with champagne and bushels of violets scattered upon the marital bed. Sweet smelling but no aphrodisiac for what was, to the scared novice, a painful gymnastic. So this was what all the shouting was about! I didn't like it. Thought I never would. It took a sprained ankle and a pair of butterflies making love to awaken a reasonable response to the prowess of my Casanova."[16] The Barhams did not at all approve of much-divorced Ernest and her English relatives wrote that it was "exactly the sort of marital mix-up" they had predicted when Nell went on the stage.[17] But Nell, true to her sense of independence, went ahead and married him anyway. Their son, Barry, was born in February 1912 and the marriage lasted until 1920—somewhat longer than average for Ernest.

When Ernest and Nell moved to Southern California in 1912, neither of their careers seemed very promising. Vaudeville and theatre might not yet be dying but, in the face of the encroaching movies, they were far from healthy. In any case, Nell was temporarily out of acting: during and after pregnancy. Ernest was bankrupt and money for the baby came only through his wins at poker. But while the touring theatre shows were dying, the movie companies were settling in a small town called Hollywood in southern California. Never one to miss an opportunity, Ernest decided to use his impressive promotional talents in this new field. Movies might be considered shoddy entertainment by some and perhaps a comedown to a man who had staged an outdoor *As You Like It* (he advertised it with the delightful malapropism "a la Fresno"), but there certainly seemed to be money in them. He persuaded a retired army officer to back his first film, *The Ball of Yarn*, in 1912. It was written by and starred Nell Shipman and was so bad it was never shown publicly. His next venture was to set up a company called the Five Continents Exchange with letterhead addresses all over the world. Nell wrote the synopses of a list of features in progress or already made while Ernest attempted to buy (without money) the film rights to the books of established authors. He inveigled financial backing from the Mormon Church to produce *One Hundred Years of Mormonism*, a six-reel film complete with fires and massacres. Universal Pictures released it and gave him a contract to promote *Neptune's Daughter*, which featured the renowned swimming star, Annette Kellerman.

Meanwhile, Nell was writing and selling scripts and "through Ernie's wire-pullings and promotional perspicacity" beginning to make a name for herself.[18] One of her scripts, *Under the Crescent*, she adapted into a novel while another, *Shepherd of the Southern Cross*, was sold to an Australian production company and filmed there in 1914. Also in 1914, she directed for Universal her first three films—each was three reels long. She also scripted

Nell Shipman.

and played the lead in all of them. In 1915, she played the lead role in *God's Country and the Woman* based on a James Oliver Curwood story. It was the first of the wild-life adventure films, enjoyed great success, and made a star of Nell Shipman. The *God's Country* tag was to follow her throughout her life. In her later career as an independent producer-director and actress she billed herself as "The Girl from God's Country" following her success in the first feature she wrote, produced, and directed: *The Girl from God's Country* in 1921.[19]

If Ernest used his contacts at Universal Pictures to help Nell's career, he was by no means neglecting his own. For several years he was to hover on the fringes of film production, establishing himself first as a publicist and agent of some repute but edging increasingly into promoting production himself. When he did, it was to exploit the idea he had in 1912 with the Five Continents Exchange: to buy the film rights to established novels, promote their production, and organize the publicity for the completed films.

His contract with Universal to promote Annette Kellerman led to contracts with other producers and by 1914 he was the "active representative" of eight independent producers in addition to handling the features of Universal.[20] He now had offices in New York though he still spent some time in California. Among the companies he represented were Arthur J. Aylesworth Pictures. Arthur Aylesworth of Edmonton, a former movie theatre manager, had shot several films of animal life in the Mackenzie River valley which Shipman was releasing. Aylesworth had also negotiated with Shipman for "the establishment of a studio at the foot of the Rocky Mountains in Canada for the production of photoplays."[21] This company, Rocky Mountain Pictures, was listed among Shipman's eight companies but was never active. Another apparently inactive Canadian production company represented by Shipman was Alex Dunbar's Great Western Film Company.

These were also the years when Shipman devised some of his most imaginative, if chimerical, schemes. In June 1913, he announced plans for a "floating studio": a boat equipped as a studio was to sail around the world producing dramatic fiction films, travelogues, and documentaries. Twenty actors and actresses, three directors, five cameramen, and two scriptwriters together with various specialists would be permanent residents of the studio. The film rights to novels set in the countries the studio would visit would be purchased in advance and the stories produced "at the exact location with which they deal. . . . One anachronism will be studiously avoided, and that is the mistake of having white actors enact native roles. It will be a set rule that native parts shall be played by native actors."[22] Despite the reported backing of "several Los Angeles capitalists," this inventive scheme seems to have come to nothing. It is, however, interesting as an early example of what was to become a Shipman trademark: the filming of novels in the actual locations in which they were set.

In April 1915 Shipman attempted to promote a feature on the "further adventures" of Princess Hassan, an American girl who had married an Egyptian prince and whose story had already been novelized and scripted into a film (*Under the Crescent*) by Nell Shipman.[23] He also tried to launch the production of an underwater drama in the Bahamas: *The Mermaid* written by the author of the successful *Neptune's Daughter*. Neither production was realized but his involvement with the latter led to his being hired in December 1916 as business manager for the Williamson brothers and the Submarine Film Corporation, famous for their underwater films including *20,000 Leagues Under the Sea*. Though underwater films were popular at the time, it is characteristic of Shipman that he should issue the extravagant claim that "the greatest motion pictures of the future will be filmed on the bottom of the ocean."[24]

A year later he was back in New York, again as representative for several independent producers. He had leased a film laboratory and studio, and advertised "Pictures financed, bought, sold, and exploited."[25] Not only was he handling some fifty-two feature and short films a year but was "also acting in an advisory capacity in connection with the actual manufacture of some of the pictures."[26]

Shipman had never lost sight of the first idea he had had in the film business, the idea behind the Five Continents Exchange and the "floating studio," the idea of buying the rights to the works of prominent novelists and filming them on location. In 1918 he got his first big chance. Nell Shipman's success in *God's Country and the Woman* had been repeated in *Baree, Son of Kazan*, a film also based on a story by James Oliver Curwood. What was now proposed was that Shipman and Curwood sign a contract under which Curwood agreed to give exclusive film rights to his stories to Nell Shipman for two years while she agreed to star exclusively in films based on his stories. Ernest Shipman was a co-signatory to this agreement, dated November 1, 1918.[27] Ernest could not have made a better deal. James Oliver Curwood was an extremely popular and very prolific author, writing two novels and ten screenplays a year, and producing a short story every two weeks. His novels were always best-sellers and his name associated with a film was a certain selling point. Most of his stories were outdoor adventures and, though he was an American, many of them were set in northern Canada where he usually spent three months of the year. They were, to some extent, responsible for the popular image of Canada as a land of endless ice and snow.

The first story selected for production was *Wapi the Walrus*, a story then being published in *Good Housekeeping Magazine*.[28] It had the usual elements of a Curwood plot: a melodramatic triangle of heroine, hero, and villain, a setting in the "wilds of North Canada," a dog as co-hero, plus "bears, moose, and elk, living amid their natural surroundings in the snow fastness of the North" and the omnipresent North West Mounted Police.

Ernest Shipman still faced the problem of raising money to produce the film. For this he went to Calgary, for reasons that are not clear. It may have arisen through contacts he had established through Arthur Aylesworth and the inactive Rocky Mountain Film Company. More likely it was at the invitation of William R. Marshall, manager of the Imperial Film Company of Canada. Marshall, a long-time theatrical manager and film journalist (working in New York where he may have known Ernest) had recently installed "a complete motion picture plant" in Calgary and produced a film *Hello,*

Dad! for the Calgary Rotary Club.[29] In December 1918 Marshall was predicting that "at some not far distant date it would not be surprising to find one of the largest dramatic studios on the continent located here."[30] Only weeks later, on January 22, 1919, Ernest Shipman was in Calgary to address the Board of Trade. Perspicaciously, he drew his listeners' attention to the "enormous profits" and the apparent potential of Alberta as a film location, but he emphasized that if Calgary were made the production centre for the Shipman-Curwood films "it would be necessary for a considerable portion of the capital to be raised locally."[31] The twin lures of immediate profits and the development of their favourite city as a rival to Hollywood could not be resisted by Calgary investors. On February 7, 1919, Canadian Photoplays Ltd. was incorporated in Alberta with a capitalization of $250,000.[32] Their prospectus stated they did not intend to compete with Hollywood "in the production of studio-made pictures, but in the great pictures of outdoor life with their intense dramatic interest." For which, of course, they claimed "no country in the world can surpass Canada." Among the principal shareholders were W. R. Marshall of the Imperial Film Company, H. P. Carver, apparently a friend of Curwood's and later to be associated with him in financing Curwood-Carver Productions, and A. E. Cross later to be president of another Calgary film company, British Canadian Pictures.[33] Ernest Shipman assigned to Canadian Photoplays the benefits of the Shipman-Curwood contract for up to two years in order to produce not less than two films, neither of which was to exceed $65,000 in cost. He was also hired by the company as business manager with responsibility for "publicity, advertising and selling." Net profits from all films were to be divided equally between Canadian Photoplays and Ernest Shipman.[34] The first production was to be *Wapi, the Walrus*, soon to be retitled *Back to God's Country* for no reason other than to capitalize on Nell Shipman's success in *God's Country and the Woman*.

Cast and crew began to arrive in late February. David M. Hartford, a Hollywood director of action films, was to direct. Joe Walker and Del Clawson were photographers, Bert Van Tuyle production manager, and Bill Colvin was involved as Shipman's personal associate and general factotum. The cast included Wellington Playter, Ronald Byram, Charles Arling, and Ralph Laidlaw. Nell Shipman herself arrived March 1, and announced that she intended to make Calgary her permanent home.[35]

Curwood had already arrived and was not at all happy with the screenplay Nell had written from his story. Ernest, aware that much of the company's financial backing was being subscribed on the strength of Curwood's name, pleaded with Nell to placate the irate author. This she did with some reluctance, having no liking for the *machismo*, big-game hunter image Curwood projected.[36] Nell had enlarged the role of the heroine and downplayed that of the dog, Wapi, the centre of Curwood's story. In her screenplay, the story was about Dolores who is finally rescued from the villain by Wapi, a dog considered vicious but which she had earlier befriended. Nell accepted Curwood's changes, planning to rewrite again once he had left. Everything was smoothed over and by mid-March the company left for Lesser Slave Lake in the Peace River country where the winter scenes were to be filmed.[37]

Their experiences on location were far from comfortable. Working in temperatures that touched fifty below zero Celsius and living in cabins abandoned by fishermen for the winter, they faced unprecedented problems. Cameras had to be left outside at all times to avoid static caused by temperature changes. Ronald Byram, playing the lead opposite Nell, contracted a severe cold which developed into pneumonia; he was taken to a hospital in Edmonton and later died. He was replaced by Wheeler Oakman. The script called for a whaling ship frozen in the ice. Studio carpenters refused to work on the second day when they realized the temperature was forty-five below. They returned south, taking their tools. Bert Van Tuyle, the production manager, had to build the ship himself with the help of a local Indian.[38] Consequently, he suffered severe frost-bite which left him with a limp for the rest of his life.

Shooting was finished by the end of March and the company returned to Calgary, en route to California where the rest of the film was to be shot.[39] While in Calgary, Nell learned that her father had died suddenly.

Production was completed in May and the film was released by First National in September 1919 to almost universal acclaim. Contemporary reviews were glowing, praise being lavished on the film's sense of atmosphere and on Nell Shipman for her ability to appear at ease with the numerous wild animals who, as she intended, became almost her co-stars. One of the most striking scenes had Nell Shipman diving, nude, into a pool while being observed by the lecherous villain. It had been intended that Nell play the scene in a discreet, pink leotard. But the leotard wrinked visibly when wet, so Nell determined to play the scene in the nude. Nell was not the first actress to play a nude scene; Annette Kellerman had preceded her by some three years in A Daughter of the Gods, successor to Neptune's Daughter. But it is some measure of the times that the scene created as little furore as it did—certainly less than that aroused in the Thirties by Hedy Lamarr's brief nude scene in Ecstasy.

Back to God's Country was seen across North America, in Britain, Japan, Europe, and Australia. It was an enormous financial success, grossing over half-a-million dollars in its first year of release, and netting the Calgary backers a three hundred percent return on their investment.[40]

The film tells the story of Dolores LeBeau (Nell Shipman) who lives in the Canadian woods with her father and who has a rapport with the wild animals of the forest. She falls in love with Peter (Wheeler Oakman), a Canadian government official and writer, and marries him after escaping from Rydal (Wellington Playter), the villain who, disguised as a Mountie, tries to rape her and then kills her father (Ralph Laidlaw). Later, Dolores and Peter travel to the Arctic on a whaling schooner whose captain turns out to be Rydal, still intent on "possessing" her. She manages to foil him until the ship becomes frozen in, then escapes on a dog-sled with her husband. Rydal and his partner pursue her but the dog Wapi, ill-treated by Rydal's partner and befriended by Dolores, assists her by attacking and crippling the dogs of Rydal's sled. Rydal dies in an ice-hole while Dolores and Peter return to "God's Country" and her animal friends.

It is not difficult to understand the reasons for the film's success. Despite some melodramatic touches in both plot and secondary characters, *Back to God's Country* has qualities that seem almost modern: the emphasis on living in sensitive accord with nature and the presence of Nell Shipman—a heroine who, for once, is not a victim but an active protagonist. It is also worth noting that Rydal, the villain, is twice presented cloaked in the trappings of authority: first as a Mountie with all that officer's well-established suzerainty over the people of the west, and, second, as a captain exercising autocratic control over everyone on board his ship. Though Rydal usurps the Mountie's uniform, it seems to confer automatically an exploitative power.

A contemporary British critic noted that the film's appeal relied on "the incidents of the narrative rather than the dramatic interest of the plot."[41] If we include Nell Shipman's role in that, it seems a fair assessment. Certainly what contemporary critics and the public acclaimed were the magnificent snow scenes, the forest scenes, dramatic episodes such as "Dolores' magnificent dive and swim through rapids," and, above all, the wildlife studies: "always interesting and occasionally irresistibly funny."[42]

Nell Shipman had been proven right in her adaptations from Curwood's original story. This is emphasized if we compare *Back to God's Country* with other contemporary films derived from Curwood stories. *Nomads of the North* (1920), for example, is a quintessential "Mountie film" incorporating several of the genre's defining characteristics: a brave, honourable Mountie forced to choose between Duty and Love (the heroine), the Canadian north as landscape, and the inevitable French-Canadian villain. In contrast, *Back to God's*

Country implies that accepted authority figures may not have a right to that authority, stresses the role of the woman as a protagonist with the will and determination to control her own destiny, and presents nature not as a backdrop but as essential associate in the action.

Nell Shipman, herself, makes a memorable heroine. Though it could be argued that the coyness of some scenes is at odds with her Junoesque presence, her talent is evident throughout whether she is struggling with Rydal, rescuing her father, or "merely" bathing. Even her scenes with the animals avoid the anthropomorphic quality associated with Disney's nature films and have a natural quality that could only have grown from an essential sympathy.

Promotion of the film was in the hands of Ernest Shipman. Having raised the money for the film he had left director and cast to produce it, only reappearing when his talents for publicity were needed. The promotional campaign for the film was as extensive as one might expect for a film costing ten times that of *Back to God's Country*. Exhibitors (still largely independent or part of small chains) must have been not a little intrigued by the advertising drawings which showed a nude girl threatened by a menacing bear and an even more menacing villain. "Don't Book *Back to God's Country*— Unless You Want To Prove the Nude is Not Rude" was the slogan Shipman used to tantalize prospective customers.

Shipman's role throughout was identical to that he played on later productions: an entrepreneur rather than an artistic contributor. As long as he felt he had brought together the right talents in terms of the author and cast needed to sell the film he stayed strictly away from production decisions. Given the situation of Canadian films at the time, this entrepreneurial role was arguably more creative than any narrowly artistic one. Shipman's talents could ensure not only that a film was made but that it was marketed—a noticeable lack in Canada before his arrival. On the strength of his success in Calgary, he was to travel across Canada for the next four years, attempting to repeat the experience though never again matching the returns of that first production.

Canadian Photoplays never produced their second, promised film, though as late as April 1920 it was being discussed.[43] The reason why is unclear. By that date they had received $170,000 on their investment and were "receiving cheques monthly."[44] There was still nearly a year to go on the company's two-year exclusive contract with Curwood and Nell Shipman. It is possible that Curwood was upset at Nell Shipman's tampering with his story and broke his contract. Certainly in February 1920 he announced formation of his own company, Curwood Productions, to produce film versions

DON'T BOOK

"BACK TO GOD'S COUNTRY"

Unless

You want to prove that
the Nude is NOT Rude

September Morn

As cooling and refreshing
as an Arctic Breeze

The Return-Date Picture of 1920

A First National
Attraction

December
Morn

Advertisement for *Back to God's Country*.

of his own novels. David Hartford (director of *Back to God's Country*) would direct; Ernest Shipman would be in charge of sales and publicity.[45] And certainly two films were produced: *Nomads of the North* (1920) and *The Golden Snare* (1921), both of which were exploited by Ernest Shipman but in neither of which Nell Shipman appeared. Ernest and Nell had separated soon after *Back to God's Country* was completed and were divorced in 1920. This, too, may have had an influence on the break-up of the Curwood-Shipman partnership. In turn, it meant Canadian Photoplays had no scripts lined up. It may also be, very simply, that the backers of Canadian Photoplays were delighted with the 300 percent return on their investment and content to retire from active production with their money secure. Whatever the reason, Canadian Photoplays, the company that produced Canada's most financially successful film, went into voluntary liquidation.[46]

Ernest Shipman seems not to have been unduly concerned. He had developed an interest in filming the novels of Ralph Connor, then Canada's most widely read and famous author. An ordained and active Presbyterian minister by profession (his real name was Charles W. Gordon), Connor's stories, if somewhat pious for modern tastes, were very much rooted in the realities of Canadian pioneer life. He was to provide Shipman with some of his best material.

Exactly when Ernest Shipman signed a contract with Ralph Connor is not known. It must have been sometime in 1919, since in January 1920 he announced "a new Canadian company is being formed to film the Ralph Connor stories in a big way upon their natural locations with Mr. Shipman in charge of production and sales."[47] This company, New York-based and not Canadian, was Dominion Films Inc., a company created to exploit control of film rights to the Connor novels.[48] In May he returned to Winnipeg for discussions with Connor on production plans and, as in Calgary, addressed himself to the local Board of Trade.[49] On May 26 it was announced: "The Board of Trade and leading citizens of Winnipeg signed contracts today with Ernest Shipman, President of Dominion Films. . . . Unlimited backing was pledged for the makers of *The Foreigner*, a story of Winnipeg. Mayor Grey, hero of the big strike, will assist Ralph Connor in story construction."[50]

Events then moved quickly. Faith Green arrived in Winnipeg in early June to write the scenario for the film.[51] A new company, Winnipeg Productions Ltd., applied for incorporation June 11, and in early July Shipman signed Henry MacRae as "supervising director" for the filming of the Connor stories.[52] At that time it was announced that twelve Connor stories would be filmed of which the following were listed: *The Foreigner*, *The Prospector*,

Ernest Shipman (left) meeting Ralph Connor (centre) in Winnipeg in 1920.

The Man from Glengarry, *Cameron of the Royal Mounted*, *Black Rock*, *The Major*, *The Sky Pilot*, *Patrol of the Sun Dance Trail*.[53] In the event, only five were filmed: *The Foreigner* and *Cameron of the Royal Mounted* in Winnipeg; *The Man from Glengarry* and *Glengarry School Days* in Ottawa. The *Sky Pilot* was sold to the Catherine Curtis Corporation (also "represented" by Shipman) and filmed in the United States by King Vidor.

It is worth noting that in all these various transactions, Shipman had established himself in a position to make money at each stage. First, as sales agent for Connor he was entitled to a percentage; second, his company, Dominion Films, also shared in the profits from any contract for the production of Connor's novels; third, as a shareholder in the various production companies, he participated in any profits earned from the film; and fourth, he was paid a fee for his services as "representative" of all the companies involved. It was less than a decade since his last bankruptcy but already he was on his way to another fortune. To mark this, he moved his New York offices to larger, more prestigious, quarters.[54]

Shipman could probably not have made a better choice for director than Henry (Hugh Alexander) MacRae. He was Canadian, born in 1878 in Stayner, Ontario (a fact much exploited when he later directed *The Man from Glengarry*), who had abandoned a career in medicine to join the North West Mounted Police. Later he became an actor and stock company manager in North America and the Orient before moving into film work, as actor and director for several pioneer film companies. Since 1915 he had been responsible for the operation of Universal City Studios in Los Angeles.[55] He was also, what was perhaps most important from Shipman's viewpoint, a businessman in his own right with sufficient independent income to enable him to cover off any possible debts on the new venture. MacRae, however, accepted Shipman's offer with alacrity. Not only did it make it possible for him to return to active directing but Shipman promised him a completely free hand in choosing the cast. His enthusiasm must have waned somewhat when he arrived in Winnipeg in early July to discover that Shipman expected him to spend his own money setting up production of the first film, *The Foreigner*, the story of a Russian immigrant who makes good in Winnipeg despite ethnic bigotry.[56]

The company of twenty-four actors and technicians arrived in Winnipeg on July 28 and were wined and dined by Manitoba Premier T. C. Norris, the mayor, and other local dignitaries. Among the cast were Gaston Glass as Ivan Kalmar, a political refugee from Russia newly arrived in Winnipeg, and Wilton Lackaye as his father. William Colvin (Shipman's personal representative) was to appear as the villain, Makaroff, a long-time enemy of the

Kalmars'. Edna Shipman (daughter of Ernest's brother, Joe) was to play Ivan Kalmar's sister, Irma. Toronto-born Edna had appeared only in minor screen roles previously but it was obviously Ernest's hope to find a replacement for Nell as a box-office attraction. It did not succeed.

Others in the cast included Bradley Barker as the Winnipeg district attorney who insults Ivan and makes him feel "A Foreigner," Gladys Coburn as the girl with whom Ivan falls in love, Ann Sutherland as the Kalmars' servant, together with Bigelow Cooper, Robert Haines, Jules Cowles, Edward Elkas, and Frances Eldridge. Kate Price made what would now be called a "guest appearance" in a character role which required her to be photographed in her bath. One reviewer acidly noted "it is quality and not quantity that makes a bathing beauty."[57]

Production of *The Foreigner* (later retitled *God's Crucible* for release) took some seven weeks, almost entirely on location in natural sets in Winnipeg and in the foothills of the Rockies where scenes were shot in which Ivan Kalmar becomes foreman of a coal mine. Locations used in Winnipeg were the provincial jail and courthouse (where both Ivan and his father are, variously, held and tried for the murder of a man who insults Irma) and the exhibition buildings; most of the interiors were shot in an ice-rink converted into a temporary studio.

The film was completed by mid-September and the company left Winnipeg—with the exception of Henry MacRae, Gaston Glass, and, inevitably, William Colvin. These three, together, with the technical crew, were to move to Calgary with a new cast to film the second Connor story, *Cameron of the Royal Mounted* (based on *Corporal Cameron*), for Winnipeg Productions.[58] MacRae finished editing *God's Crucible* in early October and it was previewed October 9, 1920, by an enthusiastic local audience in Winnipeg.[59]

In November MacRae moved to Calgary to produce *Cameron*, for which Faith Green had already written the screenplay. *Cameron of the Royal Mounted* is the story of a young man (played by Gaston Glass) who emigrates to Canada from Scotland to escape arrest for forging a cheque. He falls in love with a girl but is shot by a jealous rival. Later, his success as a railroad surveyor brings him an offer to join the Royal North West Mounted Police. As an officer he combats bootlegging, rescues his kidnapped girlfriend, and clears himself of the forgery charge.

Joining the company in Calgary were Toronto-born Vivienne Osborne to play Cameron's girl-friend, Irving Cummings as the villain, and Frank Lanning, George Larking, George McDaniel, and Gordon Griffith who had achieved some minor fame as "Boy" in *Tarzan of the Apes*.

Also featured in the film was a squadron of real North West Mounted

HODKINSON
PICTURES

Ernest Shipman
presents
"CAMERON OF THE
ROYAL MOUNTED"
Ralph Connor's Stirring Story

Scene from *Cameron of the Royal Mounted*.

Police from the Fort McLeod post. Films with stories about the Mounties were fashionable at the time but it took Ralph Connor's influence to persuade the Fort McLeod authorities to allow the men to take part in the film, together with their uniforms and horses. As extras, the men were paid five dollars a day (in addition to police pay) and are seen principally in a scene in which the Mounties chase off a band of Indians who attack a CPR train. Some of the Mounties also played roles as Indians—roles for which Winnipeg Productions did not expect them to provide their own uniforms. Shipman made much of this "official participation" by the Mounties in his promotional material for the film.[60]

Filming was completed by early December and cast and crew dispersed. MacRae left for Winnipeg to edit the film and later returned to New York to revise *God's Crucible*, which had not yet been released.[61] In fact, Shipman was experiencing rather more problems in marketing both Winnipeg Productions' films than he had with *Back to God's Country*. By December the shareholders were becoming restless. Most of the original investment of

$100,000 had been spent on *God's Crucible* and an additional $100,000 of stock had had to be issued in order to produce *Cameron of the Royal Mounted*.[62] Though Shipman had promised from the first that both films were committed for release by First National, it appears First National had made no such commitment. Their representatives did not view the film until December 1920.[63] First National apparently rejected it following this screening since Shipman was already writing by then that "an offer has been received from an independent company hinting at very favourable terms."[64] Whether such an offer existed is not known but in fact nothing happened for six months. In May 1921 the W. W. Hodkinson Corporation acquired *God's Crucible* for September release and in September acquired *Cameron of the Royal Mounted* for December release. The contract was for a percentage of distribution rentals with no advance payment to Winnipeg Productions, despite promise of this by Shipman.[65]

God's Crucible, which was released first, received a mixed critical reception.[66] The acting was uniformly praised as was the sense of atmosphere. But there were difficulties with the adaptation of the novel. Faith Green and Henry MacRae had crammed too many incidents into the film with the result that Connor's novel was turned into "bald melodrama that is not in keeping with the spirit of the original work. The titles are often cheaply sensational." *The Exhibitors' Herald* commented cryptically: "Here is a picture with a splendid cast minus the story to equal it."

Cameron of the Royal Mounted fared considerably better.[67] *Motion Picture News* described it as a "vivid, thrilling dramatization" while *Exhibitors' Herald* found it "another good story of the Northwest Mounted Police type and with better exhibition values than most of those which have gone before." *Moving Picture World* praised its "spirit and background," noting that its "quality of authenticity" eliminated the "theatrical effect" common in similar films. "The exciting rides and pursuits accomplished by experienced riders amid the magnificent natural settings of the hills and woods of the Northwest are highly convincing." *Canadian Moving Picture Digest* praised the film's "realism" and urged every Canadian exhibitor to inaugurate an "All-Canadian Week" in his theatre as the Allen Theatre in Toronto had done. "Such pictures as *Cameron of the Royal Mounted*, *Camera Classics*, *Fox-Canadian News*, and a Canadian produced comedy like the *Toonerville Trolley* make up an excellent bill and should pack your house."

Shipman's desire to seek "realism" through use of natural locations and avoid high studio overheads seemed to have merit. All other questions aside, all three films so far had been praised for their atmosphere and sense of natural background. But, in the event, it is not known whether Winnipeg Productions made a profit from the two films. It is difficult to imagine *Cameron* being a failure at the box-office: too many of the right ingredients were there. And although W. W. Hodkinson was not as powerful as Associated First National Exhibitors, his company was still in 1921 a major distribution outlet. A year after the films' release it was announced that the company was "in receipt of $1,500 weekly as their share of the profits."[68] It was further reported that "Ernest Shipman also is in receipt of a considerable sum weekly for his share." But whether the investors made a profit or not, Shipman did not return to Winnipeg and the company quietly surrendered its charter in 1928.

Shipman himself, in any case, was a very busy man through 1921 and 1922. In New York, he was handling the films of the Renco Film Company which was producing Myrtle Reed's stories, including *Lavender and Old Lace*.[69] The Legend Film Corporation was established to make short films featuring Edna Shipman and he was involved in promoting the San Gabriel Producing Company. In August 1921 he was married, for the fifth time, to his former secretary, Sadie. More interestingly, in April 1921 he made his first forays into the international film scene with a trip to Italy, taking with him "prints of a number of his recent productions."[70] This visit grew out of a deal with Ferdinando and Mario Luporini of the Luporini Brothers who had had the idea of producing films in Italy with American directors and technicians and American financial backing.[71] The idea appealed to Shipman; Italian production was at a nadir in the early Twenties and Shipman saw the possibility of applying his Canadian approach in Italy. As a result of his visit, a five-year contract was signed with the Ultra Film Company of Rome (which controlled the Nova, Bernini, and Italia studios) to produce an average of four films a year.[72] A year later Shipman bought out the interests of the Luporini Brothers in the Ultra Film Company, giving him an equal share of the company with Francesco Stame, the president.[73] By that time, the first production had been completed in Italy: *Sant' Ilario* based on a story by F. Marion Crawford and directed by Henry Kolker. Shipman's friend and staunch supporter, William Colvin, again represented Shipman's interests during the production. It appears this was the only film completed even though several film adaptations of the novels of F. Marion Crawford had been planned.[74] However, Shipman's pioneering venture was to be followed, more successfully, by several American film makers over the next couple of years: Henry King shot *The White Sister* and *Romola* in Italy, George Fitzmaurice, *The Eternal City*, and J. Gordon Edwards, *Nero*. The legendary *Ben-Hur* was also initially in production in Italy in 1923.

On to Ottawa

Shipman reappeared in Canada in late 1921. He had been saying for more than a year that Ralph Connor's two stories of the Glengarry lumber industry, *The Man From Glengarry* and *Glengarry School Days*, would be produced in Ottawa. There were other Canadian authors whose novels could, with advantage, be produced in the locale which they depicted—and the financing raised in that same locale. In 1922 Shipman was criss-crossing eastern Canada and five new Shipman-promoted film companies were created: Ottawa Film Productions, Sault Ste. Marie Films, New Brunswick Films, Newfoundland Films, Halifax Films, and Prince Edward Island Films. Only the first three were to produce any films and Halifax Films and Prince Edward Island Films appear not to have been actually incorporated. Ottawa Film Productions were to produce the two Connor stories, Sault Ste. Marie Films an adaptation of Allan Sullivan's novel *The Rapids*, and New Brunswick Films an adaptation of *Blue Water* by Frederick William Wallace. All were to be produced during 1922.

It is interesting to note that Shipman assiduously avoided the two major Canadian metropolitan centres of Toronto and Montreal. Both had on-going film production and both had seen the rise and fall of more than a few feature film companies. Investors there might have been more sceptical of Shipman's projects. They might indeed have asked the inevitable, if unanswerable, question, "How can you guarantee a return on my investment?" (It is recorded that when Shipman was once asked this question by a group of potential investors, he replied with perfect aplomb, "Gentlemen, I always burn my bridges." The investors are reported as being so dumbfounded at this response they gave him their money.)[75]

Shipman made his first public appearance in Ottawa on February 10, 1922, for the Canadian première of *Cameron of the Royal Mounted*. Before an invited audience of a thousand people, including Sir Robert Borden and other notables, Shipman announced that the two Connor stories would be filmed in Ottawa by a local company.[76] True to form, Shipman knew exactly how to stimulate local interest and ease money from potential investors. Ottawa Film Productions was incorporated February 27, 1922, and, as usual, all the directors (except Shipman) were from Ottawa. Among them were Senator Girroir as president, author Robert Stead, John Bain, and Duncan Campbell Scott.[77] J. R. Booth, head of the Booth Lumber Company, offered his company's facilities. (Later, Booth was himself to become involved in production, first with an inactive Ottawa-financed company, Tesa Films, which planned to produce at the Trenton Studios and secondly with Booth

Dominions Films which produced two quota films in Toronto in the Thirties.) *The Man from Glengarry*, a drama of the rivalry between two lumbering families, was selected as the first production.

Director, cast, and crew arrived in May 1922. "Locally born" Henry MacRae was again to direct from a script by Kenneth O'Hara who had scripted *Sant' Ilario* for Shipman in Italy. The ubiquitous William Colvin was also back from Italy to supervise the production for Shipman and appear in the film. The cast for *The Man from Glengarry* included Warner Richmond as Ranald MacDonald, Harlan Knight as the Reverend Alexander Murray, and Marion Swayne as Ranald's sweetheart, Kate. E. L. Fernandez was to appear as the French-Canadian "heavy," Louis Lenoir, who kills Ranald's father (played by Anders Randolph) and, after fighting Ranald, extricates him from the jealous intrigues of Maimie, played by Montreal-born Pauline Garon. Others in the cast included Jack Newton, William Colvin, Marion Lloyd, as well as Frank Badgley, who had only recently arrived in Ottawa to join the Canadian Government Motion Picture Bureau. Warner Richmond was added to the cast only later after the original lead actor, Ralph Faulkner, broke his leg during the first week's shooting. Cameramen were Barney McGill and Jacques Bizeul.

Production got underway in early May with location shooting of logging scenes on Booth Company land and on log slides in the Mattawa area. As in Winnipeg, locations were also used across the city: in the Chateau Laurier Hotel, Rockcliffe Park, and St. Stephen's Church with other interiors shot in a temporary studio constructed in one of the Exhibition buildings at Landsdowne Park. Even the film processing was done locally in a laboratory fabricated out of a local house.[78]

MacRae completed the film by mid-July at a cost of $50,000—$20,000 under budget—and immediately began work on the second Connor story, *Glengarry School Days*, from a script by Garett Fort. Barney McGill and Jacques Bizeul were again to handle the camerawork, William Colvin would supervise the production, and Pauline Garon was retained to play the leading role of Margie Baird. *Glengarry School Days* (later retitled *The Critical Age* for release) was a story of young love and a political drama rather than an adventure film as the previous film had been. The story is of the rivalry between two men, Tom Findlay and Bob Kerr, for the love of Margie Baird. Bob's father attempts to pass a bill in Parliament detrimental to the interest of the farmers and Margie's father opposes it. Bob's father attempts to frame Mr. Baird but Tom and Margie discover the plot. Naturally, Margie chooses Tom over Bob. James Harrison played Tom Findlay and Wallace Ray his competitor, Bob Kerr. The rival politicians were played by William Colvin and Ray Peck, head of the federal government's Motion Picture Bureau. Other roles were played by Alice May, Harlan Knight, and Marion Colvin, wife of William Colvin.

The production budget was much tighter than that of the previous film to the extent that often only one camera was used. When needed, this was supplemented by equipment from the Motion Picture Bureau. Again, natural locations in and around Ottawa were used and many local people played supporting roles in the film—including scenes shot in the Senate Chamber of the Houses of Parliament and at a children's party at a farmhouse.[79] When shooting was completed in late August, the company left for the United States. It was to be almost a year before either film went into general release through W. W. Hodkinson.

But once the Ottawa company was established, Shipman had moved on to Sault Ste. Marie where his visit followed the pattern established in Winnipeg and Ottawa. In March 1922 a local production company was incorporated and a contract signed with Ernest Shipman (now being described as "the well-known Canadian film producer"), to produce *The Rapids*, a novel of limited merit by Alan Sullivan.[80] The novel has been called "a thinly disguised interpretative account of one of the greatest entrepreneurial adventures in Canadian history, the rise and fall of Francis H. Clergue's industrial empire at Sault Ste. Marie, Ontario, between 1894 and 1903."[81] Again the project was custom made to appeal to local investors. Among the directors of Sault Ste. Marie Films were the presidents of the Algoma Steel Corporation, the local Board of Trade, and the Algoma Central Railway, and the vice-president of the Spanish River Pulp and Paper Company—plus Ernest Shipman himself, of course. The film was budgeted at $200,000 and Shipman hinted that it would be "Canada's first million dollar picture" (presumably in its earnings, not its cost).[82] David Hartford returned to Canada to direct the film which was scripted by Faith Green. William Colvin moved up from Ottawa, again to supervise production, and Harlan Knight and John Newton also joined the company from Ottawa to play supporting roles. Leading roles were played by Harry T. Morey as Robert Fisher Clarke, entrepreneur of the town of St. Mary's, and Mary Astor (then unknown at sixteen) as Elsie Warden who is pursued by Clarke but who finally chooses Jim Belding, played by Walter Miller. Other roles were played by Charles Slattery, Edwin Forsberg, Charles Wellesley, John Dillon, Peggy Rice, and Frank Andrews. As with Shipman's other films, many local people appeared in small roles.

Shooting, through September 1922, was again largely on location: at St. Mary's Rapids, on the Algoma Central Railway, and in the city itself.

Some indoor scenes were shot in a temporary studio erected on the local skating rink with the rest shot in a New York studio.

Hartford completed the film by the end of September and moved to St. John, New Brunswick. Here he was to direct *Blue Water*, adapted by Faith Green from the novel by Halifax author Frederick William Wallace, a story of a fisherman in the Bay of Fundy. Shipman had acquired the film rights to Wallace's novels and planned to film *Blue Water* in St. John and *Viking Blood* in Halifax.

New Brunswick Films was incorporated August 23, 1922, with a capitalization of $99,000. It had the same kind of local support Shipman had gained elsewhere, with the additional boast that New Brunswick's lieutenant-governor and premier were directors of the company.

Accompanying Hartford to St. John from the Sault were the technical crew together with Harlan Knight, John Dillon, Alice May, and, inevitably, William Colvin. Playing leading roles would be Pierre Gendron as Jimmy Westhaver, a fisherman with "a love for the sea and strong drink," and Jane Thomas as his sweetheart who leaves the home village and jilts Jimmy. Norma Shearer played Lilian Denton, "sent to him from the sea," with whom he finds true love after almost wrecking his ship in a storm while drunk.[83] Montreal-born Norma Shearer was then just beginning her film career and *Blue Water* was to become a film she preferred to forget. Production got underway in October with most of the scenes being shot in the fishing village of Chance Harbour. Though completion was promised by "mid-November," the film had still not been finished a month later.[84] Certainly the weather was a problem; it was discovered that the "New Brunswick sea water was too chilly for many of the situations required."[85] Cast and crew disappeared from St. John, somewhat ingloriously, and David Hartford completed *Blue Water* in Florida. *Viking Blood* was never produced.

The first of Shipman's 1922 films to be shown publicly was *The Rapids* which had its première in Sault Ste. Marie on October 30, 1922, with Shipman present to give it his personal touch. Not surprisingly, it was greeted warmly by the local audience; nearly ten thousand people queued for admission on opening night and the local reviews were full of praise.[86] But six months were to pass before W. W. Hodkinson released the film commercially. Critical reaction was less positive than had been the response of the local audience but tended to follow the pattern of the earlier films.[87] The background and natural atmosphere were praised but there were reservations about the story which *Film Daily* found "fairly unconvincing and conventional." For *Motion Picture News* it was only an "adequate picture of program houses" but *Moving Picture World* described it as "commendable entertainment. . . . The directing is good . . . and the story and acting are the more forceful because of [the film's] naturalness." Warmest praise came from a British critic who found it "difficult to speak too highly of the production." Recommending it "for discriminating patrons," he described it rather curiously as a successful "attempt to combine a pretty love story with an industrial-scenic." Box-office returns were modest and did not come close to Shipman's "million dollar" prediction. Indeed, for once, he made no claims about the film's lucrative financial returns to the local investors.

The two Ottawa films were next to be seen. *The Man from Glengarry* was first publicly previewed in Ottawa, December 11, 1922, "under the distinguished patronage" of the governor general, Lord Byng.[88] Once more, commercial release was delayed, the film opening only in March 1923. Promotional material emphasized that it was an "all-Canadian" production being shot, processed, and edited in Canada; Shipman had made his film "amidst the scenes which inspired the writer," not against a "background of makeshift and incongruous sets" in a foreign studio. In his "super-productions" Shipman had "given to the world true, vital, and interesting pictures of Canadian life," believing the "struggles, passions and achievements of these [Canadian] people" would appeal to audiences everywhere.[89]

But despite the fact that films featuring Canadian locales and stories had been popular for the past few years, *The Man from Glengarry* was none too well received.[90] Though Ray Lewis in the *Canadian Moving Picture Digest* felt "the scenes in the north country were sure-fire realism and could not be surpassed in interests and thrills," few other reviewers agreed. Something seems to have gone wrong in the screen adaptation of the novel—one of Connor's most acclaimed and popular. A British critic, for example, found the story "undeveloped and colourless with practically no dramatic value or thrill" and suggested its appeal lay entirely in its "scenic value." Another British critic agreed, finding the atmosphere more convincing than the "rather conventional" story. American critics, too, tended to praise the backgrounds and dismiss the story as melodrama. *Film Daily* noticed that it offered "a realistic idea of life in a lumber camp." *Moving Picture World* commented, rather superciliously, that it would make "a fine choice for the theatre where heavy action of a somewhat primitive character is liked." The quality of the acting was uniformly either ignored or condemned; typically, "Warner Richmond shows skill at his timber work but little histrionic ability."

The release of *The Critical Age*, retitled from *Glengarry School Days*, followed in May.[91] "Rather modestly produced, but offering some refreshing qualities . . . with simple country scenes and an atmosphere of wholesome-

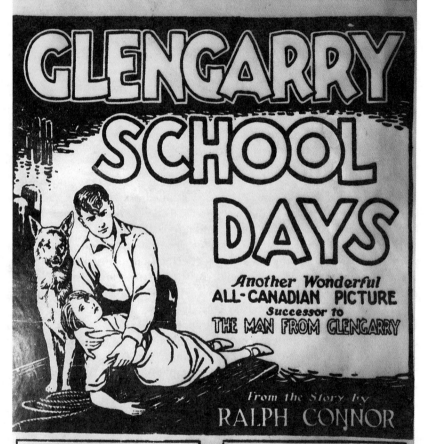

Advertisement for *The Critical Age* (*Glengarry School Days*).

ness about it all," concluded a New York critic. Pauline Garon, then approaching the peak of her popularity, came in for some praise, being described as "charming and vivacious" and "well qualified to act." *Film Daily* found it a "thoroughly pleasing attraction," though not as thrilling as one might expect.

Whether the Ottawa backers of these two films ever recouped their investment is not known. A year after their release Shipman announced that Ottawa Film Productions "will declare another five percent dividend this month." He suggested these payments would continue "for a considerable period of time" until foreign sales were concluded "when the present percentage will be appreciably increased."[92] This report was hastily denied by the directors of the company who pointed out that they were "not yet in a position" to pay any dividends.[93] However, given the modest cost of both productions, it is likely the initial investment was recovered, though clearly nobody—Shipman probably excepted—made much of a profit.

As for *Blue Water*, the St. John investors lost everything they put into the film. The film, completed by David Hartford in Florida sometime in 1923, never gained a major theatrical release. It was shown in the Maritimes a year later and was praised by the *Canadian Moving Picture Digest*'s critic in May 1924 as "a good story of the coast [with] plenty of adventure and love interest."[94] Thereafter the film disappeared from view and lived out the rest of its existence in a vault in New York. Even David Hartford's career suffered and he made no more features until 1926.

Dark Day's Morning

The failure of *Blue Water* marked, ignominiously, the end of Shipman's career as a Canadian film producer. His Canadian venture was over. In the summer of 1923, when it became evident that the financial returns of his four 1922 features would not match the expectations of investors, he began to diversify his activities again. June found him sending an emissary to France to establish a company to produce films in Morocco;[95] by July he was president of the Long Island Cinema Corporation which was to produce three features on Long Island "this Summer."[96] And by October he had moved to Florida where he planned to repeat the Canadian experience. Deciding to commit "my associates to Florida for future film activities," he publicly predicted that "independent studios soon will dot Florida."[97] But his predictions failed and nothing came of the venture. His subsequent career is something of a mystery. At one time he was the representative of prizefighter

William (Young) Stribling, for whom he made film contracts.[98] In the mid-Twenties he was in England, probably lured by the possibilities of the British quota, attempting to promote an actress protegée, Eleanor Goldsmith.[99] This again failed. In 1929 he was a journalist for the *Exhibitors Trade Review*.[100] He died in his Jackson Heights home in New York on Friday August 7, 1931. He was survived by his wife Sadie and two sons, Robert and Ernest Junior.[101]

Why did Ernest Shiprnan's Canadian venture fail? It is not enough to suggest that his promotion deals finally caught up with him. The Shipman method could have gone on almost indefinitely. Profits may not have matched Shipman's predictions but as long as the films were released and the investors saw at least some return on their original investment, there was no reason why other cities could not have been tapped. There were other novels to film against their appropriate backgrounds and in fact several of the popular Connor novels to which Shipman held the rights were never filmed. He always stayed on the right side of the law and no one ever sued him in Canada or called him a rogue in print. There is no evidence, except in St. John, to suggest any of the investors felt cheated or ill-used by Shipman. The mood of nationalism in the country was exactly right; the newspapers and the Canadian film trade paper backed his efforts to create a viable Canadian film industry. The style of his films, their use of real-life locations, was, if anything, ahead of its time and never harmed them at the box-offices. On the contrary, all critics found this the most appealing quality in all his films.

What went wrong? Quite simply, Shipman was caught in a squeeze play which everywhere was forcing independent producers and distributors out of the film business. Even W. W. Hodkinson, a pioneer distributor, founder of Paramount Pictures (which he lost to Adolph Zukor), and a staunch believer in independent production, was forced out of his own company in 1924 and retired from the industry. By the early Twenties, three companies were already beginning to dominate the industry: Paramount, First National, and Fox. All three companies owned or had contracts with first-run theatres; all three companies produced films on their own account with leading stars and directors. Independent producers found it increasingly difficult to sell their films to these three and, having to release through one of the smaller distributing companies, then found it difficult to have their films shown in major theatres. Only seventy-five percent of the films produced at this time were shown and, because of this over-production, competition was intense.[102] Shipman himself had first felt this pressure when First National turned down *God's Crucible* in December 1920 though eighteen months earlier they had accepted *Back to God's Country*. In 1919, when Shipman began his Canadian venture, the distribution and exhibition systems in the United States, Canada, and abroad were still relatively open to the independent producer. By 1922, Shipman's busiest year of production, the vertical integration of production, distribution, and exhibition interests in the United States was well on its way to becoming a reality. Eventually it was to defeat Shipman as it was to defeat many other independent producers. Shipman well knew that American release was an essential element in recovering production costs. It is interesting to note that revenue from Shipman's films fell drastically from the half-a-million-plus dollars of *Back to God's Country* to the near zero of *Blue Water*—a drop that paralleled exactly the integration of production, distribution, and exhibition interests in the United States.

Shipman was well aware of what was happening. In September 1922 he called a meeting in Ottawa of nine Shipman-promoted production companies.[103] This meeting decided "to reserve for Canadian management the distribution of all productions made with Canadian capital on Canadian soil." The intent of this decision was to ensure that Canadian producers could sell their films directly to foreign countries without selling the rights first to an American distributor who then subcontracted distribution in other foreign countries. It was a reflection of the difficulties Shipman was already beginning to experience in selling his productions to American distributors. It was intended as a threat, a way of saying, "We Canadians don't need you. We can go it alone." Unfortunately it was too late.

Shipman persisted, however. In December 1922, after moving to bigger New York offices at 565 Fifth Avenue, he set up his own distribution company in Toronto, the Ernest Shipman Film Service.[104] But this company was far too weak to affect the interests of established distributors in the United States.

Thereafter, things became increasingly difficult. Though he still exuded confidence in an interview in March 1923 about future plans for producing more Canadian films that "portray real life," his statements became increasingly desperate.[105] In March 1923 he paid for a series of large advertisements in *Moving Picture World* to promote all his films.[106] Using the headline "Telling the Truth in Motion Pictures," he announced he would defy all "trusts and booking combines" and continue to exploit the ten films "until every foreign country and a reasonable quota of theatres in the English-speaking world have been contracted for." But there is an element of desperation in his plea to "the eleven million Canadians on this North American continent to get behind the local exhibitors in boosting these dramas of the

Canadian northland." He continued through mid-1923 to plead the cause of Canadian films but, with the release of three of the 1922 films to less than spectacular box-office returns, he must have known the cause was lost. It is at this point that he suddenly developed an interest in the potential of Florida as a production centre. But even this failed. The new major film interests in New York were not nationalistic; they were not against Canadian production *per se*, just any independent production, including Shipman's.

Shipman's passing from the Canadian film scene also marked the end of the minor boom in Canadian feature film production that had begun during the First World War.

Perhaps Shipman's most lasting testament lies in the fact that his approach to film making, the production of films in "the exact locales called for by the story," was a method that was to be repeated with some success by many others including Varick Frissell on *The Viking* and, more significantly, on much Canadian production of the Sixties. And more than this. Reading his speeches and statements gives one a strange *déjà vu* feeling. So much of what he said about and claimed for Canadian films and the development of an indigenous film industry, more than fifty years ago, was to be repeated by many others in more recent times.

CHAPTER 5

The State and the Movies

Among the most significant defining characteristics of film in Canada is the manner in which governments have had a persistent involvement in film production. Indeed, the Canadian experience with government film production is unique. Since 1900, the federal and provincial governments have sponsored the production of films. Production units have been maintained at various times by several provinces—notably by Ontario. And, since 1918, the federal government has operated a national film production organization: the oldest continuing operation of its kind in the world.

It seems remarkable that the Canadian experience is, in fact, unique. Film is an efficient and effective medium for disseminating information, education, and propaganda and has been recognized as such since its first years. One might expect many national governments to exploit its potential. Yet, until relatively recent times, few governments have perceived the merits of maintaining a permanent film unit to produce films "in the national interest." Which is not, of course, to say that many governments have not sponsored or produced films at various times, particularly during wartime. And there are exceptions to the generalization, including the British government's sponsoring documentary film production under John Grierson, and the United States government's Department of Agriculture productions under Pare Lorentz. But direct government involvement in both cases was relatively brief. In contrast, government film production in Canada began during the First World War and has continued, despite changes of name and structure, ever since.

There is something in the Canadian experience with government film production that reflects a more general Canadian attitude towards state owned enterprises. In this century at least, there is apparent a continuing concern in Canada that the forces of the free marketplace must be tempered.

in the public interest through government involvement. Most commonly this has found expression in state owned enterprises either taking over commercial companies or operating in competition with them. Examples are numerous, running from provincially owned telephone and power corporations to such operations as CNR and the CBC. Rarely argued philosophically —and certainly never on socialist principles by governments in power—it seems more of a pragmatic response to the peculiar needs of Canadian society than an articulated doctrine. Certainly the measures taken do not reflect the actions of any one political party at any single period of time. All political parties, at both the federal and provincial levels, have nationalized existing corporations or established state owned companies, actions that in any other country would have been defined as socialistic.

Given this approach and, in particular, the operation of publicly owned film units by several governments in Canada, it is curious that those same governments almost completely ignored the commercial film industry. Supporting a publicly owned film unit might seem to reflect an awareness of the significance of motion pictures to Canadian society. But apparently not. The operation of government film units was paralleled by a sweeping official neglect of private film production. Throughout this period, governments refused to accept the possibility that there might be measures which could protect and promote a domestic film industry as there were measures that protected and promoted other industrial and cultural enterprises in the national interest. Though there were numerous examples in other countries of what was possible, federal and provincial governments maintained an almost total *laissez-faire* policy in relation to Canadian film production outside of their own film units. It is almost as if there were an unwritten policy which suggested that, apart from the production of films to promote trade and tourism and the occasional provision of services to foreign producers wishing to film location scenes, it was not somehow *proper* for Canadians to produce films, and certainly not fiction films. It is a paradoxical picture of governments willing to pay civil servants to make films while at the same time refusing to recognize or support the existence of anything outside their own bureaucratic circles.

Direct involvement by government in film began in 1902 with the federal government's sponsorship of James Freer's tour of Britain with his films. It continued sporadically through the first decade of the century with the sponsoring of production by British producers of films designed to promote immigration and trade. This has been described earlier but it is worth recording that the federal government did not concentrate all its activities in Britain. There is at least one instance of a "Paris film maker" being commissioned by the federal government in 1906 to take films of the city of Winnipeg in order to stimulate emigration from France and to remove "the common conception existing in France of Canada as a place with an arctic climate."[1]

In 1913, a British film producer, M. D. Kinniard, persuaded the federal government's Industrial Bureau to finance the production of a four to five thousand feet "huge motion picture creation." Designed "to impress the investing British public with the rapid and enormous growth of Canada and her resources," the film was to include not only scenes of current life but also "photographs of Canadian life and affairs in days gone by."[2] However, it appears that this ambitious venture was never completed and the experience may have played a role later when the federal government was considering establishing its own unit.

The outbreak of war in 1914 stimulated government film activities just as it stimulated private film production. Government sponsorship of films on the war has already been discussed but the interest in film by several departments of the Canadian government was not by any means restricted to war themes. By 1915 many of them, including Agriculture and Railways, were making use of motion pictures. The Canadian Geological Survey had films of bird and wildlife photographed by P. A. Taverner.[3] Between 1913 and 1916, George H. Wilkins (later Sir Hubert Wilkins) produced film records of Eskimo life and of the Canadian Arctic Expedition under the leadership of Vilhjalmur Stefansson.[4] The Parks Branch of the Department of the Interior was interested in films to promote conservation and the proper use of natural resources while the Department of Trade and Commerce wanted to use films to promote the development of Canadian trade.[5] In the early months of the war, the ministers of the interior and of trade and commerce exchanged views on "a more adequate representation of the resources and productive activities of Canada through the medium of motion pictures and photographs."[6]

Those earlier films sponsored by government and others and designed to encourage immigration were felt to have been successful. Perhaps there were possibilities for a much broader use of the motion picture as a medium of information. Though no immediate action was taken, the minister of trade and commerce, Sir George Foster, did use the occasion of a wartime visit to England in 1916 to initiate some inquiries. As a result, Sir George received a solicitation from the Cartoon Film Company of London, England which offered to produce and distribute films to advertise Canada at a cost of approximately $50,000 per year.[7] Perhaps as a result of the not entirely happy experience with the M. D. Kinniard production in 1913, the offer was declined.

Meanwhile, even while Sir George was in London, other events began to bring the discussions to a head. Early in 1916, the Bureau of Commercial Economics in Washington D.C. approached the Canadian government with a request for films and other visual material on the resources and economic development of Canada. The Bureau of Commercial Economics had been founded in 1913 as an educational, non-profit organization. It owned a collection of twelve million feet of educational films dealing with industry, commerce, and manufacturing in all parts of the world which were loaned free of charge in the United States and South America. A lecturer was usually provided to accompany the films and in 1916 the Bureau claimed its films were seen by twenty million people every year in the United States. The Bureau had the support of the American government and cooperated directly with the governments of twenty-nine countries. The Canadian government had been working with the Bureau since 1914 and several Canadian scenic films had already been provided for distribution. It was, in fact, the Bureau's interest in Canadian films that had first stimulated the attention of the ministers of trade and commerce and of the interior. Now, Francis Holley, director of the Bureau, asked for films on industrial development, particularly Canadian grain and water power resources. The Canadian government could see the obvious publicity advantages and a committee of ministers recommended that a series of films on these topics should be produced.[8]

The Canadian Pacific Railway Company was known to have experience in film production so the general publicity agent of the CPR was consulted for his recommendations on suitable production companies to carry out the commission. The general publicity agent replied, surprisingly, that since there were "no moving picture firms in Canada" the best company for the work would be the Essanay Film Manufacturing Company of Chicago.[9] The CPR had cooperated with Essanay the previous summer when Essanay sent several cameramen across the country (by CPR) from Toronto to Vancouver to create a series of scenic films.[10] Obviously, the CPR were happy with the results since they recommended Essanay over the existing Canadian film companies in Toronto and Montreal. In any case, Canadian producers did not get the contract, which was signed with Essanay. Early in June 1916, four cameramen led by Arthur Reeves, were sent into Canada to film the grain industry and the developed and undeveloped water resources. Filming took most of the rest of the year.[11] Since much of it had to be done in areas controlled by the Water Powers Branch of the Department of the Interior, Ben Norrish, a chief draughtsman with the branch, was put in charge. Norrish was not only scientifically qualified but an energetic man with a keen interest in film. On his own initiative, he had visited the Essanay Company in Chicago, the E. I. and S. Corporation in New York, and the Ford Motor Car Film Unit in Detroit in order to learn about motion pictures and how they were produced. He was a natural choice to supervise the filming. In fact, said Norrish later, "at least 90 percent of the direction of this undertaking was entirely in the hands of government officials" (i.e. Norrish himself)— even though Essanay had been paid liberally for their work.[12]

From the footage shot by Essanay's cameramen, a series of non-theatrical, educational films was created under Norrish's direct supervision while Essanay produced eight films for theatrical release.[13] The Essanay films were of good quality, received much favourable critical comment in the United States and elsewhere, and were a popular addition to the Essanay series, *The Wonders of Nature and Science*. But then there was no way Essanay could have lost on the deal: they had been paid by the Canadian government for production of the films, now they could earn money through distribution. Canadian officials would have been a good deal less than intelligent if they had not realized the implications of this. Couldn't similar films be produced more efficiently and cheaply by an in-house government film unit and might there not be some financial return to be earned on these films through their theatrical distribution?

Civil Servants as Film Makers

The deputy minister of the Department of Trade and Commerce, F. C. T. O'Hara, was aware of these questions even while the Essanay films were being completed. He was also an imaginative man with a keen awareness of the potential value of films for propaganda purposes. He and his minister, Sir George Foster, discussed this many times. They were also concerned about the interest in producing films expressed by other government departments. In May 1917, O'Hara wrote a long memorandum to the minister urging that Trade and Commerce be first in the field. "If we were to go into it a little more actively," he wrote, "we could save considerable duplication and establish an important work in this line."[14] One of the responsibilities of the department was the promotion of Canada and Canadian products abroad; it seemed sensible for the department to supervise the production of films designed to do exactly that. He pointed out that the department would have to make films, purchase others, and develop a system of distribution using the Canadian Trade Commissions abroad. He suggested that Ben Norrish be transferred from the Department of the Interior to Trade and Commerce and, finally, estimated that the cost of a film production unit within the department would be three to four thousand dollars a year.[15]

Sir George Foster was very receptive to the idea of a departmental film unit though he was temperamentally inclined to dislike advertising films *per se*. What was needed, he felt, were films made with what was later to be called "the soft-sell" approach: films to promote the image of Canada, its industries, and natural resources in general, not films which would sell specific products. On June 14, O'Hara proposed a list of possible film subjects to Sir George, a list which included natural resources, Canadian shipping facilities, industries, National Parks, the CNE, and other exhibitions. He mentioned the need for someone to view existing films on Canada made by other companies to decide which should be purchased and urged again that Norrish be transferred to the department to begin this work.[16]

Two more months were to pass before O'Hara succeeded in having Norrish transferred. Though Norrish joined the department on September 1, 1917, for a time little activity was evident.[17] In September, Norrish directed filming in and around Shawinigan Falls and Trois-Rivières on behalf of the Quebec government and the Shawinigan Water and Power Company. This was to be a film designed to promote the marketing of a bond issue for the Shawinigan Water and Power Company. As Deputy Minister O'Hara wrote at the time to the Bureau of Commercial Economics, the department had as yet neither proper facilities nor a clear idea as to what would be involved in developing a motion picture branch.[18]

But Norrish did not intend to let the issue die. He had a forceful personality, a good head for business, and believed in the logic of a centralized government film unit. Though he undertook the purchase and distribution of industrial films on Canada produced by others,[19] he was also busy planning facilities for the new film unit and attempting to define its role. By February 1918, studios and laboratory facilities were almost completed in the Arnold Block at the corner of Kent and Wellington streets in Ottawa and Norrish announced his plans to release ten short films a year at a cost of $1,500 each with distribution projected in Canada, the United States, Britain, Australia, New Zealand, and South Africa.[20] He urged the appointment of a staff cinematographer and finally succeeded in hiring Arthur Reeves, formerly senior cameraman at Essanay, who began shooting film "in the field" that July. It was planned that some revenue would accrue from film distribution since the government would take a percentage from its distribution agents, but Norrish went to some lengths to emphasize that the "greatest returns would come, not to the department, but the country in general" in terms of propaganda.[21] It was also essential, he noted, that the new branch be properly equipped since this would enable it to service the film needs of other departments.[22]

Action was swift. Within a month, $5,000 worth of photographic and processing equipment had been purchased and the new branch was given the name of Exhibits and Publicity Bureau by the minister.[23] The draft of an order-in-council, officially establishing the Bureau, was written in April[24] and in May the department held a special screening of Canadian industrial and travelogue films in order to make its activities known.[25] By August, six films were in production, distribution arrangements set up with trade commissioners abroad, and lantern slides were being prepared.[26]

On September 19, 1918, an order-in-council officially recognized the Exhibits and Publicity Bureau,[27] set out its functions, and instructed other departments to carry out their film propaganda and publicity work "in co-operation and consultation" with the Bureau.[28] Its principal function was to be the production, acquisition, and distribution of motion pictures; the "Exhibits" part being a permanent display of trade items from around the world. This was the first government film production unit to be established anywhere in the world. Though the Ontario Motion Picture Bureau had been founded in 1917, its productions in the early years were commissioned to private film companies while the federal Bureau was already producing films with its own staff in the summer of 1918. Ben Norrish and Arthur Reeves were the first two film makers whose salaries were paid directly by Canadian tax payers and who worked directly for the state. In fact, there is something a little comical in the contortions the civil service must have had to go through to respond to the pressure of Norrish and O'Hara to hire Arthur Reeves since there was no category for cinematographers! Reeves was eventually hired at the somewhat high civil service salary of $2,100 a year—$200 more than Norrish himself received.

The Bureau grew rapidly, from a staff of four in September 1918 to a staff of fourteen, including three cameramen, by November 1919.[29] Among those hired were John Alexander (who was later to become a major cinematographer and director for Associated Screen News) and Raymond S. Peck who was to succeed Norrish as head of the Bureau in 1920. Peck's hiring illustrates the circumlocutory struggles the Bureau had in dealing with the civil service's ignorance of motion pictures. Peck was hired as "editor" (obviously a term the civil service understood since it was used in publishing) though it is clear from the description of his functions ("to supervise the taking of government motion pictures") that he was a film director.[30]

By November 1919, the Bureau could also boast of "the largest and best equipped studio and laboratory in Canada."[31] Its films were receiving wide and popular theatrical distribution through Canadian Universal in Canada, Jury's Imperial Pictures in Britain, plus theatrical and non-theatrical distribution in the United States, Australia, New Zealand, South America, and Japan. Some attempt had been made to enter the European market and fourteen films were screened in 1919 at the trade fair in Lyons, France in a special theatre. This was heady success for an organization barely a year old, run by civil servants on a comparative shoestring budget. Reviewers pointed to the films' "magnificent photography. . . . Technically they are practically flawless, being well photographed and edited and cleverly subtitled, [they] deserve a much better position in the programme than that of a 'fill-up'."[32]

The films which stimulated such fulsome praise were all part of a series designed by Ben Norrish for release beginning in February 1919: the *Seeing Canada* series. With the development of the series, Norrish's conception of the role of the Bureau clearly began to move beyond the narrow definition of industrial propaganda implicit in the order-in-council. The months following the end of the war were a period of strong nationalist sentiment. There was considerable agitation against the dominant influence of American films and in fact, the growth in the Bureau was a reflection of a wider concern and a more intensive level of production in Canada generally.[33] Though the *Seeing Canada* films were originally prepared for foreign release, "the recent agitation for more Canadian films in our theatres" led to a contract with Canadian Universal for Canadian theatrical release "on a rental basis in the same way that they have been handled in foreign countries."[34]

It is difficult now to imagine the impact those first releases of the Bureau had. Canadians were hardly familiar with seeing themselves depicted in their own movie theatres. They had had a taste of it during the war; film production was moving to new levels and now the *Seeing Canada* films offered the possibility of Canada being appreciated abroad. *The Canadian Moving Picture Digest* was ecstatic to the point of hyperbole:

> Already millions of people in Great Britain, the United States, New Zealand, and Australia have seen Canada flash in pictures before their eyes—Canada as she actually is—Canada, a nation of wonderful industrial possibilities, a wonderland that will attract

millions of tourists when her beauties and opportunities for sport, sight-seeing, and recreation become known. This is the purpose of the development of these films—to enable the people of the world to know the Canada which they have heard so much about in the last four years of war; to attract to Canada, as a result of showing a new and fertile field for industrial development, thousands of bona-fide businessmen and millions of foreign capital. As flashes of lightning across the sky, so is Canada being flashed across the world on the motion picture screen.[35]

A new film was released in the series every two weeks. Among the films produced in the first year were *The Most Picturesque Spot in North America, Lake Louise*; *Wooden Shipbuilding in Canada*; *A World of Scenic Wonders*; *Building Aeroplanes in Canada*; *Harvest of the Sugar Maple Tree*; *A Fish and Bear Tale*; and *Peace Hath Her Victories*. The titles in themselves convey the content that was to mark much of the Bureau's production, but not the quality of the films. One Canadian newspaper reviewer confessed that their quality "proved a surprise to many of the audience. The direction was most effective, the photography comparable to the best work of the big American producers, and the titles very attractive and in good taste."[36]

The *Seeing Canada* films rapidly became a popular addition to film programs in Canadian theatres. One year after the series began, the general manager of Canadian Universal, Claire Hague, could report that the films were being booked by all the major theatres in Canada and that he had received many unsolicited letters from Canadian exhibitors praising the films. "Every exhibitor who is showing this series on his screen is a booster for the government pictures," he declared.[37]

Not everyone was pleased by the Bureau's success. There were rumblings from the private film industry that the Bureau's activities were financially damaging since the Bureau deprived them of potentially lucrative government film work. This was to be a recurrent theme in complaints about government film production, a theme that has not abated in later years. Most incensed at the government's actions was the Pathescope Company of Toronto which was already producing films for the Ontario Motion Picture Bureau. It submitted a proposal to do the same for the Canadian government but had received no response before the Bureau released its first films. The president of Pathescope, H. Norton DeWitt, argued in a letter to the minister that the Canadian film industry was still "in its infancy," that it was not comparable to the British or American industries, and that the Department of Trade and Commerce ought to be encouraging new Canadian enterprises, not depriving them of their livelihood.[38] Pathescope must have had some political clout because six months after DeWitt's complaint, the president of the Privy Council made an arrangement for government financial backing for Pathescope to produce a weekly newsreel, *Canadian Pictorial News*. Norrish's resentment at the decision—which went against his advice—was evident and understandable. But the federal government continued subsidizing the newsreel until July 1921.[39]

From the first, Ben Norrish was concerned about the quality of the Bureau's films. The effectiveness of the program was directly dependent, he felt, on the films' acceptability in theatres. They had to be good enough to compete on equal terms with commercial films from the United States. And to do that the Bureau needed not only good technical equipment but also the funds to pay competitive salaries to qualified production staff. Norrish won the battle for equipment: by March 1920, the Bureau installed new laboratory equipment that enabled it to process ten thousand feet of film a day, but in other directions he was frustrated.[40] He had difficulty persuading the Civil Service Commission to offer a high enough salary to attract a competent cameraman to replace Arthur Reeves—who left the Bureau to go to another job at more than double his Bureau salary.[41] While other Bureau cameramen were proficient in exterior work, Reeves had been the only one with the skills to shoot the technically more demanding interior scenes. Norrish was also irritated by seemingly endless demands to justify the Bureau's existence and to keep costs down. Though he went to some pains to draw the minister's attention to the favourable reviews the Bureau's films were receiving, Sir George seemed most concerned about the fact that the Bureau had cost the Department $90,000 in 1919 while only $1,600 had been received as the Bureau's share of film rentals.[42] Sir George was also concerned that most of the films produced were "scenics" to which Norrish could only respond that the lack of industrial films was a direct reflection of the difficulties he had had with the Civil Service Commission in hiring a competent cameraman to replace Reeves. The Bureau's concentration on "scenics" to the exclusion of other subjects was ultimately to prove self-defeating.

In the spring of 1920, Norrish received an offer to join the publicity department of Canadian Pacific Railway in Montreal.[43] The CPR was continuing its long association with film in Canada. They had recently sponsored a seven-reel film by Tracey Mathewson of the Canadian tour of the Prince of Wales.[44] Now there were plans to finance and develop a film production company. (Curiously, there seem to have been no discussions of the Bureau's producing a film covering the Royal Visit—an obvious topic one would have thought for a government production unit.) Norrish almost certainly felt the bureaucratic frustrations he had suffered at the Bureau could be avoided in private enterprise. He resigned in June 1920 and was replaced by Ray Peck. In July 1920, the CPR incorporated Associated Screen News in Montreal, with Norrish at its head.[45] He was to remain there for the remainder of his professional career.

Ben Norrish's two-year tenure at the Bureau had been crucial. He had transformed a vague idea on the part of government officials into a functioning operation, a competent, well-equipped film unit whose work was well respected in Canada and abroad, and whose films had already been seen by millions of viewers. It was the first permanent government film unit to be established anywhere in the world. Whatever judgements might be made of his later career, to Ben Norrish must go the credit for giving practical expression to the idea that Canada deserved to be seen on the movie screens of the world. The foundation he laid was to be put to good use by the new director, Ray Peck, during the Twenties, the most active and successful years of the Bureau's existence.

Ontario—And Two Producers, Rampant

In Toronto, the Ontario government had established its provincial Motion Picture Bureau in May 1917, more than a year before that of the Canadian government.[46] However, unlike its federal counterpart, it did not produce its own films until 1923. Until then, all production work was contracted to private film companies in Toronto with the Ontario Motion Picture Bureau being responsible for the content of the films and for arranging their distribution.

Interest in the use of film by the Ontario government goes back at least to 1914–15 when Toronto film and newsreel producers, W. James and Sons were commissioned by the province to film the construction of the new concrete highway between Toronto and Hamilton.[47] In the Department of Agriculture there was an agricultural expert and author, S. C. Johnson, who saw in the motion picture an educational tool with wider potential than the written word. As the author of several books on farming techniques, he felt films could be used to train farmers who had little formal education.[48] During the war years, Johnson was responsible for the production of several films on farming methods which were shown to various groups around the province.[49] The provincial treasurer, T. W. McGarry, whose department was responsible for the motion picture industry, had also become convinced of the educational value of film—both in and out of the classroom.[50] In cooperation with the minister of agriculture (later premier), W. W. Hearst, it was decided to centralize the province's film production activities and to combine these with the distribution of films which had been acquired by other government departments.[51] In May 1917, the Provincial Motion Picture Bureau was established by order-in-council as part of the provincial treasurer's department. Its first director was S. C. Johnson and its principal purpose was to carry out "educational work for farmers, school children, factory workers, and other classes." A distribution section was planned "to handle the large number of films to be made under official auspices [or which] will be purchased from outside sources." Films would be used to advertise Ontario and "to encourage the building of highways and other public works." In addition, the lectures on agricultural topics already available would be supplemented by films.[52]

Though it was hoped that some of the films would have a regular theatrical release, the main thrust was to be toward educational screenings in churches, schools, and other institutions. This immediately created a problem since the standard 35mm film was on inflammable nitrate film and could not be easily used in such situations because of the fire hazard. To solve this the Bureau decided to release its films on safety film stock, the 28mm film designed for non-theatrical use. Projectors for this gauge were portable and could be operated in any room where an electrical connection could be made. Agents in Canada for the French-developed 28mm film were Pathescope of Canada and the Bureau decided to purchase several projectors from Pathescope.[53] Not surprisingly, Pathescope also received the first contract to produce films for the Bureau.

Pathescope of Canada had been established in 1914 with H. Norton DeWitt as president and principal shareholder.[54] Its initial activities had been concentrated on selling 28mm projectors and distributing entertainment and educational shorts and features through its links with Pathescope in the United State and the Pathé company of France. When the level of Canadian production increased during the war, Pathescope began to concentrate its activities directly on production. Always this was to be production sponsored and paid for by others. Pathescope never risked its own capital to produce for its own account. Films were made for industrial companies, the federal government, and several provincial governments—most notable that of Ontario. They were perhaps the most active Canadian producers of propaganda films during the war and one of their cameramen, William J. Craft, was a leading official war photographer who worked for three years with the Canadian Expeditionary Forces in Canada, Britain, and France.[55] But American born Bill Craft was only one among several foreign cameramen and

Dick Bird making a film on the potato industry for Pathescope Co. of Canada.

technicians imported by Pathescope as the company's production activities expanded rapidly in 1917 and 1918 through its contracts with the Ontario Motion Picture Bureau.

Among them was Dick Bird whose almost sixty-year film career was to concentrate on documentary, newsreel, and educational film production. Born in England in 1892, he moved to the United States when he was fourteen years old, became interested in film a few years later, and shot his first newsreel footage in 1912. He worked as an independent, supplying film to the *Selig Tribune* newsreel. His first work in Canada was in 1914 when he photographed troop mobilization and training, footage which he sold to the federal government. After working again in the United States, he was hired by Pathescope in 1917 as a staff cinematographer and was to photograph hundreds of films for Pathescope of which some six dozen were for the Bureau. He also worked on the only theatrical production in which Pathescope was involved: *Canadian Pictorial News*, the newsreel backed by the federal government. He was in fact, offered a job with the federal Bureau in Ottawa but since the pay was less than at Pathescope (Norrish's perennial problem) he stayed in Toronto.[56] In 1920, Pathescope sent him on a tour of Japan, Korea, and China. Pathescope had a contract with the Presbyterian, Anglican, and Methodist Missions and Bird's job was to film the work of the missions so the films could be used in Canada to raise money. The result was three films, each two-hours in length, and each detailing the work of one church.[57] Bird also spent some time in Saskatchewan and Nova Scotia shooting film for Pathescope on behalf of the Saskatchewan and Nova Scotia governments. Then he realized there was no reason why he should not produce these films himself. He was, in any case, actually making the films—Pathescope was acting only as a middleman. So, while continuing to work as a freelance news cameraman (mostly for the Canadian edition of the Fox newsreel) he set up his own company in Regina to produce sponsored and wildlife films. And it was to be in Regina that his most creative, personal contribution to Canadian film was made.

Another Pathescope cameraman, Michael J. Shiels, was an expatriate American as were many at Pathescope. From a background as a still photographer, he joined Pathescope during its major expansion and worked for them for five years specializing in films of northern development. In 1921 he was active in the Cinematographers and Motion Picture Craftsmen of Canada, a union of employees from educational and industrial film production companies.[58] Its prime purpose was not, however, to protect the interests of the employees but to attack any company attempting to promote feature production in Canada. Though there were good grounds for exposing some of the prevalent stock promotion frauds, there are also curious overtones to it. Could it be that Pathescope and Filmcraft Industries (the two major educational and industrial film companies) resented any attempt to threaten their dominant role in film production in Toronto? There is support for this view in that the union also attacked an apparently bona-fide enterprise, Educational Motion Pictures Ltd., whose aim was not to produce features but educational films for Toronto schools.[59] As "business representative," Michael Shiels was the union's key investigator and he was very active in publishing "exposures." When the Ontario Motion Picture Bureau went into production for itself in 1923, Shiels joined the staff at the Trenton studios and continued working there until his death in 1927.

For Pathescope, the contract with the Ontario Motion Picture Bureau was to be the prime force in its development into a major production company. Though Pathescope worked for others between 1917 and 1923, it was the production of films for the Ontario government which was its lifeblood.

When the Bureau moved into direct production in 1923, it signalled the decline of Pathescope. Though it continued for some years (changing its name to the Film and Slide Company and, later, General Films) it never again played a major role on the Canadian film scene.

But for now, these were good years. In April 1918 Pathescope established a "model film factory" in new headquarters at 156-158 King Street in Toronto. Under technical director William Redpath (a pioneer Canadian exhibitor and one of Pathescope's first employees) the studios had "twelve distinct working departments" with all "the latest and most approved equipment" for film production.[60] Perhaps the Ontario Legislature's recent voting of $52,000 for an extension of the Bureau's work in 1918–19 was responsible for Pathescope's optimistic expansion. In any case, the Bureau's films were receiving much favourable comment in some quarters. One writer asserted that "Ontario now leads the world in visual education work. . . . These films are strictly educational films, planned and produced under the direction of well known experts . . . with the sole object of depicting the 'right versus the wrong way' of getting the farm work done."[61]

Given the interest and background of Director S. C. Johnson, it is not surprising that the bulk of production was initially directed towards farmers. One popular example was *The Marketing of Livestock*; another was a film on the grading of wool which five thousand farmers had seen in the winter of 1917.[62] There were, however, some non-agricultural films. Five films had been made on road building and repair while ten thousand feet of film "show the new farms, mines and other attraction in New Ontario for settlers." With the use of these films, it was claimed, average attendance jumped from fifteen to eighty-five at district meetings arranged by the province's agricultural representatives. In order to keep interest and attendance high, the Bureau also decided "to add an entertainment feature to its agricultural film shows" by including dramatic and comic films.[63] Pathescope owned the Canadian distribution rights (on the non-theatrical 28mm gauge) to many hundreds of entertainment films (including cartoons, Chaplin comedies, serials like *The Exploits of Elaine*, and such features as *The Life of Christ*) and they again benefitted considerably from the Bureau's decision.

By May of 1919, the Bureau had made considerable progress. It had a library of some two hundred films—not all of which had been made for it, of course. The forty-seven district representatives of the Department of Agriculture had each been equipped with portable 28mm projectors and a battery for use when local electric power was not available. Any group could borrow films and there was no charge made except for transportation costs. (The mechanics of distribution were in fact handled for the Bureau by Pathescope which charged the province $1,200 a year for the service.) It was said that almost 700,000 Ontario citizens had seen the Bureau's films since 1917.[64]

Arrangements had also been concluded for theatrical release of several Pathescope-Bureau films through Regal Films. The first four releases *A Springtime Harvest*, *Vocational Training in Ontario*, *The Story of Paper*, and *Ontario Fisheries and Farmerettes* were to be distributed through the company's six offices across Canada.[65] But the high hopes the Bureau had for theatrical distribution were not to be fulfilled. Regal Films obviously gave little or no promotion to the Ontario films, since only seven months after the original contract, theatrical distribution of the Bureau's films was transferred to Canadian Universal, which was releasing the films of the federal Bureau with such good results.[66] Even this, however, had little effect in gaining wider distribution.

The reason for this has its roots in the impetus behind the Bureau's initial existence. The first films of the Bureau were strictly educational, geared to specific audiences. Even later, when more general films were produced, they still tended to have a didactic tone. In Ottawa, by contrast, Ben Norrish saw the primary purpose of the federal Exhibits and Publicity Bureau as the promotion of the Canadian image at home and abroad and realized that, to do this effectively, his films had to gain theatrical release. There was, in fact, an evident difference in quality between the films of the two Bureaus. Even when the Ontario Bureau's films were shown in theatres, they tended to be ignored by the critics whereas those of the federal Bureau were widely praised. Though the several directors of the Ontario Motion Picture Bureau attempted to correct this failing, the films of the Ontario Bureau never had much more than a minimal theatrical impact.[67]

More characteristic of the Bureau's repute in the early years is its 1919 expedition to Bear Island, a Hudson Bay post in the Temagami Forest Reserve. Led by William Dawson (who had replaced S. C. Johnson as director of the Bureau) the group photographed the life of the Indians of Bear Island and produced other scenic films of the far North. They also took with them a collection of films including Chaplin comedies, newsreels, educational films, and travelogues to show to the people of Bear Island who had never before seen films.[68] This use of films in remote areas as an educational tool was to be a recurrent activity of the Bureau and is arguably its most important contribution to the development and use of film in the province.

In late 1919, the Bureau began to express some dissatisfaction with Pathescope's efforts on behalf of the province. During the summer of 1919, Pathescope had sent salesmen across Canada to promote production by other provinces. Saskatchewan, Manitoba, Nova Scotia, and Quebec all expressed some interest. But Bureau Director William Dawson complained that Pathescope had offered free copies of Ontario government films to any province which signed a production contract with Pathescope.[69] Dawson was understandably disturbed at Pathescope's assumption of its ownership of the Bureau's films. Then, too, there was the problem of quality. Pathescope's films seemed to arouse little excitement among either theatre owners or the public. Whereas the Allen theatre chain had already expressed interest in the films of a new Toronto film company.[70]

The Canadian Aero Film Company, whose film *Toronto, the Gateway of Ontario* had sparked the Allens' interest, was established in 1919 by Blaine Irish, a former cameraman for Ernest Ouimet's *British Canadian Pathé News*. Irish and a Hamilton aviation pioneer, Irwin Proctor, had acquired seven "war surplus" aeroplanes and the necessary film equipment. Sales manager was Sidney B. Taube and Charles Irish (Blaine's brother) was camera director. Four pilots, all stunt specialists, worked for them. The company's aim was to produce what were then called "novelty" films, photographed from the air. By the time the Canadian Aero Film Company was incorporated in July 1919, they had already produced four films for theatrical release, including one on London, Ontario shot largely from the air.[71]

Among the first employees of the new company was Roy Tash, a cinematographer who was to make a continuing contribution to film in Canada for almost fifty years. Born in Brooklyn, New York in 1898, Tash began his film career as a projectionist in a Chicago movie theatre and by the age of seventeen was a newsreel cameraman for *Pathé News* in Chicago. Joining the exodus of other American newsreel cameramen to Canada at the end of the war, Tash moved to Toronto to work with Blaine Irish whom he had known in Chicago. One of his first assignments was the filming of Sir Wilfrid Laurier's funeral in Ottawa. After a brief absence to travel in the United States, he rejoined Irish's new company, Filmcraft Industries, in February 1922 to work on that company's *Camera Classics* series and the feature *Satan's Paradise*.[72] When Filmcraft folded in 1924 after Blaine Irish's death, Tash travelled to the Arctic as official photographer to the Canadian Government expedition to the Eastern Arctic on the patrol ship, C.G.S. *Arctic*. Later, he worked for Associated Screen News in Montreal where he remained throughout the rest of his career, photographing documentaries and shooting newsreel footage for all the major American newsreels. Perhaps his most envied assignment was the filming of the Dionne quintuplets in 1932, but he was also to photograph every notable Canadian and foreign politician and almost every member of the British Royal Family. It was often said that no Canadian news event was complete without Roy Tash and his camera—the same camera he had used for almost fifty years.[73]

The Canadian Aero Film Company was the brainchild of Blaine Irish. Irwin Proctor might be president, but it was Irish as general manager who was the company's prime mover. A man of considerable energy and persuasive powers, described by some as "a hustler," Blaine Irish was to contribute much to Canadian film in the four years he was active. Born in 1891 in Ernesttown, Ontario, Irish's first film experience, like Tash's, was as a projectionist and cameraman for *Pathé News* in Chicago. He helped persuade Ernest Ouimet that a Canadian newsreel was a viable proposition and, when Ouimet established *British Canadian Pathé News* in January 1919, Irish was hired to head the newsreel in the Toronto area.[74] It enjoyed an immediate success and Irish decided that Toronto was fertile ground for production other than newsreels. With Irwin Proctor (and, reportedly, financial backing from Clifford Sifton) he founded the Canadian Aero Film Company. By October 1919, he had set up another company, Filmcraft Industries, equipped with its own laboratories and facilities for titling and producing advertising trailers.[75]

As with Pathescope, the expansion of Irish's two companies was rapid in an atmosphere that encouraged Canadian production. Early in January 1920 the two companies moved to new, more spacious, quarters at 39 Queen Street West and announced that they had "the largest producing laboratory ever attempted in the Dominion of Canada" and were the first commercial producers "to introduce a complete tinting and toning process" to give a colour effect to their films.[76] By May 1920, they were responsible for producing the Canadian edition of the Fox newsreel and planned a weekly theatrical release of their own, *Filmcraft Nature Classics*. For the Fox newsreel, Irish obtained at least one major scoop when he had five cameramen photographing the attempt by George Stephens to navigate Niagara Falls in a barrel in July 1920. No other newsreel company was on hand.[77]

The first *Filmcraft Nature Classics* appeared in August 1920. Advertised as "Dominion Scenes for Canadian Screens" and released weekly by the Allen brothers' Famous Players Film Service, the films received praise comparable to that given the productions of the federal Bureau. The first two releases *Winter Wizardry* (Niagara Falls, again!) and *Hamilton, the Birmingham of Canada* had shots "of rare beauty" that demonstrated "the cameraman has the selective faculty of the true artist."[78] However, though the films were seen widely in Canadian theatres, they gained no foreign distribution.

Late in 1921, Blaine Irish switched the title of the series to the less restrictive *Camera Classics*. Though the new series included the inevitable "scenics" (*Fishing—Just for Fun* was the first release), Irish broadened the range of subject matter considerably.[79] Beginning in April 1922, the series included several animated cartoons featuring a cat (called Tom) with a "wondrous tail." Some of these cartoons had live photographic backgrounds with superimposed animation—as had *A Happy Thought*, released in April. Others were silhouette cartoons. Irish succeeded in persuading the Toronto *Daily Star* and *Star Weekly* to back the series. Not surprisingly, their reviewers were fulsome in praise for the films, but others were equally warm. Generally considered "good from an artistic and novelty angle," the series was "worthy of taking its place beside any other product of its kind produced outside of Canada."[80] Public response was also evident and release of the series was extended west of Ontario in association with the *Winnipeg Free Press*. Irish optimistically planned to expand into producing dramatic films and appealed, through the theatres, to Canadians to submit scripts for consideration. In the event, none were produced—except for the feature *Satan's Paradise*, described earlier.

Though exhibitors in Canada reported "business excellent" in relation to *Camera Classics*, the series received no foreign distribution.[81] A group of American exhibitors were brought to Toronto for a special preview—Irish was nothing if not ambitious—but no bookings followed.[82] This was, of course, 1922, the most active year for Canadian production and the one that presaged its downfall. *Camera Classics* might be good but why should American theatres show them when they were already deluged by comparable films produced by Hollywood companies to whom they were linked?

In any case, production of the series seems to have fizzled out by the end of 1922. Blaine Irish must certainly have been feeling a financial squeeze since Filmcraft Industries was never again active in theatrical productions, apart from *Satan's Paradise*. This feature probably sapped the company's remaining free capital and a fire which destroyed the studios of Filmcraft Industries in September 1923 may not have been entirely fortuitous.

Blaine Irish himself died of erysipelas on October 27, 1923.[83] He was only thirty-two and it seems likely that he had the potential for making an even greater contribution to the Canadian film scene.

Though Filmcraft Industries concentrated more on producing films for theatrical release than did Pathescope, the production of sponsored educational and industrial films was an important part of its activity. The company's continuing financial stability depended on it. And, given the successful releases of both the Canadian Aero Film Company and Filmcraft Industries, it is hardly surprising that they came in for an increasing share of the business of the Ontario Motion Picture Bureau after 1920.

The change of government in Ontario in 1919 may have had some impact. That October, the United Farmers of Ontario had been elected to power and several radical changes were instituted. In 1920, the new provincial treasurer, Peter Smith, decided to centralize several of the province's film activities—including film censorship, theatre inspection, and the Motion Picture Bureau—under the Amusements Branch in his department. Otter Elliott, the new director of the branch (and of the Bureau), was sent to Hollywood in July 1920 "to make personal observations of various moving picture production activities" since the new government intended to expand its film activities through the Motion Picture Bureau.[84] Otter Elliott had been a member of the first Ontario Censor Board and had worked since 1912 for the province's moving picture branch. He was more concerned than his predecessors about the quality of production and far less concerned about agricultural training films. The Bureau had already acquired for distribution several productions by the Canadian Aero Film Company and in 1920 it was commissioned to make a film for the Bureau on flying boat operations in Northern Ontario.[85] From that point the number of productions commissioned to Canadian Aero (and later Filmcraft Industries) increased rapidly. Those to Pathescope decreased proportionately. Some idea of the comparative shift can be gauged from the fact that in 1918–19 almost all the Bureau's production budget went to Pathescope; in 1920–21 Filmcraft Industries received $55,000 while Pathescope received only $28,500, of which more than half was for routine laboratory work.[86]

Competition between Pathescope and Filmcraft was fierce and often bitter. Both made it a practice to file extremely low bids in an effort to secure a contract, then added on charges for "extras" during production. Each company accused the other of this practice and there were more than a few disputes, some of which were only settled by arbitration.[87] In May 1921, Pathescope used its influence to provoke questions in the Public Accounts Committee of the Legislature regarding over-charges by the Canadian Aero Film Company. Elliott was forced to defend himself and his decision to use this company rather than Pathescope. He pointed out that, when he became director, the Bureau had been in a "terribly unsatisfactory and irregular condition . . . a legacy left by the previous Administration which has taken many months and great patience to clear up." The Canadian Aero Film Company had cooperated fully in checking back over previous work and he could "state definitely" that there was not a duplication of charges on *A Day's Plea-*

sure and *The Shores of Lake Ontario* as alleged. He defended the amount of work being given to Canadian Aero on the grounds of both quality and service: two films on the same theme had been made at the same time (under the previous director) by, separately, Canadian Aero and Pathescope. He invited the minister to see both films since the quality of the Canadian Aero film "will speak for itself." In addition, Elliott continued, Pathescope maintained that negatives shot for the Bureau belonged to Pathescope not the province, while Canadian Aero agreed these negatives were the property of the Bureau. The Canadian Aero Film Company had also been helpful in distribution and with its help "we have attained a circulation of films and revenue from same absolutely unknown in the past."[88]

Elliott's annoyance at Pathescope's attempt to embarrass him was reflected in a continuing decline in Pathescope's work for the Bureau. In September 1921, Pathescope lost the contract for the non-theatrical distribution of the Bureau's films, worth $1,200 a year. The Bureau had decided to handle its own distribution—though the cost would soon be very much greater than $1,200.

Filmcraft Industries under President Irwin Proctor and General Manager Blaine Irish pressed home their advantage. In December 1921, Proctor urged the provincial treasurer, Peter Smith, to consider the production of political propaganda films. These films would reach many more people than could be reached, say, in a political meeting and since "the propaganda would be given to the people in an indirect way and without their knowing it" it would not stir up the same criticism as at a meeting. He suggested films which would depict the economic progress made by the government, films made attractively enough to be accepted in theatres in order to get "the maximum effect in as hidden a way as possible" and overcome the influence of "a largely hostile press." Such films, Proctor suggested, could have an enormous impact on the next election. While "the political part of it is something about which there need be no correspondence or discussion . . . it would be working for you every day of the year and would be a great help to the progressive movement not only in Ontario, but all over the Dominion."[89]

Though some films were made that dealt with economic development, the United Farmers of Ontario did not sponsor any embracing the powerful "political propaganda" envisaged by Proctor. Such films were not to appear for several more decades, perhaps not truly until the age of television. In any case, the Bureau's films did not prevent the change of government during the next election.

Disputes over charges continued between the Bureau and Pathescope during 1922. In August 1922, Filmcraft Industries joined the fray, claiming that a settlement made in favour of Pathescope entitled them also to additional payment. Filmcraft, in fact, were at least a match for Pathescope in charging the province for "extras," a form of behaviour that led some in Toronto to dub the company "Film graft." Eventually the disputes over charges were to bring about the downfall of both companies. George Patton had been appointed director of the Bureau in June 1922 in an administrative change which had again separated the Bureau from the Amusements Branch. He must have found horrendous the squabbling between Filmcraft and Pathescope. The situation came to a head in October 1922 when the Bureau called for tenders for "the exclusive supply of motion pictures" for the Bureau. Amid charges and counter-charges (including one that Patton had worked with Proctor and Irish to prepare the Filmcraft tender) a firm of chartered accountants adjudged the Filmcraft tender the lowest.[90]

But the province had had enough. Patton and the new provincial treasurer, Colonel W. H. Price, were determined to solve the problem. It was pointed out, rightly, that the federal government's Motion Picture Bureau in Ottawa operated its own studios and laboratory, that it functioned more efficiently than the Ontario Bureau, and that its films had more impact.

The decision was taken in 1923 to abandon the system of commissioning production to private companies. Now the Ontario Motion Picture Bureau would produce its own films directly. Temporary production facilities were set up in the Bureau's offices on Richmond Street, Patton hired several film makers away from Pathescope and Filmcraft, and brought in new people. Among them was twenty-four year old Gordon Sparling, hired as a title artist, but soon to make a major contribution to Canadian cinema.

(It is worth noting, parenthetically, that Filmcraft Industries lost a major share of its income when the Bureau moved into production itself. This, and the almost simultaneous collapse of its theatrical shorts program, may have been not without influence on the timing of Filmcraft's fire in September.)[91]

The Richmond Street facilities of the Bureau were crowded and meagre. However, the Trenton studios of Adanac Films had been unused since *The Great Shadow* had been produced there. The ubiquitous George Brownridge, promoter of Adanac, suggested that the province purchase the studios. This would amortize Adanac's debts, help solve his personal financial problems, and, of course, provide the Bureau with excellent facilities. The proposal appealed to Provincial Treasurer Price and the government agreed to purchase the studios for the very low cost of $29,000.[92] At the same time George Brownridge was hired to check the Bureau's films and prepare an audit of its facilities so the Bureau could prepare its first catalogue for publication.

By February 1924, the first film directed, photographed, and printed by the Bureau's staff at the Trenton studios was delivered to Patton.[93] The studios were officially opened by Colonel Price on October 9, 1924, before a crowd of six thousand people. At the opening, Colonel Price announced that the Bureau intended to produce "features of an historical and dramatic nature in addition to the one and two-reel scenic and educational releases."[94] Under Patton's vigorous direction and a concerned minister the Bureau had suddenly taken on an apparent new life and significance. On that sunny day in October 1924, the Bureau's future looked very promising.

British Columbia, *et al.*—and Trenton Again

Film production by other provinces was by no means as extensive as it was in Ontario. Though several provinces, notably Manitoba, Saskatchewan, and Nova Scotia made use of films for agricultural training and general education, production was contracted out to private companies. Initially, Pathescope and Canadian Films of Montreal got the major share of this work but eventually local firms were included. In some cases, production companies (such as that of Dick Bird in Regina) were developed to meet provincial needs.

Most active of the provinces for a brief period, and potentially the most interesting, was British Columbia, which had its own Educational and Patriotic Film Service headed (astonishingly for 1919) by a woman, May Watkis. And the story of how she got the job offers an interesting commentary on the film industry at the time.

British Columbia had been concerned with motion pictures from an early date. It was the first province to establish film censorship and one of the first to use motion pictures to promote immigation. May Watkis had applied for the position of film censor in 1913. She wanted to work in movies but knew she "wasn't a 'type' and would have little chance as an actress."[95] The attorney-general gave the job to a man but, not at all daunted, May Watkis went to the new censor and offered herself as his assistant. He agreed, but only if she would also act as his projectionist. Though she had no idea how to project films, she accepted, assuming it would be easy enough to learn. But then she met a snag. The projectionists' union in B.C. (and that in Washington State across the border) positively refused to teach her anything. In 1913, women did not even have the vote in B.C. and there was a marked disinclination to give women positions doing what were considered strictly "men's jobs." "Having tried to learn by fair means," said May Watkis, "I was now determined to learn by any means at all." So she persuaded a friend who projected films at a local theatre to explain the techniques involved, without of course telling him why she wanted to know. "He really became quite interested in me," she recalled, "and under his tutelage I projected successfully for several shows—with him beside me of course." The new censor, somewhat less distressed than the projectionists at the idea of women working in films, was amused at her determination and she got the job. Even then, the projectionists' union and other men who felt deprived of a civil service job, launched a protest against her appointment. The agitation continued for a month but accomplished nothing.

After a time, May Watkis became an inspector in the Theatres Branch, checking for breaches of the Amusement Tax Act, and later worked in California in the script departments of Hollywood companies. When the B.C. Educational and Patriotic Film Service was established in 1919, she applied for, and got, the job of "directress."

In British Columbia during the war, as elsewhere in the country, the desire for more domestic production began to find expression in local film activities. The government itself became directly involved. Films were sponsored of B.C. troops leaving for the war in Europe and a cinematographer, Harold Sintzenich, hired to supervise filming. In 1915, films were made of the industries of British Columbia for presentation at the Pan Pacific Exposition in San Francisco. Francis Holley, director of the Bureau of Commercial Economics in Washington, declared them "the best I have ever witnessed." [96]

With the creation of the Film Service in 1919, more active production got underway and several films had been made by June 1920 when Ernest Ouimet's Speciality Film Import was appointed official distributor. [97] But not content with ensuring the release of its films, the B.C. government went a great deal further in ensuring that they were seen by the public. In June 1920 the B.C. Legislature passed a law compelling every theatre in the province to present at least one ten-minute B.C. educational film or travelogue in every program. [98] The howls from exhibitors were predictable. The measure was declared reactionary, confiscatory, and vicious. Though not denying that showing the films might be a "good thing," they bitterly resented the compulsion. The exhibitors were not alone in resenting the films. The Vancouver *World* sarcastically declared: "The B.C. government continues to wish its educational films on the long-suffering public. The film is good in every detail except photography, sub-titles, and editing." [99]

The truth is that the Film Service's *Pacific Coast Scenics* were not particularly good. Though the government enforced its legislation, only eighteen months later it decided to restrict the activities of the Film Service.[100] The production of theatrical shorts was dropped (thus eliminating the reason for the 1920 legislation) and from that time the B.C. Film Service stayed strictly within the bounds of producing educational and training films.

The use of film as an educational tool developed rapidly at the provincial level during the Twenties. Quebec became the first province to use films in the schools, though Alberta had established a film library at the University of Alberta in 1917.[101]

In Saskatchewan both the Departments of Agriculture and of Education purchased films and slides for their libraries in addition to commissioning film production to Canadian Films of Montreal and Pathescope.[102] One of the most interesting of these is *Nation Building in Saskatchewan: The Ukrainians* (produced in 1920 by Pathescope and directed by Dick Bird) which depicts the immigration of the Ukrainians and their life in the province. Later, by 1924, the film activity of the Saskatchewan government was centralized in the Motion Picture Branch of the Bureau of Publications under a professional agriculturalist, Harry Saville. As in Ontario, non-theatrical prints were distributed on the non-inflammable 28mm gauge, processed by Pathescope. Typical titles were: *Hog Raising in Saskatchewan*, *Saskatchewan's War on the Grasshopper*, and *Farm Boys' Camp, Regina*.[103] Though the Motion Picture Branch was active for a while, it never developed to the extent of its Ontario counterpart.

The opening of the Trenton studios of the Ontario Motion Picture Bureau promised a new level of activity and influence for government film production. And there were not only the studios. The Bureau now had a young, energetic director in George Patton and a provincial treasurer in Colonel W. H. Price very much aware of the importance of film as an educational and cultural force. Patton, a graduate of Guelph Agricultural College, was in those first years at Trenton a man full of ideas for extending the work and influence of the Bureau. Within a year after the Trenton purchase a second cameraman had been added to the Bureau's staff to support the work of B. J. (Bert) Bach, formerly with the federal Bureau.[104] Within eighteen months, Patton had commissioned George Brownridge to prepare a report on the possibilities of foreign distribution.[105] As a result, distribution contracts were established in Japan, Cuba, and other South American countries. Non-theatrical distribution was promised if the films were re-edited and re-titled for the American market.[106] Within twenty months, Patton had negotiated new contracts for theatrical distribution in Ontario[107] and decided to purchase the Pathescope Library of entertainment and educational films for distribution by the Bureau.[108] And, even with all this activity, the Bureau was now operating more efficiently and at less cost than under the former system. In 1922–23 the Bureau had cost $120,000; in 1924–25 it cost $91,000 and that included the paying of several more staff salaries than two years earlier. By 1925, the Bureau had two thousand films in its library and was distributing fifteen hundred reels of film every month.

Yet after those first two years of fresh blooming, things began to go wrong for the Bureau. Within ten years it was to become so moribund, sterile, and unimaginative that the decision to disband it seems almost inevitable.

Certainly one of the factors in its final collapse was the Bureau's decision to continue releasing its films non-theatrically on 28mm, a decision which locked it into a situation from which, by 1930, it would have been extremely expensive to extricate itself. The federal Bureau in Ottawa did not make the same mistake, choosing to release non-theatrically on the non-inflammable 35mm film that had been available since 1918.[109] In January 1925 when Patton and the Bureau were deciding whether to acquire the large collection of 28mm prints from Pathescope, 16mm film had been on the market for only a few months. Colonel Price was astute enough to question the advisability of the Bureau being so dependent upon a film gauge which might be replaced.[110] But Patton was determined to expand the Bureau's loan library and impressed on the minister the fact that if the Pathescope films were not purchased, then the Bureau would have to invest considerable funds in acquiring films from elsewhere. Perhaps rightly at the time, he saw the acquisition of the Pathescope films as a relatively inexpensive way of extending, rapidly, the Bureau's usefulness. Whatever the reasons, it proved to be a bad decision. The use of 16mm film spread quickly in the late Twenties and early Thirties. Its advantages were manifold. The projectors were lighter and simpler to operate by teachers and other non-professional film people; when sound was introduced, 16mm projectors became available with sound equipment whereas those for 28mm never did; the film itself was lighter, easier to handle and, though its image quality was not as satisfactory as that of 28mm, it was more than acceptable for small group film presentations. Such was the growth of 16mm usage that by 1930 the Bureau had to begin issuing some of its releases on 16mm though even then, most of its prints were released on 28mm. In 1934, the fact that the vast bulk of the Bureau's film collection was on the out-dated 28mm and its laboratory equipment designed for 28mm only was to be a major factor in the decision of the new Liberal government to close the Bureau.

There was also the factor of bureaucratic interference which niggled at Patton until his initial enthusiasm waned. In his early years as director, Patton was continually sending off memoranda to the minister, suggesting some new idea or asking approval for a project. By the late Twenties, this was reversed and Patton appears able only to respond to memoranda from the minister asking why something hadn't been done or proposing a subject for a film.[111] Once an energetic initiator, Patton was to become cautious and conservative.

One example of Patton's increased caution only four years after his appointment is his reaction to a proposal that the Bureau develop a role in newsreel production. Four years earlier he had been willing to fight to develop a direct role in production even though this meant taking business away from two commercial companies. Now, though he felt the Bureau was "in shape to produce" newsreel items, it should not "compete unfairly with existing Canadian firms or individuals who are making their livelihood by producing motion pictures."[112] There may have been valid grounds for the point of view that the provincial government should encourage private film production but the fact remains that the Bureau *was* in competition with private industry. Patton's two page memorandum on the topic carefully avoided saying yes or no to the proposal, avoided commitment, and helped neither the Bureau nor private industry.

Unfortunately, Patton's judgement, when exercised, was not always what it might have been. In what may have been his initial enthusiasm, he made several bad decisions that a more experienced film professional might have avoided.

The story of George Brownridge's involvement with the Bureau is an example of this. Brownridge, the hustling promoter of several production companies, had experience in the film industry though not, perhaps, of a kind that should have given Patton confidence. But Patton obviously respected Brownridge's knowledge and apparent contacts in the American film industry and continued to defend his abilities despite increasing evidence to the contrary. In October 1924, Brownridge had submitted a report, at Patton's request, extolling the glowing possibilities for distributing Ontario films in the United States.[113] As a result, Brownridge was sent to New York to supervise the American adaptations of five films and to set up theatrical distribution. He was not paid a salary but was able to claim living and travelling expenses. Almost his first act was to promote, and persuade Patton to accept, a deal that was the most extraordinary in the Bureau's history.

Brownridge proposed that the Ontario government sponsor a three-week visit to the province of S. L. Rothafel (better known as "Roxy") and his Capitol Theatre broadcasting group. "Roxy and His Gang" were then famous radio personalities and Brownridge proposed that Roxy broadcast three of his shows from Toronto (and thus publicize the province) and at the same time appear in ten Ontario travelogues which, said Brownridge, would find an immediate theatrical market in the United States. On the surface, it seemed a reasonable proposal. But Patton had not reckoned on Brownridge. By the time the three-week visit was finished, it had cost the province over $23,000, of which Brownridge's personal share was $1,231—almost as much as Patton's salary for a year. Six months later, in April 1926, questions were to be asked in the Legislature that embarrassed the government and eventually cooled Patton's enthusiastic backing of Brownridge.[114]

Provincial Treasurer Price was not so naive. In a memorandum to Patton on January 30, 1926, he noted that Brownridge's "travelling expenses are very high and I do not see there was very much result from anything he has done." Peremptorily he asked Patton: "I want a report on what this man has accomplished in the year he has been in New York."[115] Patton rushed to Brownridge's defence in a long, detailed, reply that seemed only to repeat more of Brownridge's promises. In tangible terms he could only point to the showing of six Ontario films in three American theatres.[116]

By April, the minister was becoming quite tetchy. "The time has now been reached," he wrote Patton, "when Brownridge must fish or cut bait. If he cannot make progress in New York then we do not want him there." He instructed Patton to "take a positive, aggressive attitude with Brownridge . . . so that the matter may be brought to a successful termination."[117] Even Patton was now becoming a little wary and his reply to this merely notes a telegram from Brownridge promising results within a week. When the week was up, Brownridge's proposals consisted only of a report of some modest sales (which he claimed would gross the province $4,000) but no overall distribution arrangement. He also announced his intention of "severing his connections" with the Bureau since he felt the newspaper publicity over the Roxy deal had been very harmful. He was particularly incensed at an editorial in the *Canadian Moving Picture Digest* and wrote that "anyone with such little brains as Ray Lewis [the editor of the *Digest*] should not be allowed to write or edit a paper of that kind."[118]

But the minister was not to be put off. He sent Patton to New York with an ultimatum to produce definite offers in a week.[119] Forced to produce, Brownridge set out three proposals, only one of which had any real merit. This was an offer from the firm of Cranfield and Clarke to distribute the Bureau's films world-wide on a percentage basis. Cranfield and Clarke had already announced their intention of opening a Canadian branch.[120]

Patton felt they were "an exceedingly well established firm of high standing."[121] The decision to sign a contract with Cranfield and Clarke in June was to have its ultimate consequences in the debâcle of *Carry On, Sergeant* two years later. And, more immediately for the Bureau, in yet another failure to penetrate the theatrical market in any real way. Even the few showings Cranfield and Clarke won for the Bureau's films produced limited revenue. When the firm went bankrupt, it still owed money to the province.

The minister was still not content however. Reacting to news from Brownridge that Colonel Clarke had left for England in June to "develop affiliations" and promote British financing for Canadian film production, the minister insisted on returning to the main point. "I would feel much better pleased," he wrote, "if I had word that the Roxy pictures were being shown."[122]

What the minister was probably not aware of, but which others certainly were, was that the province's difficulty in securing theatrical distribution was a reflection of the quality of its films. The Bureau's productions were simply not good enough to compete for theatrical showings with comparable films. The integrated Hollywood production-exhibition system may certainly have played a role. But some comparison may be gained from the fact that in 1927 the Canadian Government Motion Picture Bureau films were still being shown widely in Canadian and foreign theatres while those from the Ontario Bureau had difficulty in gaining theatrical showings even in Ontario.

How aware Patton and others at the Bureau were of this lack of quality is impossible to say. Certainly one who was aware was a bright, young film maker, Gordon Sparling. Keen to learn, he had persuaded a somewhat reluctant minister to send him to New York for a week in 1926 to study film production in action at the Astoria Studios. On his return, his appraisal of the Bureau's current production was sharp and to the point: "We are depending far too much on the ways and means generally used ten years ago . . . recording accurately but dully the subject being shot. . . . We shall need to introduce a great deal more pictorial work and modern practice into our films if we wish to keep pace with the very great advances of the motion picture."[123]

For the next year, Sparling kept up a steady stream of proposals and memoranda on modernizing the Bureau's production and distribution. Patton passed on the proposals to the minister without much evident support and no action resulted.[124] Sparling was soon to leave the Ontario Bureau for the federal Bureau in Ottawa and eventually joined Ben Norrish's Associated Screen News in Montreal.

Sparling's comments were, however, keenly accurate. The Bureau's films by the late Twenties were technically competent in their photography, but lifeless and dull. They lack pace and imagination in their construction and vision in their design. In fact, most of them appear to have been made by film makers who had not seen another film since before the First World War.

There is a handful of films which have retained more interest, less perhaps for their intrinsic qualities than for the fact that they shine amidst the enveloping mediocrity. George Rutherford's *The Drive*, a documentary on the annual log drive, has at least some sense of rhythm. And there are a few films in which an attempt was made to combine a documentary approach with scripted drama. Not unlike those films by Ernest Ouimet a decade earlier and, superficially at least, comparable to *The Silent Enemy* and *The Viking*, the Bureau's dramatized documentaries used acted-out scenes to accentuate an educational point. In films such as *Someone at Home*, *The Adventures of George S. Fishog*, *Mailing Trouble*, and *Spare Time* (Gordon Sparling's first film) there is evident a conscious attempt to increase their interest for a general audience, an awareness that a personalized drama would be more appealing. The same approach is apparent in the feature-length *Cinderella of the Farms* by John French, described earlier. Though far from the stature of *The Silent Enemy* and *The Viking* (whose dramas grew directly out of actual realities), these films at least suggest the presence—albeit sporadically and barely exploited—of a more developed sense of imagination than was evident in the Bureau's other work. It is worth noting that the approach was never even attempted by the federal Bureau in Ottawa.

But the bulk of the Ontario Bureau's output remains a testament to artistic mediocrity. Once the content was out-dated, the films themselves remain as mere curiosities of another age. Once the decision was taken to close the Bureau, it would have been difficult to argue for its continuing existence on the basis of the quality of its films. Even its most loyal supporters were aware how out-dated its work had become.

Part of the difficulty in production quality stemmed from the fact that the Bureau paid such relatively low salaries to its professionals. Canadian salaries for cinematographers outside the Bureau (though far from Hollywood levels) were more than double those for Bureau staff. However, as far as the province was concerned, they were still civil servants and were graded accordingly. So bad was the situation that in 1929 the province received representations from the Canadian Society of Cinematographers and Photographers, Local 665. The society pointed out that, despite the risks Bureau cameramen were asked to take as part of their work, "their remuneration was little better than that of a bank clerk." It asked for an increase from "$2,100 per year to $5,200 per year with bonuses for special tasks such as aerial photography."[125] The request was denied and Bureau staff were still being paid at the same rates, or even less, when the Bureau was dissolved in 1934.

(It is a depressing sidelight on this attempt at collective action, that the secretary of the Cinematographers' Society in 1929, W. H. Graham, joined the Bureau in 1931 as a cameraman at a salary of $1,800 per year.)

Patton complained repeatedly (as did his counterparts in Ottawa) of the difficulties in keeping good professionals at civil service salaries. He observed several times that young, inexperienced people joined the Bureau, then left as soon as they were trained and could command a better salary elsewhere. The situation was, however, more complex than this. What happened was that young film makers with real ability, such as Gordon Sparling, *did* leave after being trained—not only for better salaries but also for work that gave them a more creative outlet. Conversely, those with less ability who would have found it difficult to survive in commercial film production, found a comfortable, relatively secure, haven at the Bureau even though it meant less money. Of the Bureau's twenty-six full-time staff at its dissolution in 1934, ten had been with the Bureau for a decade. At least one of these ten-year-men, George Rutherford, was to observe that the closing of the Bureau was justified in view of its inefficiency which, he said, was due to the political appointment of inexperienced men.[126]

Certainly, in its last six years, the Bureau became increasingly top-heavy with personnel. Although the Bureau's total expenditures declined from $111,000 to $82,000 between 1928 and 1934, salary expenditures rose in the same period from $35,000 to $56,000. The total number of employees increased from twenty-four in 1928 to thirty-eight in 1934.[127] So, although there was less money available with which to produce films, there were more people on staff to produce them.

The end when it came was swift and brutal. The new Liberal government under Mitchell Hepburn had already made known its intention to reduce government expenditures by cutting much of the bureaucracy of the previous administration. Less than a month after the Liberals came to power the Motion Picture Bureau came under scrutiny.[128] In July 1934, Patton was asked for, and produced, a report on the purposes and activities of the Bureau. Though long and detailed there was nothing in it to change the attitudes of a government determined to sweep out wastage. In his innocence he even claimed the "Roxy" deal to the benefit of the Bureau![129] Two days after Patton's report, the deputy provincial treasurer pointed out to the premier that the Bureau competed with private industry and that commercial producers could make at less cost any films the province required.[130]

In October, the premier asked R. C. Buckley, chief inspector of theatres (later director of the Amusements Revenue Branch) for his recommendations on the future of the Bureau.[131] Three days later his report spelled out the Bureau's death. After describing the inadequacies of a film rental library based on the out-dated 28mm film, Buckley pointed out that the Bureau's equipment was antiquated, could produce only silent films, and would require an expenditure of thousands of dollars to make it more efficient. He laughed at Patton's attempts to produce sound films on "home made apparatus"; the large sums of money spent on these experiments had been a total waste and the money would have been better spent on purchasing professional equipment. The Bureau's equipment he valued at only $10,000 while the studios themselves were worth only the value of the land and buildings. He recommended that the Trenton studios be closed immediately and disposed of; all film production should cease. The Still Pictures Branch was to continue as was the Film Rental Branch which should however, wrote Buckley, move quickly into having more prints available on 16mm. (The library had 3,000 reels of 28mm film and only 171 reels of 16mm.) Under this reorganization twenty-six of the Bureau's thirty-eight full and part-time staff, including director George Patton, would have no jobs.[132]

Hepburn's government acted swiftly. On October 23 Patton was advised by the premier of the decision to cease film production and dissolve the Bureau. He was also advised that his services would "no longer be required."[133] Not a word of thanks for his work nor a word of regret at the decision.

When the order-in-council relating to reorganizing the Bureau was signed by the lieutenant-governor on October 26, 1934, the Ontario Motion Picture Bureau ceased to exist.[134] Few mourned its passing. Even the *Canadian Moving Picture Digest* was moved only to protest the Liberal government's apparent indifference to using films as a means of promoting the province.[135] But the argument was made only in a general way; there was not a word of support for the Bureau itself.

The land and buildings of the Trenton studios were donated to Trenton for a community hall.[136] Eventually they were adapted for commercial use. If it was a sad end for studios on which so much Canadian film activity had focused, the demise of the Bureau itself was regretted by few.

How To Take Care of the Means—And
Forget the Meaning

In Ottawa, the federal government's film Bureau was to suffer from some of the same problems. But when Ray Peck took over as director from Ben Norrish in 1920, the groundwork laid by Norrish held out considerable promise. Indeed, under Peck, the Bureau was to enjoy its most effective years, in its impact at least. And this despite the fact that he never developed further the style of the Bureau's films which Norrish had created in the first two years. Perhaps he felt it dangerous to change a successful formula established in the *Seeing Canada* series. Whatever the reasons, the Bureau's films through the mid-Twenties could increasingly be characterized as Sparling characterized those of the Ontario Bureau: "depending far too much on the ways and means generally used ten years ago." A film style which had been appealing and imaginative in 1920 would be far less so in 1930. But that was in the future. In 1920, the Bureau was just beginning to hit its stride and Peck seemed just the man to move it forward.

Raymond S. Peck was born in Ridgetown, Ontario, February 2, 1886. He began his career as a journalist, serving with newspapers in London, Windsor, and Detroit before becoming a salesman in the United States. He returned to Canada in 1917 as publicity manager for Universal Pictures. He also edited Universal's house journal, *Motion Picture Bulletin*, which eventually developed into the *Canadian Moving Picture Digest*, Canada's first film trade paper, with Peck as the first editor. In September 1918, he became Montreal branch manager for Mutual Films but left in 1919 to become "editor" at the Bureau in Ottawa.[137] As editor, he was responsible for developing scripts, writing titles, and directing the Bureau's cameramen on location. He was, in fact, the Bureau's first film director since he worked only on production and had no administrative functions as had Norrish.

When he became director of the Bureau in November 1920 (he had served as acting director since July), he had well developed ideas for the expansion of the work of the Bureau. Its films, he felt, were of good quality. They were, he said, "a commercial product and as such must be distributed on a marketable basis."[138] For the next two years, Peck devoted much time and effort to developing international theatrical and non-theatrical distribution. His experience in the commercial film industry (in contrast to that of any of the Ontario Bureau's directors) was to prove invaluable to the Canadian government. He had no interest in free distribution to theatres since he knew exhibitors would assume the films were not good enough to compete on the open market. All of his contracts were designed to produce revenue, either through a share of the rental with the distributor or through the outright sale of prints.

His efforts were highly successful. By 1923, theatrical distribution had been established through major distributors in Canada, Britain, the United States, France, Belgium, Switzerland, Australia, and New Zealand.[139] The Bureau's films were also being circulated in Japan, South America, China, Holland, South Africa, and Hawaii. Peck reported proudly that the *Seeing Canada* films "have been well viewed by the general public and most favourably commented upon for their artistry."[140]

Financial returns to the Bureau kept pace with the increasing level of distribution. In 1921–22, revenue was only $2,800. The following year it jumped to $16,000 and by 1924–25 it was in excess of $27,000—an amount more than double the Bureau's direct expenditures for that year.[141]

Perhaps Peck's most significant success was in the United States, by far the largest potential market but also the most difficult to penetrate. It took Peck nearly three years to develop an acceptable distribution program but the delay may have been worthwhile. In 1924 two Bureau films, *Unblazed Trails* and *Nipigon Trails*, had Broadway first-run showings and the distributor estimated that they would be seen throughout the United States by five to ten million people. Canadian government films eventually became an accepted part of the American theatrical circuit and by 1927 the Bureau had over one thousand prints circulating in the United States, far more than in any other country.

The increased activity produced strains on the Bureau's facilities and by 1922 the demand for films was outstripping the Bureau's capacity. There was some discussion about whether the Bureau should contract out its laboratory work to commercial companies, a discussion stimulated by a submission from Filmcraft Industries in March 1922. This raised yet again the old question of whether the government's film activities were depriving the commercial industry of work. "From time to time," wrote Peck, "it has been my experience to run against a strong current of opposition in connection with our film activities."[142] However, the experiences of the Ontario Bureau in commissioning their work were a telling argument. It seemed apparent that it was both less expensive and more efficient for the government to operate its own facilities. Deputy Minister O'Hara was also adamant that the department should retain full control and it was mainly due to his efforts that the Bureau was able to purchase new laboratory equipment.[143]

At this time, in 1922, the Bureau had a staff of six: Peck himself, Frank

Badgley who, since 1921, had held Peck's previous job as editor, three cameramen who also did laboratory work—W. S. Carter, B. J. Bach (soon to leave for the Ontario Bureau), and C. Ross—plus a title artist, E. S. Turnbull. Peck was having the same difficulties hiring and keeping good cameramen as had his predecessor and as later his successor, Frank Badgley, was to have. It was a constant source of irritation that was to help precipitate the decline of the Bureau. The Civil Service Commission, as in Ontario, was adamant in insisting on fitting film craftsmen into its existing job classifications and salaries. At one point, Peck suggested hiring temporary cameramen and an obviously exasperated Deputy Minister O'Hara agreed: "If necessary I will do anything I can to ignore the Commission and fight them afterwards." [144]

O'Hara, deputy minister of trade and commerce from 1908 to 1931, seems to have been a continuing source of strength. Committed as he was to the basic concept underlying the Bureau's activities, he fought many battles on its behalf, obtained additional funds for capital expenditures whenever necessary, helped defend it from occasional political attack, and was a constant booster of the Bureau's films. He was always ready to help when needed yet never interfered with the Bureau director's professional decisions. He never "suggested" topics for the Bureau to film, unlike his Ontario counterpart. The Ontario Bureau was not infrequently asked to film an event in which a political friend of the government had an interest. This never happened in Ottawa.

It was O'Hara who was responsible for having the "Exhibits" part of the Bureau removed. Though the reputation of the Bureau's film activities had increased with the years, the permanent trade exhibit housed in the same building had been neglected. As O'Hara remarked, "it is a disgrace to the department." [145] The trade exhibit was scrapped in 1922 and the Bureau became concerned solely with motion picture and photographic publicity. Peck suggested that the Bureau's name be changed to reflect its principal activities more closely and O'Hara agreed. [146] On April 1, 1923, its title was changed to the Canadian Government Motion Picture Bureau, a name it retained until absorbed by the National Film Board in 1941.

The Bureau's films of this period have a style, structure, and choice of subject matter that was to become characteristic. They are well-photographed, if a little static, and tend to concentrate on interesting scenery to the frequent exclusion of urban scenes and people. The editing is ponderous. Interspersed between shots are explanatory art titles, often cutely humorous, designed to increase audience interest. Even the titles of the films themselves often have something of the same quality: *Where the Moose Run Loose*, *Coining*

Money, *Where Snow-Time is Joy-Time*, *Canada's Cosy Corner*, *Fishing Gamely for Game Fish*, *The Apples of Annapolis*, *Winter Witchery*.

One should not make too much of this. In the early Twenties, the Bureau's style was typical of travelogue and interest films produced in Hollywood and elsewhere. Humorous art titles were expected, and enjoyed, by audiences. Often the Bureau's films were better in quality than similar Hollywood films. But the cinema moved on and the Bureau stayed behind. A style, approach, and titles that produced an enjoyable film in *Where the Moose Run Loose* in 1920 was to be hopelessly outdated by 1928 when the Bureau produced *Falling Waters*. Characteristic of the Bureau at its worst, this consists of a series of static shots of dozens of waterfalls across Canada interspersed with ponderously poetic titles.

The Bureau's output during the Twenties was concentrated on travelogues depicting Canada's scenic wonders. There were a few educational films produced for other government departments, such as *Marketing Canadian Hogs*. There was a handful on Canadian cities: *Ottawa, Edinburgh of the North*; *Victoria, City of Sunshine*; and *Canada's Queen City*, a travelogue on Toronto, unusual for its split-screen effect in one sequence.

There was even the occasional, unusual, scenic film, such as J. Booth Scott's *Down North* produced by him in 1920 and pictorializing a trip down the Mackenzie River as far north as Fort McPherson. But there were no films on industrial development. Badgley recognized the problem in 1927, soon after he became director. Expressing the hope that he could increase the quality of production, he noted "that the majority of the existing stock of films lack either pattern or human interest. So far they have been turned out chiefly with the object of encouraging tourists to visit the Dominion."[147]

The reason for the Bureau's inordinate emphasis on tourist films is not hard to find, given Peck's interest in theatrical distribution. He felt, it would seem, that Americans were not interested in "Seeing Canadians" building cars or making paper; they were interested in "Seeing Canada" as an endless fish and game reserve with stunning scenery coast to coast, peopled by friendly guides and interesting natives. His judgement seems to have been right. Such non-scenic films as the Bureau produced received limited or no theatrical distribution in the United States. It was also the scenic films which were most in demand by non-theatrical audiences in the United States, the Bureau's biggest market. The judgement may have been right but it was ultimately to prove a burdensome and self-defeating trap for the Bureau, a trap from which Badgley was not able to extricate it.

Peck's interest in the exploitability of Canadian scenery went beyond the production of films by the Bureau itself. He was an early exponent of the idea that foreign production companies should shoot dramatic features on location in Canada. It was through his encouragement that foreign production activity in Canada reached new peaks in the Twenties. Having witnessed the failure of so many stock promotion deals in the film industry in Canada, he might be excused for his view that a viable commercial feature film industry was impossible. It was, after all, the view held by many of his peers (including Ben Norrish at Associated Screen News) who had witnessed the failure of the major thrust to develop an industry in the immediate post-war years. It was more sensible, Peck argued, for Canada to encourage a more accurate depiction of its image by cooperating with Hollywood. This could result in much valuable indirect publicity for Canada in addition to bringing Hollywood dollars to Canada when producers filmed here. According to Peck, the average Hollywood company spent $30,000 to $40,000 while on location for a few weeks in Canada. He pointed proudly to the results of Fox's *The Country Beyond* which had been shot at Maligne Lake in the Canadian Rockies. The critics, he said, praised not the film's story but the scenic backgrounds and he quoted one critic as acclaiming "the most glorious scenes ever used to tell a film story."[148]

Peck believed that it was part of the Bureau's role to encourage such developments and to act as liaison between the government and the commercial film industry. In 1925, he announced (obviously with the approval of O'Hara) that "the Canadian government offers a warm welcome and all possible co-operation to legitimate American motion picture producers who care to take advantage of her great resources and beautiful scenic backgrounds."[149] The offer was more than goodwill. It carried tangible benefits since the government could, through one or another of its departments, offer technical assistance and guides, arrange for Indians and Mounties as extras, and set up lodging facilities.

Peck's offer found ready acceptance. It was during this period that such films as *The Alaskan*, *Calgary Stampede*, *The Knockout*, *The Country Beyond*, *The Winds of Chance*, and *The Canadian*, were shot in Canada. There were also such films as *The Last Frontier*, *The Covered Wagon*, and *Flaming Frontier* in which a Canadian setting played no part but for which Canada was a useful place to send a Second Unit to photograph buffalo herds in stampede.

Such fine cooperation between Canadian government officials and Hollywood producers was not to be found again until the Canadian Co-operation Project in the years following the Second World War.

Peck also argued at this time against the advisability of the British

Cameramen of the Canadian Government Motion Picture Bureau, circa 1925. Frank Badgley (right) and Ray Peck (left) are standing next to each other on the steps.

quota plan. Feeling that "any such restrictive legislation would not remedy matters," he suggested that "the only way to meet the American film was to create one which was just as good."[150]

His efforts on behalf of Hollywood were appreciated. In the spring of 1927 he was invited for a two-month stay in Hollywood to visit the major studios and confer "with prominent producers regarding producing possibilities in the Dominion to meet the proposed British quota law."[151] In other words, to find ways the Canadian government (represented by the Bureau) could assist Hollywood producers circumvent the intent of the British quota. It is not going too far to suggest that the Hollywood branch plants which sprang up in Canada in the Thirties were a direct result of that visit by Peck to Hollywood in 1927. There may even have been some sort of trade-off. Certainly, Peck returned from Hollywood with advantageous contracts for American distribution of Bureau productions which it was announced would make the studio "self-supporting during the coming year."[152]

With all these major activities, Peck had little time to devote to the ongoing production work of the Bureau. This had continued under Assistant Director Frank Badgley. Consequently, when Peck died suddenly of meningitis on May 27, 1927, the transfer of the Bureau's direction to Badgley was relatively easy.[153]

But Badgley's tenure as director was not to be at all easy. He did make efforts to increase the quality of the Bureau's films, broaden their appeal, and expand the kinds of subjects filmed. But he was ultimately to be thwarted by the Depression, lack of financial resources, and a government which no longer seemed in the least interested in the Bureau's activities. Unfortunately, Badgley was a technical man, not a political in-fighter. Finding it impossible to do things the way he wanted he finally allowed the Bureau to sink into oblivion much as Patton had done in the Ontario Bureau. This is regrettable since Badgley had qualities which could have given much to government film making if the times had been more propitious.

Frank C. Badgley was born in Ottawa in 1893 and educated at McGill University. A journalist when war was declared, he joined the Canadian Expeditionary Forces as a private, later gaining a commission as lieutenant and then as captain. He fought on the Western front until late 1916 when he was wounded and invalided home. He was awarded the Military Cross for bravery during the battle of Courcellette. After a year as instructor at the Royal Artillery School in Kingston he was posted to the British and Canadian joint recruiting office in New York where he was responsible for publicity. During this time he wrote short stories and newspaper articles that were published in Britain and Canada. In November 1918 he married June Elvidge, then a minor stage and screen actress. He, too, was involving himself increasingly in film work. He had already acted as military adviser on several war films and, with the end of the war, he went to work as an assistant director for Metro Pictures. By 1920, he had made his acting debut with a small role in D. W. Griffith's *Way Down East*, following this with several other, more major, roles including a prominent role in the Broadway play *Scrambled Wives*.[154] The American trade paper, *Moving Picture World* described him as an "excellent screen type, tall, slender, handsome with an inside knowledge of motion pictures, and a broad experience as a writer," while a colleague at the Bureau recalls him as "a handsome brute in uniform."[155]

Badgley returned to his hometown in the spring of 1921 to appear in Ernest Shipman's *The Man from Glengarry* and work with the Bureau.[156] His first production was *Where Salmon Leap*, photographed by Bert Bach, and described as "one of the finest fishing pictures ever produced." It must have been a strange shift for the twenty-eight year old Badgley from the lights of Broadway and the bustle of feature film production to the quiet of a six-man production unit in small-town Ottawa. He seems to have settled in happily enough and, certainly, the Bureau was delighted to get a man with his writing experience and technical ability. Peck was an organizer, administrator, and developer of policy. He was less capable of—and less interested in—the actual craft of film making. (Though the rumour that he knew nothing of the technical side of film is an obvious *canard*.) Badgley was exactly the opposite and the pair made a good team.

Badgley was to play an increasingly major role in the Bureau's work through the Twenties as Peck concentrated his efforts on the "policy of co-operating with commercial film producers, especially the large producers in the United States." When he became director he made it clear that there would be changes in the Bureau's films. It is also likely he felt Peck's "policy" in relation to Hollywood was not something in which the Bureau ought to be involved. Most of the Bureau's express activity in this direction ceased except for assistance to foreign newsreel companies.

Given his expressed concern in August 1927 that the principal aim of the Bureau's films had been only to encourage tourism, it is somewhat remarkable that one year later he toured the Pacific Coast and the western provinces to direct "the shooting of many thousands of feet of scenic film" for the *Seeing Canada* series.[157] Though these films were somewhat more lively than their predecessors, making greater use of film techniques such as slow motion and split screen, it was to be some years before the content of the Bureau's production shifted away from the traditional "scenics"—and even then, not significantly.

But then, Badgley had more important concerns on his mind than film content in the first years of his directorship. "Sound" films had hit the exhibition business and their popularity was rapidly forcing silent films out of the theatres. Badgley rightly pointed out in 1929 that, if the Bureau did not produce sound films, it would lose its theatrical markets.[158] His prediction proved correct. Lacking sound facilities, the Bureau rapidly lost its theatrical distribution and never regained it. When sound equipment was acquired in 1934, it was six years too late.

In addition to this, Badgley had to argue for the acquisition of new equipment.[159] Much of what existed was obsolete and had been in constant use for a decade. Further, 16mm film was rapidly gaining a major share of the non-theatrical market and, if the Bureau were to meet this new demand, it required 16mm laboratory facilities.[160]

Badgley succeeded in getting money for new equipment in 1928, and 16mm facilities were added in 1931. But additional staff and facilities to produce sound films were out of the question. For Badgley and the Bureau, the timing could not have been worse. The Depression had begun in 1929 and there was little hope that requests for further capital expenditures would be looked upon with any favour. Despite Badgley's desperate pleas for sound equipment and an improvement in salaries for senior staff such as Don Bartlett, Stanley Hollebone, and Ernie Wilson, the Bureau's expenditures remained the same in 1930–31 as in the previous year. Over the next two years they were successively cut and it was not until 1933–34 that the Bureau's budget was increased to $70,000 to provide for the purchase of sound equipment.[161] And, even at that, it was still lower than the Bureau's expenditures in the peak year of 1929–30.

Perhaps understandably, the Bureau produced little that was memorable in the 1928–33 period. As expenditures were cut so were staff salaries. The staff knew their films were technically outdated and destined for non-theatrical showings only. Inevitably, morale was extremely low.

In 1932, production of films was down, for the first time in the Bureau's history. In other hands, this might have been used as the impetus to break the Bureau out of its perennial preoccupation with tourist films. But Badgley, by 1932, seems to have lacked the drive to push for change, and the Bureau settled into a somewhat demoralized routine. Even its "prestige" production designed for the Imperial Economic Conference held in Ottawa, a seventy-minute feature titled, unimaginatively, *Canada, From Coast to Coast*, was only more of the same and seemed little more than seven *Seeing Canada* films strung together.[162] The Canadian Government Motion Picture Bureau, unlike its Ontario counterpart, may have survived the Depression

Film processing facilities of the Canadian Government Motion Picture Bureau.

and the introduction of sound but over a decade something of the reason behind the Bureau's existence had been lost. The Bureau still existed but its meaning and usefulness had been dissipated.

Badgley was also facing threats from other government departments which were circumventing the order-in-council of 1918 that attempted to ensure that all film activities were centralized in the Bureau. The Department of Agriculture had been specifically exempted in 1919[163] and during the Twenties other departments, including the National Museum, National Parks, the Department of the Interior, and the RCAF were to find loopholes.[164] Such departments, and others, excused themselves from the order-in-council when Badgley complained—as he frequently did—on the grounds that the films were not for general public release, were merely "record" films, or were too esoteric in subject matter for the Bureau to handle.

Most significant of these "exceptions" was the National Parks Bureau which was part of the Departments of the Interior and of Mines and Resources at various times. The interest of National Parks in motion pictures had begun in 1922 with the appointment of J. C. Campbell as director of publicity. Campbell was an energetic man with an instinctive feeling for the value of visual material in publicity work.[165] Though his initial activities were mainly in the use of slides on lecture tours through the United States and Canada, he had already had a dispute in 1922 with Peck about his involvement in motion pictures.[166] Peck and Campbell were not at all compatible and from their first meeting their contacts were unfriendly. Campbell argued that the Bureau was incapable of producing the kinds of films he wanted to promote the National Parks and its conservation work. Peck, and later Badgley, considered the films Campbell wanted beneath their dignity.

None of this might have been at all relevant, nor the films produced of any greater importance than those produced by the Department of Agriculture, if it had not been for the fact that National Parks had the good fortune to have most of its films made by Bill Oliver, a freelance Calgary photographer. Bill Oliver was unquestionably one of the best film makers of the period. The films he made for National Parks have a quality in their visual style and structure that gives many of them an interest even today— when most of the Bureau's films of the same period have faded into a deserved obscurity. They have a superior photographic quality (some of his mountain-top panorama shots would be difficult to match even today) but his films also have a unity, warmth, and human interest that contrasts favourably with the Bureau's static, impersonal, products.

William J. Oliver was born in England, July 28, 1887.[167] He immigrated to Canada in 1910, settling in Alberta because of an interest in cattle. He had difficulty getting work and after various odd jobs he became a photographer, working for the *Calgary Herald* and selling wild life and scenic photographs to the National Parks Bureau. He purchased his first film camera in 1917 and established himself in free-lance work, supplying news footage to the *Fox Canadian Newsreel* and shooting films for the CPR and CNR.

In 1924 the Thomas Ince Company visited Wainwright to shoot buffalo scenes for the feature *The Last Frontier*. Oliver was hired as an assistant cameraman. When the director wanted photographs of stampeding buffalo shot from a pit while the buffalo thundered overhead, the cameramen refused to do the scene. Oliver agreed and produced such spectacular shots that Ince offered him a Hollywood contract. But Oliver did not want to leave Calgary. Some years later those same scenes were used by Oliver in a National Parks film, *Home of the Buffalo* (1930). Its qualities are so striking that, twenty-five years after it was made, it won an award at a Film Festival in West Germany.

Oliver's films for National Parks were personal creations. He wrote and designed them, in consultation with J. C. Campbell and other Parks officials. He photographed them himself, often with the help of his long-time assistant, Bud Cotton. Later, in Ottawa, he edited them himself. His name does not appear on any of his films (he was a modest man) but they were Oliver creations from first to last.

Oliver would take considerable risks: film from a canoe when he could not swim, climb mountains carrying heavy equipment with experienced mountain climbers (*She Climbs to Conquer*), crouch behind a flimsy blind to get close-up shots of a grizzly bear (*Hunting Without a Gun*). His mountaineering and skiing films tell the story of the protagonists in a direct way: making a film about the climbing of a difficult peak, he would go up the peak with the climbers. There is a kind of direct involvement in his work which comes through on the screen. They are adventure films in the best sense of the term.

As for his wildlife films, a friend described his work as requiring "the efforts of the big game hunter, the endurance of the explorer, the courage of the RCMP, the patience of Job and the kindness to animals of St. Francis of Assisi." "Oliver cared wholeheartedly for his work," the friend wrote. "He developed a poetical treatment for each shot. He visualized not so much black-and-grey against a white background, but a thing of loving beauty which had to be presented in an artistic manner. His pictures are so sincere that they cause audiences to voice understanding and sympathy for the images at which they look."[168] Oliver's productions were widely seen and

Bill Oliver (standing at camera) photographing one of his mountaineering films. With him are Rudolph Ammer and a guide.

admired—not only for their qualities as films but for their championing of wild-life and nature conservation. (The National Parks Bureau was many years ahead of fashion in this.)

His best-known films were those he made between 1928 and 1935 featuring Grey Owl: *Beaver Family*, *Beaver People*, *Strange Doings in Beaverland*, *Pilgrims of the Wild*, and *Grey Owl's Neighbours*. Several of these were adapted into sound versions under Gordon Sparling's direction by Associated Screen News: *Grey Owl's Strange Guests* and *Grey Owl's Little Brother*, which were released world-wide in theatres as part of the *Canadian Cameo* series. They did much to foster the public image of Grey Owl (now known to have been the Englishman, Archie Belaney). But the contrast between Oliver's and Sparling's films is telling. Sparling's films have an anthropomorphic quality of the kind best known in Walt Disney's nature films. They have "cute" commentaries and belong in style very much to their period. Oliver's films respect the material with which he was dealing. They reflect Oliver's own concerns with the importance of conserving the wilderness and suggest the deep empathy he felt for what Grey Owl was trying to do. In fact, Oliver's work greatly impressed Grey Owl, so much so that he was to produce two films of his own just before his death. *The Trail—Men Against the Snow* and *The Trail—Men Against the River* were both photographed by Bert Bach but in Grey Owl's direction there is a reflection of Oliver's approach.

On another film, *Sea Lions of the Pacific*, he set about to accomplish what many told him was impossible. The seals of the Pacific coast islands had never been filmed and he was advised that it was impossible to land people on the rocks. Not at all daunted, Oliver had a boat specially adapted with steel-reinforced sides and a heavily padded landing platform and secured the most spectacular shots of the islands ever made. Even today that filming has never been repeated.

Oliver's films may have been popular with audiences but Badgley and the Bureau staff disapproved of them. They found them "unprofessional" and not up to Bureau standards. When complaints began to arrive from London about the quality of the Bureau's films, Badgley rejoined that there were other Canadian government films (particularly those of National Parks) in circulation. He noted that people thought all of them were Bureau films but that it was these other films, not the Bureau's, which were responsible for the poor reputation of Canadian government films abroad.

Badgley was wrong: the Bureau's films were precisely the problem. Despite Badgley's hopes for changing both the content and quality of production, the kinds of films produced remained depressingly similar. The Bureau's *Annual Report* for 1935 stated that "particular attention was given to films illustrating the basic industries and products of Canada, as also those designed to advertise Canada's tourist attractions and promote tourist travel."[169] The basic industries to which "particular attention" was given consisted almost solely of films on timber production. The Bureau seemed never to tire of such films: *Conquest of the Forest* (1928), *The Drive is On* (1931), *Big Timber* (1935), and *The Story of Canadian Pine* (1937) are only a few of their efforts to depict lumbering in Canada. Though other resource industries, particularly mining, were shown, they received nothing like this extensive coverage.

And the style of the films, even after the Bureau was able to make sound films, changed little. There was still a tendency to concentrate on the inanimate and impersonal. Where once there had been pseudo-poetic titles on the silent films, now there were circumlocutory commentaries bombarding the viewer with inappropriate metaphor. Perhaps the most unforgettable of these is in *Big Timber* in which the movement of logs is described as being "like a boa-constrictor bounding through the forest." Apart from the hyperbole, this suggests the Bureau's writers had a limited knowledge of biology.

This was hardly the departure from Peck's methods that Badgley had argued for in 1927. In fact, it was business as before—but now with less impact than in Peck's day. One can hardly cavil at the opinion of Canadian government films given to John Grierson by a friend: "If life in the Dominions is as these films represent, we might expect Canadians to engage only in fishing, golf, and the observation of wild animals. There are practically no industries, very little work, and no working people."[170] Viewing the films in retrospect, one can only wonder at the self-image the Bureau was offering Canadians. For the Bureau, at least, Canada was a vast playground for tourists full of rich, natural resources ready for exploitation; the Depression, apparently, never happened.

By 1934, the Bureau had been given the money for sound equipment, had moved into new studios on John Street, and now tried to make up for lost time. Perhaps its most notable effort was *Lest We Forget*, a ten-reel film history of Canada's role in the First World War compiled in 1935 from actuality newsreels, graphics, and re-enacted scenes. It was a striking departure from the Bureau's characteristic approach, being both well-paced and engaging, and received an enthusiastic reception in Canada and abroad.[171]

(It was not the Bureau's first feature-length production. In 1928 it had released *In the Shadow of the Pole*, a six-reel record of the Canadian Arctic Expedition of 1928.)[172]

However, *Lest We Forget* had no successors, though two later productions broke out of the tourist and trade promotion mould. Both were actuality record films, though longer than usual. *Salute to Valour*, made in 1937, depicted the dedication of the Canadian National Memorial at Vimy Ridge in France;[173] *The Royal Visit*, though undoubtedly important as historical record, is vapid and quickly becomes a dull repetition of cheering crowds, officials, and regal speeches as King George and Queen Elizabeth travel across Canada.[174]

Only one other film of the period stands out: J. Booth Scott's *Heritage*, a moving tribute to prairie settlement and the effects of the drought in western Canada. It is the only Bureau film that bears any real relation to contemporary social conditions in Canada—and it was completed only under Grierson's leadership.

But, by November 1937, the end was in sight for the Bureau. There had already been some rumblings from within the Department of Trade and Commerce itself about the disorganized distribution of Canadian films abroad,[175] when Vincent Massey, Canadian high commissioner in London, submitted a report on the paucity and quality of films on Canada then available in Britain.[176] The report, written by Massey's private secretary, Ross McLean, suggested that a survey be made of Canadian film publicity activities. McLean's proposal started a chain of events that eventually brought John Grierson to Canada, led to the creation of the National Film Board, and the eventual demise of the Canadian Government Motion Picture Bureau in 1941.[177]

The decision was long overdue. The Bureau had, quite simply, ceased to be an effective film unit. It had lost touch with both social reality and film itself. The Bureau had once provided an effective international screen for Canada and Canadians, but by the Thirties its films had become largely irrelevant. Though Badgley had had to cope with the sound problem during a period of economic crisis, this, in itself, does not explain the uninspired quality of the Bureau's films in the late Twenties and Thirties. A different director might have handled the situation with more drive and imagination. As it is, Badgley allowed the Bureau to drift into ineffectiveness as did Patton with the Ontario Bureau. Both increasingly behaved as defeated men. And the end for both Bureaus, though brutal for those involved, can only be endorsed.

CHAPTER 6

The Years of the Quota

"You in Canada should not be dependent on either the United States or Great Britain. You should have your own films and exchange them with those of other countries. You can make them just as well in Toronto as in New York."[1] These words of American director D. W. Griffith in Toronto in 1925 might have offered timely encouragement for rescuing Canada's film industry from the desert to which it had been consigned. The optimistic expansion that had marked film production during the war and the ensuing years had long evaporated by 1925. In the face of Hollywood's determined and successful attempts to bring the benefits of the American way to the film industries of the world, the nascent Canadian film industry had crumpled quietly. At the time Griffith spoke in Toronto, most of the distribution companies in Canada were American controlled; so were first-run theatres in all major cities. Film production, outside of government, had virtually ceased. The several independent Canadian newsreels had disappeared under a torrent of cheaper—for the theatres—American newsreels. Feature production had come to a complete halt. There were still a few private companies, such as Associated Screen News and Pathescope, producing short films, but their work was hardly evident to the Canadian public in general. What the Canadian public was aware of were Hollywood films shot in, and about, Canada: films such as *The Canadian*, *The Knockout*, and *The Country Beyond*, shot on location in Canada with the active support and encouragement of the Canadian government. D. W. Griffith must have been aware of the bleakness of the Canadian film scene. It is ironic that his speech in Canada should have coincided with statements by the Canadian government's official film spokesman, Ray Peck, that argued exactly the opposite.[2]

During that earlier period of optimistic expansion, the Canadian film producer had had two principal problems: raising sufficient capital to sustain production through more than one film (and hence allow time for money to be returned on the first) and access to experienced, creative talent. They were critical problems but, once the producer had completed a film of reasonable quality, he could at least ensure its release to theatres. By the mid-Twenties that had changed and the independent producer—American as well as Canadian—found it well-nigh impossible to get his film shown.

The seeds of this situation were planted in the United States in the immediate post-war years. The continued economic growth of Hollywood during the war while the film industries of many European countries suffered, together with the size of the American domestic market, gave Hollywood incomparable advantages internationally. Enormous fortunes could be made in the film industry and many struggled to control the means of winning them. The independent, entrepreneurial, producer (and distributor and exhibitor) was buried in the process, as Adolph Zukor or William Fox, or Marcus Loew bought up, bought out, or destroyed what they did not control. Adolph Zukor was far from the only one involved in this bid to annihilate competition, but he was perhaps the most successful—and, certainly, through his control of Famous Players Canadian Corporation, of somewhat more moment for the Canadian film industry. Zukor's strategy was simple. With the aid of a massive loan from the Morgan Bank he embarked on a process of acquiring theatres in cities across North America. Since he controlled a production company and a distribution company, films made by Zukor production companies would be released by Zukor distributors to Zukor theatres. This vertical nexus of producer-distributor-exhibitor created a model on which the international success of Hollywood was based.[3] In Canada, Famous Players Canadian Corporation under its managing director N. L. Nathanson had acquired the Allen theatre chain in 1923, then through the Twenties it had embarked on a major program of theatre acquisition and building. By the late Twenties, it controlled first-run theatres in all major cities. This may not have been, in itself, a problem but, directly or through subsidiaries, the company also controlled the supply of films to theatres, owning the franchise to films from Paramount, MGM, Pathé, and British International. "Block booking" and other protective techniques made it difficult for the independent theatre owner to get the films he wanted at a price he could afford. Many were forced to sell. It became practically impossible for an independent producer to get his film into a downtown theatre for a first-run. The stifling control by Famous Players Canadian Corporation of the film industry in Canada was to lead, in 1930, to an investigation under the Combines Investigation Act. Despite the mass of evidence and the persuasive conclusion by Commissioner Peter White in 1931 that Famous Players

Canadian Corporation's operations were detrimental to the public interest, no remedial action resulted.[4]

The problems for a Canadian producer in the late Twenties and Thirties were virtually insurmountable. Not only were there still the original problems of a decade earlier, there was the difficulty of raising financing during the Depression. These, combined with the impossibility of release to Canadian theatres if a film was made, led to a virtual cessation of meaningful feature film production.

Canada's film industry was not alone in falling under Hollywood domination during the Twenties. Canada, being geographically and economically closest to the United States, suffered perhaps more quickly than European countries but by no means less intensely. But the European countries differed from Canada in that most of them moved quickly to protect their domestic film industries. There were various devices to do this but by far the most controversial, even today, was the British legislation which obligated British theatres to show a fixed percentage of British films each year: the so-called "quota" system.[5]

Prior to the war, the British film industry had enjoyed considerable economic and artistic success both at home and abroad. But during the Twenties, Hollywood production gained an ever-tightening stranglehold on the British domestic industry. By 1926, only five percent of the films exhibited in Britain were of British origin.[6] This was a serious situation, both economically and culturally for the British. A memorandum prepared for the Imperial Conference in 1926 pointed out:

> It is clearly undesirable that so very large a proportion of the films
> shown throughout the Empire should present modes of life and
> forms of conduct which are not typically British and, so far as
> setting is concerned, tend to leave on the mind of untutored
> spectators the impression that there are no British settings whether
> scenic or social which are worth presentation.[7]

There may be echoes of another age in this somewhat jingoistic argument but the concern was real. And the British were determined to protect their film industry. There had been talk through the early Twenties of establishing a quota system to favour domestic production and by the time of the Imperial Conference in London in 1926 the British had settled on this approach.

The Canadian delegation to the conference, led by Prime Minister Mackenzie King, took some pains to argue that the definition of "British"

Canadian Moving Picture
DIGEST

Established in 1915 for
Exhibitors
Subscription: $5.00 yearly
Telephone: Trinity 1481
Cable: Ontocanada

RAY LEWIS
Editor and Managing Director

Published by Canadian
Moving Picture Digest
Company, Limited

259 Spadina Ave. - Toronto

Vol. 22, No. 3   TORONTO 2, CANADA   May 17th, 1930

"At Your Risk!"

Indicative of the debate over Famous Players Canadian Corporation in 1930
was this front page cartoon in the *Canadian Moving Picture Digest*.

within any quota system should be expanded to include any film produced within the Empire. Other delegations agreed that this approach was a useful one; it could offer protection to their own domestic industries while opening up the potentially lucrative market in Britain. A resolution was passed which noted the need for an increased showing of Empire films within the Empire and recommended "the remedial measures proposed to the consideration of the governments of the various parts of the Empire with a view to such early and effective action to deal with the serious situation now existing as they may severally find possible."[8]

The federal government in Canada took no action whatsoever. Given King's arguments in London, this is surprising. In fact, the only reactions out of Ottawa were several statements by Ray Peck, director of the Canadian Government Motion Picture Bureau. As pointed out above, he declared himself, forcefully and on several occasions, as being opposed to any British quota, arguing that if the British made good films there would be no need of one. "To put a quota law against the United States in Great Britain," he argued, "would tend to place a bonus on inefficiency."[9] This somewhat naive view overlooks the fact that the cinema is very much an industry and is subject to the same economic stresses as occur in other industries. Economically, it made good sense for Hollywood to buy up distribution and exhibition interests in a foreign country and then ensure that its own productions were exhibited. This may not, necessarily, have anything whatsoever to do with the quality of that country's production. Peck's argument is a little like suggesting that, if only Canadians could make good automobiles, McLaughlin's Oshawa company would not have been taken over by General Motors. In any event, neither the federal nor any of the provincial governments (which have jurisdiction over film exhibition in Canada) took any action to protect Canadian film interests at that time. The Australian government, in contrast, took almost immediate action.[10]

What seems most puzzling about the official inaction is that it took place in an atmosphere conducive to action. Many were disturbed, as they had been nearly a decade earlier, over the predominant influence of Hollywood movies in Canada. And, more than that, it was distressing to see the image of Canada which Hollywood perpetuated. Canadian teachers in 1928 were incensed when shown an American educational film which depicted Canada as a land of snowdrifts with the "forest primeval" still predominant. Its people were either trappers, lumberjacks, or wheat farmers while the RCMP "often rescue trappers lost in the wilds." When told, however, that "Newfoundland, like Canada, has recently been given self-government" the teachers could do little more than collapse with laughter.[11]

Distortions of Canadian life and history in Hollywood films were plentiful, so plentiful that contemporary Canadian critics despaired of having to reiterate the same points. Typical of many others was the James Oliver Curwood story, *Flaming Forest*, supposedly depicting the Riel Rebellion on the prairies but set mostly in a forest and entirely produced in California. Not infrequently, Hollywood even ignored Canadian political sensibilities. As Ontario Provincial Treasurer Price noted in 1924, he had seen many films set in the Canadian North "in which a cabin was shown flying a flag that was not Canadian."[12] Not surprisingly, many writers—and even government officials—voiced the opinion that Canada was "cynically treated as a mere convenience" by Hollywood. Canada was useful "as a market for Hollywood films" or as a source of stories or locales.[13] In the late Twenties several writers urged the establishment of a Canadian feature film industry "by Government assistance to whatever degree is necessary."[14] Though there seemed some sympathy for this approach at one time—the Ontario government was particularly encouraging[15]—no specific action was taken. It was, however, against this background that Canadian International Films received such enthusiastic financial support for the production of *Carry On, Sergeant*.

But, on the other side of the Atlantic, the British quickly took "remedial action" following the Imperial Conference in 1926. The Cinematograph Films Act, passed in December 1927, required that seven and a half percent of all films rented for exhibition in British theatres be of British origin. From October 1928, five percent of all films shown in theatres were to be British and these percentages were to increase gradually each year up to twenty percent. For the purposes of the act, all films produced in the Empire qualified, provided that at least seventy-five percent of the salaries were paid to British subjects. The long-term aim was "to establish an industry under British control . . . for the production of these films."

Ray Peck's opposition to the British quota plan had been in vain. But, as discussed earlier, Peck had very definite ideas about the role of the Motion Picture Bureau in encouraging Hollywood producers to film in Canada. He often expressed admiration for Hollywood films and, in contrast, considered British films technically and dramatically shoddy. And he was pessimistic about the possibilities of developing a viable Canadian feature film industry. Given his attitudes, it seems almost inevitable that he should encourage the notion of Canadian film production as a "branch plant" of Hollywood. Even as early as 1925, he was proposing the establishment of American production facilities in Canada to make films that would "secure a British classification for them."[16] And then there was his two-month visit to Hollywood in the spring of 1927. The principal purpose of this was to encourage Hollywood producers to establish subsidiaries in Canada and thereby (with the collaboration of the Canadian government) circumvent the clear intent of the British quota to encourage more British and Commonwealth production.[17]

Peck's views were expressed most plainly in a letter to Captain H. V. S. Page who was interested in the production and distribution of British and Canadian films. He had pointed out to Peck the dangers of encouraging Hollywood producers to work in Canada. Peck replied that while he favoured more British films, he felt this was a question of quality; if the films were better there would be no need for a quota. He did not agree with Page on the question of American producers in Canada. On the contrary, he felt we "have a great deal to learn from American producers." He continued: "We are attempting at all times, as Canadians, to induce American capital and manufacturing interests to come into Canada and establish branch factories. I look on the American film industry much as a branch factory idea in so far as it affects Canada. American motion picture producers should be encouraged to establish production branches in Canada and make films designed especially for British Empire consumption. I do not entirely agree with the thought expressed in your letter that the experiment of allowing American producers to get a footing in Canada would be a dangerous one. We invite Americans to come over to Canada to make automobiles and a thousand and one other things, and why not invite them to come over and make pictures, but make them the way the British markets demand?"[18]

Though Peck was not to live to see it, his vision of a "branch-plant" feature film industry in Canada became a reality. Peck had correctly reasoned that Hollywood producers would need to be sure that there were enough British or Empire films available in Britain in order to get their own films shown. An easy way of doing this was to finance the establishment of a registered Canadian film company, import enough British-born Hollywood actors and technicians to satisfy the quota, produce a feature film as cheaply and quickly as possible, and ship it off to London for showing. Often, the films were not taken seriously by the recipient theatres: they were simply a device for satisfying the letter of the quota law. It was reported for example that American owned theatres ran the Canadian "quota quickies" in the early morning while the theatres were empty of anyone except the cleaning staff.[19]

Many "quota quickies" were of course, produced in Britain itself. Few were of good quality but they were mostly produced by British companies and at least provided economic support for the industry and those who worked in it.[20] The same was true in Australia. Only Canada allowed itself to be exploited without protest by Hollywood for the production of quota quickies. And Canada reaped small benefit—except the injection of a little money into the cities where production was based.

Peck's "branch plant" film industry came to full fruition in the decade between 1928 and 1938. During those years, twenty-two feature films were produced solely for the British market—almost the entire Canadian feature film output. When the British changed their quota law in 1938 and excluded Dominion productions (mainly because of the way Canada had allowed Hollywood to circumvent the intent of the original law), the Canadian companies involved closed their doors and disappeared. The Canadian feature film industry collapsed.

None of the quota films produced during that decade can be considered Canadian in any cultural sense. As a classic example of a branch plant economy and Canadian short-sightedness, the production of quota quickies is sadly typical. There are all the traditional arguments Peck used to favour the development: Hollywood has the technical know-how and the capital and it provides jobs for local workers. But what Peck did not see was that in terms of developing a domestic, continuing, industry the effort counted for nothing. Once the reason for the Americans having branch plant production no longer existed, they removed themselves, their capital, and their technical know-how. And Canada was left with nothing.

North of 49

The British Quota Act was to stimulate a number of film production schemes in Canada, many of which never got off the ground. Some of these were nothing more than stock promotions attempting to defraud the public; others were sincere and well-intentioned but simply came to nothing.[21]

The first Canadian company established specifically to produce quota films is characteristic of many later ones—perhaps less so in the extent of local financing involved, than in the kind of production and the manner of its release. Calgary had been the site of Shipman's triumph in 1919 with *Back to God's Country*. Calgarians may well have remembered the profits from that venture when they provided financing and production money for British Canadian Pictures Ltd.[22]

The venture began on the initiative of Guy Weadick, founder and manager of the Calgary Stampede and a man of drive, enthusiasm, and great persuasive powers.[23] In February 1928 he invited to Calgary William Steiner, an independent New York distributor, and Neal Hart, a Western star then all of forty-nine and past his prime. Hart had been producing and directing independently for some time under contract to William Steiner and he and Steiner had visited Calgary the previous summer to shoot footage of the Stampede. It was this visit and the discussions in February that led to the incorporation of British Canadian Pictures in March 1928. A. E. Cross (a director of Shipman's 1919 company) was president and Guy Weadick general manager. It was agreed that the first film would be a "Western" action film, directed by and starring Neal Hart, from a script by Daniel E. C. Campbell, city editor of the *Calgary Herald*. The cast, apart from Neal Hart, were to be entirely Canadian or British. Chosen as heroine was Barbara Kent, a Hollywood starlet born in Alberta.[24] In supporting roles were Mary Cross (a "well-known Calgary society girl" and daughter of president A. E. Cross), Frank Newton of Calgary, Charles Wellesley, and Joseph Quinn (both Hollywood actors but born in London, England and Toronto respectively). Cameraman was Alvin Wyckoff, a highly creative cinematographer, famous for his work on Cecil B. DeMille's films but out of favour in Hollywood after his establishment of a union for cameramen.

Campbell's script was written deliberately to take advantage of local action and scenery, often to the detriment of the plot. Even the *Calgary Herald*'s critic noted later that "the producers have sacrificed continuity of story theme in the interests of action, with the result that the audience at times may find difficulty in holding the story connection."[25] On the other hand, the plot was the rather common one of a hero falsely accused of cattle rustling, who escapes from prison, meets and falls in love with an adventure loving girl, and eventually clears his name. However, Weadick, Campbell, and Hart wanted to emphasize the action and the scenery rather than the plot as the British magazine *The Bioscope* noted in its review. Pointing to the "selling angles" being "an escape from prison, a stampede of horses, and the annual Calgary sports [stampede]," it added, "the bucking horses, wild cow milking, and steer decorating contests are certain to make a strong appeal . . . [as are] the interesting glimpses of the ranch owned by the Prince of Wales." It concluded: "There are so many glimpses of impressive Canadian scenery that the picture might almost be termed a travelogue."[26]

During the months of production from May to August 1928, Guy Weadick took pains to ensure that *His Destiny* presented "a faithful reproduction of ranch and cowboy life on the Western Canadian plains for the benefit of the people of the British Empire."[27] There was even a prologue to the film depicting pioneering life, the arrival of the first white settlers and the North West Mounted Police, and the growth of ranching. This was done so that the film's audiences could see "that Western Canada is no longer a wild and lawless land. . . . the events of the past lead through to the present showing Calgary as a modern city with tall and costly buildings and all the conveniences of present-day life."[28]

His Destiny was premièred at the Palace Theatre in Calgary on December 10, 1928, and was well received. One local film critic found it "a more truthful picture of the west, as its residents know it, than we have ever had before in a movie . . . [it] will serve as a wonderful advertisement throughout the Empire for the Province."[29] Guy Weadick's aims had been met and the principals of the company had high hopes for the future. There were tentative, but optimistic, discussions on the next production to be started as soon as some financial return was received from the film's distribution. But there was to be no second film and the fate of *His Destiny* was not to be much different from that of *Carry On, Sergeant* released a few months earlier.

From the subsequent history of the film, it appears that British Canadian Pictures was well and truly swindled by William Steiner, the New York distributor.[30] Though Steiner had been involved throughout the production, had approved the script, and had claimed the film would be a "box-office winner" when he first screened it, his subsequent actions reflect an apparent difficulty in marketing it. Steiner did nothing to promote the film in advance of offering it for sale, contrary to standard procedure in the film industry, and consequently had to sell it "cold" without any prior build-up.[31] He sold British rights to Paramount for $25,000 advance and, at that time, predicted British grosses in excess of $125,000. From the advance paid by Paramount, Steiner deducted $5,000 expenses, his own sales commission of thirty percent, and $3,000 he claimed was necessary to bribe British officials in order to get the film accepted as a British quota film. On the strength of the film's clear "British" content this would seem to have been totally unnecessary.[32] When the film failed to gross as much as he predicted, Steiner began to offer excuses for its failure: that the film was badly edited, that Westerns were no longer popular and, later, that sound films were driving silent films off the market. The film may, indeed, be criticized as being badly edited (it is somewhat disjointed in continuity) but the other two arguments are nonsense. Westerns were still popular and silent films were still very much in demand. The same argument had been used in relation to *Carry On, Sergeant* but the fact is that, in 1928–29, the number of theatres in North America and Europe equipped for sound films was still a minority.[33] However, financial returns were so small that British Canadian Pictures finally accepted Steiner's arguments and invested another $15,000 to prepare a synchronized dialogue version. This was released in late 1929 under the title *North of 49*.[34] It, too, did not do as well as Steiner predicted.

The company folded and the only person for whom it was profitable was William Steiner.

Another American producer, Sam Bischoff, was quick to take advantage of the possibilities of exploiting Canada as a base for the British quota market. His first effort in November 1928 to release a film in Britain as a Canadian production was blocked. The British excluded it from the quota after it was discovered that the only performer of British extraction in it was a dog.[35] The film was *Code of the Air* (1928), an adventure story of robbery from a fleet of commercial planes. It was not a Canadian story and was not apparently shot in Canada. For his second effort, Bischoff was somewhat more circumspect. The production of *The Wilderness Patrol* (1929) was backed by a British company, British International Films, produced by an Australian (J. P. McGowan), based on a novel about Mounties by Harold Blindloss, and with several British born Hollywood actors in the cast— though Hollywood Western star Bill Cody played the lead. The film was shot in North Vancouver with the cooperation of the RCMP, released quietly, and quickly buried.[36]

There were other companies that appeared and disappeared quickly in the early years of the quota. In Toronto, the Exclusive Canadian Film Company produced *Destiny* (1927).[37] George T. Booth's Ontario Film Company produced *The White Road* (1929), a six-reel feature with synchronised sound about how a Canadian girl saves a Chinese boy's life in China and how, years later, he repays her. The players were from the Hart House Theatre and the production cost only $3,120.[38] George Booth, a magazine and scenario writer, incorporated Booth Canadian Films in July 1929, announced in 1931 that his company would begin producing shorts, and completed *The Bells* in 1932. Though other plans were announced—including *Under the Circumstances* by John French—the company ceased production of dramatic films.[39]

One of the most curious companies of the period was based in Fort William, Ontario. Thunder Bay Films was incorporated in April 1927 to produce "Canadian stories from Canadian themes with purely Canadian atmosphere and background."[40] The company owned the rights to six stories, the first of which to be filmed was *The Spirit of the Wilderness* with a script by Sargeson V. Halstead, directed by Louis W. Chaudet, with leads played by Peggy Olcott, Dorothy Dwan as "Fernleaf of the Wildwood," Mitchell Lewis, Carroll Nye, and Bobby Mack, all minor Hollywood actors.[41] (It seems to have been Canada's fate during this period to acquire the services of Hollywood rejects: the aging, the unknown, and the minor.) Sargeson

Halstead was born in eastern Ontario and had previously been a mining engineer in the North. All six of his stories were based on "personal experience."

In October 1927, the company left for Hollywood "to complete the film" and in November Sargeson Halstead announced that the film was finished.[42] "The story material is Canadian and essentially British in its epical value although many of the players and technical staff were recruited in Hollywood."[43] A rough-cut of the Canadian scenes was apparently seen in Port Arthur-Fort William but then the story becomes confused.[44] In February 1928 it was reported that the "first film" was being finished (still) in Hollywood,[45] in September 1928 that interiors for *The Spirit of the Wilderness* were being shot in Hollywood,[46] and in October 1928 that "Thunder Bay Films is bringing to completion its own first offering *The Spirit of the Wilderness*, a Canadian and English epic."[47] Thereafter, all references to *The Spirit of the Wilderness* cease but in January 1929 a film called *The Devil Bear* was previewed in Buffalo, produced by Thunder Bay Films, directed by Louis Chaudet from a script by Sargeson V. Halstead. It seems likely they are the same film, retitled.

The Devil Bear is an adventure thriller about a ship's captain with a tame gorilla as a pet. During a mutiny the captain is injured by a blow on the head which makes him insane but the gorilla (called by Indians "The Devil Bear") rescues him and hides him in a cave. The plot becomes more complicated as "The Devil Bear" foils some villains and rescues a missionary's daughter who turns out to be in love with an engineer whose partner is trying to cheat him out of their mine. "The Devil Bear" helps sort out their problems too and, when another blow on the head restores the captain to his right mind, all ends happily. If this was one of Sargeson Halstead's "personal experiences," he must certainly have had an interesting life.

Ray Lewis compared *The Devil Bear* favourably to *Carry On, Sergeant* which had also just been released: "It is the best picture from a standpoint of being professional which has yet been produced in Canada. . . . it has a good story, a fine cast of players, it shows that pictures can be made in Canada which will be entertainment without the necessity of spending half-a-million dollars on them or even one-half of that sum."[48] *The Devil Bear* was released by Gaumont British Films but without creating much impact. Thunder Bay Films ceased production. Apparently well-intentioned, the company nonetheless ended in a financial loss to the local investors.

Fort William-Port Arthur was also the site of two feature films produced by amateurs. *A Race for Ties* (1929) and *The Fatal Flower* (1930) were both produced on 16mm by the Amateur Cinema Society of Thunder Bay.[49]

Dorothea Mitchell wrote the script for *A Race for Ties*, a drama of competition between a local, small lumbering concern and a large lumbering company. It is a surprisingly adept effort for amateurs who had never made a film before, well written and photographed, even though the acting is often too obviously by amateurs. It was successfully shown in local theatres but not released elsewhere. Titling on *The Fatal Flower* was never completed and it was not shown publicly.

The only other comparable efforts by non-professionals are a feature-length documentary, *Gold Is Where You Find It*, produced in 1937 in Flin-Flon by Carl Ango (who also made several other similar documentaries in the same period) and *Talbot of Canada*, produced and directed in 1938 by Melburn Turner with members of the London Little Theatre. Based on a play by Hilda Smith, *Here Will I Nest*, about Thomas Talbot, founder of the Talbot Settlements, it is most notable as the first Canadian dramatic feature produced in colour.

Western Canada was by far the most popular locale for quota companies, with Vancouver and Victoria favourite locations for possible studios because of their climate and closeness to Hollywood. Toronto and Montreal were not neglected however and had the distinction of being the location of perhaps the three worst quota films to be produced in Canada.

In 1935, Booth Dominion Productions was incorporated, headed by Ottawa J. R. Booth—no relation to George T. Booth but formerly involved with Ernest Shipman on the production of *The Man from Glengarry*.[50] It had a contract with MGM for the production of twelve quota films. In the event, only two, *The King's Plate* and *Undercover*, were produced. Their scripts were so incompetent and the acting so bad that the project was scrapped.[51]

In Montreal, Coronet (under contract to William Steiner) produced *From Nine to Nine* (1936) at the Associated Screen Studios. Directed by the talented German-born director, Edgar Ulmer (who had worked with Max Reinhardt in the theatre and with Murnau on the classic *The Last Laugh* and *Faust*), and featuring the famous star of silent serials, Ruth Roland, it promised more than it delivered. So crudely produced was it that it quickly disappeared from release lists and no further films were produced.[52]

The Pacific coast of Canada had long been a happy hunting-ground for film promoters with glib tongues and schemes for million-dollar production companies. The new possibilities of quota production drew many of them, yet again, to Vancouver and Victoria.

Even while the Imperial Conference was meeting in London in 1926, Famous Players Canadian Corporation incorporated a Victoria-based subsidiary with an authorized capital of fifteen million dollars to produce "British

Empire-made" films in Victoria.[53] Nothing came of the scheme which seems to have been designed less to actually produce than to confuse the issue for the Imperial Conference in London as to what was a "British Empire-made" film.

Others were quick to follow. A "Cinema City" was announced for Victoria in 1926—and never built.[54] In 1927, Vancouver had both the Lion's Gate Cinema Studios (which claimed financial backing from the First National Company of the United States)[55] and the National Cinema Studios headed by famous European producer Nils Olaf Chrisander.[56] Only months later the promoters of National Cinema Studios were charged and found guilty of conspiring to defraud the public.

Over the years several producers had attempted to exploit the evidently warm interest by the city of Victoria in encouraging the establishment of a film studio there. All had failed, some because the scheme simply collapsed, others for legal reasons when the City Council could discover no way to provide the financial support demanded by the producer. It remained for an Australian producer, Claude Flemming, to direct the city fathers out of their difficulty. Flemming proposed that the city invest $200,000 in his production company and give him rent-free land for a studio if he could raise an additional $400,000 from British sources.[57] In order for the city to do this, it would be necessary to pass a by-law incorporating the agreement, and the by-law would have to be approved by the electors of the city. In July 1927 the citizens of Victoria approved the by-law by a three-to-one majority.[58] Flemming left for London to raise financing. He never returned and the scheme collapsed.

Two months later, another company, British Northwestern Development Company, approached the city with a similar proposition.[59] More wary now, the city merely took the proposal under advisement.

Despite all the plans, promotions, and flurry in Victoria it was not until 1932 and the arrival of Kenneth Bishop that anything of practical consequence developed.

Victoria's Quota Quickies

Kenneth Bishop remains something of an enigma. Apparently Canadian born (in 1893), he claimed to have been a producer in Hollywood since 1918 though there is no record of his activities there. Certainly he was a highly persuasive believer in Victoria as a base for producing quota films. So much so that, from his suite at the Dominion Hotel, he not only persuaded British

Columbians to invest in Commonwealth Productions and Central Films, but also convinced municipal and provincial politicians to argue his case on the British quota and on Canadian taxes and import duties. The city of Victoria (relieved not to be asked again for direct financial support) happily leased him studio space at the Willows Exhibition Grounds. And, over a five-year period from 1932 to 1937, he produced fourteen features, all of them competently made, if routine, B-movies. Better certainly, than previous quota companies—if only in quantity—but hardly much to give pride to a Canadian film industry. Budgets were low ($65,000 or less for each film) with shooting averaging three to four weeks in the Willows Studios or on locations around Vancouver Island. No one was under any illusions. Bishop was always frank about the fact that Commonwealth Productions and Central Films existed expressly for the purpose of producing British quota films. Some of them—such as *Lucky Corrigan*, *Secret Patrol*, *Tugboat Princess*, *Death Goes North*, and *Special Inspector*—were Canadian stories depicting lumbermen or the RCMP but the rest were comparable to any other Hollywood produced B-film. As a British critic commented about *Vengeance*, one of Central Films' gangster thrillers: "The film comes from Canada and for quota purposes counts as British, but in content, treatment, and acting it is indistinguishable from the everyday American second-feature melodrama."[60] It was this, not untypical, reaction to Canadian made quota films that was to lead in 1938 to the elimination of Canadian (together with all other Commonwealth) production from the British quota.

Kenneth Bishop's first Victoria company, Commonwealth Productions, was incorporated in July 1932 in British Columbia. Kathleen Dunsmuir (Mrs. Seldon Humphries) of the wealthy Dunsmuir family of B.C. was not only a major investor and director of the company but was also to play a lead in the first production. This was announced as *The Mystery of Harlow Manor* but, despite the fact that sets were constructed and the cast and director selected, the film was never made.[61] The company's first production was in fact to be *The Crimson Paradise*, filmed in three weeks on Vancouver Island. Based on the novel *The Crimson West* by British Columbia author Alexander Philip, it was set in a logging camp and concerned the rivalry between a rich Bostonian, sent to B.C. in disgrace, and a French-Canadian, for the affections of the boss's daughter. The plot (reflecting the notions that one is only sent to British Columbia "in disgrace" and that French-Canadians are always the villain) seems oddly reminiscent of those Hollywood "Canadian-content" films of two decades earlier. It was directed by Bob Hill, a Hollywood director born in Port Cohen, Ontario, and photographed by an aging Hollywood cameraman, William Beckway, whose hands were too

Scene from *Death Goes North*.

shaky to focus the camera. An assistant had to be brought from Hollywood to do this for him. Two of the leads, Nick Stuart and Lucille Brown, were brought in from Hollywood but many local actors were also used: Kathleen Dunsmuir and James McGrath in lead roles and Reginald Hincks, Michael Heppell, and others in supporting roles.[62]

The film was premièred in December 1933 at Victoria's Capital Theatre. Local reaction was rosy, the actors were individually praised, and a great future was predicted for Commonwealth Productions and Victoria's own movie industry. Unfortunately, what Victorians found interesting was not equally well regarded elsewhere. As with some of his predecessors, Bishop had neglected to check the details of the British quota law. *The Crimson Paradise* was found wanting since too few members of the cast and crew were of British origin.[63] Bishop had obviously assumed that if the company were Canadian and the story Canadian it would get by.

When this happened, the New York distributor with whom Commonwealth had a contract cancelled the agreement, and Commonwealth was left with an unsaleable film. Meanwhile, Bishop had produced a second film, *The Secrets of Chinatown*, from a story by Canadian author Guy Morton about the drug smuggling of a gang of Chinese in Vancouver and how the ring was smashed by a dauntless police inspector. The film has obvious echoes of the Fu Manchu stories and in the hands of Hollywood director Fred Newmeyer (once director for Harold Lloyd) it was little more than a routine adventure film. The cast again included Nick Stuart and Lucille Brown in lead roles, together with H. B. Warner, James Flavin, Harry Hewitson, and James McGrath.[64]

The film was completed in January 1934 but with the cancellation of their distribution contract, Commonwealth was in serious financial difficulties. The company went into receivership in February 1934 and its assets (including *Secrets of Chinatown*) were used to pay the company's creditors. Kathleen Dunsmuir attempted to obtain personal possession of *Secrets of Chinatown* on the basis of her $20,000 investment in the company but the court ruled against her.[65] *Secrets of Chinatown* was finally released in the United States in 1935 by Northern Films, a company apparently linked to Commonwealth and in which Bishop also had an interest.[66] As with the earlier film, *Secrets of Chinatown* did not qualify under the British quota.

For two years after this failure, no features were produced in Victoria. But Kenneth Bishop reappeared again in Victoria in 1935, this time with a firm contract to produce quota films for Columbia Pictures. And this time he would not make the mistake of failing to ensure that his films fulfilled the requirements for British films under the Cinematograph Films Act. If the British wanted British actors and technicians then Central Films (the new company incorporated in B.C. in October 1935) would ensure they got them. Hollywood was scoured for minor actors, writers, directors, and technicians who were British by birth. Occasionally, Americans were also used. And as with Commonwealth Productions, local actors were used in supporting roles, including James McGrath, Reginald Hincks (who was also casting supervisor for local actors), and Michael Heppell, Kenneth Bishop's assistant in Victoria.

Throughout the production of twelve films over the next two years,

Kenneth Bishop kept an eagle eye on things, seeing that none of them ran over budget or were behind schedule. Between films he made frequent trips to Hollywood to supervise processing and editing (which were not done in Canada) and to ensure that Columbia Pictures were happy with the product. Certainly, Columbia seemed to be. The films were released regularly in Britain as quota films and most were released also in the United States. And if reactions of critics and audiences were not ecstatic, at least the films did not meet the outright negative reaction and resistance to the earlier Canadian quota quickies.

The films themselves tend to merge into each other, so similar in theme and style are they.[67] Indeed they are not only similar to each other, but indistinguishable from a hundred other B-movies produced in Hollywood in the Thirties. This even embraces the Mountie and lumberjack stories since Hollywood filmed many similar stories during the same period. Only the occasional location scene in Victoria itself offers a clue to the films' ostensible Canadian origin.

Minor Hollywood directors who worked for Central Films included Ford Beebe (*Stampede*, *Secret Patrol*), Leon Barsha (*Manhattan Shakedown*, *Murder is News*, *Special Inspector*, *Convicted*), Nick Grinde (*Lucky Fugitives*), and David Selman (*Tugboat Princess*, *Secret Patrol*, *Woman Against the World*). One of the technicians involved, William Thompson, had worked also for Canadian Bioscope in Halifax more than twenty years earlier. Among the lesser known Hollywood performers, now forgotten except by late movie buffs, who appeared in the films were David Manners, Maxine Doyle, Charles Starrett, J. P. McGowan, Lyle Talbot, Marc Lawrence, and Charles Quigley. Two actresses who worked for Central Films were later to become better known: Valerie Hobson, only eighteen when she appeared in *Tugboat Princess*, and Rita Hayworth, only nineteen and two years in movies when she appeared in *Special Inspector* and *Convicted*.

The people and city of Victoria took great pride and interest in the company, the comings and goings of the actors and technicians, and in the location filming. Though this may now seem a little excessive, it is more understandable if one remembers that any industry was welcome during the Depression years. Central Films claimed to be putting over $400,000 annually into Victoria's economy. That was not to be ignored, quite apart from the reflected glamour of being a movie city—even a minor league one. Certainly Victoria made every effort to support and encourage Central Films, both providing facilities and using its political influence to accommodate Central Films' needs in relation to duty-free importation of technical equipment. But the best efforts of the city, the Chamber of Commerce, the prov-

A young Rita Hayworth (centre) featured in Central Films' *Convicted*.

ince, the local M.P., and the Canadian high commissioner in London were ineffective in preventing a change in the British quota act which excluded Canadian films from preferential treatment.

In 1937 the British Parliament debated the renewal of the Cinematograph Films Act which was due to expire in 1938. During the course of the debate, the clause which allowed Commonwealth production to count as "British" was at various times included and deleted. As one might expect, the British expressed some resentment against the Canadians for the manner in which they had allowed the Americans to get round the act. The "quota quickies" of Central Films and others may have satisfied the letter of the law but they most certainly ignored its spirit and intent. Finally, the crucial clause was deleted: after March 1938 Canadian production would no longer receive preferential treatment in Britain.[68]

It is relevant to note that although three Canadian provinces—Ontario,

British Columbia, and Alberta—enacted legislation allowing for the establishment of a quota for *British* films none of the necessary steps were taken to put this legislation into effect. None of the three provinces ever entertained legislating a quota for *Canadian* films, only one for British. This is in marked contrast to Australia where quotas were established for both Australian and British productions. The result for Canada was that when the British changed their legislation the only protection offered Canadian production was removed. Inevitably, production ceased. The Hollywood producers took their money, performers, and equipment, and went home.

The Canadian government, through its high commissioner in London, did make some representations in an effort to stop the legislative change. But it must have been a pretty difficult case to argue when neither the federal government nor any of the provincial governments had made any attempt to assist Canadian production. Indeed they had done the reverse by allowing, and even encouraging, branch-plant Hollywood production under the guise of Canadian companies. Understandably the British wondered why they were expected to help Canada when she was not prepared to help herself.

With the disappearance of the quota protection, Central Films was finished. Columbia Films had only bought its productions because of the quota. Kenneth Bishop left Victoria in 1938 and died three years later in Vancouver at the age of forty-eight.

Central Films, as active and as economically useful to Victoria as it was, produced nothing that could in any sense be considered an organic growth from Canadian culture. It was, on the other hand, an exact fulfillment of everything Ray Peck had preached in the Twenties. He would have been delighted with the establishment of Central Films. He would have pointed out that the company was pumping nearly half-a-million dollars into Victoria's economy, was providing local jobs, and all at no cost to Canada since the Americans provided the capital and imported the famous technical know-how of Hollywood. And, in the Thirties, these would have been pretty potent arguments.

But in terms of developing a domestic film industry Central Films and its sister companies contributed absolutely nothing. Indeed, as Peck himself might have finally realized, its effect was exactly the reverse. Being totally dependent on a set of circumstances well beyond domestic control and operable only at the whim of a New York or Hollywood distributor, the effort sapped the drive of those Canadians who might have been able to take advantage of the positive possibilities the British quota law offered to Canadian production.

As for quality, the worst of the quota quickies are as bad as expectations might imagine. Those of Central Films are generally better. But even at their best, the quota quickies are no more than efficient, routine, B-movies. It was a gloomy period, the Thirties, for Canadian film production. If it were not for those Canadians who concentrated their creative efforts at this time on short film production it would have been even more dismal.

All But Canadian

There were, however, two films released in 1930 and 1931 which offer more relevant reflections of Canadian culture than all the quota quickies. Neither is Canadian in the legal sense. (A film's nationality is defined as derived from the country in which the production company is incorporated.)[69] But in spirit, style, and feeling both are more Canadian than any of the legally "Canadian" productions of Central Films. These two films, *The Silent Enemy* and *The Viking*, are both set in Canada. Both were made by men—explorers first, film makers second—passionately engaged by their subjects. Each used the concept of a "dramatized documentary," using authentic locations and non-professional actors to evoke the relationship between a people and their environment. Both were made with affection and humanity by men who were not mere observers of an ethnological or sociological state but participants in the dramatic struggle they depicted; men who cared about the people whose story they were filming. *The Silent Enemy* by Douglas Burden and *The Viking* by Varick Frissell are extraordinary documents about the lives of ordinary people.

This approach, blending actuality and dramatic narrative, in which the film maker lives with and seeks the active cooperation of the people he is portraying, is in sharp contrast with the traditional documentary method. Here, the film maker is observer, journalist, sociologist, or propagandist— or sometimes a blend of all four—but in any case he maintains a distance from the material, a certain sense of objectivity. John Grierson, "father of the British documentary film" and founder of the National Film Board of Canada, was first to give theoretical form to the documentary film. From his first writings in the Twenties he laid down a coherent philosophical approach to the development of the documentary. Most documentary film makers have continued working in the tradition about which he wrote, theorized, and taught so persuasively.

But the other tradition, more poetry than sociology or reportage, has an equally long history. In fact, the attempt to blend drama and actuality goes back at least to *In the Land of the War Canoes* filmed on Vancouver Island in 1914 by Edward Curtiss. It was used—in a less clearly defined but not insignificant manner—in several Canadian features, including Ernest Ouimet's *The Scorching Flame* and *Sauvons nos bébés*, and the Ontario Motion Picture Bureau's *Cinderella of the Farms*. The same concerns are apparent also in, for example, Ernest Shipman's insistence on the use of real life locations for his dramas. But, more precisely, the approach owes its origin to Robert Flaherty and the classic documentary he made in Canada: *Nanook of the North*. The methods Flaherty developed to make this film became the foundations of a whole tradition of film making.

Despite John Grierson's later, direct, influence on Canadian documentary as head of the NFB, Flaherty's approach, in retrospect, seems more relevant to Canadian film and has consistently affected the course of Canadian cinema.[70] Both Douglas Burden and Varick Frissell were influenced by Flaherty's work and Frissell, in particular, was a "friend and protégé" of Flaherty. Several decades later, another generation of Canadian film makers witnessed that the lessons Flaherty taught had not been forgotten and that his vision was at least still as germane to the questions that generation was asking.

Robert Flaherty came to film not as an aesthete or technician but as an explorer.[71] It was the sense of discovery that must be so much a part of the explorer's nature which made a major contribution to his qualities as a film maker. He was also a romanticist—in the Jean Jacques Rousseau sense—in love with man and the natural world, fascinated by primitive traditions, and appalled by the dehumanizing technology of the modern world. His interests took him from the Canadian Arctic to the South Seas, from the coast of Ireland to the Louisiana bayous. Always he would live for a year or more in the communities he was to film, assimilating the attitudes and life of the people, getting to know them as friends. Then he allowed the form and story of his film (in Flaherty's words) "to come out of the life of the people." And in that story—for Flaherty's films always involved a narrative—the people themselves "acted out" their own lives. In doing so they were not mere characters in a drama but representative of all men who must live in response to the challenge of nature. His four major films—*Nanook of the North*, *Moana*, *Man of Aran*, and *Louisiana Story*—for all their physiographic differences, are all celebrations of the human spirit. They are not social documents nor even exposés of the corrupting influence of the white man on so-called primitive peoples. Faced with the cultural destruction wrought by white men on the Indians and Inuit with whom he came into contact, Flaherty's response was to banish the intruder, to portray "the former majesty and character of these people while it is still possible."[72] Flaherty's films are humanistic statements not political ones. But, while many social documentaries have become increasingly irrelevant with the passage of time, Flaherty's films have retained a validity that seems timeless.

Robert Flaherty spent much of his early life in Canada.[73] And it was in Canada that he evolved his special sensibility to the qualities of native peoples living outside the mainstream of technological development. Though born in Michigan, he often travelled with his father, a mining engineer and prospector, through the Canadian wilderness searching for mineral resources. His nomadic youth, with miners, Indians, and Inuit for companions, taught him the practical aspects of exploring, map making, and prospecting. More significantly, it also gave him a deep respect for the unpredictability of nature and for man's physical and spiritual relationship with the world around him.

In 1910, after schooling at Upper Canada College in Toronto and technical studies at the Michigan College of Mines, he began an independent career as explorer and prospector. He was commissioned by Sir William Mackenzie, builder of the Canadian Northern Railway, to explore the mineral resources in the eastern Hudson Bay area. Within a few years, in four expeditions for Sir William, he had gained no small fame as an explorer, mapped unknown country, and charted mineral and other resources.[74] He had also, for himself, discovered the Inuit. "In that harsh country, depending on them for companionship and daily bread, Flaherty found in the Eskimos a humanity so golden that he carried it with him ever afterwards as a touchstone of judgement. To him, the Eskimos were 'we the people' as we should be."[75]

In 1913, as he prepared for the third expedition, Sir William Mackenzie suggested he take along a motion picture camera.[76] Sir William had not forgotten the beneficial public relations that had accrued through the use of films produced for his railway company in 1909. Flaherty liked the idea and, though he had no plans for using film except for "taking notes of our exploration," he bought a camera and processing equipment and took a three week cinematography course. During his next two expeditions he shot many thousands of feet of film of life in the Arctic and became so obsessed with his film making activities that it almost eliminated his search for minerals.[77]

Back in Toronto, between the third and fourth expeditions, he edited the footage into the semblance of a narrative. In April 1915, his six-reel documentary was shown in public for the first time at the University of Toronto's Convocation Hall. Reviewers described it as including "the most complete and extensive pictures of their kind ever taken"[78] while the director of the Ontario Museum of Archaeology wrote that he had "never known anything received with greater enthusiasm."[79]

But Flaherty was not satisfied. On the fourth Mackenzie expedition he obtained more footage, returned to Toronto and continued editing. Then, in 1916, while packing the negative for shipment to New York, he dropped a lighted cigarette onto scraps of film on the floor and his entire negative went up in flames.[80] Flaherty himself was badly burned and barely escaped with his life.

He persuaded himself the accident was for the best. Though his film had been warmly received, he himself was not satisfied with it. It was, he felt, too much like a travelogue—"simply a scene of this and that."[81] Showing the film to friends, he noticed that the interest they took in it was in relation to him, the outsider. That was not what he wanted. "I wanted to show the Inuit. And I wanted to show them, not from the civilized point of view, but as they saw themselves, as 'we the people'."[82] He became convinced that his mistake lay in showing the picturesque strangeness of the North rather than the characteristic, ordinary way of life. He determined to return to the North and make a different kind of film which would centre on one Inuit family.

But raising funds was a problem. The financing of trips to Hudson Bay was not of prime concern to potential sponsors during the First World War. Film people were even more indifferent to the idea. Then, as the war ended, he convinced Jean Revillon and Captain Thierry Mallet of Revillon Frères, the French fur company, to finance the project.[83] It was not entirely an altruistic decision. Revillon Frères had competed for years with the Hudson's Bay Company and felt that the film would make a new, impressive, kind of promotion for them in vying for the northern fur trade.

By August 1920, Flaherty had retraced his steps to western Ungava. He was to remain in the North more than a year, shooting film under the most adverse conditions with the help of his non-professional cast and crew recruited in Port Harrison.

But this time he knew how to proceed. The full collaboration of the Inuit was already the key to his method. It was to be a film not only about the Inuit but also a film by them. In line with this method, they soon became involved in every phase of the production, from "acting" in front of the cameras, to planning scenes and assisting in processing the exposed film, and repairing the equipment.[84] As his principal character, Flaherty chose Nanook, a celebrated hunter in the district. Nanook became totally engrossed in making the film and was a constant source of ideas. One of his first suggestions was to film a walrus hunt, done as in the old days before the white men came with their rifles. It was an extraordinary event and the sequence became one of the most famous in *Nanook of the North*.

For another sequence, Flaherty wanted to film interior scenes in an igloo. "The average Eskimo igloo, about 12 feet in diameter was much too small. On the dimensions I laid out for him, a diameter of 25 feet, Nanook and his companions started to build the biggest igloo of their lives." They worked for days to build it and then, when they discovered the light from the iced windows proved inadequate for filming, "the dome's half just over the camera had to be cut away, so Nanook and his family went to sleep and awakened with all the cold out-of-doors pouring in." [85]

It is sequences such as these (and there were others "staged" for the camera) which have led many traditional ethnologists to condemn the Flaherty method. But Flaherty was not here, nor in later films, concerned with documenting facts but in revealing and dramatizing a way of life. He was intent on authenticity of result.

Given both its unusual subject and even more unusual filming approach, it should perhaps not be surprising that Flaherty experienced great difficulty selling *Nanook of the North*. But then this was 1922 and the few independent distributors were reluctant to take a chance on an unpredictable product. The Hollywood production-distribution-exhibition combines were rapidly standardizing film production and films had to fit into what the corporations' executives felt audiences wanted. As one executive for Paramount (first to reject *Nanook of the North*) remarked to Robert Flaherty, such a film "just couldn't be shown to the public." He was very sorry, especially since Flaherty had "gone through all that hardship in the North" for nothing. [86] Four more major companies reacted similarly. Another executive explained to Flaherty that the public was not interested in Eskimos; it preferred actors in dress suits. Such closed doors and minds might have continued indefinitely had not Flaherty turned in desperation again to Revillon Frères, his sponsor. Revillon brought patriotic pressure to bear on the Pathé Company in the United States—which, like Revillon, was of French origin. Pathé, somewhat reluctantly, accepted it but it was not shown theatrically until the New York impresario "Roxy" Rothafel saw it, called it a masterpiece and opened it at his prestigious Capitol Theatre. [87] It was an immediate success. Audiences loved it and most critics were impressed. The *New York Times* critic found it "far more interesting, far more compelling purely as entertainment, than any except the rare exceptions among photoplays." [88] Robert Sherwood, reviewing the best films of the year, said: "It stands alone, literally in a class by itself." [89]

It was an enormous box-office success in Europe, running for six months in London and Paris, and its fame spread throughout the world. European critics had no doubts that the film was a masterpiece. One French critic compared its power to that of Greek classic drama.

But in the United States, financial returns were less spectacular. The American film industry was unwilling, or unable, to give it the special kind of promotion it demanded. Still, everyone (including Revillon Frères and Flaherty) made a profit from the theatrical release.

Nanook himself knew nothing of his fame. He died of starvation on a hunting trip two years after the film's release. But the film has lost nothing of its artistic stature. At the 1964 Mannheim Film Festival, documentary film makers from all over the world were asked to select the greatest documentaries of all time. *Nanook of the North* headed the list.

That it continues to appeal to audiences is a tribute to the Flaherty method. *Nanook of the North* has no immediate social value nor does it help solve the problems of native peoples. But it does illuminate the human condition. Nanook is a very ordinary man living in circumstances which are ordinary to him but extraordinary to us. If he seems noble, larger than life, it is because "Nanook is more than the master of his environment; he is the master of himself, a hero who endures and prevails and who, without pride, has the humility that comes only to a man who lives close to nature."[90] And Flaherty's portrait is not an outsider's detached observation. Caring for the Inuit, sharing their lives, Flaherty could transmit to the screen what is essentially the *self-image* of Nanook and his people. It is a philosophy of creation that remains perhaps Flaherty's greatest legacy to the cinema.

Douglas Burden's *The Silent Enemy* has a similar quality. It is not surprising to find critics in 1930 comparing it favourably with *Nanook of the North*. It, too, is a reflection of a people's self-image—in this case of the Ojibway people and of their life before the white man came. It, too, involved a dramatization, acted out by the people themselves, combined with a meticulous authenticity.

Set in the early fifteenth century, *The Silent Enemy* tells the story of a small band of Ojibways who have enjoyed six years of plenty but now face famine: the silent enemy. The hunters find no game and return empty-handed. Baluk, "the mighty hunter," urges their chief, Chetoga, to lead the band out of the forest into the northern barrens to search for the migrating caribou. Though Dagwan, the medicine man, taunts Baluk with cowardice, the chief decrees that the tribe must move North. It is a long, weary journey as, cold and hungry, the tribe travels through unbroken forests and a wilderness of snow to the rim of the Arctic Circle. After terrible suffering and discouragement, the tribe finally meets the caribou herd and, once again, for a time, there is plenty.

Woven through this tale, is the love story of Baluk and Neewa, Chetoga's daughter, and the conflict between Baluk and Dagwan, the medicine man, who plots Baluk's downfall in order to gain Neewa for himself. But the real drama lies in the people's unending fight for food and survival.

William Douglas Burden was principally responsible for *The Silent Enemy* though, unlike *Nanook of the North*, many people were involved in the technical aspects of its production.[91] Still in his twenties at the time he produced *The Silent Enemy*, Douglas Burden had rapidly established a name for himself as an explorer and ethnologist after graduating from Harvard. He was an active trustee of the American Museum of Natural History, with a special interest in the customs and way of life of the Ojibway. As had Flaherty, he wanted to make others aware of the special qualities of the indigenous peoples of North America. Their way of life had already changed substantially over the past four centuries and might soon vanish altogether. Burden felt that producing a film would leave "a visual record for the America that is to come of the America that used to be."[92] To reach a wide public it would have to be both authentic and entertaining, both factual and dramatic. It would have to be produced in a natural environment with Indians "living again the lives of their remote ancestors," recreating the use of tools and equipment long since relegated to museums.[93] This idea was eventually to involve Burden in two years of concentrated effort and the expenditure of considerable funds. It was to involve the cooperation of the Ontario Department of Lands and Forests, the American Museum of Natural History, and more than one hundred and fifty Indians. And, though a great critical success, the film was to be a financial disaster on its theatrical release.

The production site selected by Burden was the Timagami Provincial Forest of northern Ontario. There, preparations for the production began in the summer of 1927, one year before any filming was to be done. A base camp was constructed at Temiscaming, together with a film processing laboratory and animal compounds, and a second camp erected at Rabbit Chute where most of the dramatic scenes were to be filmed. Live specimens of wolves, moose, black bear, mountain lions, and deer were captured and housed.[94] Many of these were to feature in some of the film's most exciting scenes— including one in which wild animals attempt to steal the tribe's food during the trek north but are fought off by the men using only their bare hands.

Some of the clothing and other objects necessary for the film were loaned by museums; a few of the Indians gathered together to make the film brought with them their family heirlooms. But most of the tools, clothing, and equipment had to be recreated. "Some old men we found could build birch bark canoes; some old women could sew bark and erect wigwams; others could make skin clothing. We formed groups of workers who taught the others."[95] Nothing was forgotten in the search for authenticity. For example, no beads were used to decorate the clothing since the Indians knew nothing of beads until the Hudson's Bay Company introduced them. "Then, with all the equipment and props ready, we had to teach the Indians their use. Old games, old dances, old methods of making fire and cooking, and many other customs forgotten by disuse were revived."[96]

For the lead roles, Burden selected three chiefs: Chief Yellow Robe to play Chetoga, the tribal leader, Chief Buffalo Child Long Lance to play Baluk, and Chief Akawanush to play Dagwan, the medicine man. All were to receive high praise from critics for the freshness and spontaneity of their performances. As Flaherty had realized a decade earlier, when people act out their own lives they create "performances" so natural and believable as to surpass any professional actor in the role.

None came in for more adulation than Chief Buffalo Child Long Lance. Described by one critic as "a superb figure, agile as a catamount and utterly fearless," his performance astonished all who saw it.[97] Even seeing the film today it is difficult to believe he was a newcomer to acting. One magazine, dubbing him "Chief of the Heartbreakers," swooningly described him as "tall, barrel-chested, thin-hipped, and with hands strong enough to strangle a bear."[98] Given that description it is perhaps not surprising that he enjoyed some small fame as Manhattan's new social idol.

Chief Buffalo Child Long Lance had already had a picturesque career before making *The Silent Enemy*. Born in Montana, he had been a circus performer, cowboy, football player, captain in the Canadian Army, journalist in Calgary, and archeologist for the Canadian government. His book, *Long Lance*, was a best-seller and had been published in five languages. It was soon after this success that Douglas Burden cast him in the lead role in *The Silent Enemy*. For Long Lance, the production of the film was an unforgettable experience. "It was a life of real adventure. We were free. . . . We lived for twelve months the lives my remote ancestors lived five hundred years ago."[99]

That experience began in June 1928 when shooting finally got underway after a year of preparations. Filming was to continue through the winter and spring of 1929, often under extremely adverse conditions. Several more months were spent on editing.

Burden-Chanler Productions (the company established by Douglas Burden and William C. Chanler to produce the film) had arranged distribution with Paramount. On May 19, 1930, with a minimum of publicity,

Scene from *The Silent Enemy*. Baluk (Chief Buffalo Child Long Lance, left) greets the old chief.

The Silent Enemy opened in New York. It was an immediate critical success. The *New York Times* wrote that there were not enough superlatives to describe it and that "it deserves a rating as the Great American Film."[100] An editorial in the New York *Post* recommended it for a Pulitzer Prize, noting that it was "no ordinary moving picture [but one] so faithful, so honest, so beautiful, and so romantic as to make a permanent contribution to the mysterious story of the North American continent."[101] Everyone praised, rightly, the remarkable photography and the many extraordinary animal sequences. Most stunning of these is the final caribou hunt, with the herd "first appearing in faint black outline upon the snowy horizon of the Canadian plain, then rushing past the camera in a thundering stream."[102]

However, *The Silent Enemy* was conceived before the universal adoption of sound and was premièred on Broadway without synchronized dialogue, though there were "a few sound effects and a music score."[103] And, as the reviewer for *Motion Picture World* predicted, "no silent film ever again will succeed on Broadway." Despite its superb qualities, concluded the reviewer, its life would be short in "this land of subways and doughnut shops." [104]

It was an accurate prediction. Notwithstanding the lavish praise of critics, *The Silent Enemy* disappeared rapidly from movie theatres. Its lack of dialogue was not, however, its only problem. The distributor failed, or was not prepared, to give the film the special treatment and promotion it deserved and needed. As had happened with *Nanook of the North*, Hollywood was at a loss when it came to handling a film which did not fit into a predictable mould.

Following its theatrical failure, *The Silent Enemy* was shortened and adapted for educational use. In this form it survived for years, being shown regularly in schools and museums. Only recently has the original version by Douglas Burden become available again. Viewing it today, one can only share the opinions of those enthusiastic New York critics in 1930. *The Silent Enemy* is a rich, warm, and impressive film, full of evocative imagery, and staged with great sensitivity. An artistic achievement in its time, comparable to the best of Robert Flaherty's work, it is a film whose stature has only increased in the half-century since it was made.

Varick Frissell was a contemporary of Douglas Burden (though Frissell was at Yale while Burden was at Harvard) and both came from similar backgrounds. Though they apparently never met, they shared, with Flaherty, a neo-Rousseauesque concern for those parts of the world as yet untouched by the hand of industrialization.

Varick Frissell was only twenty-seven when he died in 1931. Yet, by then, he had already explored the interior of Labrador, discovered and named a river and a falls there, worked for the famous Grenfell Mission, and created three remarkable films. Two of these films, *The Great Arctic Seal Hunt* and *The Viking*, were about seal hunting in Newfoundland. Or, more accurately, they were about the people whose way of life it was, about their courage, skill, and hardihood—and the constant threat of death they faced. And that threat was real. Frissell himself was to die at sea with two dozen seal hunters in an incident not dissimilar to that he depicted in his films.

He was loved and admired by the people of Newfoundland; and this love was reflected in the way they mourned his death. Though American, he was far more to the Newfoundlanders than a visitor. He had shared their lives. He knew their problems by experiencing them. He was not an outsider filming them but someone who cared enough to discover what the seal hunt was really like—and only then to film it. It was, indeed, the Flaherty method and it is not surprising to learn that Frissell was a great admirer of Robert

Flaherty. There had, in fact, been plans for collaborating on a film of the Indians "of the farthest far northwest."[105] After Frissell's death Flaherty was to describe him as "my good friend and protégé."[106]

He was a good friend to many others, a man much loved by his contemporaries. Sir Wilfred Grenfell said that everyone sensed something exceptional about Frissell, "not merely his wonderful physical body, handsome, tall, athletic, naturally attractive to everyone though it was. . . . He was every inch a real man, and yet he was as gentle as a child. His size, his strength and his reactions to all the impulses of life were just such as I have always associated with those I love best."[107] His height alone—six feet, seven inches—was impressive enough but he also had "the smiling disposition of a boy and the heart of a lion."[108] One anonymous author dubbed him "gentlest giant" in a special poem which began:

Child-hearted lover of the northland,
Gentlest giant, eager-eyed and strong . . .[109]

Lewis Varick Frissell was born August 29, 1903. While still an undergraduate at Yale University he volunteered to work with Sir Wilfred Grenfell in Labrador. Grenfell, sometimes known as "Newfoundland's Albert Schweitzer," was then at the peak of his international influence. He had begun his medical missionary work in 1892, sailing the coasts of Newfoundland and Labrador, treating the sick, and holding religious services. In winter he travelled by dog sled. To make the public aware of the unusually difficult living conditions and to publicize his work and raise funds, he lectured throughout the United States, Canada, and Britain. As a result, branches of the International Grenfell Association were formed to support his work. Funds were raised to build an orphanage and school and Sir Donald Smith, then president of the CPR, donated a specially equipped hospital ship, the *Strathcona*. Scores of young men, fired by Grenfell's tales of adventure in the service of others, volunteered to work for the mission without pay. Among them was Varick Frissell. Like Grenfell, Frissell relished danger. He spent the winter of 1922 as a dog-team driver and later worked on the hospital ship *Strathcona* and at the mission at St. Anthony. It was at this time that his interest in and love for the people of Newfoundland and Labrador was formed.

In 1925, at Grenfell's urging, Frissell made a canoe trip with another Yale student and two trapper guides up what was then called the Hamilton River and is now known as Churchill River. His principal purpose was to take moving and still pictures of Grand Falls (now Churchill Falls) which Grenfell could use to illustrate his lectures on Labrador. Grenfell also suggested that Frissell visit the aptly named Unknown River and establish some basic geographical facts about the Labrador interior. Frissell's explorations resulted in the discovery and naming of Yale Falls, the description of a considerable portion of the Unknown River (which he named Grenfell River), and won for him a fellowship at an unusually early age in the Royal Geographical Society.[110] The motion pictures he had shot of Churchill Falls (the first ever taken) became part of his first film, *The Lure of Labrador*. As a documentary, it enjoyed a modest success and was, in fact, being shown in London, England, at the time the Privy Council was deciding the Quebec-Newfoundland boundary dispute over Labrador. The Newfoundland government in 1928 used Frissell's photo of Churchill Falls for its thirty-cent postage stamp. And, more significantly, it was through Frissell's "camera record that Newfoundlanders came to a full realization of the veritable gold mine in the form of water power that was hidden away in their northern territory."[111]

Frissell continued to spend his summers in Labrador. "While 'jiggin' for cod in open dories out in the ocean, he learned a great deal about the lives of his comrades and was almost tempted to make Newfoundland his country by adoption. He heard about shipwrecks, exciting whale hunts, and 'the swilin' racket' (the seal hunt)."[112] It was the seal hunt that most interested him. It seemed to typify the special qualities of the Newfoundlanders. Sealing is high risk for small recompense. Sealers face six weeks of incredible hardship for a possible pay of fifty dollars—if there is a catch. And sealing history is full of disasters. Every year some ships never returned and the crews of others were frozen to death or lost on the ice. Yet, in Frissell's time, ten thousand men clamoured for berths every year—and only half could be taken. "Every ship is crowded with 200 or more men who are squeezed into every available cubic foot of space not reserved for the seals. Every ship is a rival, guided by the experience of her skipper who wants to reach the seal herd first—and, if possible, alone! Since the herd occupies a mere pinpoint on the Atlantic, it is often difficult to find."[113] In order to find the herd and enjoy a modest share of the catch, the men faced bitter cold, hurricane force storms, and the chance of the ship being frozen into the ice. That men should accept such risks as part of their livelihoods was, for Frissell, a remarkable testament to the human spirit.

Even the ships themselves had that character of romantic adventure that appealed to Frissell. Many had been used on Arctic expeditions by such famous explorers as Robert Peary, A. W. Greeley, Donald MacMillan, and Bob Bartlett; the S.S. *Terra Nova* had carried Scott and Shackleton to the

South Pole. "But," said Frissell, "in the swilin' racket these ships have reverted to their true destiny."[114]

In 1927, a year after graduating from Yale, Frissell was offered a berth as a sealer on the S.S. *Beothic*. His intention was to make a film of the voyage but for six weeks he had to be a sealer first, film maker second. The *Beothic* (on which David Sarnoff had sailed as a radio operator before his fame as chief executive of RCA) was one of the largest, and reputedly luckiest, ships in the fleet. But the drama Frissell experienced was none the less for that. Two days out of port, the ship faced a terrific hurricane which almost destroyed it. Ventilators were torn away, dories smashed, the radio broken, and the decks strewn with wreckage. Later, the ship became frozen hard into the ice and the men left on foot to search for the seals. Frissell's "watch" walked twenty miles away from the *Beothic*. He enjoyed wandering about in the wilderness on the heaving ice-floes but found it "no fun killing seals."[115] When the time came for the hunters to report back to the ship, Watch No. 3 was missing. A bad storm broke, the men were almost given up for lost, and were located only after a four day search. Frissell was later to use this incident as the dramatic focus of *The Viking*.

After six weeks at sea, the *Beothic* returned to St. Johns with 23,000 seals. Frissell received $53 as his share of the catch. He had also shot ten thousand feet of film which, a year later, he edited into *The Swilin' Racket*, a film about forty minutes long.

But there was still the problem of getting it shown in public. So Frissell began that odyssey so well known to independent film producers: hawking his film around to distributors and theatres in New York. He convinced the Cameo Theatre (which was not allied with any of the theatre chains) to run it for a week in April and in June the independent Film Arts Guild contracted to handle national distribution.[116] Now re-titled *The Great Arctic Seal Hunt*, it excited considerable critical attention—unusual for a film of its type. *Variety* wrote that "unlike many of its kind [documentaries], it holds its various shots together with the thread of a story," while the *New York Times*, noting that it contained "infinitely more drama than many a Hollywood piece of film fiction," found it "absorbing from beginning to end." It was, said the New York *Post*, "even more realistic" than *Nanook of the North*, *Grass*, and *Chang*, films "which were intended to free us from seeing the drama of faraway places through rose-colored glasses." Audiences, reported the theatre managers, appeared to find the film fascinating and were pleased with it as a "supporting attraction."[117]

Frissell, it seems, had achieved his stated aim of producing a dramatic film of "man's struggle for existence against an overwhelmingly cruel environment."[118] But he was not satisfied. As a short film, *The Great Arctic Seal Hunt* had an inevitably limited audience. Might not a feature-length film, perhaps with more plot than merely "a thread of a story," have a greater impact and carry to more people the story Frissell wanted to tell?

But meanwhile there were other projects. There were plans for a film on Sir Wilfred Grenfell following his knighthood in 1927, plans which collapsed when several directors of the International Grenfell Association appeared less than enthusiastic.[119] The hoped-for collaboration with Robert Flaherty on a film about Indian life also came to nothing. In 1929, Frissell was in Mexico, photographing the *Cristero* revolution. But, later that year, he returned to his idea for a dramatized feature film about the seal hunt and set about making practical plans for financing and producing it.

He had drafted a story which embraced some of the actual events he had witnessed on his earlier sealing trip.[120] Two men, Luke and Jed, are rivals for the love of a girl. Luke, the hero, has a reputation as a "jinker": someone who puts a jinx on, or brings bad luck to, those with whom he sails. Since Jed does not want Luke left alone with the girl while Jed leaves for the seal hunt, he obtains a berth for Luke on the same ship, headed by Captain Bob. After several misadventures on board ship—accidents for which Jed always makes Luke appear responsible—the two are isolated on the ice during the hunt. Jed attempts to kill Luke but a fierce storm cuts them off from the ship. Jed, who has lost his smoked glasses, becomes snowblind. Luke leads him back to land by crossing the ice-floes on foot and, of course, wins the girl. Extensive actuality sequences of ship-board life and the hunt itself were to be woven into this story.

To raise the money to produce his film, Frissell formed the Newfoundland Labrador Film Company under the lenient incorporation laws of the State of Delaware. Vice-president of the company was W. C. Chanler who was simultaneously working with Douglas Burden on the filming of *The Silent Enemy*. As the company's president, Varick Frissell was to "supervise and direct" the production of the proposed film, select the actors and actresses, furnish the story, and arrange for services and supplies, plus ensure the cooperation of the "fleet of sealing vessels operating from St. John's, Newfoundland." He agreed to devote himself full-time to the production and, in return, was to be paid a salary in the form of shares in the Newfoundland Labrador Film Company to be delivered when the film was completed.[121] In other words, he was to be paid no money for his work on the film; the recompense for his contribution would come only if the film were successful.

By the time filming began in early February 1930, $100,000 of the $125,000 production cost had been raised and the company had tentatively arranged distribution with Paramount Pictures. Paramount, true to form, insisted not only that the love story should be emphasized but also that an established Hollywood director be hired to handle the scenes with professional actors.[122] To do this, Frissell hired George Melford, a free-lance Hollywood director whose most notable work was to have directed Rudolph Valentino in *The Sheik* a decade earlier. His principal function was to direct the scripted, dialogue scenes (written by Garnett Weston) with the three professional actors hired to play the leads. All three actors—Charles Starrett, Louise Huntington, and Arthur Vinton—were from the New York stage and probably more familiar to Frissell than West Coast movie actors. Charles Starrett had, however, recently signed a film contract with Paramount and is perhaps better remembered by movie buffs for his starring roles in innumerable B-Westerns of the Thirties and Forties than for his work at Central Films in Victoria.

To play the captain of the sealing ship, Frissell selected Captain Bob Bartlett. Known as "Newfoundland's most famous son,"[123] he had first gone seal hunting at the age of seventeen in 1892; he had also captained *The Windward* on two of Peary's expeditions to the North Pole and *The Bowdoin* during the Arctic expeditions of Commander MacMillan. The claim he was to make in Frissell's film, that he had "never lost a man," was true. Bartlett was famous far beyond Newfoundland. He had already appeared in a documentary, *Bob Bartlett's Labrador*, filmed by Maurice Kellerman, who was to be one of the cameramen on *The Viking*.[124]

In early February 1930 the company shot the dramatized scenes which open and close the film.[125] The climactic scene was to take place in church during a memorial service for Luke and Jed who are thought to be dead on the ice. For these scenes the famous little Christ Church at Quidi Vidi was used. Some local residents were upset by the thought of "sinful" movie people desecrating the church and the church fathers found it necessary to issue a notice regretting "the wild tales which have been circulating about mock weddings, etc." Far from blaspheming on church property, the film people had not only "conducted themselves with due reverence for sacred things" but had also "made a generous contribution to the church funds."[126]

In March, cast and crew left for the ice-fields. Frissell had originally selected the S.S. *Viking* as the featured ship of the film. Not only did its name coincide with his proposed title for the film (*Vikings of the Ice-Fields*)[127] but it was also one of the oldest wooden ships of the sealing fleet with a long history of successful hunts. It had been built in 1881 and had been at one time commanded by Captain Bob Bartlett's father. However, the *Viking* proved unavailable and the S.S. *Ungava* was chartered so that the company could film the seal hunting scenes. Later, when the sealing fleet returned, the *Viking* was chartered and, in command of Captain Bob Bartlett, returned to the ice-fields so that the ship-board scenes could be filmed.[128]

One of Frissell's most ambitious decisions was to use authentic sound and dialogue recorded on location.[129] No one had dared do this before. Sound equipment for movies was not only primitive in reproductive capability but also extremely cumbersome. Sound was recorded, in the early years, on large discs—making synchronization of sound and image a highly exacting technical task during shooting and curtailing freedom of editing later. Microphones had none of the selectivity of later years and picked up every stray noise to which they were exposed. And, unlike today's tape-recorders, all the equipment was heavy, yet delicate and difficult to adjust. Most producers solved the problem by eliminating all exterior shooting from their films and working entirely on sets in the studios. There was a handful of directors, even in the early years, who tried to use sound more creatively but there was no one in 1930 who had thought it possible to film a dramatic feature entirely on location. And, in Frissell's case, it was not just any location: for much of the time filming and recording had to take place in the middle of the ice-fields and on the ice itself. Thomas Sweeney (who went on location with Frissell) later described "the great difficulty of setting up the delicate sound recording apparatus and the impracticability of transporting anything even slightly cumbersome over the broken fields of ice which twist and heave as the great Atlantic swells roll under them."[130] Impractical or not—and those heaving fields of ice described by Sweeney can be seen in *The Viking*—Frissell did it. Perhaps his innocence in technical matters led him to ignore the advice of Hollywood experts who told him it could not be done. Perhaps he just wanted to try it anyway. His demands for authenticity certainly made imperative the use of location sound.

Producing *The Viking* that spring in the ice-fields was an unforgettable experience for all involved. The full paraphernalia of a typical movie studio was set up amid complete desolation. "Batteries, cameras, microphones, props, director, assistants, technicians, actors, and script boys all functioned as though at work in the studio."[131] And when Frissell's desire for authenticity created new technical demands, solutions were found on the spot. For example, Frissell wanted film shot right in among the sealers actually attacking the seals. The problem was that the seals scattered at the first sign of danger and long before standard camera equipment could be set up. Then it was discovered that one of the cameras could be thrown with its tripod at-

Production of *The Viking*. In this photograph the microphone and sound equipment can be seen.

tached over open water and caught without damage. "When open water was encountered which defied leaping without the use of all fours, the Eyemo [camera] would be grasped by the end of the tripod and, by a long pendulum swing, be sent flying over the obstacle into the arms of another member of the party, and so relayed up the line into the centre of action where it was quickly put to work."[132] Inevitably someone miscalculated the throw one day and the camera ended up in the ocean. But not before the unorthodox technique had produced some of the most extraordinary shots of *The Viking*.

There were many other extraordinary shots too, scenes which had never before been recorded on film. When shooting was completed in late April and the actors and crew disbanded, Frissell was contented with what had been achieved. He still had some doubts about the dramatic love scenes but Paramount had insisted and his financing was dependent on Paramount's backing. In any case, the footage was shipped to Hollywood for editing and Frissell himself left St. John's with it.

The edited film was first seen in a pre-release test screening in Hollywood on January 5, 1931.[133] The response from critics and audience alike was identical. Everyone admired the actuality scenes (with their "shots that make your hair stand on end") but many felt these scenes sat rather incongruously alongside the melodramatic episodes. One reviewer described it as "a gripping tale which is capable of telling its own story as was *Nanook of the North*," but unfortunately this was mixed up with a lot of "impossible love stuff." Frissell was advised, forthrightly, that most of these scenes "should be tossed into the waste basket."[134]

Frissell needed no more encouragement. He had always been less than happy with the scenes directed by George Melford. The test screening had proved him right and now—with or without Paramount's agreement—he was determined to revise the film to bring it closer to his own conception. The basic plot would remain but the professionally acted sequences would be shortened in length and more actuality scenes inserted. Frissell particularly wanted spectacular shots of an iceberg turning over.[135] It was evident that another spring voyage on the S.S. *Viking* was necessary.

Frissell set sail on March 9, together with his new cameraman Alexander G. Penrod (who had shot the whaling film *Down to the Sea in Ships*), Harry Sargent, his friend from Boston, and a local assistant, Fred Best. From the beginning it was a difficult voyage.[136] For the first four days there were gale force winds and unusually heavy seas which kept all hands busy at the pumps. Frissell and his colleagues were no exception, as Clayton King, radio operator on the *Viking* was later to recall. Frissell, Penrod, and Sargent "proved to be sailors of the finest quality. Especially Mr. Frissell. Working day and night, he never ceased his untiring efforts." Even cooked meals became an impossibility after an exceptionally heavy sea washed overboard the galley house and all its equipment.

On Friday, March 13, there was a lull in the weather and Captain Abram Kean decided to anchor in Bonavista Bay in order to make repairs and send ashore for new equipment. The next day, with the weather considerably more moderate, the *Viking* set sail again for the sealing grounds. The crew, many of whom were sailing for the first time, were again in good spirits and that evening Frissell showed them a print of his film shot the previous spring.

On the evening of the following day, Sunday, March 15, the ship encountered heavy ice. Captain Kean decided to hold the ship in the ice for the night, ready to break out in the morning. He then retired to his stateroom.

A short time later, Varick Frissell was in the saloon with Harry Sargent, Ted Carter, the bos'n (he had appeared in Frissell's film the year before), Dr. Roche, the ship's surgeon, Clayton King, the radio operator, and the navigator, Captain Kennedy. Frissell's dog, Cabot, was, as usual, with him. Frissell was writing out a sign: DANGER—POWDER. There was a plentiful supply of dynamite and gunpowder on board, necessary to blast the ship free of ice jams. Frissell was concerned that the men coming down the companionway with lighted cigarettes might cause an explosion. He was also worried that several old flares on the ship were damaged and inherently dangerous. Bos'n Carter said he wanted to keep the flares "and make some experiments on the ice tomorrow" but Frissell insisted they be immediately thrown overboard. "If you fool with them," he said, "we'll all be blown to Hades before daylight."

Carter picked up the flares and left the saloon, heading towards his cabin which was directly opposite where the explosives were stored. "A few seconds after Carter's departure," Clayton King recalled, "the ship gave a terrific lurch and listed over to an angle of about forty degrees. . . . Captain Kean came running out of his stateroom and headed for the deck to determine the cause of the racket. Getting to our feet, we started to clean up the saloon. Almost immediately there followed a terrific blast from the after-end of the saloon."

The explosion was loud enough to be heard on Horse Island, eight miles away, at nine o'clock that evening. Within minutes there was a second explosion and flames were seen. By morning, the few inhabitants of the island could see the burning wreckage of the ship and make out dozens of men struggling over the ice toward the island. Twenty-four hours later, 118 survivors had landed safely, though several were in weakened condition from exposure, and all of them now faced possible starvation and further exposure since both supplies and shelter were inadequate on the island until rescue ships could arrive.[137] Most of these men had been below decks at the time of the explosion and later escaped the fire. Captain Kean, who had been on the bridge, was blasted off the ship by the explosion and sustained bodily injuries from the fall.

Of those in the saloon before the explosion, only Harry Sargent and Clayton King survived—and King lost both his legs. Captain Kennedy died on the rescue ship. Ted Carter, Dr. Roche, and Varick Frissell were never seen again. In all, there were twenty-eight missing and eight urgent hospital cases.

As the survivors were picked up and told their stories and when the rescue ships could find no traces of other survivors, it became clear that those still missing were dead. The official search was called off. But the Frissell family, led by Varick's father, Dr. Lewis Frissell, refused to accept the official verdict. An aeroplane was purchased and a personal search organized, headed by Burt Balchen and Merian C. Cooper.[138] Both men were World War I pilots and Cooper had co-directed two films comparable to Frissell's: *Grass* and *Chang*. Later, he was to enjoy a different kind of fame as co-director of *King Kong* and production chief of RKO Studios.

Their week-long aerial search was fruitless. The only glimmer of hope —that Frissell's dog, Cabot, had been seen roaming a small island—led nowhere. The search was abandoned.

As the search was underway, Sir Richard Squires (Newfoundland's most notorious prime minister) announced that a commission of inquiry headed by the chief justice of the Newfoundland Supreme Court would investigate the disaster.[139] After a month of public hearings, the commission issued its report. In the carefully guarded language of such documents it concluded that the disaster occurred because the explosives were "insecurely fastened," with the result that powder escaped and "was found on the deck of the ship."[140] No blame was attached to anyone for the explosion or its aftermath, not even to Captain Kean, even though one might presume he had the responsibility for ensuring that the explosives were properly stored. In any case, Captain Kean had the last word about the fruitless search for Varick Frissell. "He was making a film about a jinker," he is reported to have said, "he is bound to be dead. No reason to look for him."[141]

Frissell's "jinker" film was released in the form it had first been seen the previous January. Now titled, finally, *The Viking*, it was released in Toronto in May, in New York in June, and in London, England in August.[142] Given that the disaster to the ship had made headlines around the world, the deaths of Frissell, his cameraman Alexander Penrod, and the sealers were fully exploited in the film's publicity. "The picture that cost the lives of the producer, Varick Frissell, and 25 members of the crew . . ." was a typical advertisement.[143]

Predictably, the reviews echoed the sentiments expressed at the prerelease test screening in January.[144] The story was "old melodrama" but "it is chiefly with the adventures of the men as a whole that the interest lies and, in this respect, the film is a truly remarkable record." There were "brilliantly photographed scenes of men's hazarous work," while even the sound engineers had "overcome their difficulties with marked success."[145]

Despite the awkwardness of the film's opening and closing scenes (which seem even more melodramatic today) Frissell most assuredly succeeded in his aim of portraying the Newfoundland people's "dramatic struggle for existence." *The Viking* is a Newfoundland film, in true spirit if not in law, and a remarkable testament by Frissell to the people of that island.

CHAPTER 7

Supporting Program

Though less glamorous than making feature films, the production of sponsored industrial films, documentaries, and travelogues has always been an important part of the Canadian film industry. Such films can provide a basic commercial underpinning, a pool of trained technicians, and the laboratory facilities necessary for the development and maintenance of a viable, ongoing film industry. The production of feature films may have a high profile in the public's eyes but, even at the best of times, it is a high risk business. The production of films sponsored and paid for by industrial companies or institutions can be predictably profitable. It is difficult to imagine a film industry, in the western world at least, operating without such production. It ensures that film processing facilities are available, that cameramen, editors, and technicians have continuing work, and—for the more adventuresome producer—provides an income that he can use to finance the production of theatrical shorts and features.

It is not at all unusual for such production to exist. What was unusual in Canada was that, after the collapse of the post-war thrust to produce Canadian feature films, it became almost the only domestic production. There were the rather dubious "Canadian" efforts that arose through the protection provided under the British quota. There were sporadic attempts to produce theatrical short films. There was the more consistent effort of Gordon Sparling on the theatrical *Canadian Cameo* series. But most of the activity was in government or in those companies specializing in the production of sponsored films and of Canadian newsreel footage for foreign companies.

It is a depressing picture and one that was not to be relieved for some three decades. If you were a Canadian in the Thirties and wanted to work in films you did so at the moribund Canadian Government Motion Picture Bureau in Ottawa, at Associated Screen News in Montreal, or at one of the handful of similar, but smaller, companies across the country. There were many technicians—Roy Tash, Frank O'Byrne, J. Booth Scott, Harry Pollard, Jack Chisholm, Bert Mason, Jean Arsin, John Alexander, Bert Bach, W. H. Graham among others—who remained and produced highly professional work. There were others—Albert Tessier, Maurice Proulx, Harlan Smith, Richard Finnie, P. A. Taverner—who made valuable films independently, but auxilliary to their principal professions. But there were few who attempted to expand their film making in more creative directions. Gordon Sparling in Montreal, Bill Oliver in Calgary, and Dick Bird in Regina were notable rarities. And if their work stands out in retrospect, it is perhaps more for that very rarity. Amidst the dearth of quality film making in the Thirties anything above the level of the routine seems that much more memorable. Which is not to diminish their very real achievement.

The production of sponsored films in Canada goes back at least to the Edison produced film for Massey Harris in 1898 and to the CPR sponsored immigration films. Several early Canadian film companies were to find their principal income in such production, including the Pathescope Company and Filmcraft Industries of Toronto. As the Film and Slide Company of Canada (later the Screen and Sound Service), Pathescope was to continue producing sponsored films through the late Twenties and early Thirties; Filmcraft Industries folded soon after its studio fire and the premature death of Blaine Irish in 1923. In Toronto, George Brownridge's Adanac Films, Atlas Films, Commercial Films, and Unique Photoplays (in all of which Charles Roos was involved) were all active before 1920 in sponsored production.[1] In Montreal, Canadian Films had an ongoing production program of industrial films in addition to producing health education films for the Saskatchewan government. By 1920 they had made films for Bell Telephone (*Speeding the Spoken Word*), the Windsor Hotel, the McKinnon Steel Company, Canadian Explosives Ltd., the Montreal Dairy Company, and Holt Renfrew.[2]

Dick Bird had been one of Pathescope's most active cameramen, shooting films for the Ontario government and for industrial companies. For Pathescope he had travelled to China and had several times worked in Saskatchewan and the Maritimes on Pathescope produced films. Deciding that, if he could do this work for Pathescope, he could do it for himself, he moved to Regina and set himself up as a freelance film maker. He worked as a newsreel cameraman for the *Fox Canadian News*, produced numerous sponsored and educational films (for the Saskatchewan government, General Electric, the CNR, National Harvesters, and the anti-TB League), and became interested in and expert at wildlife filming. Later, he was to provide considerable superb footage to the Walt Disney Studios for their wildlife films and to tour with his own nature films through the Audubon Society in the United States and Canada.[3] Though never interested in feature production, two of his most memorable short films were to be dramatic in the manner first developed by Ernest Ouimet and capitalized on by George Brownridge and others—films which promoted the sponsor's message through a dramatic story. And, as with Ouimet's films, both films were designed to sell an idea rather than a product. *This Generation* (1934) sponsored by the Saskatchewan Co-operative Wheat Producers was an attempt to encourage university graduates to return to the land and bring the benefits of their education to farming. Though somewhat over-earnest, it reflects, kindly, the special qualities of rural life on the prairies in the Thirties. *Youth Marches On* (1937), a twenty-three minute drama sponsored by the Oxford Group Movement, was filmed in Saskatchewan, completed in London, and gained a major theatrical release in North America and Britain. Designed to promote "the call to the New Frontier," it featured Hugh Campbell and Cecil Broadhurst and its use of a song as an integrated part of the story gives some truth to its claim as Canada's first "musical."[4]

Jean Arsin was another early newsreel cameraman who later worked on numerous sponsored films. While at the Winnipeg Publicity Bureau in 1919, he had provided newsreel footage to *Fox Canadian News* and had himself produced a film on the Winnipeg General Strike.[5] He moved to Montreal and, in 1924, produced a dramatic film "representing incidents in the life of the Count of Frontenac." This was sponsored by the local Frontenac Brewery and was apparently a great success.[6] Later, he worked on the first Canadian sound films for Herbert Berliner, son of Emile Berliner of disc recording and gramophone fame. Herbert Berliner had become interested in movies and the possibility of combining them with his disc sound system. He organized Apex Film Parlant in 1928 and, with Jean Arsin as cameraman, created a series of films with Quebec folk singers. Among them were Juliette Beliveau, Eugène Daigneault, Arthur Lapierre, and Gaston St. Jacques singing such well known songs as *En roulant ma boule*, *Mon pitou*, *Le Vagabond*, and *L'Hirondelle*. Walter Darling, who recorded the sound for those films was later to set up sound recording facilities for Associated Screen News.

There were to be other companies involved in sponsored production but none, apart from Associated Screen News, had much real impact on the industry. Screenads of B.C. worked for the Bureau of Provincial Information,[7] Arthur Gottlieb's Audio Pictures produced some industrial films, while the Photo-Sound Corporation of Montreal, headed by J. J. Burns, was more of a film service than a production company, offering editing, processing, and sound recording facilities. It provided recording facilities to both the Canadian Government and Ontario Motion Picture Bureaus for their first sound films and edited footage supplied by industrial companies and others into a release form.

Of somewhat more interest is the work of several individuals, all amateurs in the sense that film making was not their principal profession. Most of their films were created from a desire to design visual material for their work; most now remain important ethnological and social records of their time. Indian and Eskimo life and the northern regions of Canada, received a major share of this filming.

George H. Wilkins had filmed the Canadian Arctic Expedition under Vilhjalmur Stefansson in 1913–16. In the summer of 1920, J. Booth Scott sailed down the Mackenzie river and photographed *Down North*, which was released by the Canadian Government Motion Picture Bureau in 1921. George H. Valiquette, a professional newsreel cameraman, was the official cameraman for the annual eastern Arctic expeditions of the Canadian Government in 1922, 1923, and 1925. Roy Tash provided the same service in 1924. On board the Arctic patrol ship, C. G. S. *Arctic*, in 1924 was a seventeen-year-old wireless operator, Richard S. Finnie, who acted as Tash's unofficial assistant and who from 1928 on was to make by far the most significant contribution to the filmic recording of the traditional way of life in the north. He was official photographer and historian of the eastern Arctic expeditions of 1928–29 and 1937, creating the six-reel *In the Shadow of the Pole* (1928), *The Arctic Patrol* (1929), and *Northwest Passage Patrol* (1937), the first of which was shown extensively in Canadian theatres. He was on, and filmed, the first flight ever made to King William Island and the area of the North Magnetic Pole (1930), travelled extensively throughout the Mackenzie District in the Thirties, and spent a year among the Copper Eskimos in 1930–31, creating *Winter in an Arctic Village* and the six-reel *Among the Igloo Dwellers*—later shortened for educational release as *Ikpuck the Igloo Dweller* (1934). Among Finnie's other films of the Thirties are *The Last Frontier* (1934), *Wandering Through French Canada* (1935), *Anticosti Island* (1935), and *Canada Moves North* (1939), later adapted by James Beveridge for release by the National Film Board as *Northwest Frontier* (1943). The author of a number of books and many magazine and newspaper articles, Finnie made some ninety documentary and industrial films between 1928 and 1968. [8]

There were to be other Canadian films of the Arctic (including *Big Game in the Sub-Arctic* (1925) by James C. Critchell-Bullock and John Hornby and *Sunset or Sunrise* (1927), a five-reel film on Eskimo life and the activities of the Church by Archdeacon A. L. Fleming) but no one was to film as actively, extensively, or creatively as Richard Finnie.

American born Harlan Smith came to Canada in 1911 as an archeologist with the National Museum of Canada. He travelled extensively across Canada and, partly as a result of his inaugurating weekly lectures for children and adults, he set out to provide himself with visual lecture material that would be more alive and interesting to his audiences than mere words and objects. Single-handedly, and on a shoestring budget, he filmed Plains and Northwest Coast Indian life from 1923 to 1930, creating more than two dozen films which form probably the most complete collection of ethnographic film records on the early life of these Indians. From then until his retirement in 1937, Smith's only other film was the forty-five-minute *Cheenama, the Trailmaker: An Indian Idyll of Old Ontario* (1935). An attempt to reconstruct the traditional Algonquin family life, it failed as an ethnographic record but was extensively used in schools and lectures across North America for more than two decades.[9]

Maurice Proulx and Albert Tessier, two Quebec priests, were to make major contributions in using films to document the traditional Quebec way of life. L'Abbé Maurice Proulx shot much documentary footage of the opening of the Abitibi region. His films such as *En pays neuf*, *Roque Maure*, *Défrichement motorisé*, and *Brûlage des Abatis* are a priceless record of their time and of the difficulties of building a settlement in that barren area. After 1941 his films were to receive wider circulation through Le Service de Ciné-Photographie de la Province de Québec.

Proulx's work, though it forms now a precious social record, is of minimal cinematic interest. That of l'Abbé Albert Tessier is extraordinary. Tessier was a film maker, a man with a sentient eye, able to capture the essence of life around him. Though inevitably imbued with a Catholic vision, his films are not without resemblance to those of Robert Flaherty and, in their sensitive perception of nature and wild life, comparable to those of Bill Oliver. It is a curious comment on the Canadian film scene of the period that Tessier and Oliver should have been producing not dissimilar work at the same time and yet be completely unaware of each other's films.

Tessier began filming in 1925 during his travels among the rivers and lakes of the Manouan region, the Gouin reservoir, and the St-Maurice river valley. Each summer, from 1927 to 1957, he travelled in this region under the auspices of the St-Maurice Forest Protective Association who provided him with boats, supplies, and guides. The film costs he had to cover himself. His most intensive film making period was from 1927 to 1937 though after 1937, when he was named propagandist for the Catholic Church's program in family education, he continued to make films illustrating rural life, home life, peasant crafts, and the activities of the Church's *Ecoles ménagères*. Almost all of his films were in colour and silent, designed, like those of Harlan Smith, to be used in conferences, meetings, and lectures during which Tessier himself presented the spoken commentary.

In films such as *La Chasse aux images* (1926), *Dans le bois* (1925–30), *La Pêche* (1937–40), *Arbres et bêtes* (1942–43), *La Grande vie tonifiante de la forêt* (1942–43) he captured, sensitively and movingly, the living world of Quebec forests, rivers, and lakes. *Hommage à notre paysannerie* (1938), *Conquête constructive* (1939), *Le Crédo au paysan* (1942), and *Artisanat familial* (1939–42) are poetic evocations of Tessier's belief in the rural roots and strength of Quebec. *Gloire à l'eau*, his favourite film, he was continually re-structuring—though it had been selected for the International Amateur Movie Show in New York in 1938. As with *Cantique du soleil* (1935, based on the writings of St. Francis of Assisi), *Bénissez-le Seigneur* (1942), and *Cantique de la création* (1942), it is a highly personal film in which Tessier sought to express through acutely poetic imagery, his deepest feelings about life, nature, work, and the land, and the sense of the sacred as reflected in Quebec society. In some thirty years of active film making he created more than seventy films.[10] Not all have survived since he screened his original copy in all his conferences and lectures. In all Tessier's films there is an unfailing attention to and awareness of the milieu in which he lived and worked, a sense of lyric reportage that seems not far removed from that of Pierre Perrault and Michel Brault in a later generation.

Ben Norrish Again — With Gordon Sparling

Throughout all this period only one private film company was to survive in active production for more than a few years. Associated Screen News, in fact, long held the reputation of Canada's longest surviving film production agency—though both Crawley Films of Ottawa and the National Film Board of Canada will soon surpass its record of thirty-eight years.[11] Given the Canadian film milieu in the Twenties and Thirties, the sheer longevity of ASN is itself a tribute to its founder and general manager, Bernard E. Norrish. Ben Norrish had founded the federal government's Film Bureau in Ottawa where he had developed an efficient film laboratory and an active production agency whose films were being viewed in theatres around the world. In 1920 he was persuaded by Edward Beatty, president of Canadian Pacific Railway, to leave the Bureau and set up Associated Screen News. The CPR had long been active in film production and for some years had had its own staff camera-men. Its experiences with Adanac Films and in producing the eight-reel film (shot by Tracey Mathewson) of the 1919 Canadian tour of the Prince of Wales, convinced the company of the merits of having its own film company. Charles Urban, now in New York, encouraged this idea, suggesting that the company could not only produce films for the CPR and for other companies but also shoot newsreel footage under contract.

So, in July 1920, Associated Screen News of Canada Limited was es-tablished in Montreal with the CPR as a majority shareholder, a quarter of a million dollars invested, and with Ben Norrish as general manager—and later, president.[12] As with all the CPR's forays into film production it was a remarkably venturesome and sophisticated development. For the first time, a Canadian film company had adequate financial backing, efficient business management (under the CPR's supervision), and a general manager of proven ability in film. And Norrish was to confirm the CPR's initial judgement. Associated Screen News grew rapidly from a staff of two (Norrish and John M. Alexander, formerly with Norrish at the Film Bureau in Ottawa) in July 1920, to sixty in 1927, and over one hundred in 1930. By the end of that decade it was the dominant force in Canadian film—far more significant than the Canadian Government Motion Picture Bureau, as John Grierson recog-nized—and was producing a wide range of films from theatrical shorts to sponsored industrial films and newsreels.

One of Norrish's first acts had been to build a film laboratory for ASN;[13] by 1929 that laboratory was processing twenty-two million feet of film a year and was preparing positive release prints of American films dis-tributed in Canada for all but one American company. (Before this, release prints were processed in the United States and shipped across the border.) As had Ouimet before him, Norrish recognized the merits of combining Canadian newsreel material with that of foreign newsreels. He felt that the failure of Canadian newsreels stemmed mainly from their inability to include international news in their releases. Ouimet had solved this with his *British Pathé News*, combining the British *Pathé News* with Canadian material shot by his own cameramen. Norrish was to follow much the same pattern. From the first months of ASN's existence it supplied Canadian newsfilm to foreign newsreels—*The Selznick News*, *Kinograms*, *Gaumont News*, *Gaumont Weekly*, and *Pictorial Life*.[14] Soon after, Norrish secured the contract to supply a Canadian section to *Pathé News*—Ouimet's operation having ceased. From that point, newsreel production steadily grew into an important part of ASN's activities. By 1929, ASN had staff cameramen, including Roy Tash and Frank O'Byrne, located across Canada from Saint John to Victoria.[15]

The studios and laboratories of Associated Screen News
in Montreal.

Soundtrucks for shooting location sound newsfilm were acquired in 1931 (while Brownridge was still noisily but ineffectively promoting the formation of *Canadian Sound News*) and in the Thirties ASN was to supply most major American newsreels with Canadian material. *Fox Movietone* was the only major exception: for their Canadian edition they had their own group of Canadian cameramen, which included Dick Bird, Bill Oliver, Jean Arsin, and Len Roos. ASN's supplying of Canadian footage to American newsreels was not only for Canadian editions.[16] Much of the material they provided ended up also in international editions—as did Roy Tash's famous films of the Dionne Quintuplets.

While establishing the production program of the federal government's Film Bureau, Norrish had recognized that its effectiveness depended on ensuring theatrical release for the films. He was to repeat that approach with Associated Screen News. Within a year of the company's founding, Norrish released the first of ASN's theatrical short film series, *Kinograms*.[17] Released in Canada by Canadian Universal, the *Kinograms* were travelogues about Canada and some foreign countries largely shot on routes served by CPR rail, ferry, or ship services, and were in fact thinly disguised promotions for travel by CPR. The series continued through the Twenties and not uncommonly duplicated films on similiar themes produced by the Canadian Government Motion Picture Bureau. (Though, unlike the latter's films, they had only limited foreign release.) Among them were such films as *Old French Canada* (1921), *Heap Busy Indians* (1922), *Pidgin' Land* (1923), *Land of Ancestral Gods* (1923), *Lake of the Woods* (1924), *Canada's Last West* (1924), *The Fishing Parson* (1925), *Sky Trails in the Bear Country* (1925), *The Classic Nipigon* (1926), *Rivers of Romance* (1927), *Yukon* (1928), *The Beautiful Nipigon* (1929), and, inevitably, *Niagara* (1929). Alongside them, to produce twenty to twenty-five new releases a year, were a range of other travelogue, documentary, and interest films. Plus, of course, sponsored industrial films, for the production of which ASN had been initially established. Among the better examples of ASN's documentaries of the Twenties are: *A Mooseback in the Miramachi* (1924), *Tobique Secrets* (1925), and *The Moose Spoofer* (1925); three Berton S. Moore films of Northern New Brunswick wildlife (he was to make many others for ASN); *Canada's Diamond Jubilee* (1927); *Princes and Premier* (1927) on the 1927 Canadian visits of the Prince of Wales and British Prime Minister Baldwin; *Fish and Medicine Men* (1928) on Kwakiutl Indian life and the salmon fishing and canning industries of B.C.; and *Saving the Sagas* (1927) on the work of Marius Barbeau and Ernest MacMillan in recording the music, dances, and rites of the Wolf Indians of British Columbia. There were numerous others, including *Forging the Links of Empire* (1924), *Climbing into Canada's Past* (1925), J. Booth Scott's *Kawartha Muskeys* (1928), *Tadoussac* (1928), *A New Yorker's Canadian Weekend* (1928), and *Miracle at Beauharnois* (1931)—the first film directed at ASN by thirty-one-year-old Gordon Sparling.

Inevitably, ASN was also to produce for CPR each year several films to promote immigration, including *New Homes Within the Empire* (1922), *Making New Canadians* (1925), *British Success in Canadian Farming* (1928), Roy Tash's *From British Home to Canadian Farm* (1929), and *Canada, The New Homeland* (1930). Though many of ASN's documentaries of the Twenties have gained interest over the years as social records of Canadian life, they are generally routine, if always competent, productions of a somewhat more craftsmanlike quality than the later Motion Picture Bureau efforts and at least as good as comparable films from any other country. In the manner of the times, the explanatory inter-titles of the silent films tend to seem now cloyingly sentimental or cutely comical. Author of many of the ASN titles was Terry Ramsaye, the first major historian of the motion picture and author of the classic *A Million and One Nights*, published in 1926.

This assessment is true also of the many ASN films sponsored by outside firms, films such as *Achievement: The Story of a Store* (1929) on the operations of the T. Eaton Company, which was photographed by Roy Tash, *The Toronto Star* (1929), *Petroleum, Alberta's Newest Industry* (1929), and the feature-length *Cotton* (1927), photographed by Roy Tash for the Dominion Textile Company.

In editorial charge of production during this time and "director" (though uncredited) of many of the films was John M. Alexander, who later became vice-president of the company. Major cameramen working for ASN across the country included Roy Tash and Frank O'Byrne in Toronto, Berton S. Moore who was producing wild life films in New Brunswick, J. Booth Scott (later to become head of production at the Motion Picture Bureau in Ottawa) who was filming in the Rockies and on the West Coast, and James Campbell who was making similar films on the Prairies. Later, others, such as Ross Beesley and Alfred Jacquemin, were to join ASN.

Sponsored films were to continue to play a major role in ASN's activities through the Thirties, and even later. ASN produced industrial and promotional films for most of the major Canadian companies and for many American companies with Canadian branch plants: Shell Oil, the Ford Motor Company, General Motors of Canada, Famous Players Canadian Corporation, Ottawa Hydro, Canadian General Electric, International Harvester of Canada, International Nickel Company of Canada, the Province of Quebec, Canadian Wheat Board, Sun Life, Bell Telephone, various breweries and distilleries, and many, many more. Most were designed simply to depict and publicize the activities of the company in question and now appear rather gauche in the crude way they make their point—as in Gordon Sparling's *Cold Facts* (1938) which, though ostensibly a documentary on the use of modern machinery in the north, is in fact a rather unsubtle commercial for Trac Tractors. However, not all the sponsored films were commercials for the company. Occasionally, a company would sponsor a "public-spirited" film of more general interest—as did General Motors of Canada with *Forward Canada!* (1930), designed as an antidote to the Depression and directed by Gordon Sparling for ASN before he became a staff member of the company. Or, *Wings Over the Atlantic* (1937), sponsored by Shell Oil and also directed by Gordon Sparling, which is a record of the first trans-Atlantic commercial flight between London and New York via Gander. (Though not a commercial, Shell Oil's pumps are rather evident throughout.) Or, Sun Life's Anti-

The sound stage of ASN's studios in 1939 during production of a sponsored film. Gordon Sparling can be seen leaning on the car.

Typhoid film (1927), *Canadian Firsts* (1939), sponsored by Lake of the Woods Milling Company, and General Motors of Canada's *On to Victory* (1940), directed by John Alexander. Associated Screen News also produced dozens of travelogues, repetitions often of earlier films and most commonly sponsored by the CPR—including John McDougall's *From Sea to Sea* (1936) and *Ski Trails of New France* (1938), Norman Hull's *Radiant Rockies*, Gordon Sparling's *Top of the World* (1939) with an original music score by Horace Lapp, and *Ski Time in the Rockies* (1939), not forgetting the curiously titled *Life Aboard a Duchess* and *Life Aboard an Empress*. ASN also produced travelogues for other companies such as those of Phillip Pitt-Taylor for Le Service de Ciné-Photographie de la Province de Québec: *ByWays of New France*, *Islands of the St. Lawrence*, and *Wonderland of Gaspé*. Many notable Canadian musicians composed or arranged the music for ASN: Howard Fogg, Horace Lapp, and Lucio Agostini—one of whose memorable scores was for the Ontario Hydro-sponsored *The Bright Path* (1939), directed by Gordon Sparling.

The importance in which the sponsored film was held by ASN is illustrated by its building a fully equipped sound stage at its Montreal studios in 1936 in order to produce a feature-length dramatized documentary to promote Shell Oil products and services. *House in Order* (1936), depicting the romantic adventures of a service station attendant and his wife, was directed by Gordon Sparling and featured John Pratt and Mildred Mitchell. It was ASN's only feature-length production in the Thirties—and it was very much a sponsored film. Its production did, however, result in the building of a sound stage which was the first in Canada, and, for a time, among the most modern in the world. The quota film *From Nine to Nine* was produced using ASN's studio facilities.

Associated Screen News' main departure in the Thirties from the production of sponsored documentaries and newsreels came about under the direct influence of one of its new employees, Gordon Sparling. Born August 13, 1900, he had been educated at the University of Toronto and had worked at Hart House Theatre with Roy Mitchell, co-producer of *The Proof of Innocence*. He had joined the Ontario Government Motion Picture Bureau just before its expansion and move to the Trenton Studios. After a brief—and not entirely happy—sojourn working for Canadian International Films on *Carry On, Sergeant*, Sparling spent a year in Ottawa with the Canadian Government Motion Picture Bureau, found it not at all to his liking, and moved to New York. At the famous Astoria Studios in Long Island he did various odd jobs, learning the profession. He returned, briefly, to Canada to make *Forward Canada!* for ASN and was invited by Ben Norrish to head ASN's new production department. Sparling accepted—but on condition that he be allowed to produce theatrical shorts in addition to sponsored films. Norrish was not at all averse to the idea. The *Kinograms* series had died with the

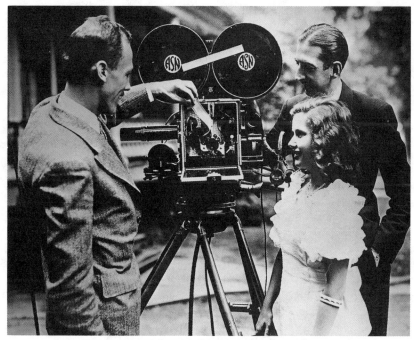

Gordon Sparling (left) with Roy Tash during production of
Back in '23.

arrival of sound but he had not forgotten his long-standing commitment
to the importance of theatrical release. He was also, however, aware of the
equal, if not greater, importance of ASN's financial stability. So he accepted
the idea, provided that the budget for each film was fixed at around three
thousand dollars, and that the production cost of each was covered by rentals
from theatrical release. (Since the budget did not include overheads and staff
salaries, they were in fact subsidized by ASN's other activities.) So, in 1932,
the *Canadian Cameo* series was born. It was to represent Canada's only continuing creative film effort in the Thirties, and, through international theatrical release, almost the full measure of Canada's image on its own and the
world's screens.[18] They were not only to be Canada's first theatrical shorts
in sound but were to include the first Canadian theatrical short in colour—
Royal Banners over Ottawa (1939) a two-reel film in Dufay colour—and to
introduce Canadian composed music (by Howard Fogg) into Canadian films.
The series was to continue, under Gordon Sparling's supervision, until

1953. Eighty-five films in all, most of which were directed by Sparling himself though occasionally other directors, such as James W. Campbell, would direct the sports films.

The *Canadian Cameos* were to be what their name suggests: short vignettes of different aspects of Canadian life. Each ten minutes in length (with two exceptions), they were far more diverse in subject matter than the earlier *Kinograms* and the *Seeing Canada* series. Topics ranged from "Sport Chats"—*Hockey, Canada's National Game* (1932), *Breezing Along* (1933), *Hockey Champions* (1933), *This Badminton Racket* (1936), *Ornamental Swimming* (1937)—to historical compilations about Canada—*Back in '22* (1932), *Back in '23* (1933), *Back in '14* (1934)—and to collections of oddities about Canada and Canadians in the *Did You Know That?* mini-series. Today, their style seems a little declamatory (their commentaries read by Corey Thomson and musical scores by Howard Fogg are especially strident) but they reflect flair, imagination, and a good deal more variety than other theatrical shorts of the same period, whether Canadian or foreign. Even the city portraits, not the most inspiring of subject matters, have a visual inventiveness that seems remarkable alongside the stolid city films of the Motion Picture Bureau. One of these, *Rhapsody in Two Languages* (1934), on Montreal, stands out from among others of its time with a flash of artistic creativity that makes one regret Sparling's lack of opportunity to extend his talents into other film making areas. Depicting Montreal from sunrise to sunrise (in a manner not unlike the "Lullaby of Broadway" number in Busby Berkeley's later *Gold Diggers of 1935*) its rapid cross-cutting blends Howard Fogg's original music with a succession of positive and negative images and optical effects, building to a dizzying climax. Only the intrusive presence of Corey Thomson's voice dates the film in a manner not evident when the theme is conveyed through images and music alone. The approach was not new; Europeans had developed the "city symphony" in the Twenties, though it is likely Sparling had never seen them. However, so imaginative is the style (and Sparling called the technique he developed for it, "the rhapsodic technique") that it is puzzling why he never again applied it with the same flair. Though other *Canadian Cameos* were to use a similar impressionistic (rather than didactic) approach, none have the same sense of rhythm and optical design.

Some of the *Canadian Cameo* films are less successful than others. A few, such as *Point of Honour* (1936), are dull and ponderous. The films adapted from those of Bill Oliver (*She Climbs to Conquer*, 1932 and *Return of the Buffalo*, 1934)—have a "cuteness" not implicit in Oliver's original work; the Bill Oliver-Grey Owl films (*Grey Owl's Little Brother* and *Grey Owl's*

Strange Guests, 1932 and 1934) have an anthropomorphic quality which neither Oliver nor Grey Owl could have intended. But, by and large, the films remain interesting, very much alive, and very Canadian. Perhaps the most important thing about the *Canadian Cameo* series is that the films were actually shown extensively in Canadian theatres, and in British, American, European, Australian, and Far East theatres.[19] As such they represented in the Thirties almost the only reflection to Canadian film audiences of their own cultural efforts. However, despite the continued success of the *Canadian Cameos*, Norrish resisted all pressure to go further and undertake feature film production.

Collage advertising Gordon Sparling's *Rhapsody in Two Languages*.

It is interesting to note that Ben Norrish shared this attitude with Ray Peck of the Motion Picture Bureau. Both men, in their time, were in better positions than anyone to do something about establishing a feature film industry in Canada. Both were adamantly opposed to it. Both loudly proclaimed on several occasions that the production of feature films was best left to the Americans who had the technical expertise. Ray Peck believed in encouraging Hollywood companies to film on location in Canada. Ben Norrish believed that Canada, with its limited population, "had no more use for a large moving picture studio than Hollywood had for a pulp mill." Noting that Florida had tried three times to establish a movie industry "and its principal business continues to be tourists and citrus fruits," Norrish advised Canadians not to invest in feature production unless "they had enough influence to move the centre of population as well."[20]

This was, indeed, the prevalent attitude in the Thirties amongst Canadians with some expertise. If you knew enough about the economic structure of the international (i.e. Hollywood) film industry it seemed foolhardy to do battle. Canadian excursions into the field only confirmed this view; though the continued success of film stock promotion swindles through the Twenties and Thirties suggests there were still Canadians with an emotional commitment to the idea of Canadian feature production, however abortive.

Perhaps Norrish's attitudes can be criticized from the comfort of hindsight as over-conservative. But such a perception must be judiciously weighed against his remarkable achievements. He did succeed in operating a successful film production company for many years. He did ensure that Canadians saw something of themselves on their newsreel screens, and he did provide Canadians with a theatrical short film series that was seen worldwide. And in this, in the Thirties, he stands alone. His achievement is all the more remarkable given the current bleakness of the Canadian film scene. Without Norrish, it would likely have been a great deal bleaker.

An End And a Beginning

By the late Thirties, that bleakness began to seem less harsh. New film companies sprang up, two of which—Crawley Films of Ottawa headed by F. R. ("Budge") Crawley and Judy Crawley, and the Vancouver Motion Picture Company headed by Leon Shelley—were to become continuing forces in Canadian film. These film makers made their first films, as independents, before the war and both companies were to grow as a result of the additional film work generated by the war. And then, in 1938, there arrived in Canada a ferociously energetic Scot who was to have profound and far-reaching effects on the course of film in Canada. John Grierson was the principal exponent of a film movement which had not yet reached Canada: the production of documentaries with a definite sense of social purpose, films which would show everyday life and ordinary people in a highly creative and exciting way, films which would help people communicate with each other. He was later to say he looked "on the cinema as a pulpit and used it as a propagandist."[21] He had established a creative documentary film unit in Britain at the Empire Marketing Board and later at the GPO. When Vincent Massey, Canadian high commissioner in London, urged on by his private secretary, Ross McLean, began to complain about the paucity of effective Canadian information films, Grierson seemed a natural choice to help improve the situation. At the suggestion of Ross McLean, John Grierson was invited to Ottawa by the Canadian government to report on its film activities.

Grierson arrived in May 1938 and hit bureaucratic Ottawa like a whirlwind. In his investigation he brooked no delays from civil servants, used to taking weeks to prepare reports and reply to memoranda. And since he had the ear of Prime Minister MacKenzie King, he got the answers to his questions with remarkable speed. It did not take him long to reach his conclusions. Working with a speed and concentration that astonished officials, he submitted on June 23, 1938, a sixty-page report replete with his characteristic prose. Terse and to the point, it avoided the euphemisms commonly found in such reports and hit hard at the weaknesses of the Motion Picture Bureau. Though Canada, said Grierson, had taken an important early initiative with the formation of the Bureau, it had fallen behind the times since 1931. The Bureau's films were competent but not dynamic enough to capture markets. The permanent nature of the Bureau's staff bred complacency (and privately he added that several of the Bureau's film makers should have been pensioned off years before). There were, he felt, three weaknesses in Canadian government film work: it lacked "a considered directive policy with regard for Canada as a whole"; there was no "strong, creative film unit" to carry out the policy; and individual government departments were too parochial in their concerns. The Bureau was treated as an unimaginative factory for supplying cameramen and equipment for departmental scripts and he had been horrified to discover that departmental "experts" often took over the directing and editing of the films they commissioned. The Bureau had to be released from "the inferiority complex" in which it had become trapped and developed "as a powerful instrument of government propaganda policy." He recommended the creation of a continuing board, headed by an appointed film commissioner, to guide, criticize, and review the work of the

Bureau. The board would include both government representatives and members of the public.[22] It was strong stuff, especially for Badgley and the Bureau's staff, who must have been horrified at the notion of making "propaganda" films.

Most federal officials found Grierson's proposals for reform rather more vigorous than they had expected. For several months no action was taken on the report. Then, under mounting pressure from the Bureau (left in limbo because of the government's inactivity) and from such interested parties as the National Film Society (now the Canadian Film Institute), the government agreed to act. In November, Grierson was invited back in order to implement his recommendations and, with characteristic energy, he set up a full round of meetings with departmental officials and representatives of the commercial film industry. Some of the film companies were concerned that the strengthening of the Bureau could only lessen the already meagre amount of work they did for the government. Grierson assured them that there would be plenty of work for all and, true to his word, was later to commission production to the commercial industry—including ASN, Crawley Films, the Vancouver Motion Picture Company, and Audio Pictures.

In December, after requesting detailed policy needs from all ministers and getting no response, Grierson himself drafted the National Film Act which would establish the National Film Board. He had considered one of the inherent weaknesses of the Bureau's structure to have been its creation through order-in-council and not through a legislative act of Parliament. If the new Film Board was to have any continuing strength and autonomy it must be created by Parliamentary action. Within three weeks of his second arrival, Grierson had a draft bill before the overwhelmed ministers for their consideration. And, on March 16, 1939, the National Film Act passed its final reading in the House.[23] The National Film Board of Canada came into being and Grierson, somewhat reluctantly, since he had other plans, accepted the position of film commissioner in October 1939.

As first designed, the National Film Board was to act in an advisory capacity; the Bureau would still continue as the active production arm. But it was inevitable, given Grierson's forceful personality, that this could not continue for long. Considerable antagonism developed between the older staff members of the Bureau and the new, young, film makers Grierson brought in. Their ideas and impatience roused hostility and resentment among the permanent civil servants of the Bureau who remained fiercely loyal to Frank Badgley, still the director of the Bureau. Although no one was aware of it at the time, the passing of the National Film Act was the first step in the dissolution of the Motion Picture Bureau. Within two years, practical expediency, Grierson's drive, and the pressures of world events during the war were to lead to the absorption of the Bureau by the more powerful NFB. In June 1941, by order-in-council, the control and supervision of the Motion Picture Bureau passed from the Department of Trade and Commerce to the National Film Board.[24] Frank Badgley was offered the insulting position of director of the Stills Division which was to remain with Trade and Commerce. Mortified, he refused the offer indignantly and transferred to the Department of Veterans' Affairs, a bitterly disappointed man. Even years later, his former staff members were to feel he had been treated cavalierly, given his years of service.

But it was to have been expected. He was of another age, and another kind of film making, the direct opposite of Grierson and the passion he brought to his work. Badgley's passing marked the end of an era in Canadian film making. With Grierson's arrival, the Canadian cinema was to take on a different shape and a different significance around the world.

CHAPTER 8

Postscript

It is possible to construct a theoretical model for the history of film in Canada, based paradigmatically on the histories of film in most European countries. This model would begin with showmen exploiting a new technical invention, exhibiting films the origin of which was irrelevant to everyone concerned. Some of the showmen might even make a few films on their own account. By 1903, as public interest in simple record and trick films began to wane, these showmen/producers would begin, gradually, to draw on the narrative tradition and its formal techniques as exemplified in the nineteenth century novel and melodrama. Throughout the first decade of the twentieth century there would be sporadic attempts to produce short anecdotal dramas alongside the actuality films. Many of those involved would have a background in theatre or vaudeville. By 1910, these attempts would consolidate themselves around studios, probably scattered across the country, headed by entrepreneurs or active producers. Gradually, one centre of studio production (usually in the capital city) would come to dominate the rest and those other (often regional) studios would tend to disappear. Narrative films would become longer, more complex in plot and character, and in the use of point of view. Production would be almost entirely studio-based and the earlier use of natural locations minimized. The First World War would be a crisis point and would either diminish production (as in France) or increase it (as in Sweden). Soon after, or by the early Twenties, the film industry would have to face the increasing hegemony of Hollywood. Government would intervene to protect the industry on economic and cultural grounds. It might legislate that theatres and distributorships had to be owned by citizens of that country, that a certain percentage of profit from the box-office be returned to finance national production, or that theatres exhibited a certain minimum content of national production. In any event, independent production would almost entirely disappear and the industry would become increasingly controlled by banks and other financial institutions. The legislative measures would have a certain success but, from the mid-Twenties until the Second World War, the industry would face a series of crises: falling attendance, the introduction of sound, the Depression. The industry might weaken but would never totally collapse. Finally, the Second World War would preface new changes. Throughout, Hollywood films would enjoy considerable, increasing, profits and many producers would seek success by imitating them.[1]

It will have been apparent from the pages of this history that this model is not applicable to Canada, even though its outlines can be seen. These are sharper in the early years but become increasingly fuzzy after 1922. Since this model does, however, represent the pattern of film history in most countries and, with some differences (most notably the role of government), even in the United States, it is important to consider the nature of the variations from the model and the possible reasons for their existence.

In the early years, up to about 1914, the production and use of films in Canada was much like that anywhere else. It is true that there seems to have been in Canada somewhat more emphasis on the pragmatic, quasi-educational, use of film than one finds elsewhere. But it would have been difficult to predict in, say, 1905 that Canada would not have developed a film industry comparable to Italy's. After this, two significant differences emerge. First, the fact that centralized studio production did not develop while regional production (often not using studios) persisted. And second, the fact that the federal and provincial governments did not, in the Twenties, legislate effective protection and support for the production, distribution, or exhibition branches of the industry. These two factors (which may be related) fundamentally distinguish Canada's film history from that of other countries. Certainly they distinguish it more fundamentally than the factor of Hollywood's economic intervention—a problem faced equally in all countries, even in the United States itself.

It has sometimes been argued that the principal problem of Canadian film has been the economic influence of Hollywood. Yet, even in 1922 with the rise of vertical integration in Hollywood, the loss of Canadian theatres to foreign control, and the disappearance of independent production (in the United States and Europe as well as Canada), the industry in Canada was not strong. Most assuredly it had considerable potential at this time and the films produced not ones of which the makers need be ashamed. But it was not strong, not as strong as, say, the British or Swedish industries which also had to cope with Hollywood. It was, in fact, so weak it collapsed entirely, leaving only government production, short film production, and, later, branch plant production.

There is, of course, the failure by governments to intervene on behalf of the Canadian industry. This failure, some would argue, relates more broadly to the Canadian scene, being based on an assumption that serious measures to counter American economic influence amount to intolerant protectionism. And one might legitimately assert that had someone of more vision than Ray Peck headed the Motion Picture Bureau at the critical point, at least some of the industry's difficulties would have been ameliorated. Certainly the industry would not have become in the Thirties such an unmistakable branch plant of Hollywood. Perhaps the seeds might have been planted that would have grown after World War II into a more lively industry.

But it is probably simplistic to lay sole blame on the head of Ray Peck and others in government. Such a conclusion begs the question since, if the industry had been stronger, more cohesive, Peck and the government could hardly have failed to act in its support. But there was, in fact, no industry comparable, even on a smaller scale, to that of Hollywood. Activities were scattered, the result of individual, uncoordinated, efforts. Production was quite distinct from distribution and exhibition (the Allens, for example, never involved themselves in production as their American counterparts did) and there was no continuing system for financing production. The activities that existed, though far from negligible, could be seen (and were seen by Peck) as of minimal economic or cultural relevance to the international film structure of the Twenties.

This aspect was not unique to Canada: vertical integration and the financial backing of Wall Street were crucial factors in Hollywood's hegemony over other national cinemas with less monopolistic capitalist structures. But those other cinemas had an industrial base that was at least comparable to that of Hollywood in that it already was, or tended to become, increasingly oligarchic.[2] Canada never, at any time, came close to developing a centralized, monopolistic, structure in its film industry. From first to last it operated within a framework of classical liberalism with full emphasis on the role of individual initiative.[3]

This is apparent throughout the history of Canadian film and is exemplified most clearly in the rise and fall of the Allens' exhibition and distribution interests and of Ernest Shipman's production companies. Both Shipman and the Allens relied heavily on local financing and the support of small investors. In contrast, their rivals (and successors) had the support of large financial institutions on Wall Street, Bay Street, and rue St. Jacques.

Whether this tendency is indicative of a weakness in or failure of the

Canadian socio-economic structure is a complex question that cannot be explored here.[4] But its prevalence was a factor that most certainly helped keep Canada out of the mainstream of the international film industry whose standards were set by Hollywood.

The lack of a centralized studio system can be discussed in similar terms. Measured against contemporaneous Hollywood standards, it represents a failure in the Canadian system: an insistence on both regionalism and possessive individualism at a time when the trend was the converse. Some, such as E. K. Brown, have argued that regionalism is, at best, a stage through which Canada should pass: regionalist art fails "because it stresses the superficial and peculiar at the expense . . . of the fundamental and universal."[5] Others find it a force of decided merit, particularly in the light of today's resistance to the oligarchic tendencies of North American civilization. It has, in any case, continued to prevail as a characterizing aspect of the Canadian experience. But regionalism, too, was a factor that served to isolate Canadian cinema from the international film industry.

Thus, the particular shape of Canadian film history is derived from the general economic and cultural history of the society itself. The economic intervention of Hollywood, while important, was secondary and finally dependent for the strength of its impact on a particular Canadian ethos. To suggest this is not to see the Canadian response as a failure in either imagination or spirit. To do so would be to impose the standards of others. And, as Northrop Frye points out, too much Canadian creative energy "has been absorbed in meeting a standard, a self-defeating enterprise because real standards can only be established, not met."[6]

The same might be said of the films themselves. Hollywood, since about 1920, has always imposed a standard of correctness (comparable to the way Parisian French was "correct" in Quebec until recently). There was, at any given time, only one proper way to "speak" a film.[7] As this history has suggested, the Canadian film only rarely spoke using Hollywood forms. Shipman and Frissell insisted on location shooting when Hollywood was studio-bound; Ouimet, Brownridge, and others leaned towards documentary dramas; Canadian film narratives in general owed little to Hollywood codes and conventions and more to Canadian literature. In fact, one finds in Canadian films, fiction and non-fiction, of this period consistent traces of what such critics as Northrop Frye have identified in Canadian literature. The "triangular conflict of nature, society, and individual" in which "the individual tends to ally himself with nature against society" is evident in several films, but quintessentially in *Back to God's Country*.[8] (Though what Frye calls "the identity of the sinister and terrible elements in nature with the death-wish in man"[9] seems more evident in the three quasi-Canadian films, *Nanook of the North*, *The Silent Enemy*, and *The Viking*.) In the films of Bill Oliver and Albert Tessier in particular, but also less precisely in the idyllic portraits of Canada of the two Motion Picture Bureaus, one finds the pastoral myth with its "nostalgia for a world of peace and protection, with a spontaneous response to the nature around it."[10] Indeed, the most dominant characteristic of all the films is nature and humanity's relation to natural phenomena. Interestingly, Frye's "elegiac and lonely tone" and Margaret Atwood's "survival equals failure" syndrome are absent from Canadian films until more recent times.[11]

This special Canadian naturalism, whose essence is the sense of the environment having a determining and decisive effect on the individual life, found its most powerful formal expression in the documentary, dramatized documentary, or documentary-drama. This is so consistent throughout the history of Canadian cinema that it is impossible not to identify it as the quintessential Canadian film form. But these have never been dominant forms internationally and Hollywood films have perhaps most often exemplified the converse. Here again, then, an approach which seemed best suited to the Canadian spirit also helped place Canadian cinema beyond the mainstream.

In the light of more recent developments in Canadian film one must conclude that this formal aspect has been at least as significant as socioeconomic forces in distinguishing the history of Canadian film. As the Hollywood narrative structure became dominant internationally, the Canadian approach became increasingly isolated from the mainstream. So, too, did the film makers. Unable to communicate in the most proper form and criticized in Canada for attempting to (consider the criticisms of *Policing the Plains* for its lack of "real drama"), the film makers either abandoned fiction films or turned to narrative structures and forms created elsewhere. So appeared such films as *Carry On, Sergeant*, *His Destiny*, and other quota quickies of the Thirties which are finally nothing better than counterfeit Hollywood films. Only in the documentary did the Canadian approach survive and even then only in an impure form. (It might be argued that the theatrical success of the *Canadian Cameos*, for example, stemmed from their following an American model; later, the National Film Board drew on British prototypes in its first years of production.) It was not until the Sixties that the earlier approach to fiction films surfaced again in such films as *Le Chat dans le sac*, *Nobody Waved Goodbye*, *Entre la mer et l'eau douce*, and *Goin' Down the Road*.[12]

Finally, of course, all these factors—liberal economics, regionalism, naturalism—stem from the same roots. These roots are identifiable with the Canadian ethos and represent both its strength and its limitations. If, on the one side, that ethos worked to prevent the Canadian film from capturing international markets, on the other, it may have created a model of what a more democratic film industry might be. If, on the one side, Canadian film makers have rarely made story films that captivated international audiences, on the other, they have offered a reflexive gentleness, a meditative feeling that is often not far removed from the Zen mood of *mono-no-aware*.[13] In the end, the apparent weaknesses of Canadian film are not inconsistent with its apparent strengths. In the end, they are the dialectic of the Canadian ethos.

APPENDIX 1

A Chronology of Film in Canada, 1894–1913

This chronology includes major film developments and activities both in Canada and of significance to the Canadian scene, together with a listing of films produced in Canada during this period. Specific dates have been included wherever appropriate.

Very few of the Canadian films of this period are available for research and study. The National Film Archives in Ottawa has an extensive collection of films made in Canada by foreign producers together with examples of the films made for the CPR by Urban and by Edison. If a copy of a film listed in this chronology is known to exist in an archive, a note to this effect is included in parentheses.

⋙ 1894 ⋘

April 14: Andrew and George Holland of Ottawa open the world's first Kinetoscope Parlor at 1155 Broadway in New York.

⋙ 1895 ⋘

December 28: First public presentation of the Lumière Cinématographe in the Salon Indien of the Grand Café, boulevard des Capucines, Paris. This date is usually considered as marking the true beginnings of motion pictures.

⊸§ 1896 §⊷

April 23: First public presentation of the Edison sponsored Vitascope at Koster and Bial's Music Hall, New York.

July 21: First public presentation of films in Canada at West End Park, Ottawa, promoted by Andrew and George Holland using the Vitascope. Later, films are presented in Toronto, Montreal, and other urban centres by showmen using the American Vitascope, the French Cinématographe or the British Animatographe.

⊸§ 1897 §⊷

September and October: First films of Canadian scenes produced (all featuring Niagara Falls) by Félix Mesguich for Lumière, by W. K. L. Dickson for American Mutoscope and Biograph, and by an unknown cameraman for Edison. (See notes 16 and 24, chap. 1, and note 2, chap. 2 for list of titles. The National Film Archives has several examples of these.)

Robert Bonine films the Klondike Gold Rush. (See note 6, chap. 2, for list of titles. The National Film Archives has several of these.)

James S. Freer films life in Manitoba; his "Ten Years in Manitoba" lecture and film show tours Britain in 1898–99 sponsored by the CPR and again in 1902 sponsored by the Canadian government.

Films are taken "on the road" by travelling showmen such as John C. Green and Frederic Conway Edmonds and begin appearing as a regular attraction in vaudeville theatres.

⊸§ 1898 §⊷

The Massey-Harris Company of Toronto commissions the Edison Company to produce films promoting its products—one of the first uses of film for advertising purposes.

A cameraman for Edison films *Sleighing-Ottawa*.

December 15: John Schuberg presents Vancouver's first film show in an empty store.

⋞ 1899 ⋟

Cameramen for Edison and American Mutoscope and Biograph photograph several films of Canadian public events and of Canadian troops training and departing for the Boer War. (National Film Archives has examples of these.)

May: John Schuberg begins touring out of Winnipeg with his black-tent theatre.

October: G. W. Bitzer films the Rockies from CPR trains for American Mutoscope and Biograph. (National Film Archives has all five of these.)

⋞ 1902 ⋟

The CPR hire the Urban Company of Britain to produce a series of films to stimulate immigration. As the Bioscope Company of Canada, Joe Rosenthal, Cliff Denham, and Guy Bradford make more than thirty-five films in the *Living Canada* series from the fall of 1902 through the summer of 1903. (The National Film Archives has examples of these films, re-released by Urban in the later *Winter Sports* and *Winter Sports in Canada*.)

February: Robert Bonine photographs *Run of a Snowshoe Club*, *Quebec Fire Department on Sleds*, and *What Ho, She Bumps* for American Mutoscope and Biograph. (National Film Archives has the latter two films.)

October: John Schuberg opens the Electric Theatre in Vancouver. By 1903 store-front theatres are common across Canada.

⋞ 1903 ⋟

September: Urban releases the first dramatic film made in Canada: "*Hiawatha*," *The Messiah of the Ojibways*, directed and photographed by Joe Rosenthal, "conceived" by E. A. Armstrong of Montreal. (Length: 800 feet.)

✎§ 1904 §❧

April: George Scott of Toronto films *The Great Toronto Fire*. (National Film Archives.)

Harry Winter of Newfoundland begins filming local events. (Newfoundland Archives.)

✎§ 1905 §❧

American, and some British, producers begin producing "interest" films in Canada. Typical examples: *Moose Hunt in New Brunswick* (1905) and *Salmon Fishing in Quebec* (1905), both photographed by Billy Bitzer for American Mutoscope and Biograph; *Honeymoon at Niagara Falls* (1907), released by Edison; *A Canadian Winter Carnival* (1909), photographed by James White for Edison. (National Film Archives has several examples of these "interest" films.)

✎§ 1906 §❧

January: Ernest Ouimet opens his first Ouimetoscope in Montreal, converting it into a permanent nickelodeon-type theatre in the fall.

March: John C. Griffin opens the Theatorium in Toronto, Canada's first permanent movie theatre.

May: Ernest Ouimet opens the first film exchange in Canada.

October: Jules and Jay Allen open the Theatorium in Brantford—the beginnings of the Allen Theatres chain.

✎§ 1907 §❧

August: Ernest Ouimet opens his second, converted, Ouimetoscope, the first luxury movie theatre in North America.

September: The American Mutoscope and Biograph Company become the first American producers to release a Canadian content dramatic film: *An Acadian Elopement: A Romance in the Land of Evangeline*, photographed by O. L. Poore and O. M. Grove on the coast of New Hampshire, not Nova Scotia. (National Film Archives.)

⋅❧ 1908 ❧⋅

Jules and Jay Allen launch their first film exchange, the Allen Amusement Corporation.

Ernest Ouimet films *Mes espérances* (Cinémathèque québécoise) and *Quebec: The Tercentenary Celebrations*. Later, he films other public events.

The Charles Urban Company is hired by the B.C. government to make films promoting British Columbia.

⋅❧ 1909 ❧⋅

The Charles Urban Company is hired by the Canadian Northern Railway Company to make films to promote emigration from Britain to Canada. At the same time, Butcher's Film Service is hired by the Grand Trunk Railway to produce similar films. (The National Film Archives has one example: *Building of a Transcontinental Railway in Canada*.)

The Kalem Company become the first American production company to make dramatic films on location in Canada. Nine films are released: *The Girl Scout* (1909), *The Cattle Thieves* (1909), *The Canadian Moonshiners* (1910), *Fighting the Iroquois in Canada* (1910), *A Leap for Life* (1910), *The Perversity of Fate* (1910), *Her Indian Mother* (1910), *White Man's Money, The Red Man's Curse* (1910), *For the Flag* (1911).

⋅❧ 1910 ❧⋅

The CPR's Colonization Department sponsors thirteen one-reel films (eleven of them dramatic) made by the Edison Company and designed to promote immigration. They were directed by J. Searle Dawley, photographed by Henry Cronjager, and featured Mabel Trunnelle in leading roles. Titles: *The Life of a Salmon*, *A Trip over the Rocky and Selkirk Mountains*, *A Wedding Trip from Montreal to Hong Kong*, *An Unselfish Love*, *The Song that Reached his Heart*, *Riders of the Plains*, *More than his Duty*, *The Cowpuncher's Glove*, *The Stolen Claim*, *The Little Station Agent*, *The Swiss Guide*, *The Ship's Husband*. (National Film Archives has three: *The Life of a Salmon*, *An Unselfish Love*, *The Song that Reached his Heart*.)

1911

First Canadian production companies established: Starland Ltd. of Winnipeg; Canadian Film Manufacturing Company of Winnipeg; Kinemacolor Company of Canada.

Quebec Provincial Legislature debates the law regarding censorship of motion pictures, the first in Canada. Other provinces follow in establishing censorship boards, all before 1914.

1912

British American Film Company established in Montreal; Canadian Bioscope Company established in Halifax; Montreal Motion Pictures established in Montreal.

Kinemacolor Company of Canada releases *The Canadian National Exhibition at Toronto* and a film on the Rocky Mountains.

Starland Ltd. release *The Calgary Stampede* (photographed by A. D. Kean) and *Sovereign Grand Lodge Oddfellows Parade*.

1913

British American Film Company release *The Battle of the Long Sault*.

Arthur Larente releases *Madeleine de Verchères*.

American producers release many Canadian content drama and interest films including *Blood is Thicker than Water*, *The Laws of the North*, *The Peculiar Nature of the White Man's Burden*, *Pierre of the North*, *Sons of the Northwoods*, and *Into the North*, between 1912 and 1914.

Premier Film Manufacturing Company established in Montreal. Several other Montreal companies established in 1914–15.

APPENDIX II

Filmography

Select List of Canadian Productions, 1913–1939

The following chronological listing of Canadian films is intended to offer a representative sample of Canadian production before 1939. It includes feature films, short fictional films, and documentaries. Though the descriptions of feature films (i.e. those five reels or longer) is as complete as it has been possible to make them, this filmography is not intended as a complete guide nor a complete index to Canadian production. For example, only a few of the hundreds of films produced by the several government film bureaus and by Associated Screen News have been included. The selection of short films for inclusion has been intended to suggest those of more than routine interest but, ultimately, the selection is somewhat arbitrary and most certainly leans on those films available for viewing by researchers as much as on any definition of "quality" or "significance." However, I hope it will provide a useful working tool for students and researchers.

Only *Canadian* productions are listed; not "Canadian content" films produced by foreign companies. The only exception to this are those films considered to have a special relevance to Canadian cinema: *In the Land of the War Canoes*, *Nanook of the North*, *The Silent Enemy*, and *The Viking*. In every case, the year in which production was completed has been used in the chronology. *Series* are listed under the year the first issue was completed for release.

It is evident there will be both errors and omissions in the filmography. I would be happy to hear from anyone able to offer corrections or additional information.

Information for each entry is given in the following order: main release title of the film (alternative or additional release titles are given in parentheses); principal production credits (see abbreviations below); length of the film (in reels, feet, or minutes); source of the film.

Source: A Note on Availability of Films for Viewing

At the end of each entry information has been included regarding the source for that film. If no source is given, the film, at the time this list was compiled, is not known to exist in any publicly accessible collection.

In each case, the source given is an archive, NOT a distributor. At the present time, very few of these films are available for loan, rental, and/or public screening. Each of the archives has its own regulations regarding viewings of films in its collection—which may indeed vary from film to film depending on copyright and/or the film's physical condition. However, researchers should note that, in general, almost all of these films must be viewed on the premises of the archives concerned.

It is possible, given permissions from the copyright owners, that many of these films could be made available on a loan basis for use in educational institutions. If you have an interest in encouraging this to happen, I would suggest that you write to the Canadian Film Institute, 303 Richmond Road, Ottawa.

As mentioned above, many of these films are not known to exist in a public collection. Anyone knowing the location of any of these "lost" films should contact the National Film Archives, 344 Wellington, Ottawa or the Cinémathèque québécoise, 360 McGill, Montreal.

Abbreviations:

Art Dir: Art Director   *Prod*: Producer
Assist: Assistant   *Prod Co*: Production company
Dir: Director   *Scen*: Script, scenario
Ed: Editor
Photog: Photography   CQ: Cinémathèque québécoise
                                  NFA: National Film Archives
                                  All other sources are given in full

ᵉ§ 1913 §ᵉ

Battle of the Long Sault (*Dollard des Ormeaux*). *Dir*: Frank Crane. *Cast*: Frank Crane and Indians from the Caughnawaga reserve. *Prod*: Frank Beresford. *Prod Co*: British American Film Co. 2 reels.

Evangeline. *Dir*: E. P. Sullivan, William Cavanaugh. *Scen*: Marguerite Marquis, based on the poem by Longfellow. *Photog*: H. T. Oliver. *Cast*: Laura Lyman, John F. Carleton, Arthur Morrison, William Cavanaugh, E. P. Sullivan, Rhea Rafuse, R. J. Leary, Michael Hannafy. *Prod Co*: Canadian Bioscope Co. 5,000 ft.

Madeleine de Verchères. *Photog*: J. Arthur Homier. *Prod*: Arthur Larente. *Cast*: A. R. Thibault and Indians from the Caughnawaga reserve. 4,500 ft., approx. (Note: There is some doubt this is the correct date for this film.)

~§ 1914 §~

In the Land of the War Canoe (The Vigil of Motana / In the Land of the Head Hunters). *Dir/Photog/Ed*: Edward S. Curtiss. *Prod Co*: Curtiss Film Corporation. 6 reels.
Source: National Museum of Man, Ottawa.

Mariners Compass. *Dir*: E. P. Sullivan. *Scen*: Marguerite Marquis. *Photog*: H. T. Oliver. *Cast*: Laura Lyman, John Carleton, Arthur Morrison. *Prod Co*: Canadian Bioscope Co. 3 reels.

The Mexican Sniper's Revenge (In the Enemy's Power). *Scen*: Marguerite Marquis. *Photog*: H. T. Oliver. *Cast*: Laura Lyman, John F. Carleton, William Cavanaugh. *Prod Co*: Canadian Bioscope Co. 3 reels.

Saved From Himself. *Scen*: Marguerite Marquis. *Photog*: H. T. Oliver. *Cast*: Laura Lyman, John Carleton. *Prod Co*: Canadian Bioscope Co. 3 reels.

The War Pigeon. *Dir*: Frederic Colburn Clarke. *Scen*: Frederic Colburn Clarke, from a story by Arthur Stringer. *Cast*: unknown. *Prod Co*: All-Red Feature Co. 3 reels.

~§ 1915 §~

"Aylesworth Animal Pictures." *Dir/Photog*: Arthur Aylesworth. 6,000 ft.

Canada In Peace and War. *Dir*: Tom McKnight. *Scen*: Archie McKishney. *Photog*: Ned Van Buren. *Cast*: Clara Whipple, Edward H. Robins, Gene Frazier. *Prod Co*: Conness Till Film Co. 3 reels.

Canada's Fighting Forces. *Photog*: D. S. Dwyer. 6 reels.

His Awakening. *Dir*: Tom McKnight. *Scen*: Paul Bern. *Photog*: Louis W. Physioc. *Cast*: Edward H. Robins, Clara Whipple. *Prod Co*: Conness Till Film Co. 2 reels.

On the King's Highway. *Dir/Scen*: A. J. Edwards. *Photog*: Louis W. Physioc. *Case*: Clara Whipple, Edward H. Robins. *Prod Co*: Conness Till Film Co. 3 reels.

ᜲ 1916 ᜳ

B.C. for the Empire. *Dir/Photog/Prod*: D. Kean. 4 reels.

Self Defence. *Dir/Scen/Prod*: Len Roos, Charles Roos. *Photog*: Charles Roos. *Cast*: Muriel Parker, Albert E. H. Grupe. *Prod Co*: United Films. 9 reels.

ᜲ 1917 ᜳ

The Adventures of Count E. Z. Kisser. *Dir/Scen/Photog/Prod*: A. D. Kean. 1 reel.

The Marriage Trap. *Dir*: Barry O'Neill. *Scen*: Archie McKishney. *Photog*: Louis W. Physioc. *Cast*: Marguerite Snow, Carleton Macy, Herbert Prior, Albert E. H. Grupe, Clifford Bruce. *Prod Co*: Canadian National Features. 5 reels.

Power. *Dir*: Barry O'Neill. *Scen*: Archie McKishney. *Photog*: Louis W. Physioc. *Cast*: Holbrook Blinn, Mabel Trunnelle, Clifford Bruce, Fred Tidmarsh, Albert E. H. Grupe. *Prod Co*: Canadian National Features. 5 reels.

ᨀ᷿ 1918 ᨀ᷿

Canada's Work for Wounded Soldiers. *Dir/Photog*: William J. Craft. *Prod Co*: Pathescope for the Department of Soldiers' Civil Re-establishment. 5 reels.

Modern Eden. *Dir*: David Gally. *Scen*: Marie Lambert. *Cast*: David Gally, Marie Lambert. *Prod Co*: Pan-American Film Co. 1 reel.

Polly at the Circus. *Dir/Scen*: Harold J. Binney. *Photog*: Charles Roos, assisted by Frank O'Byrne. *Assoc*: Charles J. Quick. *Cast*: Unknown. *Prod Co*: Harold J. Binney Productions. 5 reels.

Sauvons nos bébés. *Dir*: Henri Dorval. *Photog*: Bert Mason. *Cast*: non-professionals. *Prod*: Ernest Ouimet. 3 reels.

The Scorching Flame. *Dir*: Armand Robi. *Photog*: Bert Mason. *Cast*: non-professionals. *Prod*: Ernest Ouimet. 5 reels.

ᨀ᷿ 1919 ᨀ᷿

Back to God's Country (L'Instinct qui veille). *Dir*: David M. Hartford. *Scen*: Nell Shipman from the story *Wapi, the Walrus* by James Oliver Curwood. *Photog*: Joe Walker, Del Clawson. *Ed*: Cyril Gardner. *Prod Manager*: Bert Van Tuyle. *Cast*: Nell Shipman, Wellington Playter, Wheeler Oakman, Charles Arling, Ralph Laidlaw, William Colvin. *Prod Co*: Canadian Photoplays. 5,950 ft.
Source: NFA

Building Aeroplanes in Canada. *Photog*: Arthur Reeves. *Prod*: B. E. Norrish. *Prod Co*: Exhibits and Publicity Bureau. 1 reel.

The Great Shadow. *Dir*: Harley Knoles. *Scen*: Rudolph Berliner, with continuity by Eve Unsell. *Photog*: Philip Hatkin, George Coudert. *Ed*: Ralph Ince. *Cast*: Tyrone Power, Donald Hall, Dorothy Bernard, John Rutherford, Louis Sterne, Gene Hornbostell, E. Emerson. *Prod*: George Brownridge. *Prod Co*: Adanac Producing Co. 5,800 ft.

Oh, Joy! *Dir*: Gene Hornbostell. *Cast*: Edna Hume, Albert E. H. Grupe. *Prod Co*: Adanac Producing Co. 1 reel.

Ottawa, the Edinburgh of the North. *Dir*: Ray Peck. *Photog*: John M. Alexander. *Titles*: E. S. Turnbull. *Prod*: B. E. Norrish. *Prod Co*: Exhibits and Publicity Bureau. 1 reel.
Source: National Film Board Stock Shot Library.

Pacific Coast Scenics (Series). *Prod*: May Watkis. *Prod Co*: B.C. Educational and Patriotic Film Service. 1 reel each.

Peace Hath her Victories. *Dir*: Ray Peck. *Photog*: John M. Alexander. *Prod*: B. E. Norrish. *Prod Co*: Exhibits and Publicity Bureau. 1 reel.

Seeing Canada (Series). *Prod Co*: Exhibits and Publicity Bureau and, later, Canadian Government Motion Picture Bureau. 1 reel each.
Source: NFA has many of these releases from 1919–39.

Toronto, the Gateway to Ontario. *Photog*: Charles Irish, Roy Tash. *Prod*: Blaine Irish. *Prod Co*: Canadian Aero Film Co., for Ontario Motion Picture Bureau. 1 reel.

Vocational Training. *Photog*: Dick Bird. *Prod Co*: Pathescope of Canada, for Ontario Motion Picture Bureau. 1 reel.

❧ 1920 ❧

Down North. *Dir/Photog*: J. Booth Scott. *Prod Co*: Exhibits and Publicity Bureau. 2 reels.

Filmcraft Nature Classics (Series). *Prod*: Blaine Irish. *Prod Co*: Filmcraft Industries. 1 reel each.

God's Crucible. *Dir/Ed*: Henry MacRae. *Scen*: Faith Green, based on *The Foreigner* by Ralph Connor. *Photog*: William Thornley. *Cast*: Gaston Glass, Edna Shipman, Wilton Lackaye, Robert Haines, Ann Sutherland, Gladys Coburn, Bradley Barker, William Colvin. *Prod Co*: Winnipeg Productions. 5,960 ft.

A Motor Boat Ramble. *Photog*: B. J. Bach. *Prod Co*: Exhibits and Publicity Bureau. 1 reel.
Source: National Film Board Stock Shot Library.

Mountaineering Memories. *Photog*: Byron Harman. *Prod Co*: Exhibits and Publicity Bureau. 1 reel.
Source: National Film Board Stock Shot Library.

Nation Building in Saskatchewan: The Ukrainians. *Dir/Photog*: Dick Bird. *Prod Co*: Pathescope of Canada for Saskatchewan Department of Education. 2 reels.
Source: NFA

The Vow. *Dir*: Maurice R. Coste. *Scen*: J. Reynolds Allison. *Cast*: unknown, but apparently American. *Prod Co*: Patricia Photoplays. 5 reels.

Where Nature Smiles. *Photog*: B. J. Bach. *Prod Co*: Exhibits and Publicity Bureau. 750 ft.
Source: NFA

Winter Wizardry. *Photog*: Roy Tash. *Prod*: Blaine Irish. *Prod Co*: Filmcraft Industries. 1 reel.

The Years, The Seasons and The Days. *Photog*: Charles Irish. *Prod*: Blaine Irish. *Prod Co*: Canadian Aero Film Co. for Ontario Motion Picture Bureau. 1 reel.

◄§ 1921 §►

Cameron of the Royal Mounted. *Dir/Ed*: Henry MacRae. *Scen*: Faith Green, based on *Corporal Cameron* by Ralph Connor. *Photog*: William Thornley. *Cast*: Gaston Glass, Vivienne Osborne, Irving Cummings, Frank Lanning, George Larkin, Gordon Griffith, William Colvin, Joe Singleton. *Prod Co*: Winnipeg Productions. 5,600 ft.

Kinograms (Series). *Prod Co*: Associated Screen News. 1 reel each.

Nanook of the North. *Dir/Photog/Ed*: Robert Flaherty. *Sponsored by*: Revillon Frères. 5,400 ft.
Source: NFA

Old French Canada. *Dir/Photog*: John M. Alexander. *Prod*: B. E. Norrish. *Prod Co*: Associated Screen News. 1 reel.

A Ten Days' Trip Through New Brunswick. *Dir/Photog*: H. B. McNeil. *Prod Co*: Maritime Motion Picture Co.

Where Salmon Leap. *Dir/Ed/Titles*: Frank Badgley. *Photog*: B. J. Bach. *Prod*: Ray Peck. *Prod Co*: Exhibits and Publicity Bureau. 1 reel.

◄§ 1922 §►

Camera Classics (Series). *Prod*: Blaine Irish. *Prod Co*: Filmcraft Industries. 1 reel each.

The Critical Age (The Good-Fer-Nothin'/Glengarry School Days). *Dir/Ed*: Henry MacRae. *Scen*: Garett Fort, based on *Glengarry School Days* by Ralph Connor. *Photog*: Barney McGill, Jacques Bizeul. *Cast*: Pauline Garon, James Harrison, Wallace Ray, William Colvin, Ray Peck, Marion Colvin, Harlan Knight, Alice May. *Prod Co*: Ottawa Film Productions. 4,500 ft.

The Man From Glengarry. *Dir*: Henry MacRae. *Scen*: Kenneth O'Hara, based on *The Man from Glengarry* by Ralph Connor. *Photog*: Barney McGill, Jacques Bizeul. *Ed*: Elmer J. McGovern. *Cast*: Anders Randolph, Warner P. Richmond, Harlan Knight, E. L. Fernandez, Marion Swayne, Pauline Garon, Jack Newton, Frank Badgley. *Prod Co*: Ottawa Film Productions. 5,800 ft.
Source: NFA (one reel only)

Port Aux Basques. *Photog*: H. B. McNeil. *Prod Co*: Maritime Motion Picture Co. 6 reels.

The Proof of Innocence. *Dir*: B. C. Rule. *Scen*: Charles G. Rich. *Cast*: Louise Du Pré, John Hopkins, Dorothea Teal, Francis O'Reilly, Oliver Putnam, Carl Sodders, Don Merrifield. *Prod*: Roy Mitchell, John A. Martin. *Prod Co*: Canadian Feature and Production Co. (Casco Productions). 4,564 ft.

The Rapids. *Dir/Ed*: David M. Hartford. *Scen*: Faith Green, based on *The Rapids* by Alan Sullivan. *Photog*: Walter Griffin, Oliver Sigurdson.

Cast: Harry Morey, Mary Astor, Walter Miller, Harlan Knight, Charles Wellesley, Edwin Forsberg, John Newton, John Dillon. *Prod Co*: Sault Ste. Marie Films. 4,900 ft.

Satan's Paradise. *Dir/Photog*: Roy Tash. *Cast*: Rance Quarrington, Harold Taperty. *Prod*: Blaine Irish. *Prod Co*: Filmcraft Industries. 7 reels.

The Sea Riders. *Dir*: Edward H. Griffith. *Scen*: Edward H. Griffith, Wallace MacDonald. *Cast*: Edward Phillips, Betty Bouton, America Chedister, Charles Eldridge, Mike Brennan, Edward Lawrence. *Prod Co*: Maritime Motion Picture Co. 5,750 ft.

◅§ 1923 §▻

Blue Water. *Dir/Ed*: David M. Hartford. *Scen*: Faith Green, based on *Blue Water* by Frederick William Wallace. *Photog*: Walter Griffin, Oliver Sigurdson. *Cast*: Pierre Gendron, Jane Thomas, Norma Shearer, Alice May, Harlan Knight, John Dillon. *Prod Co*: New Brunswick Films. 5 reels.

From Quebec to Baffin Land. *Photog*: George Valiquette. *Prod*: Ray Peck. *Prod Co*: Canadian Government Motion Bureau. 960 ft.
Source: National Film Board Stock Shot Library.

Policing the Arctic. *Photog*: George H. Valiquette. *Prod Co*: Canadian Government Motion Picture Bureau. 780 ft.
Source: National Film Board Stock Shot Library.

Why Get Married? *Dir*: Paul Cazeneuve. *Scen*: William M. Conselman. *Photog*: Georges Benoît. *Cast*: Andrée Lafayette, Helen Ferguson, Max Constant, Jack Perrin, Edwin B. Tilton, Bernard Randall, William Turner, Orpha Alba. *Prod Co*: Laval Photoplays. 5 reels.

◅§ 1924 §▻

Spare Time. *Dir*: Gordon Sparling. *Prod Co*: Ontario Motion Picture Bureau. 2,100 ft.
Source: NFA

Trophies of a Screen Chase. *Photog*: Berton S. Moore. *Ed/Titles*: Terry Ramsaye. *Prod Co*: Associated Screen News. 1 reel.

⋞ 1925 ⋟

The Drive. *Dir*: George Rutherford. *Prod Co*: Ontario Motion Picture Bureau. 750 ft.
Source: NFA

Tobique Secrets. *Photog*: Berton S. Moore. *Ed/Titles*: Terry Ramsaye. *Prod*: B. E. Norrish. *Prod Co*: Associated Screen News. 650 ft.
Source: NFA

⋞ 1926 ⋟

The City of Loyalists. *Dir*: Frank Badgley. *Prod Co*: Canadian Government Motion Picture Bureau. 1 reel.
Source: National Film Board Stock Shot Library

Gold Production in Ontario. *Prod Co*: Ontario Motion Picture Bureau. 1,715 ft.
Source: NFA

Lumbering in B.C. *Dir*: Frank Badgley. *Prod Co*: Canadian Government Motion Picture Bureau. 1 reel.
Source: National Film Board Stock Shot Library.

The Lure of Labrador. *Dir/Photog/Ed*: Varick Frissell. 364 ft. (16mm).
Source: NFA

The Moose Spoofer. *Photog*: Berton S. Moore. *Ed/Titles*: Terry Ramsaye. *Prod*: B. E. Norrish. *Prod Co*: Associated Screen News. 1 reel.

⋞ 1927 ⋟

Canada's Queen City. *Prod*: Frank Badgley. *Prod Co*: Canadian Government Motion Picture Bureau. 750 ft.
Source: NFA

Cotton. *Dir*: John M. Alexander. *Photog*: Roy Tash. *Prod Co*: Associated Screen News, for Dominion Textile Co. 3 reels.
Source: NFA

Destiny. *Prod Co*: Exclusive Canadian Film Co. 7 reels.

Historic Quebec. *Prod Co*: Canadian Government Motion Picture Bureau. 1 reel.
Source: National Film Board Stock Shot Library.

Policing the Plains. *Dir/Photog/Prod*: A. D. Kean. *Scen*: A. D. Kean, based on the book by R. G. MacBeth. *Cast*: Dorothy Fowler, Jack Downing, Donald Hayes, Joe Flieger, Alfred Crump, Margaret Lougheed. *Prod Co*: Canadian Historic Features. 8 reels.

Princes and Premier. *Photog*: Tracey Mathewson, James W. Campbell. *Ed*: Terry Ramsaye. *Prod Co*: Associated Screen News. 1,098 ft.
Source: British Film Institute: National Film Archive.

Saving the Sagas. *Recorded by*: C. Marius Barbeau, Ernest MacMillan. *Ed/Titles*: Terry Ramsaye. *Prod*: B. E. Norrish. *Prod Co*: Associated Screen News. 800 ft.
Source: NFA

The Shadow Laughs (Series): *Follow the Swallow*; *One Bad Knight*. *Dir/Anim*: Bryant Fryer. *Assist*: Geoffrey Keighley. *Prod*: Norman Gunn, Allen Beattie. 1 reel each.
Source: NFA

Sunset or Sunrise. *Dir/Photog*: Archdeacon A. L. Fleming, with cooperation of Canadian Government Motion Picture Bureau. 5 reels.

⋙ 1928 ⋘

The Beaver People. *Dir/Photog/Ed*: Bill Oliver. *Prod Co*: National Parks of Canada. 786 ft.
Source: NFA

Carry On, Sergeant. *Dir/Scen/Ed*: Bruce Bairnsfather. *Photog*: Bert Cann. *Art Dir*: B. Rothe. *Assist Dir*: Gordon Sparling, Clarence Elmer, Bert Tuey. *Assist Photog*: Charles Levine, W. J. Kelly, W. McInnes, W. H. Graham. *Titles*: Charles Bruce. *Mus*: Ernest Dainty. *Cast*: Jimmy Savo, Hugh Buckler, Niles Welch, Nancy Ann Hargreaves, Louise Cardi, W. T. Stewart, Brenda Bond, Monroe Owsley, Lewis Dayton, Laura O'Hara. *Prod Co*: Canadian International Films. 9,700 ft.
Source: NFA

Conquest of the Forest. *Prod*: Frank Badgley. *Prod Co*: Canadian Government Motion Picture Bureau. 889 ft.
Source: NFA

Fish and Medicine Men. *Ed/Titles*: Terry Ramsaye. *Prod*: B. E. Norrish. *Prod Co*: Associated Screen News. 650 ft.
Source: NFA

His Destiny (Sound version: *North of 49*). *Dir*: Neal Hart. *Scen*: Daniel E. C. Campbell. *Photog*: Alvin Wyckoff. *Ed*: Fred Burnworth. *Cast*: Neal Hart, Barbara Kent, Frank Newton, Charles Wellesley, Joseph Quinn, Guy Weadick, Mary Cross. *Prod Co*: British Canadian Pictures. 6,845 ft.
Source: NFA

In the Shadow of the Pole. *Dir/Photog*: Richard S. Finnie. *Prod Co*: Canadian Government Motion Picture Bureau. 6 reels.

Kawartha Muskeys. *Dir/Photog*: J. Booth Scott. *Titles*: "Ozark" Ripley. *Prod*: B. E. Norrish. *Prod Co*: Associated Screen News. 750 ft.
Source: NFA

Little Gray Doors. *Dir*: McCall. *Scen*: Lexie Doherty. *Photog*: W. H. Graham. *Cast*: James Bach, Muldrew, Forgie, Mitchell. *Prod Co*: Ontario Motion Picture Bureau. 3 reels.
Source: NFA

The Swilin' Racket (The Great Arctic Seal Hunt). *Dir/Photog/Ed*: Varick Frissell. 3,595 ft. shortened to 3,162 ft.
Source: NFA

The Wilderness Patrol. *Dir*: J. P. McGowan. *Scen*: Ford Beebe, from a story by Harold Blindloss. *Cast*: Bill Cody, Lotus Thompson, Shannon Day, Dick Maitland, Reginald Sheffield, Bob Wilber, J. P. McGowan. *Prod Co*: British Canadian Pictures. 6 reels.

◄§ 1929 §►

Achievement: The Story of a Store. *Dir*: John M. Alexander. *Photog*: Roy Tash. *Prod Co*: Associated Screen News for the T. Eaton Co. 1000 ft.
Source: NFA

The Adventures of George S. Fishog. *Dir/Scen*: Merrill Denison. *Prod Co*: Ontario Motion Picture Bureau, for Canadian Forestry Association/Ontario Forestry Branch. 3 reels.
Source: NFA

The Beaver Family. *Dir/Photog/Ed*: Bill Oliver. *Prod Co*: National Parks of Canada. 1,328 ft.
Source: NFA

The Devil Bear (Spirit of the Wilderness). *Dir*: Louis Chaudet. *Scen*: Sargeson V. Halstead. *Cast*: Peggy Olcott, Dorothy Dwan, Mitchell Lewis, Carroll Nye, Bobby Mack. *Prod Co*: Thunder Bay Films. 6 reels.(?)

From British Home to Canadian Farm. *Dir/Photog*: Roy Tash. *Prod Co*: Associated Screen News.

North of 49. See *His Destiny* (1928)

Race for Ties. *Dir*: Harold Harcourt. *Scen*: Dorothea Mitchell. *Photog*: Fred Cooper. *Cast*: Dorothea Mitchell, H. A. Saunders, Martha Lake, Edward Cooke, Edward Linley, William Gibson, Fred Lovelady, Wally McComber. *Prod Co*: Amateur Cinema Society of Thunder Bay. 5 reels.
Source: NFA

The White Road. *Dir/Scen*: George T. Booth. *Cast*: Jolyne Gillier, Marjorie Horsfall, Ernest Sydney, Frederick Mann, Ivor Danish. *Prod Co*: Ontario Film Company. 6 reels.

✦ 1930 ✦

Forward Canada! Dir: Gordon Sparling. *Prod Co*: Associated Screen News for General Motors of Canada. 300 ft.
Source: NFA

Hunting Without a Gun. Dir/Photog/Ed: Bill Oliver. *Prod*: J. C. Campbell. *Prod Co*: National Parks of Canada. 1 reel.
Source: NFA

The Seasons of Canada. Dir/Ed: D. F. Taylor. *Prod Co*: Canadian Government Motion Picture Bureau. 649 ft.
Source: NFA

The Silent Enemy. Dir: H. P. Carver. *Scen*: Richard Carver. *Photog*: Marcel Le Picard. *Tech Dir*: Louis Bonn. *Mus*: Massard Kur Zhene. *Cast*: Chief Buffalo Child Long Lance, Chief Yellow Robe, Chief Akawanush, Spotted Elk, Cheeka. *Prod*: W. Douglas Burden, William C. Chanler. *Prod Co*: Burden-Chanler Productions. 7,551 ft.
Source: Library of Congress Motion Picture Section, Washington D.C.

✦ 1931 ✦

Cinderella of the Farms. Dir/Scen/ED: John McLean French. *Photog*: George Rutherford. *Cast*: Slade Briggs, Elaine Wadson, Brendhan Mulholland, Maurice Bodington, Geoffrey Hatton, John McLean French. *Prod Co*: Ontario Motion Picture Bureau. 5 reels (silent).
Source: NFA

Miracle at Beauharnois. Dir: Gordon Sparling. *Prod Co*: Associated Screen News. 500 ft.

The Viking. Dir: George Melford. *Scen*: Varick Frissell, adaptation by Garnett Weston. *Photog*: Maurice Kellerman, Alfred Gandolphi. *Ed*: H. P. Carver. *Sound*: Alfred Manche. *Prod Manager*: Roy P. Gates. *Cast*: Charles Starrett, Louise Huntington, Arthur Vinton, Bob Bartlett. *Prod*: Varick Frissell. *Prod Co*: Newfoundland Labrador Film Co. 7,150 ft.
Source: NFA

◀§ 1932 §▶

Among the Igloo Dwellers. *Dir/Photog/Ed*: Richard S. Finnie. 6 reels (Shortened 15 minute version, *Ikpuck the Igloo Dweller*, produced in 1934.)
Source: NFA

Back in '22. *Dir/Scen/Ed*: Gordon Sparling. *Narrator*: Corey Thomson. *Mus*: Vera Guilaroff. *Prod Co*: Associated Screen News. 957 ft.
Source: NFA

The Bells. *Dir/Scen*: George T. Booth. *Photog*: George Rutherford, John Alexander, Len Humphries. *Mus*: Roy Locksley. *Cast*: Dickson Kenwin. *Prod Co*: Booth Canadian Films. 2 reels.

Canadian Cameo (Series). *Prod*: B. E. Norrish. *Prod Co*: Associated Screen News. 1 reel each, with a few exceptions.
Source: NFA has several of the series from 1932–53.

Grey Owl's Little Brother (Le Petit frère de Grey Owl). *Dir/Scen/Ed*: Gordon Sparling. *Photog*: Bill Oliver. *Mus*: Howard Fogg. *Narrator*: Corey Thomson. *Prod Co*: Associated Screen News. 990 ft. (*Note*: Adaptation of Bill Oliver's *Beaver People* (1928) and *Beaver Family* (1929).
Source: NFA

Hockey—Canada's National Game. *Dir*: James Campbell. *Photog*: Roy Tash, Frank O'Byrne, Fred Huffman. *Narrator*: Foster Hewitt. *Prod Co*: Associated Screen News. 1,000 ft.
Source: NFA

The Pathfinder. *Dir/Scen*: Gordon Sparling. *Narrator*: Corey Thomson. *Prod Co*: Associated Screen News. 768 ft.
Source: NFA

She Climbs to Conquer. *Dir/Photog/Ed*: Bill Oliver. *Prod Co*: National Parks of Canada. 1 reel. (*Note*: Also adapted and released under same title in *Canadian Cameo* series, 1932.)
Source: NFA

Strange Doings in Beaverland. *Dir/Photog/Ed*: Bill Oliver. *Prod Co*: National Parks of Canada. 965 ft. (*Note*: Also adapted and released as *Grey Owl's Strange Guests* in *Canadian Cameo* series, 1934.)
Source: NFA

ᦸ§ 1933 ᦸ⃕

Back in '23. *Dir/Ed*: Gordon Sparling. *Scen*: T. C. B. De Lom. *Narrator*: Corey Thomson. *Mus*: Vera Guilaroff. *Prod Co*: Associated Screen News. 1,000 ft.
Source: NFA

Bye Baby Bunting. *Dir/Anim*: Bryant Fryer. *Assist*: Ed. Furness, Ralph Blaber. *Mus*: Fraser Allan. *Prod Co*: Bryant Fryer. 537 ft.
Source: NFA

Crimson Paradise (Fighting Playboy). *Dir*: Bob Hill. *Scen*: Arthur Hoerl, based on *The Crimson West* by Alexander Philip. *Photog/Assist Dir*: William Beckway. *Art Dir*: Ernest Ostman. *Cast*: Nick Stuart, Lucille Brown, Kathleen Dunsmuir, C. Middleton Evans, Michael Heppell, James McGrath. *Prod*: Kenneth Bishop. *Prod Co*: Commonwealth Productions. 7 reels.

Jack the Giant Killer. *Dir/Anim*: Bryant Fryer. *Assist*: Ed. Furness, Ralph Blaber. *Mus*: Fraser Allan. *Prod Co*: Bryant Fryer. 1 reel.
Source: NFA

Sailors of the Guard. Same credits as above.

Shadow River. *Dir*: Gordon Sparling. *Scen*: based on the poem by Pauline Johnson. *Mus*: Howard Fogg. *Cast*: Lorna McLean, Kenneth Duncan. *Prod Co*: Associated Screen News. 1 reel.

ᦸ§ 1934 ᦸ⃕

Did You Know That? *Dir*: Gordon Sparling. *Photog*: Alfred Jacquemin, Lucien Roy, Roy Tash. *Mus*: Howard Fogg. *Narrator*: Corey Thomson. *Prod Co*: Associated Screen News. 880 ft.
Source: NFA

En Pays Neuf. *Dir/Photog/Ed*: Maurice Proulx. *Mus*: Maurice Mongrain (1937). 70 mins. (*Note*: Originally produced 1932–34; revised 1934–37 and music added; revised again for 1939 release.)
Source: Office du Film, Québec

Grey Owl's Strange Guests. *Dir*: Gordon Sparling. *Photog*: Bill Oliver. *Commentary*: T. C. B. De Lom. *Narrator*: Corey Thomson. *Prod Co*: Associated Screen News. 900 ft. (*Note*: Adaptation of Bill Oliver's *Strange Doings in Beaverland*, 1932.)
Source: NFA

Home of the Buffalo. *Dir/Photog/Ed*: Bill Oliver. *Prod Co*: National Parks of Canada. 1,400 ft. (*Note*: Also adapted and released as *Return of the Buffalo/ Le Retour du bison* in the *Canadian Cameo* series.)
Source: NFA

The Last Frontier. *Dir/Photog*: Richard S. Finnie. 45 minutes.
Source: National Museum of Man, Ottawa/NFA

Rhapsody in Two Languages. *Dir/Scen/Ed*: Gordon Sparling. *Photog*: Alfred Jacquemin. *Mus*: Howard Fogg. *Narrator*: Corey Thomson. *Prod Co*: Associated Screen News. 975 ft.
Source: NFA

The Secrets of Chinatown. *Dir*: Fred Newmeyer. *Scen*: Guy Morton. *Photog*: William Beckway. *Cast*: Nick Stuart, Lucille Brown, H. B. Warner, James Flavin, Harry Hewitson, James McGrath, Raymond Lawrence. *Prod Co*: Commonwealth Productions. 63 minutes.
Source: NFA

This Generation: A Prairie Romance. *Dir/Scen/Photog*: Dick Bird. *Cast*: Frances Wilson, Robert Pringle, Vic Wade, M. Carswell, Grant Faulkner, Jean Bird. *Prod Co*: Bird Films for the Saskatchewan Co-operative Wheat Producers. 4,000 ft.
Source: NFA

◆§ 1935 §◆

Cantique du Soleil. *Dir/Photog/Ed*: Albert Tessier. 11 mins.
Source: Cinémathèque du CEGEP de Trois-Rivières

Cheenama the Trailmaker: An Indian Idyll of Old Ontario. *Dir*: Diamond Jenness. *Scen/Photog/Ed/Titles*: Harlan Smith. 45 minutes.
Source: National Museum of Man, Ottawa.

The King's Plate (Thoroughbred). *Dir*: Sam Newfield. *Scen*: based on a story by Kenneth Duncan. *Photog*: Sam Levitt. *Cast*: Toby Wing, Kenneth Duncan, Wheeler Oakman, Romeo Gaskins. *Prod*: J. R. Booth, Arthur Gottlieb. *Prod Co*: Booth Dominions. 63 minutes.
Source: NFA

Lest We Forget. *Dir/Scen/Ed*: Frank Badgley, W. W. Murray. *Sound*: J. Booth Scott. *Mus*: Edmund Sanborn. *Narrator*: Rupert Caplan. *Prod Supervisor*: J. M. Alexander. *Prod Co*: Photo-Sound Corporation, in association with the Canadian Government Motion Picture Bureau for the Great War Motion Picture Committee, Department of National Defence. 102 minutes.
Source: National Film Board and NFA

Lucky Fugitives. *Dir*: Nick Grinde. *Photog*: William Beckway, Gerald Callahan. *Assist Dir*: William C. Thompson. *Cast*: David Manners, Maxine Doyle, James McGrath, Reginald Hincks. *Prod*: Kenneth Bishop. *Prod Co*: Central Films. 68 minutes.

Undercover (Undercover Man). *Dir*: Sam Newfield. *Photog*: Sam Levitt. *Cast*: Charles Starrett, Polly Moran, Winn Barren, George Fiefield. *Prod*: J. R. Booth, Arthur Gottlieb. *Prod Co*: Booth Dominions. 60 minutes.

⋞ 1936 ⋟

From Nine to Nine. *Dir*: Edgar G. Ulmer. *Cast*: Ruth Roland, Roland Drew. *Prod Co*: Coronet. 74 minutes.

From Sea to Sea. *Dir*: John McDougall. *Mus*: Howard Fogg. *Prod Co*: Associated Screen News for Canadian Pacific Railway. 900 ft.
Source: NFA

House in Order (La Maison en Ordre). *Dir*: Gordon Sparling. *Scen*: Peggy Miller, Gordon Sparling. *Photog*: Alfred Jacquemin. *Cast* (English version):

John Pratt, Mildred Mitchell, Cecil Nichol, Jack Clifford. *Cast* (French version): Hector Charland, Oscar Coutlee, C. A. Vallerand, Gérald Desmarais. *Prod Co*: Associated Screen News for Shell Oil Co. of Canada. 55 minutes.

Lucky Corrigan (Fury and the Woman). *Dir*: Lewis D. Collins. *Scen*: Philip Conway. *Photog*: William Beckway, Harry Forbes. *Ed*: William Austin. *Cast*: William Gargan, Molly Lamont, J. P. McGowan, David Clyde, Libby Taylor. *Prod*: Kenneth Bishop. *Prod Co*: Central Films. 65 minutes.
Source: NFA

Noranda Enterprise. *Prod Co*: Associated Screen News for Noranda Mines. 7 reels.
Source: NFA

Ride 'em Cowboy. *Dir/Photog*: J. Booth Scott. *Prod Co*: Canadian Government Motion Picture Bureau. 659 ft.
Source: British Film Institute: National Film Archive.

Sea Lions of the Pacific. *Dir/Photog/Ed*: Bill Oliver. *Prod*: J. C. Campbell. *Prod Co*: National Parks of Canada. 835 ft.
Source: NFA

Secret Patrol. *Dir*: David Selman (after Ford Beebe). *Scen*: Robert Watson, J. P. McGowan. *Photog*: George Meehan. *Ed*: William Austin. *Cast*: Charles Starrett, Henry Mollison, James McGrath, J. P. McGowan, Arthur Kerr, Finis Barton, William Millman, Reginald Hincks, Michael Heppell. *Prod*: Kenneth Bishop. *Prod Co*: Central Films. 59 minutes.
Source: NFA

Stampede. *Dir*: Ford Beebe. *Scen*: Robert Watson. *Photog*: George Meehan. *Ed*: William Austin. *Cast*: Charles Starrett, Finis Barton, J. P. McGowan, William Millman, James McGrath, Reginald Hincks. *Prod*: Kenneth Bishop. *Prod Co*: Central Films. 58 minutes.
Source: NFA

Tugboat Princess. *Dir*: David Selman. *Scen*: Robert Watson, based on a story by Norman Reilly Raine. *Photog*: William Beckway, William Thompson. *Ed*: William Austin. *Cast*: Walter C. Kelly, Valerie Hobson, Clyde

Cook, Edith Fellows, Lester Matthews, Reginald Hincks, John Moore. *Prod*: Kenneth Bishop. *Prod Co*: Central Films. 69 minutes.
Source: NFA

Vengeance (What Price Vengeance?). *Dir*: Del Lord. *Scen*: J. P. McGowan. *Photog*: William Beckway, Harry Forbes. *Ed*: William Austin. *Cast*: Lyle Talbot, Marc Lawrence, Wendy Barrie. *Prod*: Kenneth Bishop. *Prod Co*: Central Films. 56 minutes.
Source: NFA

⋖§ 1937 ⋗⋗

Death Goes North. *Dir*: Frank McDonald. *Scen*: Edward Austin. *Photog*: Harry Forbes. *Ed*: William Austin. *Cast*: Edgar Edwards, Sheila Bromley, Rin Tin Tin Jr., Walter Byron, Jameson Thomas, Dorothy Bradshaw, Reginald Hincks, James McGrath, Michael Heppell. *Prod*: Kenneth Bishop. *Prod Co*: Central Films. 64 minutes.
Source: NFA

Manhattan Shakedown. *Dir*: Leon Barsha. *Scen*: Edgar Edwards, based on a story by Theodore Tinsley. *Photog*: George Meehan. *Ed*: William Austin. *Cast*: Rosalind Keith, John Gallaudet, George McKay, Bob Rideout, Reginald Hincks. *Prod*: Kenneth Bishop. *Prod Co*: Central Films. 57 minutes.
Source: NFA

Murder Is News. *Dir*: Leon Barsha. *Scen*: Edgar Edwards. *Photog*: George Meehan. *Ed*: William Austin. *Cast*: Iris Meredith, John Gallaudet, George McKay, James McGrath, Doris Lloyd, Colin Kenny, Allan Brook. *Prod*: Kenneth Bishop. *Prod Co*: Central Films. 56 minutes.
Source: NFA

The Trail-Men Against the Snow. *Dir/Scen*: Grey Owl (Archibald Belaney). *Photog*: B. J. Bach. *Prod Co*: Booth Canadian Films. 893 ft. (16mm.).
Source: NFA

Wings Over the Atlantic. *Dir*: Gordon Sparling. *Scen*: Margot Blaisdell. *Ed*: A. R. Thom, Jack Chisholm. *Narrator*: Corey Thomson. *Prod Co*: Associated Screen News for Shell Oil Co. of Canada. 1,700 ft.
Source: NFA

Woman Against the World. *Dir*: David Selman. *Scen*: Edgar Edwards. *Photog*: William Beckway, Harry Forbes. *Ed*: William Austin. *Cast*: Ralph Forbes, Alice Moore, Sylvia Welsh, Edgar Edwards, James McGrath, Reginald Hincks. *Prod*: Kenneth Bishop. *Prod Co*: Central Films. 66 minutes.
Source: NFA

⇜ 1938 ⇝

Cold Facts (Cold Facts from the Northland). *Dir*: Gordon Sparling. *Scen*: Margot Blaisdell. *Photog*: Alfred Jacquemin, Ross Beesley, Angelo Accetti. *Ed*: A. R. Thom. *Cast*: Cecil Nichol, Whitfield Aston. *Prod Co*: Associated Screen News for International Harvester Co. of Canada. 895 ft.
Source: NFA

Convicted. *Dir*: Leon Barsha. *Scen*: Edgar Edwards. *Photog*: George Meehan. *Ed*: William Austin. *Cast*: Charles Quigley, Rita Hayworth, Marc Lawrence, George McKay, Edgar Edwards, Bob Rideout. *Prod*: Kenneth Bishop. *Prod Co*: Central Films. 55 minutes.
Source: NFA

Hommage à notre paysannerie. *Dir/Photog/Ed*: Albert Tessier. 25 minutes.
Source: Cinémathèque du CEGEP de Trois-Rivières.

The Kinsmen (Prairie Gold). *Dir/Scen/Ed*: Gordon Sparling. *Photog*: Ross Beesley. *Mus*: Horace Lapp. *Prod Co*: Associated Screen News for Canadian Wheat Board. 4,500 ft.
Source: NFA

Special Inspector (Across the Border). *Dir*: Leon Barsha. *Scen*: Edgar Edwards. *Photog*: George Meehan. *Ed*: William Austin. *Cast*: Charles Quigley, Rita Hayworth, George McKay, Edgar Edwards, Eddie Laughton,

Donald Douglas. *Prod*: Kenneth Bishop. *Prod Co*: Central Films. 54 minutes.
Source: NFA

Talbot of Canada. *Dir*: Melburn Turner. *Scen*: Melburn Turner, based on *Here Will I Nest* by Hilda Smith. *Cast*: Members of the London Little Theatre. *Prod*: Melburn Turner. 90 minutes. Kodachrome.

Youth Marches On. *Dir/Photog*: Dick Bird. *Cast*: Hugh Campbell, Cecil Broadhurst. *Prod*: George Fraser, E. G. Parfitt, for Oxford Group Movement. 23 minutes.

◄ 1939 ►

The Bright Path. *Dir*: Gordon Sparling. *Scen*: Margot Blaisdell. *Photog*: Ross Beesley, Alfred Jacquemin, Robert Martin. *Mus*: Lucio Agostini. *Prod Co*: Associated Screen News for Hydro-Electric Power Commission of Ontario. 2,850 ft.
Source: NFA

Le Canada français est resté fidèle (St-Jean Baptiste Parade). *Prod Co*: Associated Screen News for France Film. 928 ft.
Source: NFA

Canada Moves North. *Dir/Photog/Ed*: Richard S. Finnie. (Adapted by James Beveridge as *Northwest Frontier* and released in 1943 by the National Film Board.)

Canadian Power (History of Canadian Power). *Dir/Scen/Photog/Ed*: F. R. and Judith Crawley. *Prod Co*: Crawley Films for Canadian Geographical Society. 760 ft. (16mm). Kodachrome.
Source: NFA

Le Cheval Belge. *Dir*: Louis-Philippe Roy. 10 minutes.

Coffee for Canadians. *Dir*: Ed. Taylor. *Prod*: Leon Shelley. *Prod Co*: Vancouver Motion Picture Co. for Kelly Douglas. 10 minutes. Kodachrome.

Heritage. *Dir/Photog/Ed*: J. Booth Scott. *Prod Co*: Canadian Government Motion Picture Bureau, for Dominion Department of Agriculture. 18 minutes. (*Note*: There is some evidence this film was completed in 1934 and its release delayed possibly because it dealt with the Depression on the Prairies.)
Source: NFA

Royal Banners Over Ottawa. *Dir*: Gordon Sparling. *Prod Co*: Associated Screen News. 1,800 ft. Dufaycolor.
Source: NFA

The Royal Visit. *Prod*: Frank Badgley. *Prod Co*: Canadian Government Motion Picture Bureau. 7,611 ft.
Source: NFA/National Film Board

Top of the World. *Dir*: Gordon Sparling. *Mus*: Horace Lapp. *Prod Co*: Associated Screen News for Canadian Pacific Railway. 838 ft.
Source: British Film Institute: National Film Archive.

Notes

⋅◦§ CHAPTER 1 §◦⋅

1. West End Park was developed by Ahearn and Soper in the Hintonburgh district as an encouragement for people to travel by their street railway. There was a similar park in the east end of the city (now Rockcliffe Park). West End Park spanned what is now Holland Avenue and ran between Ruskin Avenue and what is now the Queensway. The land was originally owned by the Holland family and the Holland family house was close by on Richmond Road. The park is now entirely covered by housing.

2. Ottawa *Daily Citizen*, July 21, 1896, p. 7; *Daily Citizen*, July 20, 1896, p. 8. In recollecting the event many years later John C. Green consistently put the date one month earlier. There have been also several published accounts claiming the first film show in Ottawa was not until 1899. The newspaper evidence proves conclusively the date given here.

There have also been accounts published (based on recollections of Ernest Ouimet) claiming that a showing in Montreal preceded that in Ottawa. There is no evidence to support this. See note 33 below regarding Ouimet's recollection of the Montreal showing.

3. *Moving Picture World*, 59 (1922): 529. May Irwin was born in Whitby, Ontario, in 1862. The exact titles of the films were: *Shooting the Chutes at Coney Island*; *The Black Diamond Express*; *The Kiss*; *LaLoie Fuller's Serpentine Dance*. No trace can be found of a film of that date depicting "four coloured boys eating watermelons."

4. Terry Ramsaye, *A Million and One Nights* (New York: Simon and Schuster, 1926), p. 258.

5. Edmund A. Robbins, "Animated Pictures," *The Optical Magic Lan-*

tern and Photographic Enlarger, viii (June 1897): 99–101.

6. Ottawa *Daily Citizen*, December 21, 1906. Andrew Holland was born in August 1844.

7. Ramsaye, *A Million and One Nights*, p. 79.

8. Ibid., p. 81.

9. Ibid., pp. 87–88.

10. Ibid., p. 88.

11. The Cinématographe had been invented by the brothers, Louis and Auguste Lumière of Lyons, France. The first public presentation was December 28, 1895 (some months before that of the Vitascope in New York), in the Salon Indien of the Grand Café, 14 boulevard des Capucines, in Paris. Though it embodied the same principles as those used by Thomas Armat in the Vitascope marketed by Edison, in practice it was a totally different machine. Films made on one device could not be projected on the other. This was true also of other projectors invented or developed in the early years of motion pictures.

12. Toronto *Mail and Empire*, July 22, 1933. Ed Houghton was Quebec born (in 1866) and Ottawa raised. He had been a page in the House of Commons before leaving Ottawa to go into show business. He toured with various stock companies prior to his involvement with the movies. He finally settled in Buffalo in 1903 and opened the Little Hippodrome movie theatre.

13. The other films shown were *Shooting the Chutes at Coney Island*, *The Black Diamond Express*, and *LaLoie Fuller's Serpentine Dance*—identical to those shown earlier in Ottawa.

14. Toronto *Mail and Empire*, September 5, 1896; ibid., September 12, 1896; Toronto *Star*, September 15, 1896.

15. Robinson's Musee was owned by M. S. Robinson of Buffalo. A fire apparently put Robinson's Musee out of business in 1897. In 1899 it was purchased and rebuilt by Jerry Shea and opened as a high-class vaudeville house. It became the Strand movie house and later one of the theatres in the Nathanson group. In the early 1930s it was converted into a burlesque theatre, then into an office building, and finally rebuilt entirely. The ornamental entrance to the Bijou Theatre of Robinson's Musee was still evident for many years.

16. Toronto *Star*, September 19, 1896. The copyrighted titles of these first scenes of Canada on film were: *American Falls from Above, American Side*; *American Falls from Bottom, Canadian Side*; *American Falls from Incline R.R.*; *Horseshoe Falls—From Luna Isle*; *Horseshoe Falls—From Table Rock*; *Whirlpool Rapids—From Canadian Side*; *Rapids Above American Falls*.

17. Unlike Edison, the Lumière Brothers never sold outright the territorial rights to their combined cameras and projectors. All presentations were organized directly by personal agents of the Lumières in conjunction with a local promoter-exhibitor. The financial arrangement usually involved payment of a flat fee, plus a percentage of the admission prices. Once projectionists were trained in a particular area, the agent moved on to another town.

18. Toronto *Mail and Empire*, August 29, 1896.

19. The films of the Derby and the Henley Regatta had been photographed by Robert Paul in Britain, originally for his Animatographe. The coronation of the Czar (seven short 75-foot films) had been photographed by Lumière's own cameraman in St. Petersburg.

20. Toronto *Telegram*, September 8, 1896.

21. Toronto *Star*, September 21, 1896.

22. Toronto *Star*, July 7, 1933.

23. Ibid.

24. These films appeared in the first Lumière catalogue published in early 1897 as No. 339 *Les Chutes* and No. 340 *Les Rapides*. Félix Mesguich's account of filming of the Horseshoe Falls is included in his autobiography *Tours de Manivelle* (Paris: n.p., 1933).

25. The Toronto papers also recorded the presentation of a movie system called "The Kinematographe" at the Toronto Opera House (operated by Ambrose J. Small for Jacobs and Sparrow) the week of October 3, 1896, "as a big feature of Hopkins Trans-Oceanic Company" due to the "foresight of Mr. Robert Fulgora." It is not known if this was the Lumière Cinématographe or some other machine. Ambrose J. Small later moved from vaudeville to movie theatres. He disappeared mysteriously without a trace on December 2, 1919. It is possible the Kinematographe was Rigg's Kinematographe, a British development patented March 27, 1896.

26. Refer to above note regarding the Kinematographe. It is likely that the Toronto and Montreal showings used the same machine since Jacobs and Sparrow owned both the Theatre Royal in Montreal and the Toronto Opera House.

27. Montreal *Daily Star*, September 26, 1896; September 29, 1896; *La Presse*, September 26, 1896; September 29, 1896.

28. Montreal *Daily Star*, September 30, 1896.

29. Montreal *Daily Star*, November 19, 1896; November 20, 1896. It is not clear whether this was the same Paul machine. Paul also marketed his machine under the name "theatrograph," but it might have been a name

invented by the showman for Lumière's machine. This could also have been the show seen by Ernest Ouimet (see Note 33 below).

30. Montreal *Daily Star*, December 15, 1896; *La Presse*, December 12, 1896; December 14, 1896.

31. The conflict of patent claims is highly complex. The subject is covered thoroughly in many books on the early development of the motion picture. The Phantoscope promoters were known elsewhere to attempt to exploit Edison's name. See especially, Ramsaye, *A Million and One Nights*, pp. 272–73.

32. Letter to Hye Bossin quoted in *Canadian Film Weekly*, July 10, 1963, p. 7.

33. There is clearly a certain confusion about dates and machines here which is difficult to resolve. On the evidence, it seems probable that the exhibit Ouimet saw was the Theatroscope on St. Laurent, but, if so, it seems unlikely that it was the Lumière Cinématographe since Lumière's agents were particular about ensuring that the inventor's name be associated with the showing. On the other hand, Félix Mesguich does recall presenting exhibits in Montreal (and Quebec and Ottawa) and from the way he describes it, prior to the Toronto show. Ouimet also recalls that he saw it in the spring of 1896 and that "by the end of September or the beginning of October" the showings were stopped as soon as the cold weather arrived. Ouimet also suggests the equipment was sold to Sohmer Park and that showings took place there in the summer of 1896. No films were shown, in fact, at Sohmer Park until May 24, 1897, when Sohmer Park re-opened and advertised "The Radiascope" with animated pictures.

The spring date is also unlikely for other reasons. Félix Mesguich and the Lumière machines did not arrive in New York until July 1896—not because Lumière did not want to open in New York earlier but because there were no machines available. Since Lumière always insisted on his own representative being present, it is impossible that Montreal had the Lumière Cinématographe until after its New York opening June 29, 1896, when more machines became available. Secondly, if the show opened in the spring and ran until late fall it must have been open from four to six months. This is unlikely: because of the limited number of films available, operators couldn't occupy a single location for that length of time.

No trace, other than the reference by Ouimet, can be found of Guay and Vermette.

In summary, it seems probable that Ouimet saw a Lumière exhibit (perhaps among others?) but, after sixty years, confused the dates and places involved.

34. Letter to Hye Bossin, quoted in *Canadian Film Weekly*, July 26, 1944.

35. *Moving Picture World*, 59 (1922): 259; *Motion Picture News*, June 16, 1925.

36. Archives of Ontario: File S 141.

37. Ibid.

38. Toronto *Star*, July 7, 1933.

39. *Canadian Film Weekly*, April 24, 1963.

40. Ibid.

41. *Vancouver Sun*, October 11, 1952.

42. *Canadian Film Weekly*, April 24, 1963.

43. The Royal Canadian Biograph Co. (also known as the Royal Canadian Animated Photo Co.) was based in England but the name suggests A. D. Thomas was, at least, Canadian born. The company was not only involved in exhibitions but also in production. See: *The Optical Lantern and Cinematograph Journal*, 1 (1905): 238; *The Optical Lantern and Cinematograph Journal*, 2 (1906): 63; *The Optical Lantern and Kinematograph Journal*, 3 (January 1907): 79; Rachael Low and Roger Manvell, *The History of the British Film 1896–1906* (London: George Allen and Unwin, 1948), p. 36.

44. *The Optical Lantern and Kinematograph Journal*, 2 (1906): 144.

45. Frederick Talbot, *Moving Pictures, How They are Made and Worked* (London: William Heinemann, 1912), pp. 132–33.

46. *Vancouver Sun*, October 11, 1952.

47. *Canadian Film Weekly*, April 24, 1963.

48. This was the original Nickelodeon, founded by Harry Davis and John P. Harris, which opened in November 1905. Unlike earlier storefront theatre operations, they extensively refurbished the theatre. Griffin was not alone in being impressed. Showmen grasped quickly the new way to make money; within a year there were over a thousand nickelodeons across the country. See especially, Ramsaye, *A Million and One Nights*, p. 430; Benjamin Hampton, *History of the American Film Industry* (New York: Dover, 1970), p. 46.

49. *Moving Picture World*, 59 (1955): 529.

50. Archives of Ontario: File S 141. Edmonds died February 13, 1930.

51. Ibid.

52. *Canadian Film Weekly*, May 8, 1963.

53. *Moving Picture World*, 29 (1916): 410–11.

54. Lewis Jacobs, *The Rise of the American Film* (New York: Teachers College Press, 1968), p. 57.

55. Material drawn from: *Canadian Film Weekly*, April 9, 1952; August 9, 1952; August 11, 1944; August 18, 1944; August 25, 1944; September 1, 1944. *The Montrealer*, August, 1966, p. 26; *La Presse*, March 11, 1972; *Hommage à M. L. Ernest Ouimet* (Montreal: la Cinémathèque Canadienne, 1966).

56. Ouimet also opened another Ouimetoscope in 1906 at 408 St. Catherine West in the Karn Hall (Dominion Square Building) in order to attract customers from the western parts of the city. It presented, a week later, the same films as the original Ouimetoscope.

❧ CHAPTER 2 ❧

1. Gordon Hendricks, *Beginnings of the Biograph*, reprinted in *Origins of the American Film* (New York: Arno Press, 1972), p. 38.

2. The titles of the Edison and Lumière films are listed in notes 16 and 24 in chap. 1. Those for the American Mutoscope and Biograph were: *Canadian Falls Table Rock*; *Canadian Falls Table Rock No. 22*; *Falls from Michigan Central Railway No. 23*; *American Falls from Luna Island*; *American Falls from Goat Island No. 25*; *American Falls from American Side No. 26*; *Niagara Gorge from Erie Railroad*; *Lower Rapids Niagara Falls*; *Pointing Down Gorge, Niagara Falls*; *Taken from Trolley in Gorge Niagara Falls*; *Upper Rapids from Bridge*; *Panorama of American and Canadian Falls taken opposite American Falls*. See Hendricks, *Beginnings of the Biograph*, pp. 38–39, 48–51.

3. Titles were: *The Gap (CPRR)*; *Fraser Canyon*; *Fraser Canyon, East of Yale*; *Down Kicking Horse Slide*; *Under Shadow of Mount Stephen*. Another series of railway films were photographed by F. S. Armitage in May–June 1900: *Gilead (Grand Trunk Railroad)*; *Victoria Bridge Montreal (Grand Trunk)*; *Approach to Lake Christopher (Grand Trunk)*.

4. The films are all various views of *Kicking Horse Canyon*.

5. The earliest of these "winter scenes" were *Sleighing—Ottawa* (1898), *Snowstorm, Quebec* (1898) and *Skating, Montreal* (1898). The cameramen are unknown.

6. Titles were: *Horses Loading for Klondike, No. 9*; *Loading Baggage for Klondike, No. 6*; *S.S. "Williamette" Leaving for Klondike*; *Rocking Gold in the Klondike*; *Rocking the Gold in the Klondike*; *Washing Gold on 20 Above Hunker, Klondike*; *Packers on the Trail*; *Pack Train on the Chilcoot Pass*.

7. Kemp Niver (ed.), *Biograph Bulletins 1896–1908*, (Los Angeles: Locare Research Group, 1971).

8. Bonine may also have photographed the *Kicking Horse Canyon* films

for Edison in December 1901 since from July to September 1901 he was filming in Asia and could have shot the railroad films on his return to eastern Canada.

9. *The Dominion Illustrated*, 24 (December 15, 1888): 372, 374.

10. This dating is taken from the fact that his public tours began in the spring of 1898; his films included harvesting scenes which must have been photographed in the fall of 1897 at the latest.

11. *Optical Magic Lantern Journal and Photographic Enlarger*, ix (April 1898): 54. Henry Hopwood, *Living Pictures* (London: Opticians and photographic trades review, 1899), p. 232.

12. The Canadian government and the CPR had for some time been using lantern slide lectures to promote emigration from Britain to Canada. Agent for these was Alfred Jury who later became British distributor for the films of the Canadian Government Motion Picture Bureau. Following the CPR's lead, the Northwest Transportation Company in the United States used films in 1899 to encourage potential immigrants to settle in Alaska.

13. Quoted in Freer's promotional leaflets, copies of which are in the National Film Archives, Ottawa.

14. Canada, Public Archives: Clifford Sifton files.

15. *Optical Magic Lantern Journal and Photographic Enlarger*, ix (March 1898): 37–38.

16. *Optical Magic Lantern Journal and Photographic Enlarger*, xi (February 1899): 18; Merrill Denison, *Harvest Triumphant: The Story of Massey-Harris* (Toronto, 1949), p. 157.

17. James H. Gray, *Red Lights on the Prairies* (Toronto: Signet Books, 1973), p. 15.

18. J. W. Dafoe, *Clifford Sifton in Relation to His Times*, quoted in Gray, *Red Lights on the Prairies*, p. 16.

19. In 1902, Charles Urban was heading the Warwick Trading Company. He left there early in 1903 and established his own company, the Charles Urban Trading Company. Urban was an American who originally went to Britain in 1894 to manage the London office of Edison's Kinetoscope. When he reorganized the company in 1898 as the Warwick Trading Company he also began producing films. Warwick had a staff of itinerant cameramen who travelled around the world and were the first war cinematographers. The most famous of these was Joe Rosenthal. Urban was a business man and entrepreneur rather than a producer. It was to his initiative that the early British film industry owes such achievements as Kinemacolor, the scientific film, and travel and war films. He was also expert at securing financial backing for his itinerant cameramen, from both commercial com-

panies and governments. For example, the North Borneo Company financed "the Urban Bioscope Expedition through Borneo" in 1903 and through Malay in 1904. The CPR, of course, did the same thing in Canada. Urban also had cameramen on both sides during the Russo-Japanese War in 1904–1905.

20. The name came from their use of the "Bioscope" camera manufactured by Urban.

21. Material derived from letter to Hye Bossin from H. H. McArthur, March 31, 1951 (Bossin Collection: National Film Board of Canada); letter from Cliff Denham to Hye Bossin, quoted in *Canadian Film Weekly*, July 11, 1951.

22. Cliff Denham quoted in *Canadian Film Weekly*, July 11, 1951.

23. *The British Journal of Photography*, January 23, 1903, p. 70. Lord Strathcona was high commissioner for Canada to Britain from 1896 to his death in 1914. He was most certainly a supporter of Freer's tours and the CPR films.

24. Ibid.

25. *Charles Urban Trading Company catalogue*, November 1903, pp. 16–17 and January 1904 *Supplement*, pp. 5–8. (British Film Institute copies.)

26. *Charles Urban Trading Company catalogue*, 1909, pp. 287–89 (British Film Institute copy). *The Optical Lantern and Kinematograph Journal*, 2 (1906): 227; *Moving Picture World*, 1, no. 8 (April 27, 1907). *Wonders of Canada* was 725 ft.

27. Cliff Denham quoted in *Canadian Film Weekly*, July 11, 1951.

28. Bossin Collection: National Film Board. McArthur to Bossin, March 31, 1951.

29. *Charles Urban Trading Company catalogue*, November 1903, pp. 31–39 (British Film Institute copy). The catalogue number 1091 would date the release in September 1903. Rosenthal is credited as director in the *British Films Catalogue*.

30. *Moving Picture World*, 3, no. 25 (June 20, 1908): 528; *The Bioscope*, September 13, 1908, p. 11; *The Bioscope*, July 21, 1910, p. 22.

31. *The Bioscope*, February 3, 1910, p. 21.

32. For synopses and reviews see *Moving Picture World*, 5 (1909): 175; 6 (1910): 797; 8 (1911): 430; 13 (1912): 684, in addition to the *Bioscope* references listed in notes 30 and 31 above.

33. *The Bioscope*, February 3, 1910, p. 21.

34. Ibid., January 20, 1910, pp. 12–17.

35. *The Bioscope*, February 10, 1910, p. 33; June 2, 1910, p. 32;

June 23, 1910, p. 39; September 8, 1910, p. 45; November 24, 1910, p. 37.

36. Rachael Low, *The History of the British Film 1906–1914* (London: George Allen and Unwin, 1948), p. 155.

37. R. M. Anderson and George H. Wilkins, *Canadian Arctic Expedition* (Ottawa: King's Printer, 1917), vol. 3, p. 24. David Zimmerly, *Museocinematography*, National Museum of Man Mercury Series, Paper no. 11 (Ottawa: National Museum of Man, 1974), pp. 3–4, 17.

38. *Moving Picture World*, 24 (1915): 426.

39. Also known as *The Vigil of Motana* and *In the Land of the Head Hunters*. The film was re-released by the Burke Memorial Washington State Museum in 1973.

40. *Moving Picture World*, 10 (1911): 731.

41. Kinemacolor was a true colour process using two colours, invented by G. A. Smith and patented and exploited by Charles Urban and Smith. Urban's practice was to grant exclusive rights under license for a particular exhibitor in one area. The process was very successful but the company which marketed it eventually collapsed in 1914 under the weight of legal claims concerning the patent. Kinemacolor was not distributed in the United States until 1912 because of restrictions imposed by the American Motion Picture Patents Trust. See Low, *The History of the British Film 1906–1914*, pp. 100–104.

42. F. A. Talbot, *Moving Pictures, How They Are Made and Worked* (London: William Heinemann, 1912), p. 126.

43. *Moving Picture World*, 14 (1912): 769.

44. Ibid., 15 (1913): 818.

45. Toronto *Daily News*, September 16, 1918.

46. *Moving Picture World*, 7 (1910): 685.

47. Ibid., 5 (1909): 556, 623; 7 (1910): 685.

48. Ibid., 5 (1909): 556, 619; 6 (1910): 658, 690; 7 (1910): 434, 476–77, 532–33, 641, 646, 685, 749; 10 (1911): 64.

49. Ibid., 1, no. 27 (September 14, 1907): 434; Niver (ed.), *Biograph Bulletins 1896–1908*, pp. 306, 404, 405.

50. Pierre Berton, *Hollywood's Canada* (Toronto: McClelland and Stewart, 1975) is a comprehensive account of this aspect.

51. Talbot, *Moving Pictures, How They Are Made and Worked*, p. 174.

52. *Moving Picture World*, 18 (1913): 472; 19 (1914): 954; 22 (1914): 1493.

53. Ibid., 26 (1915): 292.

54. Ibid., 23 (1915): 1796.

55. Norman S. Rankin, "With the Edison Players Across the Continent," *Man to Man Magazine*, 6–7 (June 1910 to January 1911): 936.

56. Ibid.

57. James B. Hedges, *Building the Canadian West* (Toronto: Macmillan, 1939), p. 279. *Moving Picture World*, 7 (1910): 113, 623.

58. Hedges, *Building the Canadian West*, p. 279.

59. *Moving Picture World*, 30 (1916): 81.

60. Ibid., 7 (1910): 623.

61. Rankin, *Man to Man Magazine*, 6–7 (June 1910 to January 1911): 937–38.

62. *Moving Picture World*, 7 (1910): 623.

63. Ibid., 7 (1910): 1178; *The Bioscope*, January 5, 1911, p. 32.

64. *Moving Picture World*, 7 (1910): 1486; *The Bioscope*, February 2, 1911, p. 27.

65. Also known as *Mary and John's Wedding Trip*. *Moving Picture World*, 7 (1910): 1004; *The Bioscope*, December 15, 1910, p. 39.

66. *Moving Picture World*, 7 (1910): 643, 646; *The Bioscope*, November 10, 1910, p. 37.

67. *Moving Picture World*, 7 (1910): 936, 942; *The Bioscope*, December 8, 1910, p. 39.

68. *Moving Picture World*, 7 (1910): 1125; *The Bioscope*, December 29, 1910, p. 39.

69. *Moving Picture World*, 7 (1910): 882; *The Bioscope*, November 24, 1910, p. 39.

70. *Moving Picture World*, 7 (1910): 1426; *The Bioscope*, January 26, 1911, p. 29.

71. *Moving Picture World*, 7 (1910): 1366.

72. Ibid., 7 (1910): 1306.

73. *Moving Picture World*, 7 (1910): 1186; *The Bioscope*, December 29, 1910, p. 39.

74. *Moving Picture World*, 7 (1910): 1065; *The Bioscope*, December 22, 1910, p. 34.

75. *The Bioscope*, January 5, 1911, p. 32.

76. Hedges, *Building the Canadian West*, p. 280.

77. *Moving Picture World*, 14 (1912): 49, 252, 273.

78. Ibid., 9 (1911): 460; 19 (1914): 827.

79. There is a possibility that Royal Films of Montreal did, in fact, produce at least one feature: *The Seats of the Mighty*, produced in 1914 and released in 1915. This was based on the story by Gilbert Parker of the conquest

of Quebec. British references credit this film as being produced by Royal Film Corporation (*The Bioscope*, September 16, 1915, p. 1291). In the United States it was copyrighted by Colonial Motion Picture Corporation in December 1914 and released by World Film Corporation. It was seven reels in length, was directed by (American) T. Hayes Hunter, and featured Lionel Barrymore, Glen White, William Cavanaugh, A. P. Jackson, and Arthur Morrison. See: *Moving Picture World*, 22 (1914): 1539.

There is further evidence that Royal Film Corporation was active. In 1921 a French producer, Louis Nacpas, signed Montreal actress Mlle. Narcita to a contract in France. She was described then as "a former star of the Royal Film Corporation of Montreal."

If Royal Films did produce *The Seats of the Mighty*, it seems not unlikely that the company would have produced others. If so, Maurice Marcelot and John William Peachy deserve a larger share of this history. However, confirmatory evidence does not currently exist. Royal Films, like Canadian Bioscope and the British American Film Company, seems to have involved considerable American financing and used American actors and technicians.

80. *Moving Picture World*, 13 (1912): 1295.

81. Ibid., 19 (1914): 1116; 20 (1914): 554.

82. Ibid., 19 (1914): 827; 20 (1914): 1426, 1726; 21 (1914): 1229. The studios were sometimes referred to as "Dominion Film Studios" though they were, in fact, used by three different companies. As with Royal Films, it is possible these companies were somewhat more active than is implied here.

83. Ibid., 21 (1914): 724, 1229, 1400; 25 (1915): 357.

84. Ibid., 25 (1915): 357.

85. Ibid., 20 (1914): 540, 1702.

86. Ibid., 24 (1915): 243, 1204, 1205; 25 (1915): 657, 1148, 1502.

87. Ibid., 13 (1912): 455.

88. Ibid., 14 (1912): 957.

89. *Moving Picture World*, 22 (1914): 78. It is not unfeasible that British American became the Premier Film Manufacturing Company in April 1913 with studios at Lachine, or the Canadian Cinematograph Co. Ltd. in April 1914 with studios at Longueuil. This latter company may also be related to that described by Larente as La Compagnie Cinématographie Canadienne.

90. Larente at various times has claimed different dates for the production, ranging from 1908 to 1914. Still photographs of the film were registered with the Canadian Copyright Office in 1922, though from the visual evidence of the scenes depicted this is long after the film was made. The most

consistent date he used was 1912 and this, too, coincides with the production date of *The Battle of the Long Sault*. The material in this paragraph is based entirely on interviews with Larente and various written statements by him. There is apparently no other documentary evidence for the film's existence.

It is possible that Larente simply shot his film on the sets of the British American Film Company. Without further evidence it is impossible to resolve this question.

91. Halifax *Mail-Star*, July 27, 1951; *Moving Picture World*, 19 (1914): 298.

92. *Variety*, January 23, 1914.

93. *Moving Picture World*, 19 (1914): 662.

94. Ibid., 20 (1914): 1145, 1602.

95. Ibid.

96. Ibid., and 21 (1914): 291, 521; *Variety*, July 31, 1914.

97. Halifax *Herald*, May 6, 1914, p. 12.

98. *Moving Picture World*, 22 (1914): 1704.

99. Ibid.

100. Ibid.

101. *Canadian Film Weekly*, April 22, 1953.

102. *Moving Picture World*, 21 (1914): 1667; *Variety*, July 3, 1914; *Variety*, August 21, 1914.

103. *Moving Picture World*, 22 (1914): 1257.

104. Ibid., 22 (1914): 1563; 23 (1915): 108.

105. Ibid., 22 (1914): 386; 23 (1915): 994.

106. Ibid., 23 (1915): 550.

107. Ibid., 23 (1915): 994, 1170.

108. Ibid., 24 (1915): 257, 426.

109. Ibid., 23 (1915): 1475; 24 (1915): 431.

110. Ibid., 26 (1915): 937.

111. Ibid., 24 (1915): 937.

112. Terry Ramsaye, *A Million and One Nights* (New York: Simon and Schuster, 1926), pp. 693–97.

113. *Moving Picture World*, 24 (1915): 1482.

114. Ramsaye, *A Million and One Nights*, p. 695.

115. *Moving Picture World*, 24 (1915): 1943.

116. Montreal was certainly the most active city in terms of the number of pre-1914 production companies established there. But few appear to have actually produced anything.

117. The Montreal *Daily Star*, September 7, 1911.

118. *Moving Picture World*, 18 (1913): 1259; 19 (1914): 66.

119. Ibid., 10 (1911): 459.

120. Ibid., 10 (1911): 273; 15 (1913): 1208; 16 (1913): 578, 1365.

121. Ibid., 10 (1911): 273, 795.

ᦾᥱ CHAPTER 3 ᥱᦾ

1. *Moving Picture World*, 54 (1922): 273. Lewis Selznick was the father of the more famous Hollywood producer, David O. Selznick.

2. *Moving Picture World*, 19 (1914): 1702.

3. *The Bioscope*, November 12, 1914, p. 669; December 12, 1914, p. 1065.

4. *Moving Picture World*, 22 (1914): 78. John Boldt was formerly with the Canadian Cinematograph Company.

5. *Moving Picture World*, 22 (1914): 1704; 23 (1915): 244.

6. Ibid., 21 (1914): 1400.

7. Ibid., 23 (1915): 1639; 24 (1915): 257, 426, 431.

8. Ibid., 22 (1914): 1236.

9. Ibid., 23 (1915): 1021.

10. Ibid., 22 (1914): 1704.

11. Ibid., 25 (1915): 1026.

12. Ibid., 26 (1915): 1531, 2226; 28 (1916): 1700; *The Bioscope*, December 14, 1916, p. i; *The Bioscope*, March 8, 1917, p. i.

13. Rachael Low, *The History of the British Film 1914–1918* (London: George Allen and Unwin, 1948), p. 35.

14. Geoffrey Malins, *How I Filmed the War* (London: Herbert Jenkins, 1920).

15. Low, *The History of the British Film 1914–1918*, p. 36. Lord Beaverbrook became minister of information in the summer of 1918 with responsibility for official film production and distribution. When the committee was disbanded in 1919, the Topical Film Company was resold to private hands at a profit.

16. *Canadian Moving Picture Digest*, April 20, 1918, p. 6; June 29, 1918, p. 21.

17. Ibid., September 7, 1918, pp. 8, 14; Toronto *Daily News*, August 24, 1918; Toronto *Daily News*, September 18, 1918.

18. *Moving Picture World*, 36 (1918): 735.

19. A listing of the original American films is given in *Classic Film Collector*, no. 39 (Summer 1973): 10.

20. *The Albertan*, December 2, 1918; *The Calgary Daily Herald*, December 4, 1918. See also Toronto *Daily News*, October 22, 1918.

21. Toronto *Daily News*, September 27, 1918.

22. *The Dramatic Mirror*, March 17, 1917, p. 35.

23. *Moving Picture World*, 29 (1916): 507, 1425; 31 (1917): 261, 565; 32 (1917): 138, 1163; 35 (1918): 553. *Canadian Moving Picture Digest*, December 29, 1917, p. 16.

24. *Moving Picture World*, 34 (1917): 562.

25. *Canadian Moving Picture Digest*, March 2, 1918, p. 5.

26. Also known as *Canadian Pictorial News*. *Canadian Moving Picture Digest*, May 18, 1920, p. 45; October 1, 1921, p. 20. *Moving Picture World*. 51 (1921): 45, 488.

27. *Moving Picture World*, 39 (1919): 789, 1064, 1224. *Canadian Moving Picture Digest*, January 25, 1919, p. 9; April 19, 1919, editorial; May 24, 1919, p. 4; September 1, 1919, p. 24; September 15, 1919, p. 34; January 20, 1920, p. 13. Toronto *Daily News*, January 21, 1919; January 24, 1919.

28. *Canadian Moving Picture Digest*, October 18, 1919, pp. 6, 22, 35; September 4, 1920, p. 99.

29. Leonard Hally Roos was born in 1896; Charles G. Roos in 1882.

30. Among the companies which apparently did not produce are: Canadian Art Photoplays (Montreal, 1915), Niagara Falls Film Corporation (1916), Uscan Feature Photoplay Company (near Cornwall, 1916), Canadian Patriotic Films (Vancouver, 1916), British Canadian Motion Picture Company (Vancouver, 1916), Dominion Film Corporation (Vancouver, 1917), Harold J. Binney Productions (Toronto, 1919), Anglo-Canadian Picture Plays (Montreal, 1920), Tesa Films (Ottawa, 1921), World Film Company (B.C., 1917), Alberta Motion Pictures (Edmonton, 1922).

31. *Exhibitor's Trade Review*, December 16, 1916; January 20, 1917, p. 501. *Moving Picture World*, 29: 507, 674. *Motography*, 16 (September 30, 1916): 762.

32. *Exhibitor's Trade Review*, June 30, 1917, p. 259.

33. *Moving Picture World*, 33 (1917): 680.

34. Ibid.

35. *Exhibitor's Trade Review*, January 20, 1917, p. 501; *Moving Picture World*, 31 (1917): 1645.

36. *Exhibitor's Trade Review*, March 24, 1917.

37. *Canadian Moving Picture Digest*, February 8, 1919, p. 5; February

15, 1919, p. 8; *Moving Picture World*, 37 (1918): 1909; 40 (1919): 388; Toronto *Daily News*, September 5, 1918; Ottawa *Citizen*, April 7, 1919; Montreal *Gazette*, October 3, 1918.

38. *Canadian Moving Picture Digest*, February 8, 1919, p. 5; February 15, 1919, p. 8; *Moving Picture World*, 37 (1918): 1919; Toronto *Daily News*, September 9, 1918.

39. *Moving Picture World*, 40 (1919): 388.

40. Toronto *Daily News*, September 5, 1918.

41. *Moving Picture World*, 36 (1918): 255. The company was not incorporated until March 1918.

42. *Canadian Moving Picture Digest*, April 6, 1918, p. 16.

43. Ibid., March 2, 1918, pp. 4–5.

44. Ibid., April 27, 1918, pp. 7, 18; May 11, 1918, cover.

45. Ibid., July 27, 1918, p. 10.

46. The company was undoubtedly active under that name by August 1918 but was not incorporated until January 11, 1919, with powers to take over "business heretofore carried on by Adanac Producing Company or George Brownridge." *Canadian Moving Picture Digest*, September 28, 1918; *Moving Picture World*, 37 (1918): 1452.

47. *Canadian Moving Picture Digest*, September 28, 1918.

48. Ibid., August 17, 1918, p. 8; September 14, 1918, pp. 7, 20; Toronto *Daily News*, August 27, 1918; November 13, 1918.

49. Toronto *Daily News*, August 19, 1918.

50. *Canadian Film Weekly*, April 22, 1953.

51. This background to the production of the film was given by George Brownridge but is supported by later evidence. See (unpublished) article by Brownridge in Hye Bossin Collection: National Film Board.

52. Ibid.

53. *Moving Picture World*, 40 (1919): 102; 41 (1919): 92, 261. Canada, Public Archives: RG 68 Volume 598: Articles of Incorporation.

54. Canada, Public Archives: Willison Papers, MG 30 D14 Volume 10. Beatty to Willison, March 10, 1919.

55. Ibid., Brownridge to Willison, April 11, 1919.

56. The association initially turned down the request for funds, but later correspondence from the association requesting information on the return of its investment makes clear that they later did make a financial investment. Canada, Public Archives: Willison Papers. Brownridge to Worthington, October 20, 1920; Willison to Brownridge, November 3, 1920.

57. *Canadian Moving Picture Digest*, March 29, 1919, p. 6.

58. *Film Daily*, May 21, 1919; *Canadian Moving Picture Digest*, July 1, 1919, p. 31.

59. *Moving Picture World*, 44 (1920): 1237.

60. Ibid., 45 (1920): 476.

61. Ibid., 43 (1920): 64.

62. Ibid., 42 (1919): 662.

63. Montreal *Daily Herald*, December 13, 1919, p. 14.

64. Montreal *Daily Star*, December 15, 1919, p. 26.

65. *Saturday Night*, February 14, 1920.

66. Toronto *Telegram*, March 18, 1920.

67. *Moving Picture World*, 43 (1920): 1275, 1494, 2071; 44 (1920): 23.

68. Ibid., 44 (1920): 1237.

69. *Variety*, May 21, 1920.

70. *Moving Picture World*, 45 (1920): 476.

71. *Canadian Moving Picture Digest*, Christmas 1919, p. 10.

72. Canada, Public Archives: Willison Papers. Brownridge to Worthington, October 25, 1920.

73. *Moving Picture World*, 33 (1917): 680.

74. *Variety*, February 2, 1920; *Moving Picture World*, 43 (1917): 1116.

75. Canada, Public Archives: Bennett Papers, MG 26K Volumes 452, 453, has considerable information on this. Briefly, the federal government, through an order-in-council in March 1931 imposed an import duty on the entry of foreign sound motion picture equipment. The situation for *Fox Canadian News* in particular was made more acute by the Ontario government's quota of thirty to forty percent Canadian or British items in newsreels. The barring of American sound trucks cut off Canadian news items in the Fox newsreels and the only Canadian items in other newsreels were purchased from ASN—giving it a virtual monopoly for a brief time.

76. *Moving Picture World*, 48 (1921): 1070; *Canadian Moving Picture Digest*, November 18, 1922, p. 7.

77. Hye Bossin Collection: National Film Board. Undated letter, Brownridge to Hye Bossin.

78. Ibid.

79. Canada, Public Archives: Bennett Papers, MG 26 I Volume 151. R. B. Bennett to Arthur Meighen, April 27, 1936; Meighen to Bennett, April 28, 1936.

80. See chap. 5 for details on this.

81. Quoted in a letter from Bairnsfather to Ontario Provincial Trea-

surer Monteith. Ontario Archives: Canadian International Films file. Bairnsfather to Monteith, June 14, 1928.

82. Ibid.

83. Ontario Archives: Motion Picture files. Patton to Price, May 19, 1926.

84. *Moving Picture World*, 83 (1926): 279; 83, no. 8 (1926): 3; 85 (1927): 705; *Canadian Moving Picture Digest*, February 19, 1927, p. 12. Direction was by Bryant Fryer from stories by Geoffrey Keighley. Only two of these (*Follow the Swallow* and *One Bad Knight*) were actually made. M. Mitchell, "The Silhouette Films of Bryant Fryer," *Motion*, 5, no. 3 (1976): 16.

85. *Canadian Moving Picture Digest*, February 19, 1927, p. 12.

86. Ibid., September 20, 1927, p. 10.

87. Ibid.

88. Ibid., July 16, 1927, p. 1; *Moving Picture World*, 87 (1927): 266.

89. The company rented the studios for five years at a rental of $500 per month. In return the company agreed to process the films of the Ontario Motion Picture Bureau.

90. Ontario Archives: British Empire Films of Canada file. Prospectus (undated, but *circa* April 1927 according to internal evidence.)

91. Rachael Low, *The History of the British Film 1918–1929* (London: George Allen and Unwin, 1971), p. 227.

92. *Canadian Moving Picture Digest*, February 23, 1929, p. 11. By comparison, it was not then unusual for Hollywood to pay $50,000 for screen rights to a well known author's work—double what Bairnsfather received for his story and directorial contribution together.

93. Ontario Archives: Canadian International Films file. Letter, Bairnsfather to Monteith, June 2, 1928. *Canadian Moving Picture Digest*, August 13, 1927, p. 10.

94. *Canadian Moving Picture Digest*, November 26, 1927, p. 12; February 23, 1929, p. 11.

95. *Canadian Moving Picture Digest*, February 23, 1929, pp. 10, 11, and Editorial. See also: *Canadian Moving Picture Digest*, February 2, 1929, p. 13; Trenton *Quinte Sun*, June 2, 1928; September 8, 1928, for background on the production.

96. Ontario Archives: Canadian International Films file. Letters, Patton to Monteith, October 3, 1927, and July 11, 1928.

97. Ontario Archives: Canadian International Films file. Correspondence between Bairnsfather and Monteith through June 1, 1928.

98. *Variety*, June 8, 1928.

99. *Canadian Moving Picture Digest*, September 1, 1929, p. 8; Ontario Archives: Canadian International Films file. Letter, Bairnsfather to Monteith, September 3, 1928, together with Bairnsfather's analysis of the changes, his original conception and the necessity for two versions—one Canadian, one American.

100. Ontario Archives: Canadian International Films file. Bairnsfather to Monteith, June 14, 1928, quotes telegrams from the Harold Lloyd Corporation and the Chaplin Corporation.

101. Toronto *Mail and Empire*, October 10, 1928. Also negative cost sheet for production, Ontario Archives: Motion Picture Bureau files.

102. *Canadian Composer*, May 1965, p. 32.

103. Toronto *Daily Star*, November 13, 1928.

104. Toronto *Evening Telegram*, November 13, 1928.

105. *Canadian Moving Picture Digest*, December 29, 1928, p. 6.

106. Toronto *Evening Telegram*, November 13, 1928.

107. *Regina Post*, November 20, 1928.

108. Ibid.

109. Toronto *Daily Star*, December 20, 1928. The film grossed $14,000 during its two week run.

110. *Canadian Moving Picture Digest*, February 9, 1929.

111. Ibid., January 26, 1929, p. 12; May 11, 1929, p. 6; June 1, 1929, p. 12.

112. Ibid., March 30, 1929, p. 6.

113. Toronto *Mail and Empire*, August 18, 1930; *Canadian Moving Picture Digest*, September 6, 1930, p. 12.

114. Toronto *Daily Star*, January 26, 1929.

115. *Canadian Moving Picture Digest*, June 21, 1930, p. 12; July 19, 1930, p. 10.

116. Toronto *Star*, September 19, 1931.

117. Toronto *Star*, August 17, 1932.

118. Michie Mitchell, "The Forgotten Feature," *Motion*, September/October 1974, p. 47.

119. Ontario Archives: Canadian International Films file. Bairnsfather to Monteith, June 14, 1928.

120. Toronto *Star*, November 12, 1932.

121. Ontario Archives: Motion picture files. French to Dunlop, February 11, 1931.

122. Ontario Archives: Motion pictures files. Cory, Mayor of Trenton, to Hepburn, July 22, 1935.

123. *Photoplay*, January 1916.

124. *Victoria Times*, March 24, 1919, p. 3.

125. *Moving Picture World*, 39 (1919): 740.

126. Ibid., 38 (1918): 596.

127. Toronto *Evening Telegram*, February 5, 1921.

128. Toronto *Daily News*, January 13, 1919.

129. Toronto *Times*, April 26, 1919. Among his companies were Masterpictures of Houston, Texas and Pyramid Pictures of New Haven, soon to be closed by creditors. See also: *Moving Picture World*, 41 (1919): 92, where it is suggested he was Vancouver born.

130. Frank O'Byrne, letter to the author.

131. Toronto *Times*, March 28, 1919. See also *Saturday Night*, April 16, 1921.

132. Neil Hamilton was still on the stage at this time and did not act in films until 1922.

133. The Dominion Film Corporation (incorporated in B.C. on February 7, 1917) was the successor to Dominion Educational Films (incorporated in B.C. on April 15, 1916). *Moving Picture World*, 30 (1916): 439, 1371.

134. *Moving Picture World*, 30 (1916): 439.

135. *Victoria Times*, January 16, 1917, p. 11; January 19, 1917, p. 14; January 20, 1917, p. 16; February 13, 1917, p. 11. *Victoria Daily Colonist*, January 20, 1917, p. 7; January 25, 1917, p. 10; January 31, 1917, p. 7; February 1, 1917, p. 8. *Exhibitor's Trade Review*, February 10, 1917.

136. *Moving Picture World*, 31 (1917): 1067; 32 (1917): 669.

137. Ibid., 32 (1917): 669.

138. Ibid., 44 (1920): 435; 45 (1920): 59. *Canadian Moving Picture Digest*, March 20, 1920, p. 12; July 3, 1920, p. 24. *Saturday Night*, April 16, 1921.

139. *Moving Picture World*, 29 (1916): 119, 229, 2007; 30 (1916): 427. Toronto *Daily Star*, September 25, 1916, pp. 4, 10.

140. *Moving Picture World*, 32 (1917): 1973. Alex Dunbar had earlier organized the Great Western Film Company of Canada in 1916 with temporary headquarters in Toronto. Ernest Shipman represented them in New York. The company apparently produced nothing. *Moving Picture World*, 29 (1916): 507.

141. This may have been titled *Dates* or *The Battle of Not Yet*, films Charles Roos had photographed after *Self Defence*. The following year Charles Roos was one of the principal organizers of Unique Photoplays. What they

produced is unknown. *Canadian Moving Picture Digest*, September 7, 1918, p. 10.

142. *Canadian Moving Picture Digest*, March 15, 1921, p. 17.

143. Ibid., November 15, 1921, p. 18.

144. *Moving Picture World*, 55 (1922): 613.

145. Mrs. E. H. Griffith, personal conversation with the author.

146. Halifax *Herald*, November 15, 1922, p. 16.

147. *Canadian Moving Picture Digest*, December 2, 1922, p. 7.

148. *Moving Picture World*, 58 (1922): 704.

149. Ibid.; *Canadian Moving Picture Digest*, December 2, 1922, p. 8.

150. *Canadian Moving Picture Digest*, November 25, 1922, p. 14.

151. Ibid., December 16, 1922, p. 6.

152. Ibid., November 3, 1923, p. 16. See also more detailed discussion of Filmcraft Industries in Chapter 5.

153. Toronto *Daily News*, August 19, 1918.

154. *Canadian Moving Picture Digest*, February 15, 1921, p. 21.

155. *Moving Picture World*, 55 (1922): 614. The company was incorporated federally February 2, 1922.

156. Ibid., 56 (1922): 40.

157. *Canadian Moving Picture Digest*, December 8, 1923, p. 15.

158. *The Bioscope*, March 5, 1925, p. 49.

159. Canadian release by Regal Films; USA release by Associated Exhibitors. *Moving Picture World*, 67 (1924): 200; 68 (1924): 17, 435; *Canadian Moving Picture Digest*, January 12, 1924, p. 6; February 23, 1924, p. 4.

160. *Variety*, August 6, 1924; *The Bioscope*, March 5, 1925, p. 49.

161. René Jeanne and Charles Ford, *Histoire encyclopédique du cinéma*, (Paris: Robert Laffont, 1952), Volume 2, p. 420.

162. *Moving Picture World*, 30 (1916): 1845.

163. Ibid., 30 (1916): 1537; 31 (1917): 1067.

164. Ibid., 34 (1917): 1221. Kean also claimed another film, *Told in the Hills*, which was shown only once. See, Toronto *Evening Telegram*, March 2, 1931.

165. *Canadian Moving Picture Digest*, July 8, 1922, p. 5. The company was incorporated May 20, 1922. Some later references refer to the company as "Western Pictures Company."

166. *The Beaver*, September 1925, p. 182; Program of première performance, Royal Alexandra Theatre, Toronto, December 19, 1927.

167. Toronto *Evening Telegram*, March 2, 1931.

168. *Canadian Moving Picture Digest*, December 20, 1924, p. 26; October 24, 1925, p. 2; April 9, 1927, p. 13.

169. Toronto *Evening Telegram*, March 2, 1931.

170. Toronto *Daily Star*, December 20, 1927; December 31, 1927.

171. There are two other films which should be mentioned, the first questionably Canadian, the other possibly unfinished.

The Lonely Trail was released in 1922. Its director, Julian Rivero, claimed it was produced for "Canadian Films Ltd."; the American Film Institute *Catalogue of Feature Films 1921–30* lists the film as having been produced by "Credit-Canada." There is no record of a Canadian company called Credit-Canada, but Canadian Films Ltd. was active about 1920 in Montreal as producers of industrial films.

The Lonely Trail was produced to take advantage of the "Stillman Case" and featured Fred Beauvais, an Indian guide whose testimony in the case had received considerable publicity. Also in the cast were W. L. Tremaine, Christine McNulty, Rose McNulty, and Fred Bezerril. The reviewer for *Moving Picture World* noted that it "has the distinction of being the worst picture that has screened itself this way in years." See: *Moving Picture World*, 54 (1922): 205; *Variety*, January 6, 1922, p. 43.

The other doubtful production is an anti-narcotics film designed to fight drug use and white slavery, apparently produced by December 1922 in Montreal by the "Anti-Narcotics Film Company Ltd." The president of the company was Harry Kaufman, former assistant manager of Regal Films. Script for the film was by S. Morgan Powell, drama editor of the Montreal *Star*.

172. Montreal *Star*, April 25, 1925.

173. Richard De Brisay, "A New Immigration Policy," *The Canadian Forum*, October 1927.

174. *Moving Picture World*, 72 (1925): 277.

175. Toronto *Star*, December 15, 1925.

176. Kirwan Cox, "The Rise and Fall of the Allens," an unpublished paper which recounts the story of the Allen theatre chain and its takeover by N. L. Nathanson; *Moving Picture World*, 65 (1923): 805.

☙ CHAPTER 4 ☙

1. Address to the Canadian Club in London, Ontario, reproduced on page 16 in a special Shipman section in *Moving Picture World*, 61 (1923): following p. 274.

2. According to his son, Barry Shipman. Interview with the author.

3. Nell Shipman, "The Silent Screen and My Talking Heart," unpublished autobiography; manuscript in National Film Archives, Ottawa.

4. *Canadian Moving Picture Digest*, April 1, 1922, p. 8.

5. *Moving Picture World*, 61 (1923): insert following p. 274.

6. Ibid., 52 (1921): 43.

7. Ibid., 57 (1922): 154.

8. Ibid., 55 (1922): 749.

9. Interview with the author.

10. Frederick was a well known theatrical impresario, manager of tours for Melba and Nordica among others. Joe invented the Shipman Photoreproduction process; his daughter, Edna, appeared in Ernest's films. Arthur, the fourth brother went into the church. Barry, the son of Ernest and Nell, has had a long acting and writing career in Hollywood. Barry's daughter, Nina, is also an actress in TV and movies.

11. Almonte was originally called Shipman's Mills. It was founded by Daniel Shipman, around 1820.

12. Letter, Nell Shipman to Hye Bossin, August 8, 1964. Hye Bossin Collection: National Film Board.

13. Shipman, "The Silent Screen and My Talking Heart."

14. Nothing is known of his two previous marriages. The only evidence for their existence is in Nell Shipman's autobiography, where she refers to herself as "the fourth Mrs. Shipman."

15. Shipman, "The Silent Screen and My Talking Heart."

16. Ibid.

17. Ibid.

18. Ibid.

19. Following her starring role in *God's Country and the Woman*, Nell appeared in another Curwood adaptation, *Baree, Son of Kazan*, and some six other similar features before making *Back to God's Country*. She divorced (painlessly she said) Ernest in 1920 and established herself as an independent producer. Both *Girl from God's Country* and *The Grub Stake* (produced, written, and co-directed by and starring Nell Shipman) were a success. She moved her studio and zoo to Upper Priest Lake, Idaho, but the films made there failed because they got caught in two bankruptcies in the industry—including that of Lewis J. Selznick in 1923. Attempts to re-finance her company also failed. Associated with her in her independent productions was Bert Van Tuyle, production manager on *Back to God's Country*. In 1925 she married Charles Ayers, an artist; they were divorced in 1934. She continued writing actively (sometimes under pseudonyms) and attempting to mount independent film productions throughout the rest of her career—though she never succeeded in recouping the reputation she had in the early Twenties. She died in California January 23, 1970. In addition to her own, unpub-

lished, autobiography, see also Murray Summers, "Fragments From Letters of Nell Shipman," *Filmograph*, 4, no. 2: 18; Tom Fulright, "Nell Shipman, Queen of the Dogsleds," *Classic Film Collector*, no. 25 (Fall 1960): 30.

20. *Moving Picture World*, 20 (1914): 1702.

21. Ibid., 20 (1914): 540.

22. Ibid., 16 (1913): 1147; 17 (1913): 34.

23. Ibid., 24 (1915): 534.

24. Ibid., 30 (1916): 1966.

25. Ibid., 34 (1917): 51, 91, 729.

26. Ibid., 36 (1918): 1267, 1173; *Canadian Moving Picture Digest*, May 18, 1918, p. 8.

27. *Canadian Moving Picture Digest*, November 2, 1918, pp. 14, 19.

28. Ibid., December 7, 1918, p. 17. The second story selected, *The Golden Snare*, was not filmed with Nell Shipman though it was produced (in the United States) as a film in 1921.

29. *Calgary Daily Herald*, December 4, 1918; Calgary *Albertan*, December 2, 1918; *Glenbow*, 2, no. 6, p. 5.

30. Calgary *Albertan*, December 2, 1918.

31. *Calgary Daily Herald*, January 23, 1919.

32. This company should not be confused with Canadian Photoplay Productions, incorporated in Ontario, March 28, 1919. This company was promoted by Harold Binney.

33. *Prospectus*, Canadian Photoplays Ltd., dated February 24, 1919.

34. Ibid. There is also a curious conflict of companies involved. Curwood-Carver Productions was formed in the United States to exploit the Curwood stories. President was R. C. Thomas of Calgary (also president of Canadian Photoplays), managing director was H. P. Carver of Calgary. Ernest Shipman was manager. The address was that of Shipman's offices in New York.

35. Calgary *Albertan*, March 1, 1919.

36. Shipman, "The Silent Screen and My Talking Heart."

37. Ibid.

38. Bert Van Tuyle, "Making Outdoor Stuff a He-Man's Job," *Film Daily Yearbook of Motion Pictures*, 1924, p. 17.

39. Harbour and ship-board scenes were shot in San Francisco; summer scenes were photographed on the Kern River and interiors at the Robert Brunton Studios in Los Angeles.

40. *Moving Picture World*, 47 (1920): 1027.

41. *The Bioscope*, June 10, 1920, p. 669.

42. *Kinematograph Weekly*, June 10, 1920, p. 96. For other reviews

see: *Film Daily*, November 9, 1919; *Canadian Moving Picture Digest*, November 15, 1919, p. 21.

43. *Glenbow* 2, no. 6, p. 7.

44. *Canadian Moving Picture Digest*, May 18, 1920, p. 33.

45. *Moving Picture World*, 43 (1920): 1243.

46. It is also possible the company was dissolved in favour of another Calgary company, Northern Pictures Corporation Ltd. In August 1920, Shipman announced that this Calgary-based company would be one of those producing films of Ralph Connor's stories: *Cameron of the Royal Mounted* and *Patrol of the Sun Dance Trail* were those selected. D. G. Campbell resigned as secretary of the Calgary Board of Trade to organize the company and "is its President." The company was never incorporated and *Cameron* was produced by Winnipeg Productions. There is however a record of a "Calgary producing company" merging with Winnipeg Productions in October 1920 and there were, in fact, several Calgary shareholders of Winnipeg Productions. See: *Moving Picture World*, 45 (1920): 1128, 1162; 46 (1920): 683.

This however still does not answer the question of why Canadian Photoplay Productions folded. Nothing in their incorporation limited them only to Curwood stories and there is no reason why the company could not have produced *Cameron* or another Connor story. The answer may be, simply, that Ernest and Nell were both partners in Canadian Photoplays and refused to agree on further activities.

47. *Moving Picture World*, 43 (1920): 272.

48. Shipman was president of this company; Stephen King vice-president and general manager. The company's policy was "co-operative, progressive and Masonic." It controlled producing contracts for "the works of Ralph Connor and other authors" with exploitation contracts "for the works of Curwood, Connor, Edgar Rice Burroughs and Myrtle Reed." Its offices at 6 West 48th Street were those of Shipman and also of Curwood-Carver Productions. With Dominion Films, Shipman had the kind of company which he had wanted since Five Continents Exchange: a holding corporation controlling film rights to literary works.

49. *Moving Picture World*, 44 (1920): 1206; *Canadian Moving Picture Digest*, May 18, 1920, p. 33.

50. *Moving Picture World*, 44 (1920): 1348.

51. *Canadian Moving Picture Digest*, June 3, 1920, p. 43.

52. *Moving Picture World*, 45 (1920): 356. Winnipeg Productions was incorporated in Manitoba July 20, 1920 and voluntarily relinquished its charter in 1928.

53. *Moving Picture World*, 45 (1920): 281.

54. Ibid., 48 (1921): 926.

55. In his later career, after Shipman, he established a reputation as "king of the serial makers" at Universal in the Thirties.

56. *Canadian Moving Picture Digest*, July 3, 1920, p. 17; August 5, 1920, p. 71. The story about MacRae's having to spend his own funds on the project is recounted by Barry Shipman (interview with the author). MacRae was also a shareholder of Winnipeg Productions.

57. *Moving Picture World*, 52 (1921): 319.

58. Ibid., 46 (1920): 930; *Canadian Moving Picture Digest*, November 1, 1920, p. 26.

59. *Moving Picture World*, 46 (1920): 1258; *Canadian Moving Picture Digest*, November 1, 1920, p. 26.

60. *Moving Picture World*, 53 (1921): 453, 1020; *Canadian Moving Picture Digest*, January 1, 1922, p. 16.

61. *Canadian Moving Picture Digest*, Christmas 1920, p. 50; May 1, 1921, p. 16.

62. Ibid., Christmas 1920, p. 50.

63. Ibid., December 1, 1920, p. 19.

64. Ibid.

65. *Moving Picture World*, 50 (1921): 309. W. W. Hodkinson was a pioneer distributor, the founder of Paramount Pictures, and a great believer in independent production and single picture sales to distributors. He opposed the rapidly growing block-booking system and the production-distribution-exhibition mergers underway in the early Twenties. He was himself to be swallowed in such a merger, having earlier lost Paramount to Adolph Zukor.

66. For reviews see: *Moving Picture World*, 52 (1921): 319; *Film Daily*, September 11, 1921.

67. For reviews see: *Moving Picture World*, 54 (1922): 321; *Canadian Moving Picture Digest*, April 1, 1922, p. 9; *Film Daily*, December 12, 1921.

68. *Canadian Moving Picture Digest*, September 9, 1922, p. 4.

69. *Moving Picture World*, 47 (1920): 1027. The company also produced *At the Sign of the Jack O'Lantern* and *The Veiled Woman*. All were released by Hodkinson.

70. Ibid., 49 (1921): 590. He did sell *Back to God's Country* and *Nomads of the North* for release in Italy but apparently not *God's Crucible* and *Cameron*.

71. *Moving Picture World*, 55 (1922): 724.

72. Ibid., 50 (1921): 695; 55 (1922): 149.

73. Ibid., 56 (1922): 538.

74. *Film Daily Yearbook of Motion Pictures*, 1921, p. 350. It appears *Sant'Ilario* was not released in the United States.

75. Described in Shipman, "The Silent Screen and My Talking Heart."

76. *Canadian Moving Picture Digest*, March 1, 1922, p. 20.

77. Canada, Public Archives: File 289-12. Articles of incorporation of company.

78. Ottawa *Citizen*, May 13, 1922; *Ottawa Journal*, May 20, 1922. *Maclean's Magazine*, July 1, 1922, has a complete account of the production. According to *Moving Picture World*, Faith Green wrote the script.

79. *Ottawa Journal*, February 17, 1923.

80. The company was incorporated in Ontario, March 18, 1922. *Moving Picture World*, 55 (1922): 468; *Canadian Moving Picture Digest*, May 27, 1922, p. 9.

81. Michael Bliss, "Introduction," to the reprint of Alan Sullivan's *The Rapids* (Toronto: University of Toronto Press, 1972).

82. *Moving Picture World*, 55 (1922): 468.

83. *Canadian Moving Picture Digest*, May 3, 1924, p. 13; *Moving Picture World*, 61 (1923): insert following p. 274.

84. *Moving Picture World*, 59 (1922): 58; *Canadian Moving Picture Digest*, December 16, 1922, p. 11.

85. *Canadian Moving Picture Digest*, May 3, 1924, p. 13.

86. Ibid., November 11, 1922, p. 13.

87. For reviews see: *Moving Picture World*, 62 (1923): 774; 63 (1923): 306, 558; *The Bioscope*, October 15, 1925, p. 33; *Film Daily*, April 24, 1923.

88. *Ottawa Journal*, December 11, 1922.

89. *Moving Picture World*, 61 (1923): 457.

90. For reviews see: *Canadian Moving Picture Digest*, November 18, 1922, p. 10; *Moving Picture World*, 61 (1923): 694–95; *The Bioscope*, May 29, 1924; *Kinematograph Weekly*, May 29, 1924, p. 45; *Film Daily*, March 18, 1923.

91. For reviews see: *Moving Picture World*, 62 (1923): 241; *Film Daily*, May 6, 1923.

92. *Moving Picture World*, 66 (1924): 375.

93. *Canadian Moving Picture Digest*, March 1, 1924, p. 21.

94. Ibid., May 3, 1924, p. 13.

95. *Moving Picture World*, 62 (1923): 522.

96. Ibid., 63 (1923): 499. The company did not produce anything.

97. Ibid., 64 (1923): 646, 724; 65 (1923): 460, 466, 604; 66 (1924): 389.

98. *New York Times*, August 9, 1931, Section 2, p. 4.

99. Barry Shipman, interview with the author.

100. *The Bioscope*, December 11, 1929, p. 20.

101. *New York Times*, August 9, 1931, Section 2, p. 4.

102. For an account of the background of the period in the United States see Benjamin Hampton, *History of the American Film Industry* (New York: Dover, 1970), pp. 248–57.

103. *Moving Picture World*, 58 (1922): 368.

104. Ibid., 59 (1922): 560, 726.

105. D. M. Leo Bourdais, "Canada's Attempt at Movie Independence," *The Dearborn Independent*, March 31, 1923.

106. *Moving Picture World*, 61 (1923): insert following p. 274.

CHAPTER 5

1. *The Optical Lantern and Kinematograph Journal*, 3, no. 1 (November 1906): 20.

2. *Exhibitors' Times*, July 19, 1913, p. 16.

3. *Moving Picture World*, 26 (1915): 1169.

4. Wilkins was the first to film extensively in the Arctic. For more detail on his work see: David Zimmerly, *Museocinematography: Ethnographic Film Programs of the National Museum of Man 1913–1973* (Ottawa: National Museums of Canada, 1974), pp. 3, 17.

5. Charles Backhouse, *Canadian Government Motion Picture Bureau 1917–1941* (Ottawa: Canadian Film Institute, 1974), p. 4; Jean Dryden, "Canadian Government Film Activities 1913–1941" (unpublished paper prepared for the Department of Industry Trade and Commerce, Ottawa, July 1972), p. 2. Both the Backhouse and Dryden texts were essential references for preparing the sections of this chapter referring to federal government film production.

6. Canada, Public Archives: P. C. 2307, September 19, 1918.

7. Canada, Public Archives: *Department of Trade and Commerce Papers*, File RG 20 163 16613, Volume 1, June 29, 1916.

8. At the same time as the Essanay Company began filming on behalf of the Canadian government, Francis Holley, director of the Bureau, began a cross-country tour to locate suitable films about Canada in several prov-

inces. This tour was backed by Prime Minister Borden who wrote the various provincial premiers requesting their support and assistance. Manitoba Archives: T. C. Norris Papers, Borden to Norris, June 16, 1916; *Moving Picture World*, 25 (1915): 1503; 29 (1916): 1735.

9. Canada, Public Archives: *Department of Trade and Commerce Papers*, File RG 20 107 24089, Volume 1, November 29, 1919.

10. *Moving Picture World*, 25 (1915): 826. Essanay had also filmed the Canadian Arctic in 1913 on an expedition composed of James K. Cornwall, M.P. for Peace River, sportsman B. K. Miller, G. B. Fraser, and cameraman C. A. Zuperti. See: *Exhibitors' Times*, July 19, 1913.

11. Canada, Public Archives: *Department of Trade and Commerce Papers*, File RG 20 107 24089, Volume 1, November 29, 1919.

12. Ibid.

13. Essanay's titles were *Salmon Fishing in New Brunswick, Northeastern Canada*; *Banff National Park*; *The Great Natural Industries of Canada*; *Lake Louise*; *Water Powers of Western Canada*; *Water Powers of Eastern Canada*; *Through Canada From Coast to Coast*; *Agricultural Opportunities in Western Canada*; *How Canada and the Farmers Co-operate in Grain Raising*. See: *Moving Picture World*, 35 (1918): 45, 72, 245, 280, 385, 1360.

Norrish's titles included *Tributary to Vancouver*; *Tributary to Calgary*; *Tributary to Winnipeg*; *Tributary to Montreal*; *Hydro-Electric System, Ontario*, all within the overall series title of *Water Powers of Canada*.

14. Canada, Public Archives: *Department of Trade and Commerce Papers*, File RG 20 107 24089, Volume 1, May 11, 1917.

15. Ibid. In fact O'Hara was not far off in his estimate. Even by 1922–23 the net expenditures of the Bureau were still only $7,000, not including salaries. Total expenditures of the Bureau up to 1939, not including salaries, were of the order of $650,000 with revenue of approximately $340,000, leaving a net cost of $310,000 or an average net cost per year of about $15,000.

16. Ibid., June 14, 1917.

17. Ibid., O'Hara to Boggs, September 19, 1917.

18. Ibid.

19. Byron Harmon of Banff, Alberta was one who supplied 6,000 ft. of negative on the Canadian Rockies.

20. Ibid., Norrish to O'Hara, February 7, 1918.

21. Ibid., February 19, 1918. Norrish also proposed that the film unit charge other government departments for producing films for them.

22. Ibid.

23. Ibid., List of equipment purchased, *circa* March 1918.

24. Ibid., April 20, 1918.

25. Ibid., May 1, 1918.

26. Ibid., undated, unsigned report, August 1918.

27. Ibid., Memorandum to governor-general-in-council from minister of trade and commerce; Canada Public Archives: P. C. 2307, September 19, 1918.

28. This order-in-council did not fully settle the issue of which department could handle film work. The Department of Agriculture had been subcontracting and distributing films on agricultural topics for about a year and protested that the Bureau's use of non-safety film would make it impossible to use the films in rural halls. Although Norrish protested that this argument was not valid (since safety film could equally well be used by the Bureau for the Department of Agriculture's films) he made little headway; nor did O'Hara in defending the Bureau against accusations of technical incompetence. The Department of Agriculture won the battle and was specifically exempted from the previous order-in-council by a new one (P.C. 596, March 29, 1919). This exemption and the precedent it created was to be a continuing problem for the Bureau throughout its existence and was one of the factors in its eventual demise. See: Canada, Public Archives: *Department of Trade and Commerce Papers*, File RG 20 107 24089, Volume 1, December 31, 1918; Norrish to O'Hara, March 31, 1919; MacLean to Crerar, April 5, 1919.

29. *Moving Picture World*, 42 (1919): 340.

30. *Canadian Moving Picture Digest*, August 1, 1919, p. 31.

31. *Moving Picture World*, 42 (1919): 340.

32. *Kinematograph Weekly*, October 14, 1920, quoted in *Canadian Moving Picture Digest*, Christmas 1920, p. 35.

33. *Moving Picture World*, 39 (1919): 757, 1481; 40 (1919): 531; *Canadian Moving Picture Digest*, May 3, 1919, editorial.

34. *Canadian Moving Picture Digest*, February 13, 1919, p. 13.

35. Ibid.

36. Ottawa *Citizen*, November 22, 1919.

37. *Canadian Moving Picture Digest*, March 20, 1919, p. 32.

38. Canada, Public Archives: *Department of Trade and Commerce Papers*, File RG 20 107 24089, Volume 1, De Witt to MacLean, March 25, 1919; De Witt to O'Hara, March 25, 1919.

39. *Moving Picture World*, 51 (1921): 488. The newsreel was also known as *Canadian National Pictorial*.

40. *Canadian Moving Picture Digest*, March 20, 1920, p. 32.

41. Canada, Public Archives: *Department of Trade and Commerce Papers*,

File RG 20 107 24089, Volume 1, Norrish to O'Hara, November 29, 1919; Norrish to O'Hara, December 11, 1919; O'Hara to Foster, December 12, 1919.

42. Ibid.

43. *Moving Picture World*, 44 (1920): 1754; 45 (1920): 86.

44. Ibid., 44 (1920): 269.

45. Ibid., 45 (1920): 475.

46. Ibid., 32 (1917): 1819.

47. Ibid., 26 (1915): 2052. Presumably related to Norman James, one of the earlier of Toronto's news film photographers.

48. Ontario Archives: Motion Picture Bureau files. Patton to John Elson, April 9, 1931.

49. *Moving Picture World*, 32 (1917): 1819. There is no record of who actually produced their films but it is likely that Pathescope were closely involved as well as W. James and Sons.

50. *Canada Weekly*, May 4, 1918, p. 13.

51. *Moving Picture World*, 32 (1917): 1819.

52. Ibid.

53. The projectors were built to the Bureau's specifications in the United States and were known as "Ontario Specials." The decision to release its films on 28mm, though understandable at the time, was to become one of the Bureau's principal problems in later years. It was partly because Pathescope released its productions on 28mm that Norrish objected to Pathescope producing films for the federal Bureau.

54. *Moving Picture World*, 21 (1914): 1667. The company was federally incorporated on July 21, 1914.

55. William James Craft was born in New York City, July 17, 1890, and began his film career in 1910 as a cameraman for Kalem. He had photographed the serial *Hazards of Helen* before moving to Canada. After working for Pathescope he was involved with George Brownridge in Oakwood Photoplays and Adanac Films. He moved to Hollywood in 1922 and worked on some forty minor features until his death in 1931.

56. Material drawn from an interview with Dick Bird by Barbara Sears, January 17, 1973.

57. Ontario Archives: Motion pictures file. De Witt to Peter Smith, November 9, 1921.

58. Ibid., Roos to Smith, May 5, 1921.

59. *Saturday Night*, January 15, 1921.

60. *Moving Picture World*, 36 (1918): 706; *Canadian Moving Picture Digest*, June 29, 1918, p. 20.

61. *Canada Weekly*, May 4, 1918, p. 13.

62. *Canadian Moving Picture Digest*, June 29, 1918, p. 20.

63. *Moving Picture World*, 36 (1918): 706.

64. Ibid., 40 (1919): 1646.

65. Ibid., 40 (1919): 1196.

66. *Motion Picture Journal*, January 17, 1920.

67. In 1931, for example, the Bureau claimed to have "three hundred reels a month" in circulation in Ontario theatres, but had then no theatrical circulation outside the province. See Ontario Archives: Motion Picture Bureau files. Patton to Elson, April 9, 1931.

68. *Moving Picture World*, 41 (1919): 1008.

69. Ontario Archives: Motion Picture Bureau files. Dawson to McGarry, November 1, 1919.

70. Ibid., Dawson to Smith, November 29, 1919.

71. *Moving Picture World*, 41 (1919): 92. The company also did advertising stunts such as dropping promotional leaflets from the air.

72. *Canadian Moving Picture Digest*, February 15, 1922, p. 16.

73. *Canadian Cinematography*, September–October 1965, pp. 14–16.

74. *Moving Picture World*, 38 (1919): 1224.

75. *Canadian Moving Picture Digest*, November 15, 1919, p. 12. Filmcraft Industries was incorporated federally in January 1920.

76. Ibid., May 3, 1920, p. 26. The Canadian government's film bureau in Ottawa also had tinting and toning facilities. Tinting and toning are technical processes for the introduction of colour effects into films and during the silent film days these effects were expected by audiences. Tinting and/or toning were necessary in films if they were to gain theatrical release.

77. Ibid., July 17, 1920, p. 9.

78. Ibid., August 18, 1920, pp. 24, 48. In March 1921 distribution was taken over by Speciality Film Import.

79. Ibid., December 15, 1921, p. 2; January 15, 1922, p. 6; February 1, 1922, p. 2; February 15, 1922, p. 1; March 1, 1922, p. 10; March 18, 1922, p. 10; April 1, 1922, p. 8; April 15, 1922, p. 5; April 22, 1922, p. 7; May 20, 1922, p. 9; June 3, 1922, p. 9.

80. Ibid., February 15, 1922, p. 1.

81. Ibid., March 18, 1922, p. 10.

82. Ibid., January 15, 1922, p. 6.

83. Ibid., November 3, 1923, p. 16.

84. *Moving Picture World*, 45 (1920): 582.

85. Canada, Public Archives: File MG 30 A32, report by W. R. Maxwell.

86. Ontario Archives: Motion pictures files. Report of the Amusements Branch, Treasury Department, November 1, 1920 to October 31, 1921. In terms of payment for negative (the original production) Pathescope received $6,000, Filmcraft $17,500.

87. Ontario Archives: Motion pictures files. Elliott to Smith, May 4, 1921; Clarkson, Gordon, and Dilworth to Smith, August 4, 1922; Proctor to Smith, October 19, 1922; Clarkson, Gordon, and Dilworth to Smith, November 16, 1922.

88. Ibid., Elliott to Smith, May 4, 1921.

89. Ibid., Proctor to Smith, December 15, 1921.

90. Ibid., Clarkson, Gordon, and Dilworth to Smith, November 16, 1922.

91. Toronto *Telegram*, September 13, 1923, pp. 13, 29.

92. Ontario Archives: Motion pictures files. Price to Martin, November 8, 1923; Martin to Price, November 9, 1923.

93. Ibid., Patton to Price, February 15, 1924.

94. *Canadian Moving Picture Digest*, October 11, 1924, p. 8.

95. This quote and others is taken from an interview with May Watkis in *Maclean's Magazine*, May 1, 1921, p. 64.

96. *Moving Picture World*, 25 (1915): 1503.

97. Ibid., 44 (1920): 1754.

98. Ibid., 44 (1920): 654, 836, 1754; 47 (1920): 207.

99. Ibid., 47 (1920): 207.

100. Victoria *Times*, December 19, 1921, p. 13.

101. The films were on 28mm. A grant from Goodyear Tire and Rubber Co. helped establish the library.

102. Saskatchewan Archives: Saskatchewan Department of Agriculture, *Annual Report* for the year ending April 30, 1921.

103. *The Public Service Monthly* (Saskatchewan), December 1924; *Canadian Moving Picture Digest*, April 5, 1924, p. 5.

104. Ontario Archives: Motion pictures files. Patton to Price, May 29, 1924.

105. Ibid., Patton to Price, October 16, 1924.

106. Ibid., Brownridge to Patton (undated); Patton to Price, October 30, 1924.

107. Ibid., Patton to Price, January 20, 1925. The contract was made with Douglas Cooper and John Gibbons; the Bureau subsidized distribution at the rate of $500 a month.

108. Ibid., Patton to Price, January 15, 1925; Patton to Price, January 22, 1925; announcement by Bureau of distribution, April 28, 1925.

The Pathescope Company had now changed its name to the Film and Slide Company. The Bureau paid $50,000 for the films.

109. Safety 35mm at that time was not suitable for theatrical use, mainly because of its lack of durability. An acceptable quality of safety 35mm did not appear until 1950. The federal Bureau did release a few films on 28mm also, but mainly used safety 35mm film for its non-theatrical releases.

110. Ontario Archives: Motion pictures files. De Witt to Bain, January 8, 1925.

111. The change may also have had something to do with the change of minister. Price was always interested in and concerned about the activities of the Bureau; his successor J. D. Monteith appears to have had little direct interest though he often asked Patton for reports.

112. Ontario Archives: Motion pictures files. Patton to Price, June 21, 1926.

113. Ibid., Brownridge to Patton (undated); Patton to Price, October 30, 1924.

114. *Moving Picture World*, 79 (April 24, 1926); *Canadian Moving Picture Digest*, April 10, 1926, editorial.

115. Ontario Archives: Motion pictures files. Price to Patton, January 30, 1926.

116. Ibid., Patton to Price, February 1, 1926.

117. Ibid., Price to Patton, April 15, 1926.

118. Ibid., Brownridge to Patton, April 22, 1926.

119. Ibid., Patton to Price, May 10, 1926.

120. *Moving Picture World*, 80 (1926): 141.

121. Ontario Archives: Motion picture files. Patton to Price, May 10, 1926.

122. Ibid., Brownridge to Patton, June 30, 1926; Price to Patton, July 3, 1926. Brownridge was to reappear in 1930 in connection with the Bureau. At that time he was "Twilight Pictures Corporation" of New York who were agents for the Ontario Bureau's films. Little distribution was arranged. Perhaps the name was prophetic.

123. Ibid., Sparling to Patton, June 20, 1926.

124. Ibid., Patton to minister, February 16, 1927; Patton to minister, March 16, 1927.

125. Ibid., Graham to Montieth, October 2, 1929.

126. Ibid., C. J. F. to Premier Hepburn, November 1, 1934.

127. Ibid., Buckley to Hepburn, February 20, 1935.

128. Barely was this known before Mr. H. N. De Witt, president of

Screen and Sound Service Ltd. (formerly Film and Slide Company, formerly Pathescope) made known his company's interest in purchasing the Trenton facilities and in producing films under contract for the provincial government. See: Ontario Archives: Motion pictures files. De Witt to Hepburn, July 19, 1934. Photo-Sound Corporation were also quick to declare their interest. See: Burns to Hepburn, August 16, 1934.

129. Ibid., Patton to J. White, July 25, 1934.

130. Ibid., White to Hepburn, July 27, 1934.

131. Ibid., Hepburn to Buckley, October 15, 1934.

132. Ibid., "Report on Reorganization of Ontario Motion Picture Bureau."

133. Ibid., Hepburn to Patton, October 23, 1934.

134. Ibid., Hepburn to Patton, October 26, 1934.

135. *Canadian Moving Picture Digest*, October 27, 1934, p. 4.

136. Ontario Achives: Motion pictures files. Cory (Mayor of Trenton) to Hepburn, July 22, 1935.

137. *Canadian Moving Picture Digest*, June 4, 1927, p. 14.

138. Canada, Public Archives: *Department of Trade and Commerce Annual Report 1922–23*, p. 43.

139. Ibid. Release of the films was in Canada through Canadian Universal; in the United States through Bray Productions; in Britain through Jury's Imperial Pictures; in France, Belgium, and Switzerland through Cinématographes Harry.

140. Ibid., p. 141.

141. In fact, one of the strange attitudes of the time is that the Department kept harping continually on the Bureau's desire to become financially self-sustaining. While this was admirable in some ways since it encouraged the Bureau's desire to compete effectively with commercial production it was ultimately harmful and self-defeating in later years when Department officials came to believe their own propaganda and adjusted the Bureau's budget in relation to its revenue.

142. Canada, Public Archives: *Department of Trade and Commerce Papers*, File RG 20 107 24089, Volume 1, Peck to O'Hara, March 29, 1922.

143. Ibid., O'Hara memo for file, April 7, 1922.

144. Ibid., O'Hara to Peck, June 18, 1920.

145. Ibid., O'Hara to Pousette, October 20, 1921.

146. Ibid., Peck to O'Hara, March 8, 1923; O'Hara to Peck, March 14, 1923.

147. Ontario Archives: Motion pictures files. Empire Marketing Board Film Committee report on government film activity in Canada, Jan-

uary 24, 1928. For additional insight into Badgley's policies see: Frank Badgley, "Canadian Government in Films," *The Film Daily Yearbook 1928* (New York: Jack Alicoate, 1928), p. 927; Frank Badgley, "Report on the Canadian Government Motion Picture Bureau," *Film Daily Yearbook 1930* (New York: Jack Alicoate, 1930), p. 994.

148. *Canadian Moving Picture Digest*, April 9, 1927, p. 9. See also, ibid., January 22, 1927, p. 14, for Irving Cummings comments on the same film.

149. *Moving Picture World*, 74 (1925): 744.

150. *Canadian Moving Picture Digest*, January 15, 1927, p. 12; *Moving Picture World*, 84 (1927): 15. O'Hara agreed with this sentiment. See: Canada, Public Archives: *Department of Trade and Commerce Papers*, File RG 20 163 16616, Volume 1, O'Hara to Secretary of State for External Affairs, January 24, 1927.

151. *Canadian Moving Picture Digest*, March 26, 1927, p. 14.

152. *Moving Picture World*, 85 (1927): 626.

153. *Moving Picture World*, 86 (1927): 325; *Canadian Moving Picture Digest*, June 4, 1927, p. 14.

154. Biographical material drawn from: *Moving Picture World*, 38 (1918): 1091; 46 (1920): 82, 515, 612; 47 (1920): 228; 87 (1927): 308.

155. *Moving Picture World*, 47 (1920): 228; Backhouse, *Canadian Government Motion Picture Bureau*, p. 15.

156. *Canadian Moving Picture Digest*, May 1, 1921, p. 5.

157. *Canadian Moving Picture Digest*, August 4, 1928, p. 7.

158. Canada, Public Archives: *Department of Trade and Commerce Annual Report 1928–29*, p. 39.

159. Canada, Public Archives: *Department of Trade and Commerce Papers*, File RG 20 13279, Volume 1 (T-253), Badgley to Parmelee, November 12, 1927.

160. Ibid., RG 20 13793 D, Volume 1 (T-255), O'Hara to H. H. Stevens, December 1, 1930.

161. Canada, *House of Commons Debates*, February 3, 1933, p. 1807.

162. This film is listed and described under Nos. 117, 118, and 119 in the Bureau's catalogue.

163. Canada, Public Archives: PC 596, March 29, 1919.

164. See chapter 7 for more details on these activities, particularly the work of Harlan Smith and Richard Finnie. Also, Backhouse, *Canadian Government Film Activities*, which has much information on the inter-departmental disputes, and Zimmerly, *Museocinematography*, which discusses the film production of the National Museums.

165. Interview with W. F. Lothian, Parks Canada, Ottawa, by Barbara Sears.

166. Canada, Public Archives: *Department of Trade and Commerce Papers*, File RG 20 107 24089, Volume 1, Peck to O'Hara, May 29, 1922.

167. Biographical material drawn from interview by Barbara Sears with Mrs. J. A. Langford, Bill Oliver's daughter, and from *Canada's Weekly*, March 29, 1946. Bill Oliver died in 1954.

168. W. H. Corkill, "As the Crane Flies," *Canada's Weekly*, March 29, 1946.

169. Canada, Public Archives: Department of Trade and Commerce, *Annual Report, 1935–36*.

170. Ottawa *Citizen*, June 4, 1938.

171. *Motion Picture Herald*, May 4, 1935; Ottawa *Journal*, March 5, 1935.

172. *Canadian Moving Picture Digest*, November 17, 1928, p. 5.

173. *Montreal Standard*, March 6, 1937.

174. *Canadian Moving Picture Digest*, February 2, 1939, p. 6; April 1, 1939, p. 24; June 3, 1939, pp. 2, 4; July 15, 1939, p. 3; November 25, 1939, p. 4.

175. Canada, Public Archives: *Department of Trade and Commerce Papers*, File RG 20 31 16613, Volume 3, Parmelee to Euler, October 15, 1937.

176. Ibid., RG 20 B1 236 31670, Volume 1, November 18, 1937.

177. The report by John Grierson and the creation of the National Film Board are discussed in chap. 7.

⋖ৡ CHAPTER 6 ৡ⋗

1. Toronto *Star*, December 15, 1925.

2. *Canadian Moving Picture Digest*, December 26, 1925, p. 7; February 13, 1926, p. 5.

3. The process of company take-overs was not, of course, quite as simple and painless as may be implied here and involved many complicated financial and legal battles. In Canada, for example, the Nathanson-FPCC takeover of Allen Theatres was a minor skirmish in a larger struggle in the United States between Zukor/Famous Players interests and those of First National (which backed the Allens in Canada). First National—an exhibitor's cooperative which produced films financed by guarantees from member theatres—tried to keep the Allens in business when bankruptcy threatened

in 1922 but lost out to FPCC, as they eventually lost to Famous Players in the United States. There are several excellent studies of this period of vertical integration in the American film industry. See especially: Thomas H. Guback, *The International Film Industry* (Bloomington: Indiana University Press, 1969); Gertrube Jobes, *Motion Picture Empire* (Hampden, Conn.: Archon Books, 1966); Garth Jowett, *Film: The Democratic Art* (Boston: Little, Brown, 1976); Philip French, *The Movie Moguls* (Baltimore: Penguin Books, 1971); Benjamin Hampton, *History of the American Film Industry* (New York: Dover, 1970).

It is also worth noting that, during this period, Hollywood first began to treat Canada, for film distribution purposes as though it were an additional State: box-office figures for Canada were included in "domestic returns."

4. A discussion of this issue lies outside the scope of this book, but it should be noted that FPCC was prosecuted in Ontario under the Combines Act. The failure to obtain a conviction arose primarily out of the restrictive wording of the act—a difficulty faced in anti-combines investigations of other industries than film.

The investigation of FPCC was set in motion principally, though not solely, because of a share-exchange deal through which Zukor and Paramount Publix acquired direct control of FPCC, rather than merely holding shares in it. The White report includes a detailed account of the background to the takeover and the trade practices of FPCC and its subsidiaries: Peter White, *Investigation Into an Alleged Combine in the Motion Picture Industry in Canada* (Ottawa: King's Printer, 1931).

For a more general account, see *Maclean's*, October 1, 1930, p. 6. The White hearings are reported and commented on extensively in issues of *Canadian Moving Picture Digest*, 1931 through 1932; and in the Toronto *Mail and Empire*, February–March 1931.

5. France also introduced quota systems in 1929, 1931, and 1936—though they involved a different approach than the British quota. See: Jowett, *Film: The Democratic Art*, pp. 203–205; James Monaco, *Cinema and Society* (New York: Elsevier, 1976), pp. 42–43; Georges Sadoul, *Le Cinéma Français* (Paris: Flammarion, 1962), pp. 60–61.

6. For background on the British quota and its effects see: Rachael Low, *The History of the British Film 1918–1929* (London: Allen and Unwin, 1971), pp. 71–106; Ernest Betts, *The Film Business* (New York: Pittman, 1973), pp. 81–83.

7. Canada, Public Archives: Mackenzie King papers, File MG 26J4, Imperial Conference, 1926.

8. Ibid.

9. *Moving Picture World*, 84 (1927): 15. As pointed out in chapter 5, Deputy Minister O'Hara supported Peck's position.

10. Ontario did establish a legislative quota for British films in 1931, British Columbia in 1932, and Alberta in 1933. All of the acts required an order-in-council to bring the quota into effect. None of the provinces actually issued an order-in-council and the acts seem to have been used primarily as a threat to encourage a greater "voluntary" exhibition of British films. None of the acts mention Canadian films, though (given the language of the day) the term "British" would have likely been assumed to embrace "Empire" films, including Canadian.

The Australian action was taken following a Royal Commission investigation of the motion picture industry in Australia which produced clear evidence of its domination by American interests. A quota of five percent of Empire-made films was imposed on exhibitors in 1928 (rising to ten percent the second year and fifteen percent the third year). The system is still in force.

11. Toronto *Globe*, October 13, 1928.

12. *Moving Picture World*, 71 (1924): 65.

13. Toronto *Daily Star*, July 13, 1929.

14. Richard De Brisay, "A New Immigration Policy," *The Canadian Forum*, October 1927.

15. See for example the speech by Ontario Provincial Treasurer Price at the opening of the Trenton studios: *Moving Picture World*, 71 (1924): 65.

16. *Moving Picture World*, 77 (1925): 215.

17. See discussion of this in chapter 5.

18. Ontario Archives: British films file. Copy of letter from Peck to Captain H. V. S. Page, received by Patton.

19. *Canadian Moving Picture Digest*, December 28, 1935, editorial.

20. The British had strict regulations regarding British production. Films had to be made by registered British companies, a majority of whose directors were British. However, it should be noted that the effects of the 1927 Quota Act in Britain were not all advantageous either. Hollywood producers made "quota quickies" there also (as they did in Australia). Though the act was designed to encourage the growth of the British film industry, it did not achieve it: the industry came increasingly under American domination. The 1927 Act certainly created jobs for technicians and actors but had little serious effect on the standards of production. Few British films of the Thirties achieved international success and perhaps only two individuals:

Alfred Hitchcock and Alexander Korda. It took a revision of the act and the impact of the Second World War to change this situation.

21. Some examples of companies which sprang up in the late Twenties and early Thirties but which never actually produced any features are: Famous Players Canadian Corporation (1926) in Victoria; British Picture Producers—Captain Page's group—(1927) in Victoria; Canada Productions Ltd. (1930) place unknown; Cinema City, Canada (1926) in Victoria; Lion's Gate Film Studio (1927) in Vancouver; Canadian Classic Productions (1928) in Montreal; Pacific Pictures Ltd. (1928) in Victoria; National Cinema Studios (1927) in Vancouver; British & Dominions Film Company (1928)—a scheme to produce one feature in each of Canada, Australia, South Africa, and India; Canadian-American Talking Picture Studios Ltd. (1930) in Montreal; British American Film Company (1933) in Victoria. As is evident, Victoria and Vancouver were favourite bases for several of these projects. In 1931 a "studio" for quota films was planned for Windsor but never completed.

22. The correspondence and files relating to British Canadian Pictures and the production of *His Destiny* are in the Glenbow-Alberta Institute, Calgary. Other references to this section: *Calgary Herald*, February 9, 1928; April 2, 1928; May 2, 1928; May 12, 1928; August 21, 1928; December 8, 1928; December 11, 1928; *The Bioscope*, January 23, 1929, p. 41; *Canadian Moving Picture Digest*, May 5, 1928, p. 9; September 15, 1928, p. 7; January 26, 1929, p. 11; February 2, 1929, p. 4; *Kine Weekly*, January 17, 1929; *Kitchener-Waterloo Record*, August 30, 1951.

23. Georgeen Barrass, "Guy Weadick," *Glenbow*, 3, no. 3 (May 1970): 6.

24. *Calgary Herald*, December 11, 1928.

25. Ibid.

26. *The Bioscope*, January 23, 1929, p. 39.

27. *Calgary Herald*, December 8, 1928.

28. Ibid., December 8, 1928.

29. Ibid., December 11, 1928.

30. Production costs had been less than $50,000. Given the $25,000 advance from Paramount for British rights plus even a modest return over and above this, together with returns from Canada and United States distribution, there is no reason why the production of *His Destiny* should not have shown a profit. Correspondence on this question from Hart and Weadick are in the files for British Canadian Pictures (Glenbow-Alberta Institute). Canadian distribution was handled by Regal Films, a subsidiary

of Famous Players Canadian Corporation. There was minimal distribution in Canada. Regal Films also handled the distribution of *Carry On, Sergeant*.

31. Glenbow-Alberta Insititute, Calgary: British Canadian Pictures file. Weadick to McFarland, March 6, 1929.

32. Though bribery to British officials seems unlikely on the evidence, there remains the possibility of a "kick-back" to Paramount personnel in London to ensure the sale.

33. Though an increasing number of films now had at least "sound" sequences, most were still also released in "silent" versions because of the number of theatres outside the major cities which were not yet equipped for sound.

34. Copyrighted in the United States in October 1929. The film's release did not apparently merit even the usual trade paper reviews.

35. *The Bioscope*, November 20, 1929, p. 23. This was the first prosecution of a distributor for failing to comply with the quota. The defence of the distributor (F.B.O. Ltd.) was that they had acquired the rights to *Code of the Air* from a Canadian company. When it was excluded from the quota as non-British they had not been able to find an adequate substitute. American born Samuel Bischoff had been production supervisor for Columbia in 1928 and, after running his own companies, became head of production at Tiffany Studios.

36. *Belleville Intelligencer*, November 22, 1928; *Screen Facts*, 2, no. 6: 52. The cast included Bill Cody, Lotus Thompson, Shannon Day, Richard Maitland, Reginald Sheffield, Robert Wilber, and J. P. McGowan. It was directed by J. P. McGowan from a script by Ford Beebe. Bischoff's company had no relationship to the Calgary company. There is evidence that the Calgary promoters objected to the Bill Cody venture which they felt was capitalizing on their own pioneering efforts to produce for the British quota market.

37. *Moving Picture World*, 87 (1927): 374. No other details are known. It *was* completed, since it went through the Ontario censor, but it appears never to have been shown.

38. Toronto *Star Weekly*, April 20, 1929. Toronto *Star*, May 22, 1929. Producer was George T. Booth and the cast included Jolyne Gillier, Marjorie Horsfall, Ernest C. Sydney (president of the Company), Frederick Mann, Ivor Danish. The film seems to have disappeared quickly after its initial Toronto showing.

39. Ontario incorporation July 16, 1929. Toronto *Daily Star*, December 19, 1931; November 12, 1932. For details on *The Bells*, a two-reel film

with dialogue sound, see editorial in *Canadian Moving Picture Digest*, April 2, 1932. Cameramen were John Alexander, George Rutherford, and Len Humphries. Roy Locksley wrote the music. The short *Under the Circumstances* (author John French, and featuring Claire Maynard) may not have been completed. See: Toronto *Star*, November 12, 1932. Booth Canadian Films also produced two Grey Owl films: *The Trail—Men Against the Snow* and *The Trail—Men Against the River*.

40. Ontario incorporation April 8, 1927. *Moving Picture World*, 87 (1927): 374; *Canadian Moving Picture Digest*, May 7, 1927, p. 16; June 4, 1927, p. 13; July 2, 1927, p. 19; December 24, 1927, pp. 18–19. President was Sargeson Halstead, production manager Louis Chaudet, other officers were Harry Cooper, W. Y. Montgomery, Percy Walker, and A. A. Rodman, all local residents. Its intent does not appear to have been to produce films for the British quota.

41. Despite his name, Louis Chaudet was American born (Kansas, 1884). He had been an actor in the early years of movies and was a minor director in Hollywood in the Twenties.

42. *Canadian Moving Picture Digest*, October 15, 1927, p. 7; November 19, 1927, p. 6.

43. Ibid., November 19, 1927, p. 6.

44. Ibid., December 24, 1927, p. 17 (reprint of comment from Port Arthur *News Chronicle*).

45. Fort William *Times-Journal*, February 22, 1928.

46. *Canadian Moving Picture Digest*, September 29, 1928, p. 8.

47. Ibid., October 13, 1928, p. 12.

48. Ibid., January 12, 1929, p. 5. See also: Ibid., February 2, 1929, p. 4; Fort William *Times-Journal*, February 8, 1929. It is also possible that the film was released in the United States as *The Gorilla Man*—the plots seem similar. The release of an independently produced film in the United States at this time was very difficult. One effect of the introduction of sound had been to concentrate further the ownership of theatres in a few corporations—which were now, themselves, increasingly controlled by Wall Street financial interests. See: Jowett, *Film: The Democratic Art*, pp. 196–97; Hampton, *History of the American Film Industry*, pp. 390–93.

49. Harold Harcourt directed both, Dorothea Mitchell wrote the scripts, and Fred Cooper photographed.

50. Incorporated federally May 2, 1935. Ottawa *Journal*, June 12, 1935. Booth also incorporated Dominion Motion Pictures Ltd. in British Columbia on November 22, 1935 but it was never active. J. R. Booth had

also been involved with another film company, Tesa Films, in 1922, which planned to produce at Trenton but never did so. Booth Dominion Productions was backed financially by Audio-Pictures Corporation and Du-Art Film Laboratory of New York, together with Arthur Gottlieb.

51. Co-producer was Arthur Gottlieb. *The King's Plate* (with Toby Wing and Kenneth Duncan) was a racing romance set at Woodbine Racetrack and centred around the running of the King's Plate. *Undercover* (with Charles Starrett and Polly Moran) was a crime story. See: *Monthly Film Bulletin*, January 1936.

52. *Monthly Film Bulletin*, April 1936. *Film Daily*, March 13, 1936. It is a story of a Montreal jewel robbery.

53. *Film Daily*, November 3, 1926; *Moving Picture World*, 83, No. 2 (1926): 3; *Exhibitors' Daily Review*, November 5, 1926.

54. Toronto *Globe*, October 29, 1926.

55. *Moving Picture World*, 87 (1926): 374.

56. Toronto *Mail and Empire*, November 16, 1927; *Kinematography Weekly*, May 27, 1927; *Moving Picture World*, 87 (1927): 374; 88 (1927): 84.

57. Victoria *Times*, June 14, 1927, p. 1; June 15, 1927, p. 4; June 16, 1927, p. 3; June 24, 1927, p. 1; July 14, 1927, pp. 1, 12; July 15, 1927, p. 1. *Moving Picture World*, 87 (1927): 374; Victoria *Daily Colonist*, July 10, 1927.

58. "Motion Picture By-Law 1927." (Victoria City By-Law No. 2393, July 15, 1927.)

59. *Moving Picture World*, 88 (1927): 78.

60. *Monthly Film Bulletin*, February 1937.

61. *Canadian Moving Picture Digest*, February 18, 1933, p. 5; May 13, 1933, p. 6; May 27, 1933, p. 6; Victoria *Daily Colonist*, April 8, 1933, p. 1; April 23, 1933, pp. 1–2; May 2, 1933, p. 1; May 28, 1933, p. 6.

62. Working title was *The Crimson West*. *Canadian Moving Picture Digest*, November 4, 1933, pp. 9–10; December 30, 1933, p. 6; May 19, 1935, p. 6; Victoria *Daily Colonist*, August 17, 1933, p. 5; August 18, 1933, p. 5; September 26, 1933, p. 1; October 11, 1933, p. 1; October 17, 1933, p. 3; October 18, 1933, p. 6; October 25, 1933, p. 1; October 27, 1933, p. 11; November 3, 1933, p. 2; November 26, 1933, p. 1; December 10, 1933, p. 18; December 15, 1933, pp. 1, 14.

63. Victoria *Daily Colonist*, April 7, 1934, p. 3; *Canadian Moving Picture Digest*, May 19, 1934, p. 6.

64. Working title was *The Black Robe*. *Canadian Moving Picture Digest*, December 9, 1933, p. 60; April 7, 1934, p. 6; May 19, 1934, p. 6; Victoria

Daily Colonist, December 13, 1933, p. 3; December 31, 1933, p. 6; January 11, 1934, p. 3.

65. Victoria *Daily Colonist*, April 7, 1934, p. 3; *Canadian Moving Picture Digest*, April 7, 1934, p. 6; May 19, 1934, p. 6.

66. *Film Daily*, February 20, 1935.

67. A complete list of the films with production credits is given in the Appendix. The Victoria *Daily Colonist* from November 1935 through January 1938 includes considerable background on their production.

68. *Hansard* (London), February 24, 1938, p. 590. Victoria *Daily Colonist*, December 21, 1937, p. 3; December 23, 1937, p. 3; February 24, 1938, p. 1; February 25, 1938, p. 1; February 26, 1938, p. 6; March 3, 1938, p. 5; March 4, 1938, p. 5.

69. It is commonly accepted (and defined as such in numerous cataloguing rules, including UNESCO's) that a film's nationality is derived from the country in which the production company is incorporated and which provides most of the financing. Useful at a time when most production was studio based and handled by companies of considerable longevity, this definition now leads to patent absurdities when much production is "international," when film makers, technicians, and actors work freely in several countries and, most particularly, when films are often made by a company formed specifically to produce the one film.

Even in earlier years, the definition is not entirely satisfactory. The productions of Central Films are defined as Canadian even though Canadian participation was minimal. In contrast, *The Viking* is of American origin despite its Canadian theme and the major participation by Canadians.

Nanook of the North is an even more curious example, especially since it is so much of a one-man effort. It is usually described as of "U.S.A. origin." Yet it was financed by Revillon Frères, a French fur company, which should make the film French—an evident absurdity. It has even been suggested that Revillon Frères was a registered Canadian company—which would mean *Nanook* was, legally, a Canadian film, an idea somewhat less absurd than describing it as "French."

70. For an account of the Flaherty influence see: Peter Morris, *The Flaherty Tradition*, Canadian Federation of Film Societies Portfolio No. 4 (Ottawa: Canadian Federation of Film Societies, 1965).

71. There is a wealth of published material on Robert Flaherty. See especially: Arthur Calder-Marshall, *The Innocent Eye: The Life of Robert Flaherty* (London: W. H. Allen, 1963); Richard Griffith, *The World of Robert Flaherty* (New York: Duell Sloane & Pearce, 1953); Flaherty Papers (Letters,

diaries, etc. of Robert and Frances Flaherty): Special Collections, Columbia University, New York, N.Y.

72. Autobiographical document in the Flaherty Papers, Box 59.

73. Flaherty was born in Iron Mountain, Michigan, February 16, 1884 and died in New York City, July 23, 1951.

74. Flaherty was the first white man to cross the Ungava peninsula; he re-discovered the Belcher Islands (sighted in the seventeenth century but later removed from maps). He found the Belchers to be a large archipelago, the largest island of which (named Flaherty Island by the Canadian government) contained a lake itself as large as the whole area formerly assigned to the "doubtful" Belchers on Admiralty charts. The numerous ore deposits he found were judged too lean for commercial exploitation. It was this judgement (by Flaherty's father) that ended the Mackenzie expeditions.

75. Griffith, *The World of Robert Flaherty*, p. xv.

76. Calder-Marshall, *The Innocent Eye*, p. 55. There are several, slightly differing, accounts of this episode. See also autobiographical documents in the Flaherty Papers, Box 59.

77. Ibid.

78. *Moving Picture World*, 24 (1915): 426.

79. Flaherty Papers, Box 15. Letter from C. T. Currelly, April 14, 1915.

80. A print of the film did survive but it was not then technically possible to duplicate it. It was this print, later lost, which Flaherty used in showings to raise funds.

81. Calder-Marshall, *The Innocent Eye*, p. 77.

82. Griffith, *The World of Robert Flaherty*, p. 36.

83. Flaherty was to get $500 a month for an unstipulated period, $13,000 for equipment and supplies, and a $3,000 credit at Port Harrison "for remuneration of natives." In return, Revillon required a credit on the final film. Flaherty's acceptance of this was, in fact, an affront to the film industry—which had long since banned advertising in films.

84. Flaherty's own diary contains an extensive account of the filming. See: Flaherty Papers and Griffith, *The World of Robert Flaherty*, pp. 38–43.

85. Flaherty's diary, quoted in Griffith, *The World of Robert Flaherty*, p. 41.

86. *Theatre Arts*, May 1951.

87. This is the same "Roxy" who was to figure in the Ontario Motion Picture Bureau story a few years later. See chapter 5.

88. *New York Times*, June 12, 1922.

89. Robert Sherwood, *The Best Moving Pictures of 1922–23* (Boston: Small, Maynard, 1923).

90. Richard Meran Barsam, *Nonfiction Film* (New York: E. P. Dutton, 1973), p. 132.

91. *The Silent Enemy* was produced by William Douglas Burden and William C. Chanler, directed by H. P. Carver, written by Richard Carver, and photographed by Marcel Le Picard and five assistants. William C. Chanler was also vice-president of Varick Frissell's Newfoundland-Labrador Film Company which produced *The Viking* shortly after *The Silent Enemy* was completed. Nothing is known of H. P. Carver but it is possible he is the same as the H. P. Carver from Calgary who, a decade earlier, was involved with Ernest Shipman on the production of *Back to God's Country* and in later partnership with Shipman on Curwood-Carver Productions. Richard Carver is presumably related. It has been said that a book by Douglas Burden on his travels in the Dutch East Indies gave Merian C. Cooper the idea for *King Kong*.

92. "How the Silent Enemy Was Made," original sourvenir program, 1930.

93. Ibid.

94. National Film Board: Hye Bossin Collection. Letter, Louis Bonn to Hye Bossin, August 26, 1963.

95. "How the Silent Enemy Was Made," original sourvenir program, 1930.

96. Ibid.

97. New York *American*, May 20, 1930.

98. *Screenland*, October 1930, p. 62.

99. Ibid., p. 118. For an account of his life and career see: Donald Smith, "The Legend of Chief Buffalo Child Long Lance," *The Canadian*, February 7, 1976; February 14, 1976.

100. *New York Times*, May 20, 1930.

101. New York *Post*, May 20, 1930.

102. *Motion Picture Herald*, May 25, 1930.

103. Ibid.

104. Ibid. In calling it "silent," the reviewer was presumably referring to its lack of dialogue. However, though it may have failed on Broadway, there is no reason to assume it could not have done well outside New York even though, by 1930, many more theatres were equipped for sound than a year earlier.

105. Library of Congress, Washington, D.C.: Varick Frissell Collec-

tion. This, as yet uncatalogued, collection includes a wealth of material on Frissell, including press clippings, correspondence, and company files. A microfilm copy of major items in the collection is in the National Film Archives, Ottawa. The film project referred to was in 1928 or 1929.

106. Ibid. Cable from Flaherty in Berlin, March 19, 1931, to Jesse Lasky of Paramount Pictures. The full text reads: "Frissell was my good friend and protégé. Do not know his parent's address. Will you please give them my deepest sympathy. Kindest regards from Mrs. Flaherty and myself."

107. Ibid. Address by Sir Wilfred Grenfell at memorial services for Varick Frissell, April 22, 1931.

108. St. John's *Evening Telegram*, March 20, 1931.

109. Ibid.

110. For a detailed account of Frissell's (and other's) explorations of the region see: W. Gillies Ross, "Exploration of the Unknown River in the Labrador," *The Beaver*, fall 1965, pp. 30–35. See also Varick Frissell's own account in *The Canadian Magazine*, September 1926, p. 6.

These falls on the Unknown River together with their twin, Twin Falls, are now called Thomas Falls. The geography of the region has changed considerably since the construction of the hydro-electric power project.

111. St. John's *Evening Telegram*, March 20, 1931.

112. *New York Times*, April 19, 1928.

113. Ibid.

114. Ibid.

115. Ibid.

116. The Varick Frissell Collection includes letters and contracts pertaining to the release. See also: *Film Culture*, No. 41, p. 90. The original length of *The Swilin' Racket* was 3,595 feet. The later version, *The Great Arctic Seal Hunt*, was shortened by the distributor to 3,162 feet. This version was also sold to Britain and Sweden in the fall of 1928 and later released on 16mm for educational purposes.

117. Varick Frissell Collection. Extracts from reviews, all undated.

118. Ibid. Foreword to *The Great Arctic Seal Hunt*, signed by Varick Frissell.

119. Ibid. Letter from Varick Frissell to Wilfred Grenfell, May 2, 1927.

120. Ibid. Several story outlines by Frissell.

121. Ibid. Varick Frissell to Newfoundland-Labrador Film Company, January 9, 1930.

122. It is interesting to note that Hollywood had imposed similar con-

ditions on Robert Flaherty. Paramount did not eventually release *The Viking* which was distributed in the United States and Canada by J. D. Williams, an independent distributor formerly associated with First National. At what point Williams became involved is not clear. He may have been involved in the company's formation and financing but it is more likely that he agreed to handle distribution only after the test screening of *The Viking* in January 1931. It was after this that Frissell decided to eliminate much of the love story—and hence probably lose the agreement with Paramount. Williams certainly handled a test screening of the film in New York in April 1931.

123. Title credits for *The Viking*.

124. St. John's *Evening Telegram*, February 24, 25, and 26, 1930. The other cameraman was Alfred Gandolphi. Other technical credits include: Roy P. Gates, production manager; Alfred Manche, electrical engineer (i.e. sound technician); Ted Eigil, assistant sound; Frank Kirby, stills.

125. St. John's *Evening Telegram*, February 7, 8, 13, and 17, 1930.

126. *The Weekly Bulletin*, St. John's, 10, no. 7 (February 16, 1930).

127. The film went through various title changes which are omitted in the text for the sake of clarity. Originally titled *Vikings of the Ice-Fields* in the company's prospectus, it later became, successively, *Thundering North*, *Northern Knight*, and *White Thunder*. The release title, *The Viking*, was selected after the disaster which destroyed the ship.

128. For an account of the filming see *Bell and Howell Filmotopics*, November 1930, pp. 2–3; St. John's *Evening Telegram*, April 9, 1930.

129. Frissell used the Western Electric disc-sound system which was used by Paramount under licence.

130. *Bell and Howell Filmotopics*, November 1930, pp. 2–3.

131. Ibid.

132. Ibid.

133. Varick Frissell Collection. Audience response cards to preview screening of *White Thunder*.

134. *Hollywood Daily Screen World*, January 15, 1931.

135. Personal recollection of Toni Frissell, Varick Frissell's sister.

136. A detailed, personal, account of the voyage and disaster is given by Clayton L. King, "Last Voyage of the Viking," *The Book of Newfoundland* (Joseph Smallwood, editor), pp. 76–85. All quotations relating to the voyage are taken from this source.

137. St. John's *Evening Telegram*, March 17, 1931.

138. Varick Frissell Collection. Correspondence and cables relating to the search.

139. Toronto *Mail and Empire*, March 23, 1931.

140. St. John's *Evening Telegram*, April 27, 1931.

141. Quoted by Toni Frissell, letter to Peter Morris, October 3, 1972.

142. As described above (note 122), the film was released by J. D. Williams to whom distribution was transferred sometime after the January preview. J. D. Williams was an Australian-born independent distributor and exhibitor who had owned and operated a theatre in Vancouver in the early years of his career. He had been a distributor of some importance before the onslaught of "vertical integration" by the major film companies in the early Twenties but by 1931 was of little consequence. Being handled by Williams meant that *The Viking* could be seen only in small, independent theatres, not those owned by the major chains.

143. *The Bioscope*, August 12, 1931, display advertisement.

144. *Film Daily*, June 21, 1931; *The Bioscope*, August 19, 1931, p. 25.

145. *The Bioscope*, August 19, 1931, p. 25.

ఆక్ష CHAPTER 7 ఆ

1. *Moving Picture World*, 32 (1917): 1973; 34 (1917): 562; *Canadian Moving Picture Digest*, December 29, 1917, p. 16; September 7, 1918, p. 10.

2. *Moving Picture World*, 43 (1920): 245; *Canadian Moving Picture Digest*, February 7, 1920, p. 10.

3. Interview with Dick Bird by Barbara Sears, January 17, 1973. See also chapter 5.

4. *Monthly Film Bulletin*, 1938, p. 177; *Motion Picture Review Digest*, December 1938, p. 106.

5. *Moving Picture World*, 41 (1919): 1358.

6. *Canadian Moving Picture Digest*, January 26, 1924, p. 6.

7. Victoria *Daily Colonist*, October 4, 1930.

8. David Zimmerly, *Museocinematography: Ethnographic Film Programs of the National Museum of Man, 1913–1973* (Ottawa: National Museums of Canada, 1974).

9. Ibid.

10. René Bouchard, *Filmographie d'Albert Tessier* (Documents Filmiques du Québec, no. 1) (Montreal: Les editions du Boréal Express, 1973). There is also a film, produced by Radio-Canada: *Msgr Tessier*.

11. In early 1958, Associated Screen News sold its studios to Edward Productions and its film laboratory to a corporation controlled by Du-Art Laboratories of New York.

12. *Moving Picture World*, 45 (1920): 475; Terry Ramsaye, *A Million and One Nights* (New York: Simon and Schuster, 1926), p. 812. Later the "of Canada" was dropped in favour of Associated Screen News Limited—and Gordon Sparling always insisted on calling it Associated Screen Studios. Edward Beatty was chairman of the Board of Directors when Norrish was president and John Alexander vice-president.

13. *Moving Picture World*, 45 (1920): 475; 50 (1921): 156.

14. Ibid., 47 (1921): 181. *Selznick News* was produced by Associated Screen News of the United States with which ASN of Canada was initially associated.

15. *Maclean's Magazine*, May 15, 1929, p. 15; *Canadian Moving Picture Digest*, July 9, 1927, p. 112.

16. Ontario and Nova Scotia both imposed a quota on the minimum Canadian content of newsreels shown in their provinces—a ruling which sustained both ASN's newsreel activities and those of *Fox Canadian News*.

17. *Canadian Moving Picture Digest*, May 1, 1921, p. 3; March 1, 1924, p. 3 and advertisement in same issue. The *Kinograms* series had no relationship to the newsreel.

18. Ottawa, National Film Archives: *Canadian Cameos* newsclipping file. The films were rarely reviewed in *Canadian Moving Picture Digest* which usually merely noted their release.

19. Ibid., also file of release lists with names of international distributors associated with each title. The French version of *Grey Owl's Little Brother* was running in a Paris theatre when the Nazis entered the city.

20. *Canadian Moving Picture Digest*, November 17, 1920, p. 9.

21. Marjorie MacKay, "The History of the National Film Board" (unpublished work, property of the National Film Board), p. 5. Grierson's work, prior to his arrival in Canada, is well documented in several standard texts on documentary film. See especially: Richard Meran Barsam, *Nonfiction Film: A Critical History* (New York: Dutton, 1973) which includes a useful bibliography; Alan Lovell and Jim Hillier, *Studies in Documentary* (London: Viking Press, 1972).

22. Canada, Public Archives: File RG 20B1 236 31670, Volume 1, June 1938.

23. Ibid. File RG 20B1 578 TA383, March 17, 1939. See also *Canadian Moving Picture Digest*, January 28, 1939, p. 11; September 9, 1939, p. 2; November 11, 1939, p. 3.

24. Canada, Public Archives: PC 3549, June 11, 1941.

ᴥ CHAPTER 8 ᴥ

1. Two additional points are worth noting. First, that the urge towards monopolistic control of the film industry was strong even in the early years. (For example, the various attempts by Edison from 1897 and, later, the attempts by Biograph to control the use of their several technical devices; also the foundation in 1909 of the Motion Picture Patents Company, a monopoly consortium of nine major producers.) Second, before 1914 the French film industry was far stronger internationally than the American. (One producer, Pathé, usually distributed in the United States twice as many films as all the American producers combined.) See Raymond Williams, *Communications* (Harmondsworth: Penguin, 1968), especially p. 29, for an account of this monopolistic tendency in the communications industries.

2. In France, Gaumont and Pathé might be cited as examples; in Sweden, Svenska Filmindustri; in Germany, UFA; in Japan, Nikkatsu. It is also worth noting that the USSR after Stalin's rise to power, modelled its film industry directly on that of Hollywood. Raymond Williams, *Communications*, p. 155, describes the general situation most succinctly: "In television, in cinemas, in theatres, and in the Press we find a scale of investment beyond the possibility of ownership by individual contributors, and a degree of profit so large as to make any attempt to assert the public interest a fight from the start." It is, of course, in this sense that Canadian film went so completely against the grain.

3. As suggested in the text, film production by government agencies themselves can be seen as an exception to this—similar to the development of the CNR and CBC, parallel to equivalent commercial companies. But it represented support for an alternative kind of film making, quite different from the fiction films that dominated the world's theatres. In any case, it cannot be considered intervention and support comparable to that of many European countries; its existence represents another exception to any American or European model.

4. For a recent examination of the role of liberalism in Canadian society see James Laxer and Robert Laxer, *Pierre Trudeau and the Question of Canada's Survival* (Toronto: James Lorrimer, 1977).

5. E. K. Brown, *Responses and Evaluations, Essays on Canada* (Toronto: McClelland and Stewart, 1977), p. 21.

6. Northrop Frye, "Conclusion to a *Literary History of Canada*," reprinted in *The Bush Garden, Essays on the Canadian Imagination* (Toronto: House of Anansi, 1971), p. 222.

7. This book is not the place for a discussion of filmic codes and conventions and the evolution of a more or less standardized textual system comparable to that of the written language. There is considerable recent theoretical discussion of these questions, but I would refer the interested general reader to James Monaco, *How to Read a Film* (New York: Oxford University Press, 1977), especially chaps. 3 and 5.

8. Frye, *The Bush Garden*, p. 245.

9. Ibid., p. 246.

10. Ibid., p. 239.

11. For a different view of Canadian naturalism, see A. G. Bailey, *Culture and Nationality* (Toronto: McClelland and Stewart, 1972), pp. 189–99. For a discussion of Margaret Atwood's *Survival* see George Woodcock, "Margaret Atwood: Poet as Novelist," reprinted in George Woodcock (ed.), *The Canadian Novel in the Twentieth Century* (Toronto: McClelland and Stewart, 1975), pp. 319–24.

12. There are, of course, many other comparable films. The reasons why they could be made and released in the Sixties and not earlier is necessarily part of another history than this one. But it is fair, if simplistic, to say that it had a great deal to do with changes in the economic structure of the international film industry.

13. *Mono-no-aware* is one of the four basic "moods" derived from Zen and applicable in aesthetics. Very much connected with Fall, and all that Fall implies, it is melancholic and nostalgic and expresses an awareness of the transience of worldly things.

Film Title Index

General Index

at Motion Picture Bureau, 166–74, 234–35
Bain, John, 117
Bairnsfather, Bruce, 74–79, 262
Balchen, Burt, 214
B. and C. Feature Co., 53
Barbeau, Marius, 225, 261
Barham, Helen Foster. *See* Nell Shipman
Barker, Bradley, 113, 256
Barker, Reginald, 28
Barrenn, Winn, 268
Barrie, Wendy, 270
Barrymore, Lionel, 284n79
Barsha, Leon, 192, 270, 271
Bartlett, Bob, 206, 209, 210, 264
Bartlett, Don, 75, 167
Barton, Finis, 269
Bastier, George, 62
Beattie, Allen, 261
Beatty, Sir Edward, 68, 80, 222, 323n12
Beauvais, Fred, 295n171
Beaverbrook, Lord, 59
Beckway, William, 189, 266–71 *passim*
Beebe, Ford, 192, 263, 269
Beesley, Ross, 226, 271, 272
Belaney, Archie. *See* Grey Owl
Beliveau, Juliette, 219
Belsaz. *See* John C. Green
Bennett, R. B., 71
Benoît, Georges, 259
Beresford, Frank, 48, 252
Berliner, Herbert, 219
Berliner, Rudolph, 67, 68, 255
Bern, Paul, 52, 53
Bernard, Dorothy, 68, 255
Best, Fred, 212
Beury Feature Film Co., 53–54
Beury, James and Charles, 52–54
Beveridge, James, 220, 272
Bezerril, Fred, 84, 295n171
Binney, Harold J., 83–84, 255
Biograph Co. *See* American Mutoscope and Biograph Co.
Bioscope Company of Canada, 34, 245
Bird Films, 140, 218, 267
Bird, Jean, 267
Bird, Richard, 62, 224, 256, 257, 267,

272; early career, 139–40; later career, 218–19
Bischoff, Sam, 185, 314n35
Bishop, Kenneth, 188–94, 266–72 *passim*
Bitzer, G. W., 29, 37, 245, 246
Bizeul, Jacques, 118, 258
Blaber, Ralph, 266
Black top tents, 15–17
Blaisdell, Margot, 271, 272
Blindloss, Harold, 185, 263
Blinn, Holbrook, 65, 254
Bodington, Maurice, 264
Boer War Films. *See* War: Boer War
Boldt, John E., 48, 58
Bond, Brenda, 262
Bonine, Robert, 29–30, 244, 245, 280n8
Bonn, Louis, 264
Booth Canadian Films, 80, 81, 185, 265, 270, 314n39
Booth Dominion Productions, 117, 187, 268, 315n50
Booth, George T., 185, 263, 314n38
Booth, J. R., 71, 117, 187, 268, 315n50
Borden, Sir Robert, 55, 117
Bouton, Betty, 86, 259
Bradford, F. Guy, 33, 35–36, 245
Bradshaw, Dorothy, 270
Bray Productions, 308n139
Brennan, Mike, 86, 259
Brenon, Bill, 62
Briggs, Slade, 264
Bright, Douglas, 78
British American Film Co. (Montreal), 47–48, 54, 58, 248, 252
British American Film Co. (Victoria), 313n21
British and Colonial Kinematograph, 37
British and Dominions Film Co., 313n21
British Canadian Feature Film Co., 22
British Canadian Motion Picture Co., 288n30
British Canadian Pictures, 80, 105, 183–85, 262, 263
British Columbia: production for, 36, 149–51, 219, 247; censorship, 55, 149; quota, 150, 193–94; Theatres Branch, 150; debate re Hollywood films, 82. *See*

Mounted Police in films
Mulholland, Brendhan, 264
Murray, W. W., 268

Nacpas, Louis, 284n79
Narcita, Mlle, 284n79
Nash, Johnny. *See* John Schuberg
Nathanson, N. L., 20, 88, 92, 176
National Cinema Studios, 188, 313n21
National Film Act (1939), 234
National Film Board, 174, 222, 234–35
National Film Society, 234
National Museum, 169
National origin of films, definition of, 195, 317n69
National Parks. *See* Canada, Parks Branch
Naturalism, in Canadian films, 241, 325n11
Nelson, J. Arthur, 84–85
New Brunswick Films, 117, 120, 123, 259
Newfield, Sam, 268
Newfoundland: production, 38, 204–15
Newfoundland Films, 117
Newfoundland Labrador Film Co., 208, 264, 319n91
Newmeyer, Fred, 191, 267
Newsreel quota, 323n16
Newsreels, 29, 30, 38, 46, 47, 51, 52, 57–63, 70, 153, 175, 223–24, 290n75. *See also* individual titles
Newton, Jack (John), 118, 119, 258, 259
Newton, Frank, 193, 262
Niagara Falls, early films of, 8, 9, 29, 276n16, 277n24, 280n2
Niagara Falls Film Corporation, 288n30
Nichol, Cecil, 269, 271
Nickelodeons, 21, 23
Noble, John W., 86
Norris, T. C., 112
Norrish, Bernard E., 159, 231, 255, 256, 258, 260, 261, 262, 265; and Motion Picture Bureau, 131, 132–37, 159; and ASN, 222–24, 228, 231–32, 323n12; views on film industry, 232
Northern Films, 191
Northern Pictures Corporation, 298n46

North West Mounted Police, films of. *See* Royal Canadian Mounted Police in films
Nova Scotia: production for, 140, 149; newsreel quota, 323n16
Nye, Carroll, 185, 263

Oakman, Wheeler, 106, 107, 255, 268
O'Byrne, Frank, 62, 83, 218, 223, 226, 255, 265
O'Hara, F. C. T., 131–33, 160, 161, 162
O'Hara, Kenneth, 118, 258
O'Hara, Laura, 262
Olcott, Peggy, 185, 263
Olcott, Sidney, 28, 40
Oliver, H. T., 50, 253
Oliver, William J., 169–72, 218, 221, 224, 230, 241, 261–69 *passim*; background, 169–70; production for National Parks, 169–72
O'Neill, Barry, 65, 254
Ontario: censorship, 53, 55, 146; quota, 180, 193–94; newsreel quota, 62, 323n16; Agriculture, 137, 141; Amusements Branch, 146, 148, 158; Lands and Forest, 201; involvement with *Carry on Sergeant*, 73; involvement with private film industry, 137–48, 153. *See also* Ontario Motion Picture Bureau
Ontario Film Co., 185, 263
Ontario Motion Picture Bureau, 70, 133, 220, 241, 256–64 *passim*; Brownridge involvement with, 71, 72, 153–55; establishment of, 137–38; and Pathescope, 138–43; and Filmcraft Industries, 143–49; Trenton purchase, 71, 148–49; under Patton, 151–58; production by, 78, 80–81, 155–56; Roxy deal, 153–55; dissolution, 157–58
Ontario Museum of Archeology, 198
O'Reilly, J. Francis, 87, 258
Osborne, Vivienne, 113, 257
Ostman, Ernest, 266
Ottawa: first exhibition, 1–3, production, 117–19
Ottawa Electric Railway Co., 2, 3, 12
Ottawa Film Productions, 117–19, 123, 258

Ouimet, Léo Ernest: first view of films, 10–11, 275n2, 278n33; career, 23–25, 38, 61, 88–90; Ouimetoscope, 24–25, 246, 280; first films, 38, 247; newsreel, 61; later production, 88–90, 255; Laval Photoplays, 88–90; documentary-dramas, 67, 88, 156, 196, 240
Ouimetoscope, 24–25, 246, 280n56
Owsley, Monroe, 262

Pacific Pictures, 313n21
Page, H. V. S., 181
Pan American Film Corporation, 61, 66, 255
Paramount Pictures, 124, 184, 199, 202, 209, 212, 299n65, 320n122
Parfitt, E. G., 272
Parker, Gilbert, 88, 284n79
Parker, Muriel, 254
Pathé Film Co., 25, 37, 62, 199, 324n2
Pathescope Co., 60, 61, 66, 86, 135–36, 151, 152, 175, 218, 255–57 *passim*, 306n108, 307n128; newsreel, 61, 136; founding, 138; and Ontario Motion Picture Bureau, 138–43, 145–48; rivalry with Filmcraft, 146–48; name changes, 306n108, 307n128
Patricia Photoplays, 85, 257
Patton, George, 73, 81, 148, 149, 151–58; and Cranfield and Clarke, 73, 154–55; and Trenton purchase, 148–49; and Brownridge, 153–55; and distribution, 151, 154–55
Paul, Robert, 5, 6, 8
Peachy, John William, 46, 47, 284n79
Peck, Raymond S., 119, 133–34, 169, 175, 256–59 *passim*; at Motion Picture Bureau, 133–34, 159–65; views on film industry and quota, 163–65, 175, 179–82, 194, 232, 239; visit to Hollywood, 165; influence on Bureau's films, 159–60, 162; letter to Page on branch plant industry, 181
Penrod, Alexander G., 212, 214
Perrin, Jack, 90, 259
Perron, J. L., 85
Phantoscope, 10
Philip, Alexander, 189, 266

Phillips, Edward, 86, 259
Photo-Sound Corporation, 219, 268, 307n128
Physioc, Louis W., 52, 53, 65, 254
Pickford, Mary, 28, 60
Pidgeon, Walter, 28
Pitt-Taylor, Phillip, 228
Playter, Wellington, 105, 107, 255
Pollard, Harry, 218
Poore, O. L., 247
Porchet, Arthur, 84
Powell, S. Morgan, 69, 295n171
Power, Tyrone, 68, 255
Pratt, John, 228, 269
Premier Film Manufacturing Co., 46, 249, 285n89
Price, Kate, 113
Price, W. H., 79, 148, 149, 151, 152, 154–55, 180
Price Waterhouse Co., 68
Prince Edward Island Films, 117
Pringle, Robert, 267
Prior, Herbert, 65, 254
Proctor, Irwin, 143, 144, 147, 148
Promotional films, 32–37, 41–45, 66–67, 88, 129, 138, 145–46, 147, 150, 217–19. *See also* individual company names
Proulx, Maurice, 218, 221, 267
Publicity films. *See* Promotional films
Putnam, Oliver, 87, 258

Quarrington, Rance, 87, 259
Quebec: production for, 132, 143; use of films in schools, 151; censorship, 55, 248; Le Service de la ciné-photographie, 221, 228
Quebec City, 41
Quick, Charles J., 62, 83, 255
Quigley, Charles, 192, 271
Quinn, Joseph, 183, 262
Quota, 175–95; Australia, 179, 181, 194, 312; Britain, 73, 163, 177–78, 180–82, 185, 191, 193–95, 312n20; response to in Canada, 163, 177–79; Alberta, 193–94, 312n10; British Columbia, 150, 193–94, 312n10; Ontario, 180, 193–94, 312n10; France,

Shearer, Norma, 28, 120, 259
Sheffield, Reginald, 263, 314n36
Shelley, Leon, 232, 272
Sherwood, Robert, 199
Shiels, Michael J., 62, 140
Shipman, Arthur, 296n10
Shipman, Barry, 99, 101, 296n10
Shipman, Edna, 113, 116, 256, 296n10
Shipman, Ernest, 47, 57, 64, 82–83;
    characteristics of approach, 95–99, 103,
    108, 115; 124–26, 196, 239, 240;
    early career, 99–104; and Nell Shipman,
    100–10; Canadian productions, 104–
    23; in Calgary, 104–10; in Winnipeg,
    110–15; in Ottawa, 117–19; in Sault
    Ste. Marie, 119–20; in St. John, 120;
    location filming approach, 96, 97, 103,
    115, 126, 196, 240; end of career, 123;
    and vertical integration, 124–26
Shipman, Frederick, 296n10
Shipman, Joseph, 113, 296n10
Shipman, Nell, 28, 95, 255; career,
    100–02, 296nn12–19; and Back to
    God's Country, 104–10; special contri-
    butions to, 107–08
Shipman, Nina, 296n10
Sifton, Clifford, 32, 144
Sigurdson, Oliver, 258, 259
Singleton, Joe, 257
Sintzenich, Harold, 150
Slattery, Charles, 119
Small, Ambrose J., 277n25
Smith, Donald Alexander, 35, 205
Smith, Harlan, 218, 221, 268
Smith, Hilda, 187, 272
Smith, J., 77
Smith, Peter, 146, 147
Snow, Marguerite, 65, 254
Snyder, Bozo, 78
Sodders, Carl, 87, 258
Sohmer Park, Montreal, 10–11, 278n33
Solax, 37
Sound: early uses of, 13, 14, 15, 25; intro-
    duction and economic impact of, 79,
    158, 167, 184, 314nn33, 39, 319n104;
    use of in The Viking, 210
Sparks, Ned, 28
Sparling, Gordon, 77, 148, 172, 218,

259, 262–73, passim; and Ontario Mo-
    tion Picture Bureau, 148, 155–56; and
    ASN, 225, 226, 228–31; career, 228;
    and Canadian Cameos, 229–31
Speciality (Specialty) Film Import, 25, 38,
    61, 88, 150
Sponsored films. See Promotional films
Squires, Sir Richard, 214
Stame, Francesco, 116
Starland, 46, 248
Starrett, Charles, 192, 209, 264, 268,
    269, 316n51
Star Weekly, 145
Stead, Robert, 117
Stefansson Canadian Arctic Expedition, 38,
    129
Steiner, William, 182, 184–85, 187
Stephens, George, 144
Sterne, Louis, 68, 255
Stewart, W. F., 80
Stewart, W. T., 262
Stock promotions, 63, 80, 83–85, 182,
    187–88
Store-front theatres, 12, 13, 17–18, 21
Strathcona, Lord, 35
Stribling, William, 124
Stringer, Arthur, 51, 253
Stuart, Nick, 190, 191, 266, 267
Submarine Film Corporation, 103
Sullivan, Allan, 117, 119, 258
Sullivan, E. P., 49, 253
Sutherland, Ann, 113, 256
Swayne, Marion, 84, 118, 258
Sweeney, Thomas, 210
Sydney, Nova Scotia: production, 86
Sydney, Ernest C., 263, 314n38

Talbot, Frederick, 17
Talbot, Lyle, 192, 270
Tanguay, Marcel, 62
Tansey, Denis, 67
Taperty, Harold, 87, 259
Tarté, J. L., 85
Tash, Roy, 62, 87, 218, 220, 223, 224,
    225, 226, 256, 257, 259, 261, 263,
    265, 266; career, 143–44
Taube, Sidney B., 143
Taverner, P. A., 129, 218